Railroad Reorganization

Railroad Reorganization

BY

STUART DAGGETT

BeardBooks
Washington, DC

First Edition 1908, Harvard University Press
By Stuart Daggett, Ph.D., Instructor in Economics at Harvard University

Reprinted 1999 Beard Books, Washington, D.C.

ISBN 1-893122-10-7

PREFACE

It sometimes happens that experiences long since past seem to be repeated, and that knowledge apparently forgotten proves again of service. This is illustrated by the subject of railroad reorganization. In the years between 1893 and 1899 an imposing group of American railroads passed into receivers' hands. In 1893 alone more than 27,000 miles, with an aggregate capitalization of almost $2,000,000,-000, were taken over by the courts, and in the following years the amount was largely increased. Foreclosure sales aggregated 10,446 miles in 1895, 12,355 in 1896, and 40,503 between 1894 and 1898. Among the more important failures were those of the Richmond & West Point Terminal, the Reading, the Erie, the Northern Pacific, the Atchison, and the Baltimore & Ohio; — to say nothing of the Norfolk & Western, the Louisville, New Albany & Chicago, the Ann Arbor, the Seattle, Lake Shore & Eastern, the Pecos Valley, and many other smaller lines.

The railroads which failed between 1893 and 1898 were subsequently reorganized. In order to restore the equilibrium between income and outgo the companies turned to their creditors, and demanded the surrender of a part of the rights of which bondholders were then possessed. This demand the creditors were forced to concede. Some of them yielded without legal compulsion, assenting to "voluntary reorganizations"; some insisted upon the sale of the property securing their loans, but without escaping the loss which fell upon their more pliant associates. Much injustice to individuals came to light at this time. Men who had invested in good faith were obliged to sacrifice their holdings through no fault of their own. The savings of years were swept away. The demand of the railroads was one, nevertheless, which the courts supported, and rightly. The companies could not be operated unless the creditors were deprived of part of their legal rights. At the same time, these rights no longer had a material basis on which to rest, and their surrender meant but the recognition of a loss which had already taken place.

Most of the reorganizations were completed by the year 1899. Since that date the improvement in railroad earnings has been marvellous. Gross earnings from operation were $1,300,000,000 in 1899, they were $2,300,000,000 in 1906, the last year for which the figures of the Interstate Commerce Commission are at present available. Total income, after the deduction of operating expenses, was $605,000,000 in 1899, and $1,046,000,000 in 1906. It is not to be wondered at that the distress of the years 1893–9 has not been duplicated during the years 1900–7. On the contrary, weak roads have had opportunity to strengthen their positions, and strong ones have spent enormous sums for improvements, and have declared liberal dividends besides. In no year save 1905 has the new mileage put into receivers' hands been greater than 800 miles, and in but one has the mileage sold at foreclosure equalled that figure. Operating expenses have increased because the amount of business has exceeded the ability of the railroads to handle it. Equipment has been so inadequate as to provoke drastic legislation by the legislatures of many states; yards and terminals have been crowded until a prominent railroad officer has declared the expenditure of over five billion dollars to be necessary to restore the equilibrium between facilities and traffic.

These conditions have caused the earlier problems of failure and reorganization to be lost to view. Nevertheless, the financial panic of October, 1907, and the recession in activity which has become more and more apparent since that time, have again brought these problems forward. The Seaboard Air Line, one of the important railroad systems of the South, failed on January 5, 1908. The Chicago Great Western followed three days later. The Detroit, Toledo & Ironton, the Chicago, Cincinnati & Louisville, the International & Great Northern, the Western Maryland, and the Macon & Birmingham have since been put in receivers' hands. In all, the operation of 5938 miles of railroad, with a capitalization of nearly $415,000,000, and total liabilities of $462,000,000, has been taken over by the courts during the first ten weeks of 1908. Whether this is but the beginning of still more extended trouble it is of course impossible to say. There are a number of weak lines in the American railroad system, and the difficulty in obtaining credit is bound to reveal weaknesses where they exist. At present new loans have for some months been difficult to obtain, and even strong railroads have resorted to the issue of short time notes. The Erie, indeed, escaped bankruptcy on April 8, 1908, only through the timely aid of important bankers who took up its maturing notes. This points to serious consequences for the weaker lines. It is true, on the other hand, that American railroads are generally in better financial and physical condition than they were in 1893. It is not probable that any railroad collapse will be so widespread now as it was then. Whether this be so or not, the failure of nearly 6000 miles of railroad in ten weeks invests reorganization problems at present with an importance which they have not had for ten years. How, it will be asked, shall the financial operations necessary to reorganization be performed? What methods shall be adopted, what dangers avoided, and what results expected?

The experience of earlier years will provide answers to many of the questions asked in 1908. In the hope, therefore, that a study of railroad reorganization, on which the author has been intermittently engaged during the last six years, will prove of service, the following pages have been published. They discuss in some detail the financial history of the seven most important railroads which failed from 1892–6, and that of one railroad, the Rock Island, which was reorganized in 1902; and summarize in a final chapter the characteristics of the various reorganizations in which these roads have become involved. In some respects the history of each road considered is peculiar unto itself. The Reading had coal to sell, the Atchison did not. The Southern ran through a sparsely settled country, the Baltimore & Ohio through a thickly settled one. The Erie has never recovered from the campaigns of Gould, Drew, and Fisk from 1864–72, the Northern Pacific was not opened until 1883. In other respects, however, the roads have had much in common. Excepting only the Rock Island, each of them has found itself at one time or another unable to pay its debts, and has had to seek measures of relief. The problems of the different companies at these times have been strikingly alike. However caused, their financial difficulties have been expressed in high fixed charges, and, usually, in excessive floating debts. Greater annual obligations have been assumed than the roads could meet, and current liabilities have accumulated while pressing demands have been satisfied. To this state of affairs the remedy has been sought in comprehensive exchanges of old securities for new. The exchanges, it is true, have been carried out in different ways, and the collateral expedients employed have not been the same. To similar problems different solutions have been applied. It is possible, for this very reason, for a careful study of the alternative reorganization methods which have been developed to point out some policies which have been dangerous, and to make clear others which are both just, and likely to be successful. Such a study also throws light upon the history of the companies upon which it is based.

For the way in which the different roads have been handled, the reader is referred to the text. The order of treatment is very roughly determined by geographical location; that is, the Eastern roads are first considered, then the Southern, and then the Western. Each chapter, except the last, should be examined as a "case" in reorganization experience, and as part, therefore, of a united whole. No one has been so continuously with his work as the author himself, and no one can more keenly realize its defects. It is offered as a contribution in a field in which very little has as yet been done, and it is hoped that it will prove of value to those concerned with reorganization plans, as well as to those interested in the development of corporation finance during the last generation.

Without the unselfish and intelligent assistance of the writer's Mother, the preparation of this book would have been long delayed. To her, first of all, thanks are due. To Professor William Z. Ripley, of Harvard University, should be made warm acknowledgment of his constant interest and helpful suggestions. To the Carnegie Institution the author is indebted for grants in aid of research in this special field. Grateful acknowledgment should also be made of gifts by friends of the University to cover the expenses of publication.

CONTENTS

CHAPTER I

CHAPTER II

CHAPTER III

CHAPTER IV

CHAPTER V

CHAPTER VI

CHAPTER VII

CHAPTER VIII

CHAPTER IX

CHAPTER X

RAILROAD REORGANIZATION

CHAPTER I

BALTIMORE & OHIO

Early history — Extension to Chicago — Trunk-line rate wars — Effect on the company — Extension to New York — Sale of bonds to pay off floating debt — Unsatisfactory traffic conditions — Receivership — Mr. Little's report — Reorganization — Subsequent history.

THE Baltimore & Ohio Railroad was the first important railway company to be incorporated in the United States. It was designed to aid the city of Baltimore in securing the Western trade, and not only private citizens but the city of Baltimore and the state of Maryland early subscribed to its stock. When in the course of construction it became expedient to extend into Virginia, the city of Wheeling and the state of Virginia likewise subscribed, though the action of the latter was subsequently withdrawn.[1] As a result the funds required for first construction were obtained from the sale of stocks instead of bonds. In 1844, seventeen years after the granting of the charter, the annual report showed $7,000,000 in stock as against $985,000 in 6 per cent bonds; while in 1849, though the loans had been increased, they yet stood in the proportion of one to two.[2]

On December 1, 1831, the first train was run over the line, then 72½ miles in length.[3] The early history of the road does not much concern us. It was one of steady growth, not through an unsettled territory, as with our Western roads, but through a country the industries of which were already established. Tracks led, not into prairies, but to populous cities; and the future of the company, once the initial difficulties should have been overcome, was at no

[1] Milton Reizenstein, The Economic History of the Baltimore & Ohio Railroad, Johns Hopkins University Studies, July–August, 1897.

[2] Reizenstein estimates the original cost of the first 379 miles to have been $37,612 per mile, and, adding the cost of reconstruction and extension to 1853, he gets a figure of $41,237 per mile. Vide infra, p. 75.

[3] 6th Annual Report, 1832, p. 4.

time uncertain. Thus extension to Cumberland increased the gross receipts from $426,492 to $575,235, and that to Wheeling in 1853 likewise brought a great increase in traffic.

The Civil War bore upon the Baltimore & Ohio heavily because of the peculiar location of its mileage. On May 28, 1861, possession was taken by the Confederates of more than one hundred miles of the main stem, embracing chiefly the region between the Point of Rocks and Cumberland.[1] Government protection was temporarily restored in 1862, but raids occurred until the end of the war. Each time the Confederates occupied the line they tore it up, and as soon as they retired the company hastened to make repairs. The road did not default. A portion of the track yielded a revenue from first to last, and presumably the Government paid generously for the transportation of its troops.

It was after the Civil War that the real history of the road began. The key-note was competition; — competition of the fiercest sort between parallel lines from Chicago to the seaboard, intensified by the rivalry of the great seaboard cities, and involving traffic in both directions. The decade 1850–60 had seen the extension of Eastern roads to Western connections. In 1851 the Erie had reached Lake Erie; in 1853 the New York Central and Lake Shore, and in 1855 the Pennsylvania and Fort Wayne had opened continuous routes from the Atlantic to Chicago. In 1857 the Baltimore & Ohio had obtained connection with Cincinnati and St. Louis; and in 1858 the Grand Trunk had arrived at Sarnia on its way from Portland to Chicago. After the Civil War there was both consolidation and extension. The New York Central was united with the Hudson River, and the Pennsylvania leased the Pittsburgh, Fort Wayne & Chicago in 1869. The Baltimore & Ohio reached Chicago in 1874, and the lines which in April, 1880, were consolidated into the Chicago & Grand Trunk were completed between Port Huron and Chicago in February of that year. The completion of these through routes opened the way for very bitter competition. Five independent lines struggled for Chicago business, and all of them were prepared to cut rates deeply in order to test their rivals' strength. In particular the Baltimore & Ohio was aggressive. "At the time of its [Chicago branch] opening," said Mr. Blanchard before the Hepburn

[1] 35th Annual Report, 1861.

Committee, "it was heralded all over the Northwest as a 'Relief for the Farmer,' 'the Grangers' Friend,' and all other sorts of headlines were put into the Chicago and Northwestern papers; and President Garrett's public utterances, and those to his Board, were filled with enough statements to show what he intended to do. . . . I heard him [say] that upon the completion of his lines, like another Samson, he could pull down the temple of rates upon the heads of these other trunk lines." [1]

Under these circumstances a dispute between the Baltimore & Ohio and the Pennsylvania in 1874 over the former's connection with New York had far-reaching consequences. [2] The Pennsylvania refused to carry Baltimore & Ohio cars over its line north from Philadelphia, and as a retaliatory measure the Baltimore & Ohio reduced passenger fares from Washington and Baltimore to Western points from 25 to 40 per cent. [3] The reduction in rates thus begun inaugurated the first of the great railroad wars. The cuts soon extended to east-bound passengers and to freight, and forced corresponding cuts on the Pennsylvania, the Lake Shore & Michigan Southern, the Michigan Central, the New York Central, and the Erie. Rates on fourth class and grain from Chicago to New York, which had been 60 cents per 100 pounds in December, 1873, and 40 cents in December, 1874, fell to 30 cents in March, 1875. Rates on special, or sixth class, [4] went as low as 12 cents from Balti-

[1] Testimony of Mr. Blanchard, Hepburn Committee Report, p. 3171. See also Chron. 20: 547, 1875.

[2] The Baltimore & Ohio had no line to New York. The Pennsylvania had had one since 1873, and over it Mr. Garrett was forced to send all his New York business. Disputes arose over the proper pro-rating of charges. President Garrett alleged that the terminal charge of four cents per 100 pounds which the Pennsylvania Company imposed on freight coming to or going from New York was exorbitant, and that he was paying for 100 miles of transportation when the real distance was only 90. President Scott replied that the rates for terminal services in New York were not sufficient to cover the cost of doing the business, and that the Pennsylvania's New York and Philadelphia line was open to the Baltimore & Ohio on the same terms as to all others. R. R. Gaz. 7:71–2, 1875.

[3] R. R. Gaz. 6: 8, 1874. The outcome was an agreement whereby the Baltimore & Ohio restored rates and fares, and the Pennsylvania agreed to haul two of the former's trains daily each way between West Philadelphia and Jersey City, to sell through tickets West over the Baltimore & Ohio, and to give that road all necessary facilities for the handling of through freight.

[4] Sugar, coffee, salt, etc.

more and Philadelphia to Chicago. Passenger fares from Chicago to Baltimore and Washington were reduced from $19 to $9, to Philadelphia from $19 to $12, to New York from $22 to $15, and to Boston from $22 to $15. The New York Central and the Erie quoted fares from New York to Chicago of $18 and to St. Louis of $20, and the Baltimore & Ohio replied by a cut to $16.25 to Chicago. In April, 1875, the Baltimore & Ohio cut freight rates from Cumberland to Baltimore over 50 per cent on the four regular classes, and the Pennsylvania at once announced still greater reductions.[1]

The effect of this warfare on railroad revenues was sufficiently serious to cause the Baltimore & Ohio to recede somewhat from its independent position and to enter into negotiations with the Pennsylvania;[2] but the terms of the resulting agreement proved unsatisfactory to the other trunk lines, and no general pacification was obtained. Late in 1875 rates nevertheless generally advanced, and in December a general agreement was concluded, followed by a general increase. This agreement was again hopelessly disrupted by the following April, when cuts in east-bound rates followed each other with rapidity. The published rates on grain, which had been 45 cents at the beginning of March, 1876, fell to 40 cents on March 7, 35 cents on April 13, 22½ cents on April 25, and 20 cents on May 5. In June rates on west-bound freight fell to 25 cents first class to Chicago, and 16 cents fourth and fifth class, actual rates going

[1] The traffic between Cumberland and Baltimore was mostly coal. In an interview the last of May or first of June, 1875, President Garrett said that as soon as the right was conceded to his road to enter New York over the Pennsylvania Railroad as he had been doing for thirty years, and to make such rates from Baltimore and Chicago as he chose, he was ready for peace and not sooner. . . . The Saratoga combination, which had been gotten up to ruin the Baltimore & Ohio Railroad, had only served to establish the road and give it a standing in the West. . . . It had been and was now his firm object to maintain the freight rate on fourth class, the principal freight shipped from the West, at 35 cents per 100. This was a reasonable rate and gave his company a fair profit. The other lines had to submit to this rate or there could be no peace. R. R. Gaz. 7 : 237, 1875.

[2] R. R. Gaz. 7 : 261, 1875; Ibid. 7 : 270, 1875; Ibid. 7 : 289, 1875; Chron. 20 : 593, 1875. The compact was to last for ten years, the companies to agree upon and to maintain moderate rates between all competing points. Each board of directors was to appoint a special committee to which was to be referred all differences which might arise. The Pennsylvania opened its lines to the Baltimore & Ohio between Philadelphia and New York on the same terms that it gave other connecting roads at Philadelphia.

much lower; and it was possible to travel from New York to Chicago first class for $13.[1]

Warfare between railroads became intensified by the competition between the cities which the railroads served, and by 1876 the question of relative rates to New York, Philadelphia, and Baltimore had grown to be of primary importance.[2] By an agreement in 1869 Baltimore had been given a differential on east-bound freight of 10 cents per 100 pounds, which had been reduced to 5 cents on grain in 1870. On west-bound freight Baltimore had enjoyed a differential in 1875 which had ranged from 10 cents on first class to 5 cents on special class freight, and Philadelphia one which had been 2 cents less except on first class, where the Philadelphia differential had been 3 cents less than that to Baltimore. A temporary agreement of March, 1876, had replaced these allowances by differentials of 13 per cent in favor of Baltimore and 10 per cent in favor of Philadelphia as against New York. This relation was fought over in the rate war of 1876. In December of that year another agreement was reached on the basis of equal rates from Western points to Europe on export traffic via all four competing seaboard cities, and reduced percentage differentials on local traffic to those cities; but this proved temporary, the subsequent advances in rates were not general, and final agreement was not secured until April, 1877. The contract then executed was in the nature of a compromise. The differential to Baltimore was reduced from 13 per cent to 3 cents, and from Philadelphia from 10 per cent to 2 cents, to apply equally to local and to export traffic. Rates to Boston were at no time to be less than those to New York. Differentials on west-bound traffic were to be the same as those on east-bound on third class, fourth class, and special freight, and on first and second classes to be 8 cents less per hundred from Baltimore and 6 cents less from Philadelphia than from New York.[3]

[1] See Interstate Commerce Commission, Railways in the United States in 1902, part 2, entitled, "A Forty-year Review of Changes in Freight Tariff," p. 79.

[2] For an account of the differentials at different times see the argument of counsel and the opinion of the Interstate Commerce Commission, "In the Matter of Differential Rates to and from North Atlantic Ports," April 27, 1905, in Elkins Committee Report, vol. 5, Appendix E. See also 7 I. C. C. Rep. 612.

[3] Albert Fink, Report on Adjustment of Railway Rates; also Testimony of Mr. Blanchard, Hepburn Committee Report, pp. 3171 ff.

The years following the agreement of 1877 were marked by low and fluctuating rates, extensive cutting under the published schedules, and frequent attempts at pooling and at apportionment of traffic. At a meeting at Chicago on December 19, 1878, tariff rates were agreed upon by all lines, but the existence of time contracts depressed receipts for months thereafter. Another meeting on May 8 was followed by sharp competition. In June an agreement to raise rates was made, but proved unsatisfactory owing to long time contracts. "During the period between December 18, 1878, and July 5, 1879," said Mr. King in a letter to the Trunk-Line Arbitrators on July 17, 1879, "the Baltimore & Ohio Company has practically been out of the market, on account of the low rates by the Northern lines. It has not secured enough east-bound freight to give return loads for the small west-bound traffic sent over its lines to that city, and has repeatedly moved its cars empty from Chicago to other points on its lines east of that city." [1]

Early in 1881 the cutting of rates became sufficiently important to force official recognition by the chairman of the trunk-line pool.[2] By June 17 quoted rates on grain were 15 cents per 100 pounds from Chicago to New York, and a railroad war was in full swing.[3] By October the grain rate had been reduced from 15 cents to $12\frac{1}{2}$ cents; by August passenger fares were $7 from New York to Chicago, and $16 from Chicago to New York, and there was quoted besides a $5 Boston to Chicago rate over the Grand Trunk. The radical nature of these cuts can be appreciated from Mr. Albert Fink's

[1] "Additional Arguments on the Division of [Dead] Freight from Cincinnati of the Atlantic & Great Western," etc., N. Y. 1879, p. 5. Speaking from the standpoint of an impartial observer, Mr. Fink declared that $1,840,494 had been lost between December 19, 1878, and May 1, 1879, through the failure of the Michigan Central, Lake Shore, Pennsylvania, and Baltimore & Ohio and their connections to observe their published tariffs. Chron. 28: 578, 1879.

[2] By agreement of March 11, 1881, the chairman of the Joint Executive Committee, Mr. Fink, was given authority to proclaim a general reduction in published rates when it should be shown that any pool line had been accepting traffic at less than the regular rate. This authority he exercised in April. Rates were restored almost immediately by special action of the Joint Executive Committee, only to be reduced again in June for similar reasons.

[3] The actual outbreak of the war was due to the conviction of the New York Central that traffic was being diverted to other roads by secret departures from the published tariff. R. R. Gaz. 13: 347, 1881.

testimony before the Hepburn and Cullom Committees. Fifteen cents, said he in 1879, just covered the actual cost of hauling the grain;[1] twenty cents, he asserted in 1885, was the bare cost of movement, including the general expenses, but without any profit to the road.[2] Grain was therefore not repaying the specific cost of hauling, and passengers were obviously in similar case. Temporary relief occurred through the large increase in business which took place at the end of 1881. In October the Pennsylvania and the Baltimore & Ohio advanced east-bound rates because of the abundance of traffic offering, and the New York Central, Erie, and Grand Trunk followed to a less degree. In November further advances occurred, though west-bound rates remained low ; but throughout December and January rates were low and fluctuating,[3] and negotiations were carried on for the settlement of the differential question which underlay the trouble. None of the combatants were open to conviction; the only outlet was therefore arbitration, and this was reluctantly resorted to.[4] In January, 1882, the roads divided the through trunk-line business, agreed to raise rates, and left the subject of differentials to be investigated by Messrs. Thurman, Washburn, and Cooley.[5]

This solution settled nothing. During the following three years constant disputes arose over the proper division of traffic,[6] and in 1884 the old struggle was resumed with unabated vigor. Rates on grain to the seaboard fell from 30 cents to 20 cents on March 14 of that year, and to 15 cents on March 21; remaining low and

---

[1] Hepburn Committee Report, vol. 3, p. 558.

[2] Cullom Committee Report, vol. 2, p. 98.

[3] In January the Pennsylvania announced that it would take provisions from Chicago to New York for ten cents per hundred pounds. R. R. Gaz. 14: 28, 1882.

[4] See Albert Fink, Report upon the Adjustment of Railroad Transportation Rates to the Seaboard, 1882; also, Letter to a New York Merchant, by the same, Hepburn Committee Report, vol. 2, Exhibits, pp. 106-119.

[5] For agreement see Chron. 34: 116, 1882. The Commissioners' functions were purely advisory. They reported in July that "no evidence has been offered before us that the existing differentials are unjust, or that they operate to the prejudice of either of the Atlantic seaboard cities." Senate Committee on Interstate Commerce Report (Elkins Committee), 1905, vol. 2, pp. 1243 ff.

[6] The question was passed upon by C. F. Adams as arbitrator in November, 1882 (Chron. 35: 603, 1882), and by the Trunk-Line Board of Arbitration in January, 1884 (Chron. 38: 31, 1884).

fluctuating through the year.[1] Immigrant business from New York
to Chicago was handled by the Pennsylvania at one dollar a head.
By February, 1885, rates for traffic in both directions were completely demoralized. Nominal east-bound charges on grain were
25 cents, or a 10 cent advance since the preceding March, but actual
rates were as low as 8 and 10 cents. Meanwhile published rates on
west-bound freight were a third less than the standard tariff, and
passenger rates in both directions were, roughly, one-half the regular
charges. The following month still further reductions occurred.
The warfare was finally terminated by an agreement to maintain
rates late in 1885,[2] followed by an elaborate pooling agreement between the competing lines.[3]

From 1875 to 1885 the trunk lines to the Atlantic ports were thus
engaged in active competition. What was the effect of this upon
the Baltimore & Ohio? This road was highly prosperous in 1875.
Dividends of 6 per cent and 10 per cent were being paid. The capitalization was small and the management conservative. During
the ten years following 1875 the rate of dividend was not materially
decreased. In 1876 10 per cent was paid. In 1877 the old 8 per cent
rate was restored, and the following year the distribution was made
in stock instead of in cash. After the agreement of 1878 one-half
year's dividend was paid in cash; and in 1879 9 per cent cash, and
in 1880 10 per cent cash was declared, this rate enduring until
1886. But although dividends were maintained, the effect of the
railroad wars appeared in the slowness with which net earnings
increased. A comparison of the net returns of 1884 with those of
1874 reveals a gain of 40 per cent, on a mileage 27 per cent greater;
but the figures for 1885 show an increase of less than 2 per cent
over those for 1874, while the totals for 1884 were not again equalled
until 1900. Meanwhile more bonds had been issued, and the percentage of fixed charges to net earnings had increased from 16 in
1874 to 63 in 1884. In other words, money was borrowed to put
into the road which did little more than keep the net earnings from

---

[1] The attempt of the Pennsylvania to cut off the New York connection of the
Baltimore & Ohio caused especial bitterness between those roads. See Chron.
39:420, 1884.

[2] Chron. 41:393, 1885.

[3] Cullom Committee Report, vol. 1, Appendix, pp. 237, and 240 ff.

declining. In that same time the stock increased $2,900,000, and according to the profit and loss account $15,559,636 were put into the property, making a total of $55,743,092 (of this $37,197,696 were bonds); the only result of which was the building of 313 miles of line, and the securing of an increase in net earnings for 1884, which was swept away the following year.

In 1884 the elder Garrett died, and his son Robert was elected to succeed him. The old policy of independence and competition was continued, the objective point being now an entrance into New York. "When in 1885 the other trunk lines harmonized their differences, . . ." said the Chronicle, "the Baltimore & Ohio . . . pursued its policy of aggression. . . . The road must reach Philadelphia . . . nay, must push . . . on to New York. . . . Instead of seeking to avoid rivalry, its every effort seemed to encourage it. Rates were reduced, concessions made to shippers and travellers, the one idea apparently being to get traffic no matter what the cost." [1] The necessity of a secure New York connection had been impressed upon the company in the course of the rate wars. The first step was to be actual construction to Philadelphia, the second, construction or traffic agreements from Philadelphia to New York. Bonds were issued in April, 1883, for construction of a so-called Philadelphia branch from Baltimore to the northern boundary of Cecil County, Maryland,[2] there to connect with the Baltimore & Philadelphia Railroad, which was being built through Delaware and Pennsylvania to Philadelphia. Entrance into Philadelphia was secured over the Schuylkill River East Side Railway, a corporation organized under the laws of Pennsylvania and doing business in the city only.[3] The distance was approximately ninety-nine miles; the cost was later asserted to have been $20,000,-000. Beyond Philadelphia the Baltimore & Ohio relied on an agreement with the Philadelphia & Reading for trackage to Bound Brook, New Jersey,[4] and on a traffic contract with the Central of New Jersey for its line from Bound Brook to Elizabeth.[5] Terminals

---

[1] Chron. 45: 692, 1887.

[2] The amount of issue was £2,400,000 ($11,678,400) at 4½ per cent, maturing April 1, 1933, and placed through Brown, Shipley & Co. of London. Chron. 36:426, 1883.

[3] Chron. 40: 453, 1885.

[4] Chron. 41: 555, 1885.   [5] Chron. 43: 190, 1886.

on Staten Island were secured by purchase of a controlling interest in the Staten Island Rapid Transit Company,[1] and connection between Elizabeth and the Island was obtained by new construction. The strength of this route was in its directness and in its independence of trunk-line control; its weakness was in its excessive cost between Baltimore and Philadelphia, and in its reliance upon traffic contracts north of the latter city. A proposition was advanced to unite the Baltimore & Ohio, the Philadelphia & Reading, and the Central of New Jersey with the Richmond Terminal System. This, however, fell through,[2] and the possibility still existed that the Baltimore & Ohio might some day construct a line of its own from Philadelphia to New York.

Pending the completion of the preceding arrangements rate conditions remained naturally unsatisfactory. The Pennsylvania objected to the paralleling of its Philadelphia-New York branch, and refused to allow temporary use of that line by the Baltimore & Ohio while the latter's independent connections were being established.[3] Freight rates were slowly and painfully raised after the conflict of 1884-5, and did not regain a high level. In 1886 the Baltimore & Ohio was forced to reduce its dividends from 10 to 8 per cent. The following year it cut to 4 per cent, and in 1888 no dividend at all was declared. The surplus on the year's operations, which had not since 1878 fallen below $1,000,000, dropped to $110,819 in 1885, and to $36,259 in 1886. As dividends decreased, the funded debt increased,[4] the percentage of fixed charges to net income rose from 63 to 89, and the floating debt attained the portentous amount of

[1] The Staten Island Rapid Transit possessed an extensive water front on Staten Island, besides franchises for two ferries from Staten Island to the Battery, New York City. Some trouble was experienced in securing permission to bridge the Kill von Kufl between Staten Island and the New Jersey mainland. Congress passed an act permitting construction, New Jersey protested, and the courts upheld the authority of Congress. Stockton *v.* Baltimore & New York Railroad Co., 32 Fed. Rep. 9.

[2] R. R. Gaz. 19:170, 1887; Ibid. 19:490, 1887. For an account of the Richmond & West Point Terminal Railway & Warehouse Company see the chapter on the Southern Railway.

[3] R. R. Gaz. 18:49, 1886. Interview with Mr. Albert Fink. A passenger rate war between the Pennsylvania and the Baltimore & Ohio took place early in 1886, and resulted in the indirect cutting by the former of the pool rate which it had agreed to maintain. Chron. 42:73, 1886.

[4] From $34,713,696 in 1884 to $56,868,201 in 1887.

$11,148,007. The only item which did not grow was net earnings. There was nothing occult in the situation. Every one was well aware that the competition to which the Baltimore & Ohio had been subjected had been severe, and that the cost of its New York extension had been large. In 1887 the bonds outstanding were $56,868,201, the stock $19,792,566, and the accumulated surplus $48,083,720, or a total of $124,744,487. This stood for the sums invested in the property. Net income on the other hand was $4,994,721; so that on an investment of over $100,000,000 but 4 per cent was being obtained to cover interest, improvements, and whatever dividend might be declared.

That no general apprehension was felt by investors before 1887 was due to the great prestige which the Baltimore & Ohio enjoyed. The long series of dividends counted heavily in favor of the road. The enormous accumulated surplus, said to have been invested in valuable improvements and extensions; [1] the enterprise of the company in making extensions; the large volume of business; and the confident statements of the president, all conspired to prevent a too keen analysis of the business returns.[2] Relief of two sorts was nevertheless required. In the first place the floating debt had grown so large that some means of paying it off was necessary; in the second place the road needed a sufficient reduction in fixed charges to restore some of the margin of non-mortgaged earnings which had been so great a safeguard in the early days. Only the first of these requirements was met. Cash the road had to have; the existing fixed charges, it was thought, it could endure if only some abatement of the intensity of trunk-line competition could be obtained.

The method chosen for raising cash was the sale of bonds. In September, 1887, J. P. Morgan & Co. announced that a preliminary contract had been entered into between the Baltimore & Ohio Railroad Company and J. S. Morgan & Co., Baring Bros. & Co., and Brown, Shipley & Co., of London, and their allied houses in America, for the negotiation of $5,000,000 Baltimore & Ohio Con-

---

[1] Such as connecting lines, iron bridges over the Ohio River, elevators, wharves, terminal facilities, etc.

[2] The lowest average price of the common stock before announcement of the measures taken for relief was 160, from which point the quotations rapidly dropped to 125, and on January 5, 1889, to 85.

solidated 5s and of $5,000,000 preferred stock, for the purpose of paying off the entire floating debt, and of placing the company upon a sound financial basis.[1] The consolidated bonds were to be part of an authorized issue of $29,600,000, of which $21,423,000 were to be reserved to retire the main stem mortgage indebtedness when it should fall due, and $8,177,112 were to be exchanged for securities in the company's sinking fund, the freed securities to be used to pay the floating debt in part. In case this exchange should not be made, $7,500,000 of the issue might be sold direct, and the syndicate before mentioned agreed to take $5,000,000 of this amount and to place $5,000,000 in preferred stock on condition:

(a) That the statements of the company should be verified;

(b) That the management of the company should be placed in competent hands, satisfactory to the syndicate;

(c) That satisfactory contracts should be made between the Baltimore & Ohio and other roads for New York business, which should remove all antagonism between them on the subject, and should ensure the permanent working of the first-named in entire harmony with the other trunk lines, besides avoiding the construction, or the threat of construction, of expensive lines north and east of Philadelphia.

Annual payments to the Baltimore & Ohio sinking funds were to be made in the future in consols instead of in cash.[2]

The essence of this arrangement was a funding of the floating debt, plus agreements with other roads in order to maintain earnings. The funding involved, however, a certain increase of charges through the issue of bonds, while the agreements offered but a doubtful chance of increased earnings. Only by an effective community of interest or of ownership among the trunk lines could a saving have been secured on which the new bond issues could safely have relied. That this was to take place through the syndicate, that body was emphatic in denying. "The statement," said Vice-

---

[1] Chron. 45: 304, 1887; Ibid. 45: 824, 1887.

[2] About $5,000,000 of the floating debt in March, 1888, consisted of advances by the syndicate, for which they held 50,000 shares of Western Union Telegraph Company stock, and 15,000 shares of United States Express Company stock, which at current prices about covered their loan. Statement of President Spencer, Chron. 46: 344, 1888.

President Spencer, "that the Baltimore & Ohio Railroad has
passed into the hands of a syndicate, of which J. P. Morgan is the
head, is absolutely without foundation. . . . The syndicate has
the greatest interest now in the growth of the Baltimore & Ohio,
and to secure this growth and progress absolute independence of
other corporate predominance is essential, and the road must be
worked in the interest of the states and territories it reaches." [1]
This declaration left only informal agreements as a resort; for pooling had been forbidden in 1887. It did more, it implied the necessity of a maintenance of competition, for to work the Baltimore &
Ohio in the interest of Baltimore meant to work it against the
interest of New York. In principle the plan was nevertheless
adopted. Bondholders saw no necessity for a radical reorganization, and were willing to consent only to a new issue of bonds. Certain modifications were, however, imposed. The exchange of new
bonds for securities in the sinking fund was abandoned, and the
alternative of direct sale was embraced. It was found impossible
to secure the consent of stockholders to an increase in the preferred
stock, three attempts to obtain the required authorization failing
in the week ending January 20, 1888. [2] Furthermore, the failure
of the stock issue led President Spencer [3] to request that the city of
Baltimore extend for five years at 4 per cent a $5,000,000 loan to
the company, which was to mature in two years, and that it return
the sinking fund of $2,400,000 which had accumulated in its hands
for the eventual cancellation of the debt. [4] It may be added that this
suggestion was not accepted.

[1] Ry. Age, 12:640, 1887.

[2] "If it [the stock] is sold," said a statement in the New York *Tribune*, purporting
to represent the views of Senator Gorman, a large stockholder, " it will place the
control of the road practically in the hands of the syndicate. . . . It is clearly
preferable to keep the control of the stock here [Baltimore], as the road is a city and
state institution of the first importance to our business interests." Ry. Age, 13:44,
1888. Another objection was that an issue of additional preferred stock would postpone indefinitely dividends upon the common.

[3] Mr. Spencer had succeeded Robert Garrett in December, 1887.

[4] Chron. 46:319, 1888. In connection with this proposition President Spencer
made the following statement: Of the $11,148,007 floating debt, December, 1887,
$7,769,314 consisted of loans and bills payable. This is now reduced to $6,446,173.
There will probably be added to this $1,400,000 for equipment, already either under
contract or to be constructed in the company's shops. In addition there should be,
in the near future, not less than $2,000,000 additional put into this property for the

While awaiting final settlement of the syndicate scheme the
Baltimore & Ohio obtained some cash from the disposal of all its
free resources ; that is, from the telegraph, express, and sleeping-car
businesses which it had conducted since early in the administration
of John Garrett. In August, 1887, it sold its express business to
the United States Express Company for a period of thirty years, in
return for $1,500,000 of the capital stock of the express company
plus a certain percentage of the annual earnings of the express lines
handed over.[1] In October of the same year its telegraph business
was turned over to the Western Union Telegraph Company in
return for $5,000,000 of the Western Union stock, and an annual
payment of $60,000 in cash.[2] Finally, in June, 1888, its sleeping-car
equipment and franchises were transferred to the Pullman Company
for a period of twenty-five years at a reported price of $1,250,000.[3]
The company agreed to furnish all the sleeping and parlor cars
required. This brought the incidental advantage of ending long-
continued suits over patents. The terms of sale to the telegraph and
express companies brought in no ready money, but the securities
obtained were readily salable, and being independent for their value
of the commercial success of the Baltimore & Ohio were available
for times of difficulty. It was this policy which offset the refusal
of the city of Baltimore to return the sinking fund to the company,
and which by March, 1888, rendered the road even to some extent
independent of the syndicate. At that date a modification of the
syndicate agreement took place. The bankers gave up all claim to
the $5,000,000 of stock so long under discussion, and took instead
the balance ($2,500,000) of the $7,500,000 consolidated mortgage
bonds which the company was authorized to sell. "The syndicate
acted," said the Baltimore *Sun*, "in an entirely friendly spirit, and,

purpose of improvement. The total requirements are thus $10,000,000. Of this
$5,000,000 will be disposed of by assets in the hands of the syndicate as collateral, or
in the hands of the company. Of the remaining $5,000,000, $1,500,000 is floating
debt. This will be more than provided for by the $2,500,000 of consolidated bonds
remaining in the hands of the company for its future use after the sale of the $5,000,000
to the syndicate. The remaining $3,500,000 needed for equipment and improve-
ments it is the desire of the company to provide for by that portion of the $2,500,000
not required for the floating debt, and by the $2,500,000 in the sinking-fund loan of
1890. Chron. 46:344.

[1] Ry. Rev. 28:192, 1888.   [2] Ry. Age, 12:728, 1887.
[3] R. R. Gaz. 20:417, 1888.

with a desire to continue its financial relations with the company, took the remaining $2,500,000 . . . at a better price than was paid for the $5,000,000." [1]

With temporary financial requirements provided for, President Spencer was enabled to achieve some much-needed reforms. At a meeting of the directors on March 14 a complete reorganization of the service was authorized, with changes and transfers affecting employees from the first vice-president down. Later a committee of mechanical experts was organized "to examine thoroughly all the shops, shop tools, etc., of the entire Baltimore & Ohio system, and to report on all the improvements needed." [2] The form of the annual report was improved. The much-quoted surplus, which had proved such an unreliable support, was cut in two by the writing off of bad investments, the marking down of the price of securities, and the like; and, finally, a committee was appointed to make a general examination of the financial as well as the physical condition of affairs. [3] "Great anxiety," said a resolution of the directors, "exists in the public mind as to the financial condition and the value and earning capacity of the road and property . . . [and] it is due to all interests that a full, frank, and complete statement of its affairs should be made public." So far as lay in his power President Spencer, and through him the syndicate, tried to secure a real and permanent improvement in the condition of the road, and to gain, through increased efficiency in operation, the margin which the refusal to cut down fixed charges had denied. The failure of the attempt may be ascribed to the continuance of the Garrett family in power. Any irregularities or mistakes which had taken place in the past reflected on the Garretts, so that it was to their interest to stifle investigation. Moreover, any change in policy for the future implied a criticism of their acts to which they were reluctant to accede. In 1888 the Garrett holdings amounted to from 50,000

[1] Ry. Rev. 28:192, 1888. The amiability of the syndicate was profitable to it. On May 21 the subscription books of the $7,500,000 mortgage were opened in London and New York, and the whole issue was subscribed in London before the inhabitants of the American city, in spite of their proverbial alertness, were out of bed. In September, 1888, the Baltimore & Ohio was reported as "having all the funds needed for the present." R. R. Gaz. 20:343, 1888.

[2] Ry. Rev. 28:163, 1888.

[3] Ibid. 28:236, 1888.

to 60,000 shares out of a total of 150,000 shares, or, deducting 32,500 shares held by the city of Baltimore, which were not entitled to vote, to about one-half of a total of 117,500 shares. This gave undisputed control. The effect was seen in the annual election in November. Of 12 old members of the board only 5 were reëlected, and of the 7 dropped 3 formed part of the investigating committee engaged in securing "the full, frank, and complete statement of the company's condition" promised at an earlier date.[1] The same month President Spencer was ousted and Mr. Charles F. Mayer was elected in his place.

This revolution was fatal to any radical reform, so that during the next seven years the condition of the Baltimore & Ohio improved but little. Net income grew, it is true, up to the panic year of 1893, but fell so sharply after that that the reported figures for 1895 exceeded those of 1888 by but $1,283,843, and even this gain was practically wiped out during the following year. Meanwhile fixed charges grew from $6,550,972 in 1888 to $6,934,052 in 1895, and to $7,303,781 in 1896; an increase which transformed the profits of the company the following year into a deficit. A comparison of the balance-sheets of 1888 and 1895 shows an increase of $10,207,434 in stock, of $16,261,000 in funded debt, and of $4,554,939 in floating debt. These changes were offset mainly by increases in bonds and stock owned, or in the hands of trustees, by advances to subsidiary lines, and by a reduction of $11,080,000 in bonded debt secured by collateral or by mortgage on the main line. During this time dividends were nevertheless steadily paid on the preferred stock, and, beginning in 1891, upon the common stock as well. The liberal tendencies of the management were also evinced by a 20 per cent dividend upon the common stock, declared in 1891 to compensate shareholders for expenditures in betterments and improvements of the physical condition of the property.[2] It will be

---

[1] Ry. Rev. 28 : 678, 1888 ; Ibid. 28 : 689, 1888. The coincidence was so suggestive that it was thought necessary to "credibly inform" certain bankers that the investigating committee was expected to continue its investigation and to make a full report. In December the committee was instructed by a directors' resolution not to report till its full statement was ready, and further notice does not appear.

[2] Ry. Age, 16 : 882, 1891. At the same time the directors decided to sell $5,096,600 additional common stock to meet expenditures which would be necessary in connection with the World's Fair at Chicago.

seen how different this was from the policy of retrenchment and economy which had been inaugurated by President Spencer, and which might fairly have been expected from a corporation barely escaped from bankruptcy.

Traffic conditions from 1887 to 1893 were very far from satisfactory. The difficulties between the Baltimore & Ohio and the Pennsylvania were indeed patched up, and the opening of the former's lines to New York rendered it independent of other trunkline connections; but frequent charges of rate cutting were made in 1887, and a war in dressed-beef rates was inaugurated by the Grand Trunk in November of that year. In 1888 rates were pretty much demoralized. Published rates on grain dropped from $27\frac{1}{2}$ cents in January to 20 cents in October. Emigrant rates from New York to western points became the subject of active competition; and, most important of all, the dressed-beef controversy was pushed till it developed into a war of the most active kind. The trouble here was started by cuts on dressed beef by the Grand Trunk. In May other lines retaliated by cuts in live-stock rates; by July 14 published rates on cattle from Chicago to New York were $5\frac{1}{2}$ cents per 100 pounds, and on dressed beef and hogs 7 cents. In November the New York Central extended the contest by a general reduction in west-bound rates.[1] These struggles, though terminated for a time by an agreement of February, 1889,[2] seriously diminished railway revenues, and prevented the rapid growth which the general prosperity of the country might have occasioned.[3] In fact, the Erie management stated in their annual report for 1888 that their company had retired altogether from certain classes of through

[1] Chron. 47: 575, 1888. It is impossible to give an adequate account of these wars without straying too far from our subject. Some of the methods by which rebates were granted are revealed in the case of Jacob Shamberg *v.* Del., Lack. & W. R. R. Co. *et al.*, 4 I. C. C. Rep. 630. The differential question took on a new phase in 1888 through the demand of weaker roads for protection against stronger. This had long been a demand of the Grand Trunk, and had been conceded to it in the last part of 1887. In January, 1888, the Pennsylvania and the New York Central agreed to allow besides a differential rate to the Erie, the Lackawanna, the West Shore, and the Baltimore & Ohio, which should vary from five cents per hundred pounds from Chicago to New York on first class to one cent on fifth and sixth classes. R.R. Gaz. 20: 26, 1888; Chron. 46:57, 1888. This did not prevent active warfare throughout the year.

[2] Known as the Presidents' and Bankers' Agreement.

[3] There was, however, a shortage in the wheat crop in 1888.

business for a time during the preceding twelve months, owing to the unremunerative level of rates. Conditions during the greater part of 1889 were 'better,[1] and during the following three years constant attempts at agreement and arbitration, joined with a considerable volume of business,[2] prevented a long continuance of any difficulties which arose.

It was perhaps traffic conditions such as we have described which led the Garrett family to favor a community of interest scheme which should improve the Baltimore & Ohio connections with the West. In June, 1890, Mr. E. R. Bacon formed a syndicate to control the stock of the Baltimore & Ohio Company. Acting in harmony with the Garrett family, the syndicate was made up of Philadelphia, New York, Baltimore, and Pittsburg capitalists, including the Richmond Terminal, Pittsburgh & Western, Northern Pacific, and Reading interests. The plan was to establish a community of interest between a vast network of lines reaching from the Atlantic to the Pacific, and from New York to the Mississippi. "The buyers," it was said, "came in simply as investors without condition that their other properties would be benefited, although it was of course intimated that something was to be done."[3] They were required to pool their stock for three years, and to give an irrevocable proxy for that period to President Charles F. Mayer. The amount of the syndicate purchase was 45,000 shares, of which 32,500 were obtained from the city of Baltimore, and 9686 (preferred) from the state of Maryland;[4] and the purchase brought

[1] The comparative peace of 1889 was due as much to the abundance of traffic offering as to the efficacy of the agreement concluded in February of that year. According to the Chronicle the apportionment of traffic then contemplated proved difficult to carry out, and considerable discontent arose. Chron. 50: 892, 1890.

[2] In 1890 difficulties occurred through the competition of the Canadian Pacific, and more particularly through the attempt of the Lake Shore to reduce the differential formerly granted to the Grand Trunk. Chron. 50: 850, 1890. The matter was left to arbitration, Chron. 51: 625, with the result that the lines north of Lake Ontario were allowed to charge two and one-half cents less per hundred pounds on dressed beef to the seaboard than the lines further south. R. R. Gaz. 23: 64, 1891. This had the effect of putting the Canadian Pacific on an equality with the Grand Trunk. Late in 1892 still another agreement between the trunk lines was found necessary to maintain rates. Chron. 55: 857, 1892.

[3] Ry. Rev. 30: 382, 1890.

[4] Chron. 50: 800, 1890; Ibid. 50: 833, 1890; Ry. Rev. 30: 348, 1890; R. R. Gaz. 22: 448, 1890.

the incidental advantage of removing city and state from any direct interest in the road. The preferred state stock the syndicate later exchanged for common stock owned by the Johns Hopkins University. The purchase once made, the pool was formed on well-known lines. The stock was deposited with a trust company, trust certificates were issued, and proxies transferred to Charles F. Mayer.[1] The shares to be deposited were limited in amount to 110,000; the actual amount put in was 89,750. The results of the agreement were less sensational than the forecasts made. It undoubtedly did much to promote friendly feeling among the roads concerned. When, in 1891, the Baltimore & Ohio was compelled to vacate the Chicago terminals of the Illinois Central, which it had occupied for years, it was able to make prompt arrangements with a corporation controlled by the Northern Pacific for the use of its facilities both for passengers and for freight. But the influence of the Garrett family was not lessened, and inasmuch as the main competitors of the Baltimore & Ohio were not included there was no check to competition, and earnings showed no striking change.

Matters stood thus at the beginning of 1893.[2] No progress had been made toward restoring the Baltimore & Ohio to a permanently stable condition, and the prosperity which its reports declared was fictitious only. The reorganization to which bondholders had refused to submit in the comparatively prosperous times of 1888 was compelled by the depression following the panic of 1893. In 1894 earnings fell off. The gross earnings for the year ending June 30, 1893, were $26,214,807, and the net income $9,210,666; the following year the same items were $22,502,662 and $8,719,830. The directors reduced the dividend and called attention to the losses incurred through protracted strikes in the coal and coke industry.[3]

---

[1] Application for listing of Trustee certificates, Chron. 54: 369, 1892.

[2] Certain extensions had been made, which it is not necessary to describe at length. The most important had been those of the Pittsburgh & Western in 1891, Chron. 52: 238, 1891, the Akron & Chicago Junction, Chron. 53: 756, 1891, and the West Virginia & Pittsburgh, Chron. 54: 725, 1892. In 1893 the Baltimore & Ohio Southwestern and the Ohio & Mississippi Railway companies consolidated, and the Baltimore & Ohio guaranteed the principal and interest of the first consolidated mortgage gold bonds of the consolidated company for $25,000,000. Chron. 56: 332, 1893.

[3] Chron. 59: 696, 1894. In October, 1893, the Baltimore & Ohio was borrowing in London on one year 5 per cent promissory notes, and 2 per cent commission, paying, therefore, an equivalent of 7 per cent interest. Ry. Times, 64: 499, 1893.

The following January (1895) President Mayer stated that the fixed charges, including the car trusts, sinking funds, etc., due January 1, amounting to nearly $1,000,000, had been paid without borrowing one dollar. "I name this fact especially," said he, "because it is not unusual for us to make a loan for the unusually heavy payments January 1. I doubt if the Baltimore & Ohio has owed so small a floating debt for twelve or fifteen years, perhaps longer, and it never had the large volume of stocks and bonds it now has, something over $16,000,000, not put down at their face value but rather at their market value, or far below their intrinsic value. I can safely say the road has not been in so strong a position as now for at least fifteen years." [1]

It required more than confident statements by the managers, however, to demonstrate the secure position of the road; and this all the more because the acts of these gentlemen belied their public assertions. Dividends on the common stock were passed in 1895, and again in 1896. The ratio of charges to earnings, according to the company's reports, rose from 75 per cent of net earnings in 1894 to 80.2 per cent in 1895, and to 98.2 per cent in 1896; that is, less than 2 per cent of the net earnings of $6,300,000 was admitted to be available for dividends on $30,000,000 of stock. [2] Some relief was evidently necessary. In January, 1896, it was announced that arrangements had been made with a strong syndicate to provide for all immediate financial requirements; but the appointment of receivers in February could scarcely have come as a surprise. During the two weeks just before the failure Mr. J. K. Cowen, who had succeeded Mr. Mayer in the presidency, spent a great deal of time in New York trying to borrow money to meet the

[1] Chron. 60: 42, 1895.

[2] In 1895 the directors speak of the unremunerative rates prevailing. Chron. 60: 711, 1895. At the end of the year Mr. Alexander Shaw, chairman of the board of directors, felt called upon to say, "The two subjects which are giving the new board of directors the most to think about are the floating debt and the future management of the property. We have to fund the former, and as to the latter there is a difference of opinion among the directors. . . . I deny specifically that the January interest on the bonds of the company will be passed; that a receivership, either friendly or otherwise, is contemplated; that the Baltimore & Ohio and the Southern Railway systems are to be consolidated; and the statements that there has been an irregularity in the manner of keeping the books of the company." Chron. 61: 1153, 1895.

pressing demands. On his eventual failure and return to Baltimore the directors felt that a friendly receivership was the only resource.[1]

To the well-wishers of the road this failure may have seemed an opportunity as well as a disaster. It was now possible to accomplish what the management in 1888 had refused to attempt, *i. e.* a reduction in the fixed charges of the company which should remove the burdens under which the road had labored, and should open up the way for a long period of improvement and prosperity. At least one more unpleasant experience was, however, to be passed through. With a view to determining the Baltimore & Ohio's real position, an expert accountant, Mr. Stephen Little, had been set to work upon its books, and from time to time notices had been appearing that he was at work, that his examinations confirmed the statements of the company, and that questions raised by hostile critics would be considered in his report. Thus in April a reorganization committee, composed of Messrs. Alexander Shaw, C. Morton Stuart, and six others, with whom were deposited the Garrett shares, issued a circular referring to the large amount of new capital, estimated by them at $30,000,000, which had been received by the company since 1888 "without adequate or satisfactory results," and to the floating debt, which they asserted had been increased from about $3,500,000 to $16,000,000. "We make no charges, or even intimations of wrongdoing," wrote their secretary, "but desire and require that a full explanation of the management of the property from the year 1888, when the road was set on its feet by Mr. Morgan, shall be given, and that the causes which led to the wrecking of the property shall be clearly shown." To which another committee, which directly represented the management, replied by reference to Mr. Little.[2]

The much-heralded report came out in December, having been withheld since the previous March for fear of the effect on the company's securities; and so far from sustaining the management, it contained charges of irregularity almost as sensational as those made against the Atchison at an earlier date. The books of the company, according to Mr. Little, were in error to the amount of

[1] Ry. Rev. 36: 138, 1896. The receivers were appointed February 29.
[2] Chron. 62: 777, 1896.

$11,204,858. During the period of seven years and two months which his report covered he found:

An overstatement of net income of	$2,721,068
A mischarge of worn-out equipment to profit and loss of	2,843,596
Improper capitalization of charges to income under the head of construction, main stem,	2,064,741
Improper capitalization of so-called improvements and betterments of leased and dependent roads,	3,575,453
Total,	$11,204,858 [1]

Deducting these sums from the annual income returns of the company, he found that but $971,447 had been earned which had been properly applicable to dividends, whereas $6,269,008 had been declared in the seven years, of which $3,312,089 were cash and $2,956,920 stock. Earnings had been increased by the most arbitrary of book-keeping devices. In 1892 the value of the Western Union stock held in the treasury since the sale of the Baltimore & Ohio telegraph lines in 1888 had been written up $468,038, and the stock of another company, the Consolidated Coal Company, had been written up $114,300. Not only had advances to branch lines been entered as assets, but the interest on these advances had been credited to income, the only basis being that it was hoped that such interest would some day be paid; and on the other side of the account, charges against operating expenses had been charged to profit and loss on the same principles by which the Garretts had rolled up their fictitious surplus of 1888. Turning to the capital account, Mr. Little showed an increase in liabilities from 1888 to 1895 of $22,180,000, not including $5,481,835 representing chiefly the company's endorsements of notes of its subsidiary roads which stood here for the first time revealed. This money apparently had been put into the property, and yet Mr. Little's corrected figures showed net earnings to be actually smaller in 1895 than in the earlier years. Criticisms of the report attached themselves mainly to the last items treated. That the extensive endorsement of branch-line notes, absent as any mention of the practice was from the annual reports, was most misleading and unsound, nobody could deny;

---

[1] The period covered was from September 30, 1888, to November 30, 1895. Report of Mr. Stephen Little to General Louis Fitzgerald, chairman of the reorganization committee.

but the broad question of what charges during the seven years should have been paid out of income, and what not, gave rise to lively discussion. Severe strictures on Mr. Little's statements were made by Patterson and Corwin, two accountants appointed to re-examine the books of the company. "It would appear," said they, "that Mr. Little has made some curious errors, and has been strikingly inconsistent." [1] Nevertheless the more damaging of the latter's accusations seem to have been accepted, and the Baltimore & Ohio took its place with other American corporations, the managements of which have indulged in secret juggling with the books.

Pending Mr. Little's report, reorganization was of course delayed. The receivers were then in control, [2] and under their direction a vigorous policy of improvement was carried out. The rolling stock of the system was found to be insufficient to handle its business, and the motive power was in similar condition. All testified to the consistent desire of the old management to employ every device which might contribute to greater apparent earnings. Contracts for 5000 freight cars were let as early as May, 1896, to be paid for in receivers' certificates, and bids for 75 locomotives were at the same time received. [3] During their whole administration the receivers purchased over 28,000 freight cars, 216 locomotives, 123,000 tons of rails, besides ties, ballast, new steel bridges, and miscellaneous improvements of various sorts. [4] On the financial side they had to resist an attempt to compel payment of dividends on the preferred stock. The case dragged on through 1897 and 1898, and was finally decided in favor of the company. [5]

After the publication of Mr. Little's report there remained no serious bar to reorganization, while the needs to be met were more apparent than ever before. If the proportion of charges to earnings

---

[1] Chron. 64 : 999, 1897.

[2] President J. K. Cowen, Vice-President Oscar G. Murray.

[3] Chron. 62: 907, 1896.

[4] Ibid. 69: 128, 1899.

[5] R. R. Gaz. 28: 781, 1896; Ibid. 29: 563, 1897; Chron. 65: 110, 1897; Ry. Rev. 38: 628, 1898. The status of the Baltimore & Ohio stock was somewhat peculiar, in that when first issued to the state of Maryland it had been accompanied by a guarantee, or conditional guarantee, of dividend payments; and Johns Hopkins University, to which the stock had been transferred, maintained that this contract, added to the continuous payment of dividends for over fifty years, gave them rights even against the bondholders.

had been too heavy on the management's own showing, how much more burdensome was it when the reported earnings had been proved too high, and the reported liabilities too low! The first step after the appointment of receivers had been the springing up of reorganization committees. The two most prominent were the Fitzgerald Committee, representing the directors, and the Baltimore Committee. There were besides committees representing the 5 per cent bonds of the loan of 1885, the consolidated mortgage 5s, the 6 per cent bonds of 1874, the preferred stock, and others. These were all to some extent antagonistic. It was hoped to secure a reorganization without foreclosure, but to provide against all contingencies a bill was introduced and passed through the Maryland legislature, permitting a new company to succeed, after reorganization, to the property of the Baltimore & Ohio system.

By April, 1898, a reorganization plan was ready, and was withheld only on account, first of the threatened, and then of the actual, war with Spain. Two months later this difficulty seemed no longer serious, and a plan was formally announced.[1] There were contemplated two great issues of bonds and two of stock as follows:

3½ per cent prior lien gold bonds,	$70,000,000
4 per cent first mortgage gold bonds,	50,000,000
4 per cent non-cumulative preferred stock,	35,000,000
Common stock,	35,000,000

These were to be parts of larger amounts authorized but not issued. Thus the authorized amount of prior liens was $75,000,000, of which $5,000,000 were to be reserved, and to be issued after January 1, 1902, at the rate of not exceeding $1,000,000 a year, for enlargement, betterment, or extension of properties covered by the prior lien mortgage; or for the acquisition of additions thereto.[2] The authorized amount of first mortgage 4s was $165,000,000. Since the prior liens matured in 1925, and this mortgage not till 1948, $75,000,000 were reserved for retirement of the prior issue. $7,000,000 were

[1] Chron. 66: 1235, 1898.

[2] The prior lien bonds were "to be secured by a mortgage upon the main line and branches, Parkersburg Branch and Pittsburg Division when acquired by the new company, covering about 1017 miles of first track, and about 964 miles of second, third, and fourth track and sidings, and also all the equipment now owned by the company of the value of upward of $20,000,000, or hereafter acquired in any manner by the use of the $34,000,000 reserved first mortgage bonds, as hereinafter stated."

further put aside for the new company; $6,000,000 for the retirement of the Baltimore Belt Line 5s, and $27,000,000 for enlargements, betterments, or extensions, etc., at a rate not exceeding $1,500,000 a year for four years, and not exceeding $1,000,000 a year thereafter.[1] The reserves from these two mortgages, therefore, made liberal provision for new capital requirements. All of the common stock authorized was to be issued at once; but besides the $35,000,000 preferred stock before mentioned, $5,000,000 preferred were to be held in reserve for the new company.

Of the immediate issues $60,073,090 prior liens, $36,384,535 first mortgage 4s, $17,218,700 preferred stock, and $31,178,000 common stock went toward the retirement of old securities; and $9,000,000 prior liens, $12,450,000 first mortgage 4s, and $16,450,000 preferred stock were for cash requirements. The better of the old mortgages received cash for their overdue interest, something over par in prior liens for their principal, and from 12½ to 32 per cent in first mortgage 4s and preferred stock to compensate for reductions in their annual return. Inferior bonds received new first mortgage 4s with preferred stock (except in one instance) as a douceur. The old stock, common and preferred, and the Washington City & Point Lookout 6s got mostly new stock for the principal of their holdings, and preferred stock for their assessments. The fundamental principle on which the exchanges were based was the retirement of old bonds bearing high interest rates by an increased volume of new bonds bearing lower rates; thus permitting a much smaller reduction in fixed charges than occurred in other reorganizations which we shall consider. To some extent reductions in annual yield were made up by allowance of preferred stock. The consolidated mortgage 5s of 1887, on which interest was reduced from $50 annually to $41.75, received $85 in 4 per cent preferred stock as a

---

[1] The first mortgage 4s were to be a first lien "upon the Philadelphia, Chicago, and Akron divisions and branches and the Fairmount, Morgantown & Pittsburg Railroad, covering about 570 miles of first track, and about 332 miles of second, third, and fourth track and sidings, and also on the properties now included in the present Baltimore & Ohio Terminal mortgages of 1894, when said lines and properties are acquired by the new company; also on the Baltimore Belt Railroad, if and when the same shall be acquired by the new company. They will also be a lien subject to the prior lien mortgage upon the lines, properties, and equipment covered by the latter."

compensation. The Baltimore & Ohio Loan of 1874 saw a reduction in interest from $60 to $40.41, partially made up from the dividends on $160 of new preferred stock. In fact, out of thirteen cases in which new bonds were given for old, ten included an allowance of preferred stock, thus bringing the Baltimore & Ohio in line with other reorganizations of the period. But the proportion of preferred stock given was small in each case, and the principle was not well carried out.[1]

The cash requirements of the system were estimated at $36,092,-500; being swelled by arrears of interest, receivers' certificates, need for working capital, reorganization expenditures, and the like. The plan proposed to cancel them by assessments on stockholders and by the sale of securities before described. On the first preferred stock, $2 a share was levied, $20 on the second preferred, and $20 on the common stock, with a syndicate guarantee for each. This netted $5,460,000. Stockholders received new preferred stock for their payments. Deducting $5,460,000 preferred stock from the securities reserved under the plan to be sold for cash, there remained $9,000,000 prior liens, $12,450,000 first mortgage 4s, and $10,990,-000 preferred stock, or a total of $32,440,000; all of which a syndicate agreed to take.[2] In addition the company disposed of se-

---

[1] Annual Yield of Old and New Securities:

Loan	Previous annual return	Annual return from new bonds given	Annual return from new bonds and stock given
B. & O. Loan, 1853	$40	$40.87	$46.47
Consol. Mtg. 5s, 1887	50	41.75	44.35
Loan of 1872	60	40.41	42.01
Loan of 1874	60	40.41	46.81
Parkersburg Br. 6s	60	41.75	41.75
P. & C. 1st Ex. 4s	40	40.87	42.70
P. & C. 1st 7s	70	40.00	40.00
B. & O. 5s, Loan of 1885	50	40.00	44.00
P. & C. Consol. 6s	60	40.67	48.67
Chicago Div. 5s	50	46.30	50.30
Phila. Div. 4½s	45	40.00	50.60
B. & O. 4½ Term. Bs	45	40.00	40.00
Akron & Chicago Junc. 5s	50	40.00	42.00

[2] Headed by Messrs. Speyer & Co. and Kuhn, Loeb & Co. of New York, and Messrs. Speyer Bros. of London. R. R. Gaz. 30: 733, 1898.

curities in the treasury, including $3,800,000 stock of the Western Union Telegraph Company, for $3,500,000.[1]

Both classes of stock were vested in five voting trustees, for a period of five years. The trustees might, however, deliver the stock at an earlier date in their discretion, and in fact did so in August, 1901. No additional mortgage was to be put upon the property, and no increase in the amount of the preferred stock was to be made, except in each instance after obtaining the consent of the holders of a majority of the whole amount of preferred stock outstanding, given at a meeting of the stockholders called for that purpose, and the consent of the holders of a majority of such part of the common stock as should be represented at such meeting, the holders of each class of stock voting separately. During the existence of the voting trust similar consent of holders of like amounts of the respective classes of trust certificates was to be necessary for the purposes indicated. Only a portion of the leased and dependent lines were provided for in the plan, but the various cases were left to be passed on separately. Thus the Baltimore Belt Line was finally leased at a rental equivalent to 4 per cent on the outstanding 5 per cent bonds; while the acquisition of the Baltimore & Ohio Southwestern and the Central Ohio railroads involved the payment of a cash bonus, and an increase in the preferred and common stock outstanding. The mileage of the system suffered little change. Many of the branches were sold at foreclosure, and bought in by the parent line; and a glance at the balance-sheet in 1899 shows that besides the prior liens and the first 4s, an issue of Pittsburg Junction and Middle Division bonds was the principal tool employed. These securities, bearing $3\frac{1}{2}$ per cent, and falling due in 1925, were issued; 1st, to retire branch-line securities, and to weld the system into one united whole; and 2d, to provide new capital for enlargement and betterment and extension.

The success of this Baltimore & Ohio reorganization plan was very largely due to the time at which it was put through. In other words, the reorganization was completed just when an unparalleled

---

[1] The Western Union stock was sold to the same syndicate which took the Baltimore & Ohio's securities, at a price said to be about 90. At this price the yield would have been $3,420,000; so evidently very little other stock was sold.

era of prosperity was fairly under way. The moderate reduction in fixed charges which it secured proved more than adequate when earnings rapidly grew. The net earnings of the property for the year ending June 30, 1898, were estimated at $7,724,758, and the new fixed charges were set at $6,252,351.[1] Net earnings for 1899 were $6,621,599. In 1900, on a mileage 11 per cent greater, they were $12,359,443, and fixed charges were $6,831,463 only. In subsequent years, with an increase both in mileage and in earnings, the margin between charges and income further increased. In 1903 $3,500,000 were spent out of earnings for additions and improvements; $7,370,482 were declared in dividends; and $2,947,681 were carried to surplus. In 1907 $3,000,000 were spent in additions and improvements, $6,965,245 paid in dividends, $7,480,385 carried to surplus. This situation was in no way due to the reorganization plan, and would have restored the company to solvency even if no reorganization had taken place. It may be said that the receivership did much to enable the road to take advantage of the later prosperity. The character of the receivers' work has been mentioned. By June 30, 1899, they had spent as much as $17,000,000 for cars alone, $2,500,000 for locomotives, $2,100,000 for rails, and other sums for improvements and renewals of all kinds. The maintenance of way pay-rolls in three years amounted to nearly $12,000,000, and the total expenditure aggregated about $35,000,000; of which $15,000,000 were secured by the issue of receivers' certificates, and the balance through car trusts, earnings from the property, and from the reorganization managers.[2] This was an indispensable and invaluable preliminary to a growth in earnings, but was, however, distinct from the financial problems of reorganization. In brief, the Baltimore & Ohio increased its nominal capitalization more, and reduced its fixed charges less than any of the seven other reorganizations of the nineties which we shall consider except the Erie. Its need was perhaps less crying, but not sufficiently so to explain the difference.

It will be remembered that, while provision had early been made for foreclosure, it had been hoped to avoid such a drastic step. Hopes in this respect were fulfilled, and while a number of branch lines were

---

[1] In fact they were never quite so low as this.
[2] Chron. 69: 128, 1899.

sold the main stem escaped. Vigorous objections to the plan came from the preferred stock, which was in 1898 suing to compel payment of its dividends. In July, at a meeting of sharcholders it was declared to be the sense of the meeting that the preferred stock could not justly be required to determine whether it would accept the proposition published by the reorganization committee before the case in the Supreme Court should be decided.[1] Late in July an injunction was obtained, which, however, was dissolved in October. Still later in that year the suits were settled by the sale of the bulk of the first preferred stock to the reorganization committee.[2] The only other considerable complaint came from the holders of the 4½ per cent Baltimore & Ohio Terminal bonds, and was a protest against the reduction of ½ per cent in their interest without, as they said, the smallest compensation. Suits for the foreclosure of the mortgages of 1887, 1872, and 1874 were instituted in October, 1898. Decrees were obtained in February. Decrees were also given against the Philadelphia Division, the Parkersburg Branch, the Staten Island Rapid Transit Company, and others. Separate receivers had previously been appointed for the Sandusky, Mansfield & Newark, the Central Ohio, the Washington Branch, and others. Decrees were not asked for against the main line. In August, 1898, only three months after the publication of the plan, the reorganization managers were able to pronounce it effective.

The receivers surrendered control July 1, 1899,[3] and the company started on its new career amid a buzz of satisfaction from all who had participated in its reorganization. In an address before the Maryland Bar Association Mr. John K. Cowen summarized the result as follows:

(1) Every bondholder of the Baltimore & Ohio Railroad has received new securities which substantially pay his full debt. In other words, the bondholders have been paid in full.

(2) The floating debt creditors have received every cent of their indebtedness.

(3) The first preferred stockholders have received in cash 75 per cent of the par value of their stock, the court overruling their claim of preference over the bondholders and creditors. The second preferred stockholders have received securities which, after payment

---

[1] Chron. 67: 27, 1898. [2] Ry. Rev. 38: 656, 1898. [3] R. R. Gaz. 31: 500, 1899.

of the assessment, net about $70 per share, at the market price, and at times over $80 net could have been realized.

(4) The common stockholders, instead of being wiped out, have received their common stock in the new company upon paying an assessment, the net amount of which (because of the value of the securities received for such assessment) would not exceed $5 or $6.

(5) The company saves its old charter for whatever value may be attached to it.[1]

This statement presents the favorable side of the picture. On the whole, securityholders were tenderly handled, though the bond-holders were by no means paid off in full. And on the other hand, this very tenderness made a voluntary reorganization possible, whereby the charter of the company was saved. The pertinent objections were from the point of view of the company itself, and these were silenced by the increase in earnings.

Since reorganization the Baltimore & Ohio has been enjoying great prosperity. On a mileage operated, which was some 1800 miles greater in 1907 than in 1900,[2] it earned a return increased by over $40,000,000; while its income from dividends and interest mounted from less than half a million to over $3,000,000. Ton mileage figures were about 11,300,000,000 in 1907 as against 6,800,000,000 in 1900; passenger mileage had grown from 459,000,-000 to 723,000,000. This prosperity has but reflected the condition of the country at large, but the Baltimore & Ohio has taken advantage of it in far-sighted fashion. No less than $17,000,000 have been spent from earnings for additions and improvements between June 30, 1899, and June 30, 1907, not to mention maintenance of · ᐧ expenditures which have ranged from about $1500 to over $2500 per mile of road operated. Besides the provision made by the reorganization plan, $15,000,000 convertible debentures were issued under date of March 1, 1901, for new construction and improvements. There were authorized $40,000,000 of common stock in November, 1901, to go in part for improvements, and the bulk of $27,750,000 new common stock of 1906 will be applied to similar ends. As a result the company's equipment has largely increased, grades have been reduced, curves straightened, light

[1] Ry. Age 28: 570, 1899.
[2] The chief addition has been that of the Cleveland, Lorraine & Wheeling.

rails replaced by heavy, and subsidiary track increased. There were two miles of second, third, and fourth track and sidings for every three miles of main track in 1900; there were three miles to every four in 1907. A considerable increase in average freight train load has accordingly occurred. In 1900 the average load was 366 tons; in 1907 it was 433.02. That this figure has not still more greatly increased from the 406.53 tons of 1901 is probably due to the somewhat greater proportion of manufactures handled and to a considerable decrease in average distance hauled, and is compensated for by an increase of over one cent in the average rate received.

The events of most vital importance in the Baltimore & Ohio's recent history have been connected with its control. In September, 1898, Philip D. Armour, Marshall Field, and Norman D. Ream, executors of the Pullman estate, together with James J. Hill of the Great Northern, bought a large interest in the stock, though whether or not sufficient to control no one knew. From statements by Mr. Cowen it would appear that the deal was somewhat similar to the earlier one in which the Northern Pacific had been interested: that is, it involved the sale of Baltimore & Ohio stock to secure the good will of men strong enough to support the road in case of difficulty, and influential enough to open desirable connections or to modify the stringency of competition. "The recent transaction," said Mr. Cowen, "has been the realization of my hopes about the future of the road." It was not Mr. Hill's influence, however, that was destined to be dominant. By the end of the year rumors connected the Pennsylvania with the purchase of an interest in the property and the election of Mr. S. M. Prevost, third vice-president of that company, to a directorship, gave assurance of the truth of the reports. It was, of course, impossible to purchase actual control so long as the Baltimore & Ohio stock remained in trust; but the trustees seemed very ready to accord to new buyers that representation and influence to which their stock might give them claim. At the annual election in November, 1900, an additional representative of the Pennsylvania was elected to the board, showing the probable increase of the Pennsylvania holdings, and the following year an absolute majority was said to have been passed, the shares held by Mr. Hill and his associates, and apparently sold to the

Pennsylvania, being thought to contribute powerfully to that result.[1] In May, Mr. Hill and Mr. Charles H. Tweed, chairman of the Southern Pacific, resigned from the directorate, to be replaced by two further representatives of the Pennsylvania. In June, President Cowen was replaced by Mr. S. F. Loree, fourth vice-president of the Pennsylvania lines west of Pittsburg, and in August the voting trust was dissolved.

The last step has been the sale of part of the Pennsylvania holdings to the Union Pacific system. It appears that the former's interest in the company was largely due to anxiety over the coal situation. Before 1895 rates on bituminous coal had been depressed and demoralized. Rebates had been freely given in spite of any agreements which could be arranged. Under these circumstances the Pennsylvania had determined to buy enough stock of the Chesapeake & Ohio, the Baltimore & Ohio, and the Norfolk & Western companies to control the policies of these roads, and, through stock ownership in the Reading by the Baltimore & Ohio, to influence that company also.[2] Unfortunately for the project public attention became concentrated on the coal industry at this time because of the discovery of certain flagrant abuses, and it seemed wise for the Pennsylvania to dispossess itself of a part of its stock.[3] The Union Pacific was in the market with large resources derived from its sale of Great Northern and Northern Pacific stock. It was out of the question for the Pennsylvania to sell its shares to a competitor, but there was less objection to a sale to Mr. Harriman, providing a reasonable portion should be retained. Accordingly, the Pennsylvania sold and the Union Pacific interests bought, in

[1] Chron. 72: 1079, 1901. In February, 1906, the Pennsylvania Railroad and three other companies which it controlled owned $28,480,000 of Baltimore & Ohio preferred and $42,900,000 of Baltimore & Ohio common stock out of an authorized capital of $60,000,000 preferred and $125,000,000 common. Report of the Interstate Commerce Commission on the Pennsylvania community of interest, February 6, 1906.

[2] See Chron. 76: 102, 1903; and Interstate Commerce Commission, Report on Discriminations and Monopolies in Coal and Oil, January 25, 1907. The interest of the Baltimore & Ohio in the Reading dated from 1902, and was influenced in turn by the ability of the Reading to control the Central of New Jersey, over which the Baltimore & Ohio reached New York. The latter's holdings of Reading stock were shared with the Vanderbilts. Both the Baltimore & Ohio and the Lake Shore sold a block of their Reading stock in 1904.

[3] See statement by the Pennsylvania management in Chron. 83: 563, 1906.

October, 1906, some $39,540,600 in Baltimore & Ohio common and preferred stock, being in the neighborhood of half of the former's holdings. This is the present situation of the property. The Baltimore & Ohio is independent, in the sense that it is not controlled by any single interest, but large amounts of its stock are owned by its competitor, the Pennsylvania, and by its connection, the Harriman system. On the whole the alliance with these interests augurs well for the future of the company.[1]

[1] It is not necessary to do more than to mention the recent contest between the Baltimore & Ohio and the Hill-Morgan people over the Chicago Terminal Transfer Railway. By arrangement with this company the Baltimore & Ohio had enjoyed terminal facilities at Chicago on favorable terms. When the Terminal Railway went bankrupt the Baltimore & Ohio paid off the first mortgage bonds in order to prevent the loss of its privileges. Litigation followed, to end finally in an agreement between the Hill and Baltimore & Ohio interests for joint ownership of the Chicago Terminal by the Burlington and the latter, and for the use of its facilities in accordance with an equitable division of its trackage. The Pere Marquette and the Chicago Great Western, which had shared in the use of the property to that time, were left to shift for themselves. Ry. World, August 23, 1907.

CHAPTER II

ERIE

Early history — Reorganization — Wall Street struggles — Financial difficulties — Second reorganization — Development of coal business — Extension to Chicago — Grant & Ward — Financial readjustment — New York, Pennsylvania & Ohio — Third reorganization — Later history.

THE New York & Erie Railroad was organized in 1833 in the hope of bringing to the southern tier of counties in New York State a prosperity equal to that which the Erie Canal had secured for the northern tier. It was to run from New York or some suitable point in its vicinity to Lake Erie. A six foot gauge was adopted, partly because the grades encountered were thought to require locomotives with more power than a narrower gauge could accommodate, and partly because it was wished to make the road independent of any connection which might lead trade away from the city of New York.[1]

The events of the early years may be briefly dealt with. Difficulty was experienced in getting subscriptions, and in 1836 the legislature granted a loan of $3,000,000. An assignment was made in 1842, due to the difficulty of getting the enterprise under way, which resulted in the release of the company from liability to the state on condition that it complete its line from the Hudson to Lake Erie by 1851. Stockholders were to exchange two shares of old for one share of new stock, and a first mortgage of $3,000,000 was authorized.[2] In 1851 the line was completed to Dunkirk on Lake Erie, and the following year it reported a bonded indebtedness of $14,000,000, capital stock of $6,000,000, and floating debt to the amount of $3,080,000, or a total of $43,961 per mile of line; a high figure, but probably necessarily so in view of the difficult work to be performed. Although nominally completed, the troubles of the road were not over; and a precarious existence was maintained only by the placing of additional loans in 1852 and 1855, and by the aid of Daniel Drew on two distinct occasions. A war of rates with

---

[1] E. H. Mott, Between the Ocean and the Lakes — the Story of Erie. N. Y. 1899.
[2] Ibid. pp. 79–80.

the New York Central aggravated the situation; heavy storms and ice floods in January, 1857, caused serious loss, and the panic of that year, with the ensuing depression, proved more than the road could stand. Proceedings were begun in 1859 by the trustees of the fourth mortgage, and in August a receiver was appointed.[1] The wonder was that such action had been delayed so long. The income of the road had been so far short of meeting current expenses that claims for labor, supplies, rents, and unpaid taxes, and judgments rendered against the company before the receivers were appointed, had mounted up to $741,510; while not only had interest on three mortgages fallen due in April, May, and June, but the principal of the second mortgage, amounting to $4,000,000, had matured. The settlement of claims and the reorganization of the company were put in the hands of J. C. Bancroft Davis and Dudley S. Gregory. Since the earnings of the road were at so low an ebb, wisdom would have seemed to dictate some scaling of the charges to correspond. This did not enter into the views of the trustees; instead, they proposed to give preferred stock for all unsecured indebtedness, to extend the principal of the second mortgage coming due, to exchange old common stock for new, to levy an assessment of $2\frac{1}{2}$ per cent on both classes of new stock, and with the proceeds of the assessment to pay all coupons in arrears. Provision was made for the retirement of certain fourth mortgage bonds, and for a sale under foreclosure of that mortgage. By the arrangement no saving in fixed charges worth mentioning was secured; no sacrifice was demanded of bondholders; and, save for the payment of assessments and the (new) stock given for floating debt, the stockholder's position was not made worse. The scheme was an easy and temporary means of escape from an embarrassing position. Before the reorganization the bonds outstanding had amounted to $18,006,000, the stock to $11,000,000, and the unsecured indebtedness to $8,504,000. After reorganization the totals were: indebtedness, $17,953,000, and stock, $19,911,000 (of which $8,911,000 preferred); or a capitalization of $67,728 per mile. The road was sold in 1862, and the Erie Railway took the place of the original New York & Erie Railroad Company.

With 1864 began the career of the Erie as a speculative Wall

---

[1] Mott, p. 129. Default was also made on the first, second, third, and fifth mortgages.

Street stock. Its large capitalization and the painful slowness with which its earnings grew kept the quotations of its shares normally at a low figure and invited speculation; while the location of its lines tempted more serious efforts to obtain control. Up to 1867 Daniel Drew was in power, while Commodore Vanderbilt spent his best efforts to drive him out; after that date Jay Gould and Jim Fisk became more and more prominent, and manipulated the Erie securities with enthusiastic regard to profits which they might derive both from the Erie Company itself and from operators who wished to speculate in its stock. In the course of the abundant litigation to which Gould's methods gave rise, various receivers were appointed; but the orders of appointment were subsequently vacated, and the receiverships were nominal only. The details of the Wall Street struggles have little interest for us here.[1] But the result is of importance. In the eight years from 1864 to 1872, when Gould was turned out of Erie by General Sickles and his English backers, the bonded indebtedness of the company increased from $17,822,-900 to $26,395,000, and the common stock from $24,228,800 to $78,000,000; in the one case a growth of 48 per cent and in the other of 221 per cent, at a time when the mileage increased 53 per cent and the net earnings but 22 per cent.[2] No more disgraceful record exists for any American railroad. The stock was not issued for the sake of improving the road, and it was subsequently shown that the road was not improved; but it was thrown upon the market at critical times in support of bear operations by the Erie managers, while portions of it, on at least one occasion, were bought back with the funds of the company to aid speculation for a rise. The result was to ruin the credit of the Erie, and to make it the favorite tool of cliques of gamblers. The increase in bonds occasioned an unmistakable increase in fixed charges, which rose from 20 per cent of gross earnings in 1864 to 25 per cent in 1871, 21 per cent in 1872, and 30 per cent in 1873, while the purchase of worthless bonds of subsidiary roads, such as the Boston, Hartford & Erie, lessened the assets without disclosing the real position to the casual observer.

In 1872 the control of Erie was taken from Gould through a vigorous campaign managed by General Daniel E. Sickles, and an

---

[1] See Adams's Chapters of Erie, Boston, 1871.
[2] The capital per mile rose from $81,068 in 1864 to $117,760 in 1872.

"eminently respectable" board of directors was elected. Temporary relief was obtained from the use of $6,000,000, available from an issue of bonds previously approved, [1] and dividends, first on the preferred and then on both preferred and common stock were declared. Unfortunately the dividends were not earned; and this fact, which was suspected from the previous record of the company and the marvel of its so early restoration to a dividend basis, was shown in the statements of ex-Auditor S. H. Dunan, who resigned in March, 1874, alleging that the accounts had been falsified to suit the company's purposes, and that he was unwilling any longer to be a party thereto. [2] Investigations conducted by representatives of English bondholders showed that in the three years ending in September, 1875, the profits of the road had been $1,008,775 instead of $5,352,673 as stated in the company's accounts; and the severity of this finding was scarcely mitigated by the conclusion that in the opinion of the committee the dividends on the preferred stock at least were justified by the books. [3] At the same time the report of Captain Tyler, another English representative, laid emphasis on the necessity for a change of gauge, a double track, improvements in gradient, fresh extensions and connections, and other similar matters.

The real position of the company at the time was shown but too well by the frequency of strikes upon its road. Thus in February, 1874, a strike of freight brakemen on the Susquehanna division broke out, caused principally by an order to discharge one of the brakemen from each freight crew, leaving only three on a train; and at the same time there was a strike of the switchmen on some of the divisions owing to a decrease in pay. In March occurred a serious strike among the employees of the road in Buffalo, mainly on account of irregularity and delay in payment of wages, and, finally, in April, there was trouble both in the Susquehanna shops and in the Jersey City freight yard over this same cause. The indications afforded by these troubles were borne out by the figures of the annual reports. The gross earnings of 1874 were $1,413,708 less than those of 1873,

[1] Chron. 12: 203, 1871; Ibid. 16: 489, 1873.

[2] R. R. Gaz. 6: 100, 1874. See affidavit of S. H. Dunan in the suit of John C. Angell against the Erie Railway Company and others, reprinted in Hepburn Committee Report, vol. 2, Exhibits, pp. 591–610.

[3] Hepburn Committee Report, vol. 2, Exhibits, pp. 623–643.

while the decrease in operating expenses was so slight as to reduce net earnings by nearly the same amount. If, now, there is deducted from the net earnings of the years 1871–3, inclusive, the sum which the London accountants declared to have been improperly reported as profits, there results an average of $4,175,699 net; or less than the net earnings for either 1864, 1865, or 1866, although the average charges for the years mentioned exceeded the average of the earlier period by $1,769,060 each year. These figures exclude the influence of the panic of 1873, which, as has been seen, caused a still further falling off in the earnings of the company. It was a time, moreover, when the Erie could not be content to sit still and wait, for competition was daily becoming more severe. By 1874 the Baltimore & Ohio, the New York Central, and the Pennsylvania had connections with Chicago, and the Erie was competing with them for business by means of traffic agreements with connecting lines. The next decade was to see the bitterest rate wars that the country has ever known; and the Erie, with its exceptional gauge and single track, was to compete with rivals of normal gauge, who were adding third and fourth tracks to the two which they already possessed. The one bright spot was the development of the coal traffic, which in 1874 formed the greatest item of the Erie's tonnage, and was in a measure apart from the competition of other lines.

Suit was brought in July, 1874, for the appointment of a receiver. The complaint reviewed alleged improper acts of the management in declaring dividends, in buying Buffalo, New York & Erie stock and sundry coal lands, and in issuing the new $30,000,000 mortgage before mentioned.[1] In October the Attorney-General of New York instituted suit on nominally the same grounds; not, as he explained, in the expectation that the appointment of a receiver would be required, but in order that this action might be taken if the conduct of the directors should make it necessary. Still other suits were begun before the year was out.

Meanwhile the management was changed. Whether or not Mr. Watson, who had been president since 1872, had done all humanly possible to set the Erie on its feet, his administration was not unnaturally in bad odor after the charges of Dunan and the report of the London accountants, to say nothing of the admittedly low

---

[1] Angell suit, R. R. Gaz. 6: 269, 1874.

earnings for the year 1874. An attempt was made to secure the very best man possible for the presidency, and to support him in necessary reforms, in the hope of some different results from those with which securityholders had become familiar. The man for the place was thought to be Mr. H. J. Jewett, a railroad man then in Congress from Ohio; and this gentleman was accordingly secured at an extremely liberal salary. Soon after his election a ten per cent cut in salaries was decreed, and an examination of the accounts of the stations along the line in behalf of the company was begun. It was too late, however, for the company. The business of the last of 1874 and first of 1875 was poor; floods in the spring damaged the property of the road, and rumors of a receivership were rife. On May 22 a private meeting of stockholders in New York passed resolutions to the effect that the borrowing of money by the sale of 7 per cent bonds at 40 cents on the dollar, and other means adopted by the Watson administration, would inevitably result in bankruptcy; that sound interest required that the money needed to pay interest should be raised by an assessment on the stockholders, and that the directors should be thereby requested to open books to examination, and to invite stockholders to contribute voluntarily a sum sufficient to keep the company from immediate failure.[1] The proposal showed a proper spirit, but was impracticable. Four days later Mr. Jewett was appointed receiver on application of representatives of the Attorney-General and of the Railroad.[2]

This was the second receivership which the Erie had had to face, and the situation was materially worse than at the previous failure. According to the statement of President Jewett the funded indebtedness in May, 1875, amounted to $54,394,100, and the fixed charges to $5,059,828; while the net earnings for the previous nine months had decreased 13.4 per cent from the corresponding period for the previous year, and a serious deficit was in view. Temporary measures of relief had served but to drag the company further into the mire;[3] and, most important of all, the causes for the existing diffi-

[1] R. R. Gaz. 7: 224, 1875.

[2] Chron. 20: 520, 1875.

[3] From a loan of £3,000,000 placed in London, the company had received but £1,232,029 in cash; £508,431 being retained by the London Banking Association and by James McHenry for claims and commissions on which the critical condition

culties were of a permanent nature, so that the future gave promise of still harder conditions than had existed in the past. What was needed was a reorganization which should undo the evil work of Gould, Fisk, Drew, and their associates, and which should secure the margin of surplus earnings which the reorganization of 1859–62 had failed to provide. Perhaps the chief difficulty lay in the fact that the men who were responsible for the increased capitalization were not at all those on whom the brunt of reconstruction would fall; for while the managers of the road had been Americans, the gullible investors had been Englishmen; and it was reported that much of the watered stock of the Gould régime had been unloaded on the English market.

Committees sprang up promptly. The most important of them were the English committees of bond- and stockholders, soon consolidated under the chairmanship of Sir Edward Watkin. On August 7, Sir Edward left England on a visit of inspection, accompanied by Mr. Morris, counsel for the bondholders. Conference with the board of directors and with President Jewett followed, and a provisional scheme of adjustment was decided upon. In his report to his English constituents Sir Edward outlined the results. Current indebtedness, said he, was $42,180,075; estimated net revenues for the year ending in June last were $3,715,609; operating expenses had been for that year 79 per cent, due largely to the cost imposed by exceptional gauge, while the chief lines with which the Erie competed showed proportions of only from 60 to 66 per cent. Out of fourteen branches only three showed a profit above rentals, and pay-rolls had ordinarily been months in arrears. These facts were familiar; the remedy proposed was unfortunately familiar as well. "Let it be hoped," said this English financier, "that the bond- and stockholders will have the courage now to submit to a period of self-denial, and will consent to pay their debts and complete essential obligations out of available net profits, the bondholders receiving in place of cash such equitable obligations, realized out of surplus revenue in the future, as each, according to right of priority, may justly expect." [1] What could this have meant save an issue of stock or income bonds for coupons falling due, with the result of

of the company enabled them to insist. Chron. 20: 500, 1875. For statement of the physical condition of the property, May 26, 1875, see Extracts from joint letter to Hon. H. J. Jewett, Hepburn Committee Report, vol. 2, pp. 517–518, Exhibits.

[1] See R. R. Gaz. 7:423, 1875.

adding to the unwieldy capitalization of the road instead of reducing it as should have been done! For the rest, Sir Edward Watkin concluded with Mr. Jewett the following arrangement:

(1) Three nominees of the bond- and stockholders' committee proposed by Watkin were to take seats in the Erie board;

(2) Mr. Morris was to be associated with counsel for the receiver and for the company, and was to be regarded and treated as one of the professional agents and officers of the undertaking;

(3) Mr. Jewett was to transmit a memorandum of his views on reorganization;

(4) Net earnings were to be retained for a while, and bondholders were to have a voice in their expenditure. Thus a vote was to be taken under the charge of the stock- and bondholders' committee in London on the constitution of a committee of consultation, consisting of representatives of each class of bondholders and of preferred and ordinary stock, and that committee was to designate a special representative whose consent and approval were to be taken by Mr. Jewett in the expenditure of net earnings;

(5) Monthly reports of actual earnings and expenditures, together with reports from the president and receiver, were to be regularly transmitted to the office of the committee in London;

(6) Bond- and stockholders were to be urged to give power of attorney and proxies to Watkin, or to such other person or persons as the above representatives of the bond- and stockholders should designate;

(7) Any scheme of reorganization was to include a provision giving bondholders a voting power.

On the above resolutions Jewett, with his board, and Watkin, with his committee, agreed to coöperate.[1] Under the circumstances the increased power given the bondholders was both a natural and a just demand, and it is probable that Mr. Jewett's prompt acquiescence in it had something to do with Sir Edward's advice to the security-holders "to rely on the honor, as I feel you may also upon the anxious labors and full experience of the President and Receiver."

The report did not go uncriticised. It was pointed out, first, that a majority of English proprietors could not unhesitatingly share the confidence expressed in Mr. Jewett; second, that the first mortgage bondholders were well secured, and would surely refuse to fund

[1] R. R. Gaz. 7: 423, 1875.

their indebtedness; and third, that the payment of the floating debt, according to the Watkin plan, would simply create another debt of equal or greater amount due to the bondholders whose coupons were not paid. The only sound way, said a committee of bondholders in Dundee in a letter to the Watkin Committee, is resolutely to shun an accumulation of mortgage liabilities on the one hand, and on the other to give increased reality to the bonds and stocks of the company already existing as items in capital account, *i. e.* an assessment on the stock and a sweeping reduction in the interest on the bonds secured by the second mortgage:—the first mortgage bonds are in different case — they represent investment of cash instead of mere water, and even if foreclosure is difficult, they have beyond question an absolutely good security for the ultimate payment of both principal and interest.[1]

In September, 1875, a plan of reorganization was anonymously put forward as follows: Instead of assessment on the shareholders, it suggested the issue of 50 per cent more common stock; one new share for every two shares then existing. If a price of $25 per share could be obtained a total of $10,000,000 cash would be thereby secured. Besides the new stock issued bond- and preference-holders were to capitalize their interest for two years in bonds or shares bearing their present priorities. This funding should yield $8,000,000; and the $18,000,000 in all obtained was to be expended on the road over the next two years, during which period the new shares were to be paid up by half-yearly instalments. With the line furnished and equipped as proposed, continued this optimistic plan, the working expenses could be reduced from 79 per cent to 60 per cent, and the traffic within three years would be at least $24,000,000 per year, affording a net revenue of $9,600,000 per annum, sufficient to meet all bond and preference liabilities and to leave 3 per cent for the ordinary charges.[2] The all sufficient criticism to this plan was that it required too great a combination of favorable circumstances to ensure its success. In some respects, however, it was not unlike the plan ultimately adopted.

Two months later appeared a plan by Mr. John C. Conybeare, an English bondholder, which was superior to the foregoing in that it proposed an assessment, and made some slight provision for an

[1] R. R. Gaz. 7: 479–80, 1875.   [2] Chron. 21: 277, 1875.

ultimate reduction in fixed charges. Mr. Conybeare proposed to assess preferred stock $11 and common stock $9. Payment of the assessment was not to be compulsory, but was to have the effect of giving to the stock which did pay a right to dividends before anything should be received by that which did not pay. Shares of the company by the plan would thus have ranked as follows:

(1) Preferred shares on which assessment had been paid, entitled to 7 per cent dividends before any other dividends were paid.

(2) Preferred shares on which no assessment had been paid, with rights inferior to the preferred A shares, but superior to the common shares.

(3) Common stock on which assessment had been paid, entitled to 4 per cent before further dividend on the common.

(4) Unprivileged, unassessed common stock which was to take what there was left.

In addition there was to be a pre-preference 8 per cent stock, ranking before all the above, which was to be issued to exchange in part for second preferred and convertible bonds. First consolidated bonds and sterling bonds of 1865 were to accept one or two per cent of their 7 per cent interest in bonds, secured perhaps by the coal property of the company, while the second consolidated and the convertible gold bonds were to receive 4 per cent in gold and 3 per cent in the new pre-preference stock as above. To the obvious possibility that the stockholders would refuse to pay an assessment the plan opposed no remedy. In this case the very moderate amount of interest funded would have been the only relief secured.[1]

These plans were, however, but preliminary to the elaborate Watkin scheme which appeared in December. The most prominent feature herein was, as previously indicated, the funding of coupons, both those past due and those to become due for a time into the future. Given net earnings sufficient to meet fixed charges, the postponement of interest by this plan would obviously have released revenue with which to make needed improvements on the road. This funding was to be, however, limited to the first consolidated 7s, convertible sterling 6s, second consolidated 7s, and convertible gold 7s; the six earlier issues were to be left untouched. One permanent reduction was also to be made, in that for the second

---

[1] R. R. Gaz. 7:511, 1875.

mortgage and convertible 7s were to be given two classes of ninety-year gold bonds: the first for 60 per cent of the principal, with interest at 6 per cent, and payable in bonds of the same class from the dates of default until March, 1877, and thereafter in gold; the second for 40 per cent of the principal, carrying 4 per cent until 1881 and thereafter 5 per cent, payable only out of net earnings. To start the company on its way and to meet present obligations an assessment was proposed of three dollars on the preferred and six dollars on the common stock, in return for which 5 per cent income bonds were to be given; while finally the dividends on the preferred stock were to be reduced from 7 to 6 per cent, and foreclosure was contemplated, so that the opposition of an irreconcilable minority might be more easily overcome.[1] According to the figures in the Watkin plan, the old and new capitalization and interest compared as follows:

The amount of capital stock was unchanged.

Total bonded indebtedness	Principal	Interest
Before reorganization,	$54,394,100	$4,073,106
After reorganization,	61,330,241	4,139,240
Increase	$6,936,141	$66,134

Indebtedness on which interest was obligatory:

	Principal	Interest
Before reorganization,	$54,394,100	$4,073,106
After reorganization,	46,634,134	3,316,238
Decrease	$7,759,966	$756,868

The net earnings for 1874–5 had been $3,715,609, and those from 1871–3 inclusive, with the deductions declared proper in the report of the London accountants, had averaged $4,175,699 each year, so that a safe margin seemed to intervene. The extent of the margin depended, however, on the fixed charges, such as rentals, over and above interest on the funded debt; and although it was proposed to cancel burdensome leases and contracts the actual leeway after 1880 was to be very small indeed. To speak briefly, the plan was definite but not sufficiently radical to meet conditions which were likely to arise. In counting upon the ability of the company to spare considerable sums from revenue for improvements during the next few years, it was leaning on a broken reed; in increasing the nominal

[1] R. R. Gaz. 7:533, 1875; Chron. 21:612, 1875.

amount of bonded indebtedness, it was making a step in the wrong direction; and by interposing additional claims on earnings while leaving the volume of stock the same, it took from the stockholders any very lively interest in the road's future welfare. The plan was nevertheless accepted by the English securityholders, subject to such modifications as might afterwards be found desirable.[1]

The next step was to obtain the unanimous acceptance of this Watkin scheme. Messrs. Robert Fleming and O. G. Miller were accordingly sent to New York in February, 1876, to consult with the officers of the company and the securityholders in America. No very vigorous interest was taken on this side, but the Erie directors appointed a committee to confer with the English representatives, and discussions took place for something over a month. The committee criticised the plan proposed from the point of view of the stockholders; they maintained that it would destroy all their interest in the property unless they made further sacrifices, which they were unable to do, and suggested that the funding of from four to eight coupons by the first consolidated, gold convertible, and second consolidated bonds was all that would be needed to put the road in a prosperous condition, provide for steel rails, and for the narrowing of the gauge.[2] This was so plainly inadequate that it is a matter of surprise that it was entertained by the English committee; and even they insisted that the stockholders agree to put a majority of the $86,000,000 of stock in the hands of the bondholders as a preliminary, and would do no more than lay the proposal before their constituents.

On their return home in April Messrs. Miller and Fleming stated that the essential conditions to a successful reorganization were:

(1) An effective control of the management by the real owners, — the bondholders;

(2) The restoration of the equilibrium between the compulsory interest charge on the mortgage debt and the minimum net earnings;

(3) A change of gauge from 6 ft. to 4 ft. 8½ in.[3]

"The foreclosure scheme of the committee" (Watkin plan), said they, "is certainly the soundest plan and would doubtless be preferred by those shareholders who really care for the welfare of their property." Then referring to the directors' plan, "If it were possible to present to the bondholders the scheme of proceeding by

[1] R. R. Gaz. 8:818, 1876.   [2] Chron. 22:233, 1876.   [3] R. R. Gaz. 8:178, 1876.

amicable arrangement as practicable, and therefore as presenting a real alternative for their acceptance, we should suggest to you at the same time to lay the option before them. We feel, however, that that scheme can only be regarded as such an alternative when stockholders enough have signified their willingness to vest their shares in trustees on the footing of it, and so secure an effectual control to the bondholders for a certain period. We must, therefore, content ourselves for the present with suggesting that the committee should proceed with vigor in the direction of foreclosure, at the same time inviting the stockholders to signify their willingness to vest their stock in trustees as above mentioned." [1]

The suggestion of the directors was the last alternative plan proposed, and from April, 1876, the only question was how to perfect and carry through the Watkin plan. As eventually put forward, this differed in a few points from its form as earlier announced. The fundamental principle was still the funding of coupons of the first and second consolidated and the convertible bonds. Of these the first consolidated mortgage and sterling 6 per cents were now to fund *alternate* coupons from September 1, 1875, to September 1, 1879, instead of funding *all* coupons to March 1, 1876, and receiving cash thereafter: and whereas in the earlier plan mortgage bonds of the same class had been given for funded interest, the later plan created special issues of funded coupon bonds, secured by deposit of the funded coupons, and bearing the same interest as the first consolidated bonds themselves. A more serious difference appeared in the treatment of the second mortgage and the gold convertibles. It will be remembered that it had been proposed in December, 1875, to exchange these for two classes of new bonds, of which 60 per cent were to bear interest at the rate of 6 per cent and 40 per cent were to consist of 4 per cent income bonds. The new plan did away with this permanent reduction in fixed charges. Instead, the second consolidated and convertible gold bonds funded alternate coupons from June 1, 1875, to December 1, 1879, and received a new 6 per cent bond for the principal of their holdings, and funded coupon 6 per cent bonds for the interest thus postponed; the new mortgage bonds not having the right of foreclosure until after default for six successive interest periods (3 years). The funded coupon bonds were

[1] Chron. 22:423, 1876.

to be funded at the existing rate of interest on the second consolidated and convertible bonds, *i. e.* 7 per cent, so that the reduction in interest was compensated for by the greater volume of securities given; and both classes of these coupon bonds were to bear lower interest at first than that to which they would ultimately attain. The assessment proposed in 1875 was retained in 1876, except that stockholders were given the choice of paying $6 on common and $3 on preferred stock and obtaining therefor income bonds, or of paying $4 on common and $2 on preferred and receiving nothing but new stock, dollar for dollar for their old.[1] One-half of the shares of the new company (after foreclosure) were to be issued in the name of one or more sets of trustees, who were to hold them to vote on until a dividend had been paid on the preferred stock for three consecutive years. Provision was made for an issue of $2,500,000 in prior lien bonds, to take precedence of the remainder of the second consols, the proceeds to be applied to capital requirements. Voting power was conferred on the first and second consols, funded income bonds, prior lien bonds, and income bonds, in all about $57,000,000; one vote to every $100 of bonds.[2] The property of the company was to be foreclosed by or under the direction of certain reconstruction trustees, for the choice of whom careful provisions were inserted.

Divested of all complications, what this reorganization plan proposed for the salvation of the property was the funding of the coupons on four classes of bonds from 1875 to 1879; the reduction of the interest to be paid on $25,000,000 second consolidated and convertible 7s one per cent per share; and the raising of a certain amount

[1] Amounts received from assessments to January 18, 1878, were:

$3 per share on	23,372 Preferred,	$70,116
$2	58,095	116,190
$6	72,982 Common,	437,892
$4	698,095	2,792,380
Total,		$3,416,578
Shares forfeited for non-payment, — Preferred,		3902
Shares forfeited for non-payment, — Common,		8923

R. R. Gaz. 11 : 30, 1879. Report of Pres. Jewett, Chron. 28 : 67–8, 1879. Shares with assessment paid sold in October, 1878, at $15 for common and $30 for preferred. R. R. Gaz. 10 : 516, 1878.

[2] Chron. 23 : 233, 1876; Ibid. 26 : 419; Ibid. 29 : 358, 1879; Hepburn Committee Report, vol. 2, pp. 252–7, Exhibits.

of cash by assessment upon the stockholders; while it dropped the one point of the earlier plan which might have given a key to the solution of the whole problem, viz. the exchange of mortgage and income bonds for the old second consolidated in the ratios respectively of 60 per cent and of 40 per cent. When we remember the desperate straits to which the company had been reduced, the permanent relief seems slight enough; and given the fact, which proved but too true, that the net earnings were to fall off until the road was little more than able to meet the alternate coupons which it was obliged to pay in cash, it appears to have been nothing at all. If we suppose no changes to have occurred in capital account between 1878 and 1883 save those provided for in the plan of reorganization itself, a comparison of the two periods would have stood as follows:

Before reorganization	*Principal*	*Interest*
Sterling convertible 6s,	$4,457,714	$267,463
First consolidated 7s,	12,076,000	845,320
Convertible 7s,	10,000,000	700,000
Second consolidated 7s,	15,000,000	1,050,000
	$41,533,714	$2,862,783
Old Mortgages,	13,155,500	921,062
Guaranteed bonds, etc.,	6,003,360	449,411
	$60,692,574	$4,233,256
Rentals,		742,226
		$4,975,482

After December 1, 1883	*Principal*	*Interest*
Consolidated 7s,	$20,005,794	$1,400,405
Consolidated 6s,	33,516,666	2,011,000
	$53,522,460	$3,411,405
Old bonds,	13,155,500	921,062
Guaranteed bonds, etc.,	6,003,360	449,411
Rentals,		742,226
	$72,681,320	$5,524,104
Total before reorganization	60,692,574	4,975,482
Increase,	$11,988,746	$548,622

It thus appears that this reorganization plan contemplated an immediate increase in the cumbrous capitalization of the company to the amount of nearly $12,000,000, and an eventual increase in fixed charges of over $500,000. It offered no reasonable assurance that the solvency of the company could be maintained under the average conditions existing in the past, and left no margin for contingencies of any kind. The trouble lay in the unwillingness of bondholders to sacrifice any part of their holdings to meet difficulties caused largely by inflation over which they had had no control. This reluctance was natural, — it should have been met, however, by the realization that the question was now of the future and not of the past, and that the best interests of the bondholders themselves demanded a reconstruction sufficiently radical to leave no doubt of the ability of the new company to pay its debts.

The plan adopted, foreclosure was in order, and suits which had been begun as early as 1875 were taken up and pushed. In November, 1877, a decree of foreclosure under the second consolidated mortgage was obtained, appointing a referee to conduct the sale, and providing for the sale of the road to representatives of the bondholders in case they made the highest bid. The opposition, which had not been able to prevent the approval of the plan, now appeared with a multiplicity of suits to prevent its consummation. In January, 1878, demands were made to secure a re-accounting from the receiver, and the reopening of an earlier suit of the people against the Erie which had been previously discontinued. On January 18 the postponement of the sale to March 25 was obtained. On January 19 a suit demanded the removal of Receiver Jewett, making sweeping charges of fraud; and on January 30, in still other proceedings, Mr. Jewett was arrested on a charge of perjury for swearing to incorrect statements in the annual report to the state engineer; — a culmination as disgraceful as it was absurd. In February a suit in Orange County, New York, demanded the removal of the receiver, and the appointment of a special receiver during the pendency of the action, with an injunction to prevent the sale of the road. In March a petition of one Isaac Fowler, a stockholder, for permission to examine the company's books, was granted; argument was heard on the petition of James McHenry to intervene in the foreclosure suits and further to postpone the sale; the application of Albert Betz and others to be made parties was granted; and postponement of sale to April 24 obtained. Last of all, on April 23 and 24, arguments in behalf of John F. Brown and F. W. Isaacson were heard, asking for postponement to a still later date. The litigation availed nothing. Judge Potter in the Brown suit held that the courts could relieve against any injustice occasioned by the sale, and on April 24 the property of the Erie Railway was sold for $6,000,000 under foreclosure of the second consolidated mortgage.[1] The new corporation formed to take over the railroad was called the New York, Lake Erie & Western Railroad Company, and had its articles of incorporation regularly filed at the office of the Secretary of State. Mr. Jewett was elected president. In May the receiver was discharged,[2] and a new stage in the history of the road began.

For about seven years the Erie was to be free from the necessity for further reorganization. This result, unexpected from the nature of the adjustment of 1878, was due to the vigorous policy of Mr. Jewett, first, in developing the coal traffic for which the Erie was well located; second, in improving the condition of the road; and third, in securing connections with Chicago.

For some time the Erie had been a considerable carrier of coal and a large owner of coal lands as well. In 1877, the first year in which the figures were separated in the annual report, roughly 273,000,000 out of 1,113,000,000 ton miles reported, or something over one-quarter, were due to the carriage of coal; and $2,697,776 out of a total of $10,647,807 of the freight earnings came from that business. The lands owned by the company consisted of 8000 acres in fee, and large tracts in leasehold and mining rights in the anthracite territory in the northeast corner of Pennsylvania; together with 14,000 acres in fee and 13,000 acres of mining rights in the bituminous territory in the northwest portion of the state.[3] Mr. Jewett felt that this property could be made of great value to the road, and it was under his administration as receiver that steps were taken to extend the holdings of bituminous land, and to control branch roads leading into the district. The result appeared in a remarkable extension of the company's business. While the total freight ton mileage from 1878 to 1884 increased 103 per cent, the ton mileage of coal increased 190 per cent, or nearly tripled; and while the gross earnings on ordinary freight grew from $7,950,031 to $11,687,520, those

---

[1] Chron. 26:419, 1878.

[2] Ibid. 26:469, 1878. For indenture executed by the new corporation and for text of the first and second consolidated mortgage and of the second consolidated funded coupon mortgage, see Hepburn Committee Report, vol. 2, Exhibits, pp.315-50.

[3] Mott, p. 268.

on coal increased from $2,697,776 to $5,437,000. At the same time McKean County, directly north of the coal lands, and containing large tracts purchased by the Erie in the course of its other negotiations, turned out to be an abundant oil-producing district, and made the Bradford branch, which tapped it, Erie's most valuable collateral property.[1]

It was partly because of the success of the policy in respect to coal lands that the Erie was enabled to spend large sums in the improvement of its road. In the six years from 1878 to 1883 the company put nearly $14,000,000 into improvements of the road, property and equipment, and of this about one-half was paid out of surplus earnings. In December, 1883, alone, $304,565 were spent, and in the three suceeeding months nearly double that amount; making a total of nearly $1,000,000 in the four months previous to April, 1884. The money went toward reducing grades, straightening curves, increasing weight of rails, etc., including the completion of a third rail to Buffalo by which the serious disadvantage of an exceptional gauge was removed. Its result was seen in the decrease in the ratio of operating expenses from 75.13 in 1875 and 77.16 in 1876 to 64.78 in 1883; and in the rise of net earnings per ton mile from .251 cents to .261 cents, while the gross earnings per ton mile decreased from 1.209 cents to .780 cents. No policy which the Erie managers pursued met a more crying need, and none did so much toward maintaining the solvency of the company.

The project of controlling a line of their own to Chicago was brought actively to the attention of the Erie managers by the danger of being cut off from a connection with that city. The original line of the Erie had run to Dunkirk on Lake Erie, from which a branch to Buffalo had soon been built. For western traffic the Erie had had to rely largely on the Atlantic & Great Western (later the New York, Pennsylvania & Ohio), which connected with the main line at Salamanca, New York, and extended by 1884 west to Dayton, Ohio. In 1857 the Erie first leased this property. Placed in receivers' hands in 1869, the Atlantic & Great Western was re-leased to the Erie on January 1, 1870; sold July 1, 1871, it was again leased to the Erie in May, 1874, only to enter upon a new receivership on December 9 of that year. The persistent attempt to control the road

[1] Mott, p. 269.

showed the value which the Erie placed upon it, and in fact it was invaluable as a link in a prospective line to the West. Even while the leases were in force, however, the Erie lacked that connection of its own with Chicago which seemed necessary to make it a successful competitor for trunk-line business. In 1882 it was forwarding passengers over not less than five different routes, over no one of which could it feel assured of the continuance of contracts of a favorable nature. In 1881 Mr. Jewett relieved the situation by acquiring control of the franchise of the Chicago & Atlantic Railway, extending from Marion, Ohio, on the line of the New York, Pennsylvania & Ohio towards Chicago, and soon after he entered into a contract with certain private parties for construction of the road. In 1883 he executed a new lease of the New York, Pensylvania & Ohio, which he hoped would secure for the Erie permanent control of the property, and about the same time (1882) he purchased a controlling interest in the stock of the Cincinnati, Hamilton & Dayton, which extended the Erie system to the important city of Cincinnati. These operations put the Erie upon a footing which was secure so long as the obligations which they entailed could be met, and showed a broad-minded appreciation of strategic necessities. The terms of the arrangement with the Chicago & Atlantic were as follows: For the construction of the road the Erie agreed to give to the directors the entire proceeds of the mortgage bonds of that branch ($6,500,000), and its entire capital stock ($10,000,000); making an aggregate of $61,710 per mile of line. The proceeds were, however, to be deposited with the president of the New York, Lake Erie & Western in trust, together with certain subsidies which had been voted by the counties and townships along the line, and upon him was to devolve the duty of seeing to the proper application thereof; and besides this, 90 per cent of the stock was to be deposited and an irrevocable proxy given thereon for the thirty years' life of the bonds.[1] The obligation which the Erie assumed amounted in practice to guaranteeing that the road should be constructed for the sum provided, and that interest on the bonds should be paid. In leasing the New York, Pennsylvania & Ohio the Erie involved itself more heavily. As lessee it agreed to pay the minimum sum of $1,757,055 yearly (the net earnings of 1882); the actual rental to be 32 per cent of all gross earn-

---

[1] Annual Report, 1882.

ings up to $6,000,000 and 50 per cent of all gross earnings above $6,000,000, until the average of the whole rental should be raised to 35 per cent, or until the gross earnings should be $7,200,000. If 32 per cent of the gross earnings should ever be less than the $1,757,055 to be paid yearly, then the deficiency was to be made up, without interest, out of the excess in any subsequent year. Out of the rental the New York, Pennsylvania & Ohio was to pay the interest on its prior lien bonds, the rentals of its leased lines, the expenses of maintaining its organization in Europe and America, and for five years a sum of $260,000 each year to the car trust.[1] Finally, in purchasing the Cincinnati, Hamilton & Dayton, the Erie gave to the holders of the $2,000,000 of stock which it bought beneficial certificates to the amount of $1,500,000, on which it agreed to make good any failure of the Cincinnati company to pay 6 per cent per annum.

But though the Erie managers did their best with the conditions which they were called upon to face, they were unable to hold the company up under the enormous capitalization and heavy charges left by the reorganization of 1874–8, at a time when rate wars were sapping its resources, and when contracts which it was being forced to make were entailing an annual loss.[2] In spite of the declaration of sufficient dividends on the comparatively small amount of preferred stock to terminate the voting trust, it is certain that for most of the years from 1874 to 1884 the solvency of the road was a precarious matter, and that there never was a time when any considerable falling off in earnings or any severe shock to its credit would not have driven it to the wall.

Such a shock was preparing in the early months of 1884. For some weeks before the last of April there had been a tendency for the quotations of Erie securities to fall; no reason was assigned, but it was hinted that default might be made in the payment of the June interest on the second consols, and that a receivership was not unlikely. This weakness was accompanied, and perhaps accentuated,

[1] Chron. 36:427, 1883. For the necessity of Erie's extension westward see testimony of First Vice-President Felton before the Senate Committee on Transportation Interests of the United States and Canada, 51st Congress, 1st Session, Report no. 847, pp. 130–1.

[2] For some account of the trunk-line rate wars see the chapter on the Baltimore & Ohio.

by a strike of the brakemen on the New York, Pennsylvania & Ohio in consequence of an order reducing the number of brakemen on each train from three to two. The truth of the matter came out in May, when the failure of the Wall Street firm of Grant & Ward both precipitated a stock exchange panic and laid bare the straits to which the company had been reduced. Investigation showed that a large floating debt had been piling up for four principal purposes: First, advances to the Chicago & Atlantic Railroad; second, advances for coal mines; third, advances for improvements on the Hudson River at Weehawken; fourth, equipment instalments.[1] Attempts to raise funds to cover the debt had resulted in the negotiation of promissory short time notes with the firm of Grant & Ward, for which $2,500,000 of Chicago & Atlantic second mortgage bonds had been deposited as security. The company had been attracted to Grant & Ward by their offer to purchase and dispose of Chicago & Atlantic bonds at a price 15 per cent above that offered by any other parties;[2] and had trusted so implicitly in their integrity as to deposit notes and collateral for its short time loans detached and independent, one from the other, so that Grant & Ward were able to, and did, fraudulently raise money upon them to an amount much larger than the advances they had made. The losses entailed by the transaction were serious, and the blow to Erie's credit was even more severe. The floating debt which had been so hard to carry became doubly menacing now that the possibility of further short time loans was practically cut off; and to cap the climax, the earnings for the first half of the year 1884 showed an unusually large decrease with the cessation of the fall business. Under these circumstances it was the part of wisdom to take advantage of every loophole of escape, and the peculiar provisions of the second consolidated mortgage, denying to these bonds the right of immediate foreclosure in case of default, were turned to for relief. It will be remembered that by the terms of the reorganization of 1878 no right of action was to accrue to the second mortgage bondholders until on each of six successive due dates of coupons (three years) some interest secured by the second indenture should be in default. This being the case the Erie directors decided to pass the June interest on these bonds. "As a general rule," said they in a circular, "the business

[1] Chron. 39: 234, 1884.   [2] Annual Report, 1884, p. 12.

and earnings of the company are much less for the first half than
for the last half of the year. The falling off in earnings for the first
six months of the previous year has been unusually large. The
coupons of the second consolidated mortgage bonds are due and
payable on the first of June prox. . . . Under ordinary circumstances
the board might at the present as on the former occasions provide
to some extent for the deficit of the first six months, relying on the
usual increase in earnings of the last half of the year, but in the present depressed condition of the business of the country and of the
earnings of this company, as well as of others, the board does not
feel at liberty to deal with anything but the business and earnings
as now ascertained, and therefore deems it wise to accept the provisions of the mortgage as the lawful rule for their government in
the existing emergency . . ."[1]

However necessary the action, the bondholders of the company
could not have been expected to receive it quietly; and naturally
again, the indignation was intense among the English securityholders, to whom, more than to any one else, the existing situation
was due. In June, 1884, a meeting of stockholders of the company
was held in London, at which much complaint was made of the fall
in value of the securities of the company, and an inquiry into the
management was demanded. A committee was appointed, and two
of its members, Messrs. Powell and Westlake, landed in New York
July 15, with protestations of a friendly spirit toward all concerned.
The situation was not encouraging. The day before their arrival
President Jewett had offered his resignation, and the directors were
busy selecting his successor; a large floating debt was demanding
most vigorous attention, and confidence in the company was at a
low ebb. Beyond a doubt the raising of a large amount of cash,
$4,000,000 to $5,000,000, was a pressing necessity, and the English
representatives were anxious to make it plain that at least a fair
share of this should come from American as well as from English
bondholders. Force of circumstances compelled them to give assurance that the money would be raised, and this done, Mr. John King
accepted the position which Mr. Jewett professed himself ready to
resign. Pending the annual election Mr. King took the position
of Assistant to the President.

[1] R. R. Gaz. 16:421, 1884.

On their return to London Messrs. Powell and Westlake reported the floating debt to be as follows:

Unpaid coupons, June 1, 1884,	$1,007,922
Balance of actual and early maturing liabilities other than the June 1 coupons over and above cash in hand and money assets considered good and available,	$4,447,316

"All the purposes, the expenditures on which have caused the floating debt," said they, "seem to us to have been in themselves wise and politic, but the piling up of a large floating debt for even the best of purposes is always more or less imprudent and dangerous. The company's credit might have borne the strain of the panic, but it was broken down by the Grant & Ward disaster, and the funding of its floating debt is now indispensable. . . . We have suggested to the president and directors, and now recommend to the committee that an effort should be made without delay to raise a permanent loan on the securities available for a total of $5,000,000." [1] This, it will be observed, was the old remedy. Inability to meet current expenses was to be removed by capitalizing the debts which this inability had caused.

The year 1885 was taken up with suits brought against the Erie by certain of its branch lines. In February the directors of the Buffalo & Southwestern Company brought suit to recover $345,000 interest defaulted during the previous January. The complaint alleged that the Erie was insolvent, and asked that it be restrained from using the gross receipts of the road until the default should have been made good. The Erie paid the back interest, but in July, after another default, an injunction was obtained forbidding it to divert any part of the earnings received or to be received from this property. It was recited that on May 24, 1881, the Buffalo & Southwestern had been leased to the Erie for 35 per cent of the gross earnings, subject to certain deductions; that the Erie had delayed payment of the rental due in January, 1885, and had refused to pay that due in July, 1885, but that it was still receiving the gross earnings of the plaintiffs' road, and had applied these to the payment of its debts other than the rentals of this road. [2] In November, after

---

[1] Chron. 39: 349, 1884.
[2] R. R. Gaz. 17: 446, 1885.

the Erie's other troubles were settled, the litigation was terminated
by an agreement to reduce the Buffalo & Southwestern rental from
35 per cent to 27½ per cent. Other suits arose, directly or indirectly,
because of the control which Mr. Jewett maintained as trustee
of the stock of the Chicago & Atlantic and the Cincinnati, Hamilton & Dayton railways even after his resignation from the Erie
Company. On the one hand President King was anxious to re-
possess himself of these important branches for the Erie, and on
the other Mr. Jewett was not disinclined to do what damage he
could to the managers who had succeeded in supplanting him. In
the matter of the Chicago & Atlantic Mr. Jewett gained the first
victory in a temporary injunction forbidding the Erie to divert
traffic from this line contrary to contract. This injunction was
soon, however, substantially vacated, and President King in his
turn obtained a decision that Jewett had been made trustee of
the Chicago & Atlantic simply because he had been at the time
vice-president of the New York, Lake Erie & Western Railroad
Company and could be relied upon to control the road as the western outlet of the Erie. A receiver was subsequently appointed and
the road reorganized as the Chicago & Erie Railroad Company, the
Erie agreeing to guarantee payment of its first mortgage bonds,
and receiving in return the $100,000 of capital stock and $5,000,000
in income bonds, besides $2,000,000 first mortgage bonds which
were in part payment of old advances.[1] In his action concerning
the Cincinnati, Hamilton & Dayton President King was less successful; and Mr. Jewett was sustained in his refusal to deliver proxies
for the stock held to the larger company. The result was to turn
the Erie to the Big Four, upon which, instead of upon the Dayton
road, the management was for some time to rely for an entrance
into Cincinnati.

During these various contests the suggestions of the English
committee were not lost to view, and in the latter part of 1885
they crystallized into definite propositions. The floating debt then
consisted of two parts: first, the defaulted coupons on the second consolidated bonds; and second, the current liabilities accumulated for
the purposes before described. The relief proposed was likewise in

[1] For terms of reorganization see Annual Report, 1890; also R. R. Gaz. 19: 188,
1887.

two parts, and involved the issue of a 5 per cent mortgage, secured by deposit of the second consolidated coupons maturing and to mature in June and December, 1884, June, 1885, and June, 1886, and a 6 per cent mortgage upon the property of the Long Dock Company, comprising the valuable terminals of the Erie at Jersey City.[1] The funding of the coupon issue proved simplicity itself; the funded coupons were exchanged for bonds of the new gold mortgage, which were to be redeemable at 105 at the pleasure of the company.[2] By the end of 1886 these bonds had been accepted by the holders of $32,982,500 of the outstanding $33,597,400 of the second consols, and $3,957,900 of them had been issued. Dealing with the Long Dock Company was slightly complicated by the fact that 8000 shares of that company were pledged as part security for the issue of Erie collateral bonds. To free them $800,000 in cash were deposited with the trustee of the mortgage, which were in turn employed by him to pay off $727,000 of the 6 per cent collateral bonds, thus reducing the interest charge on that issue $43,620 per annum. This done, the Long Dock Company extended the lease of its property and franchises to the Erie to 1935 at a rental of $480,000 per annum, and contemporaneously therewith placed a consolidated mortgage upon its property to secure $7,500,000 of 50-year 6 per cent gold bonds; of which $3,000,000 were reserved to retire existing indebtedness, and the proceeds of $4,500,000 were paid to the Erie for the cancellation of its floating debt. The total result was to increase fixed charges by $270,000 of interest at 6 per cent on the Long Dock bonds, and by $197,895 on $3,957,900 of the new funded 5s, less the reduction of $43,620 on cancelled collateral bonds; leaving a net increase of $424,275.[3] For its ingenuity the scheme was to be admired; from any other point of view it was to be condemned as another example of that borrowing to pay interest which had brought the Erie to its existing straits. The incapacity of the creditors of the company to realize that continued borrowing of money to pay current obligations was only to ensure repeated bankruptcy seemed complete.

[1] Annual Report, 1886.
[2] Upon such redemption a corresponding amount of the original coupons were to be cancelled.
[3] Annual Report, 1886.

After this new "salvation," the Erie started once more on its laborious attempt to pay interest on its outstanding bonds. From 1887 to 1892 the business increased somewhat, and despite a decrease in the average receipts per ton mile [1] a gain of about $4,700,000 in gross earnings was secured; from which is to be deducted an increase of $310,996 in fixed charges, and of $4,076,111 in operating expenses.

The prohibition of pooling in 1887 affected the company unfavorably. Previous to the passage of the Interstate Commerce Act the other lines had been paying it an annual average of $42,500 on west-bound business from New York for shortages under the operation of the trunk-line pool, besides about $88,000 annually on east-bound dead freight and $19,770 on live stock. These payments ceased when the Act was passed, although a differential on west-bound traffic was subsequently allowed.[2] But the leakage which was most apparent lay in the large rental and heavy operating cost of the New York, Pennsylvania & Ohio. It will be remembered that the Erie had leased that road for 32 per cent of the gross earnings when earnings were $6,000,000 or under, and 50 per cent when they should be above that figure. In 1887 this was amended so as to provide that for every increase of $100,000 over $6,000,000 in the gross earnings the Erie should pay to the lessor an additional one-tenth of one per cent of such gross earnings until the gross earnings should be $7,250,000, and the rental 33½ per cent, after which the percentage was not to increase.[3] Under the old lease the Erie had guaranteed to carry over the line 50 per cent of all its east-bound and 65 per cent of all its west-bound through traffic — under the new lease, these maxima were increased to 55 per cent and 70 per cent; but even this failed to make the branch road pay. Its grades were high, its equipment and sidings were limited, its cost of operation was well above 68 per cent; and the increase in tonnage provided for emphasized each and every disadvantage. Up to 1893 the results of operations were as follows:

---

[1] From .662 in 1887 to .610 in 1892.

[2] Testimony of Messrs. King and Felton, Senate Committee on Transportation Interests of the United States and Canada, pp. 44 and 121-2.

[3] Annual Report, 1887.

		Loss	*Profit*
First 5 months to Sept. 30,	1883		$199,540
Twelve months ending Sept. 30,	1884	$270,281	
	1885	239,820	
	1886		51,322
	1887		91,965
	1888	343,911	
	1889	331,134	
	1890		77,376
	1891	19,586	
	1892	425,888	
	1893	197,106	
		$1,827,726	$420,203
Net loss,		1,407,523	

It thus appears that the terms of the amended lease were in reality more onerous than the contract which they succeeded, and that whatever the value of the branch as a feeder, its operation involved large and fairly regular deductions from the net income of the parent line. Emphasis on these facts was laid in the annual reports, and frequent demands were made that the New York, Pennsylvania & Ohio bring its road up to the standard of like connections of through trunk lines. Meanwhile improvements were imperative on the Erie's own lines: new equipment was needed, new rails and new motive power, and at the same time surplus earnings were somewhat less. The directors adopted the expedient of allowing current liabilities to accumulate, and put $8,496,572 into the road from October 1, 1884, to September 30, 1892, of which $3,351,977 represented surplus earnings, $2,375,400 increase in bonded indebtedness, and the balance floating debt. In the matter of traffic policy they paid particular attention to the coal business, which, however, lost ground as compared with other freight, and to the local business, which it was the policy of the management to encourage. In 1890 the board declared that "the time had arrived when extraordinary expenditure for improvements and the necessities of the property were no longer necessary." [1] In 1891 3 per cent on the preferred stock was paid, the first dividend since 1884.[2]

From 1887 to 1893, with all its struggles, the Erie was continually

[1] Mott, p. 272.

[2] In 1890 a traffic agreement was made with the Cincinnati, Hamilton & Dayton, to take the place of that with the Big Four. R. R. Gaz. 22: 314, 1890.

on the verge of failure. The capitalization in 1892 was at the enormous total of $163,607,485 on an operated mileage of 1698 miles, while fixed charges were $4993 per mile, and the available net revenue but $4830.[1] Given, with this condition, a gross floating debt which amounted in 1892 to $9,163,166, and represented in a large measure the inability of the company to make necessary repairs, no further explanation is needed for the bankruptcy which soon took place.

Early in 1893 rumors were current that the Erie might be thrown into the hands of a receiver. The reports were vigorously denied, but on July 25, nevertheless, on application of the company itself, Judge Lacombe appointed President John King and Mr. J. G. McCullough as receivers of the property. The measure was taken to avoid the sacrifice of collaterals deposited. "Within the last few weeks," said President King, "during the severe money stringency the floating debt of the Erie . . . became impossible of renewal, and in order not to sacrifice the best interests of the company it was decided to place the road in receivers' hands, and preserve the system intact, and preserve and develop the transportation business for the company."[2] The action occasioned no surprise, and there was even a disposition to praise the management for having preserved the solvency of the company. "The company was bankrupt *de facto* when it passed to its new control," says Mott, and "that the time when it must become bankrupt *de jure* was held off so long was a striking demonstration of the tact and resourcefulness which the new *régime* had been able to bring to bear in the management of the company's unpromising affairs, and in judicious shifting and manipulating of the heavy burdens Erie bore upon its chafed and weary shoulders."[3] What a receivership meant was a new opportunity to put the company upon a genuinely sound foundation, by providing new capital to pay off the floating debt and to allow for future additions and improvements, and by getting fixed charges to a point well within the road's capacity to earn. We shall see what use was made of the chance.

The matter of reorganization was set about at once. On January 1 a plan appeared, prepared, at least nominally, by a special

---

[1] Figures for 1891 were, fixed charges, $4298 per mile; net revenue, $4897 per mile.
[2] Chron. 57: 179, 1893.   [3] Mott, p. 273.

committee chosen by the directors,[1] and backed by the well-known firms of Drexel, Morgan & Co. of New York and J. S. Morgan & Co. of London.[2] By its terms no mortgage senior to the second consolidated mortgage was to be disturbed save the first mortgage, which matured in 1897. The bonds to be dealt with were thus reduced to $41,481,048, besides which provision had to be made for the floating debt and for future capital requirements. The plan proposed to authorize a blanket mortgage of $70,000,000 at 5 per cent, of which $33,597,000 were to exchange at par for the 6 per cent second consolidated bonds and funded coupons thereof, $4,031,400 to exchange for the funded coupon bonds of 1885, and $508,008 for the income bonds. Of the balance, $6,512,800 were to be reserved to settle with the old first lien and collateral trust bonds, $15,915,208 to supply capital requirements in the future, and $9,915,208 to be offered for subscription in order to pay the floating debt. The new management did not conceive that these last bonds could be sold to advantage in the general market, but imposed as a condition of the exchanges as above that second consols, funded coupon, and income bonds should subscribe at 90 to the extent of 25 per cent of their holdings; hoping that the grant of the right of immediate foreclosure upon default would induce the second consols to come in. Both these consols and the funded coupon bonds of 1885, it may be remarked, were to be kept alive and deposited with the trustee for the protection of the new bonds. Stated in tabular form the distribution of securities was to be as follows:

To acquire the existing second consols,	$33,597,400
To acquire the funded coupons of 1885,	4,031,400
To acquire the income bonds,	508,008
For subscription as above,	9,915,208
To acquire the old reorganization first lien and collateral trust bonds,	6,512,800
To be expended for construction, equipment, etc., not to exceed $100,000 in any year, except that $500,000 might be used to acquire existing car trusts,	15,435,184
Total,	$70,000,000

The new mortgage was to cover the property of the New York, Lake Erie & Western, including its leasehold of the New York, Pennsylvania & Ohio, and the capital stock of the Chicago & Erie

---

[1] Chron. 57: 938, 1893; Ibid. 57: 1083, 1893.   [2] Ry. Times, 65: 3, 1894.

Railroad.[1] There was to be no assessment, no syndicate to raise money, and no voting trust.

This plan was advanced as adequate to restore the prosperity of the company. Examination will show its weakness. It comprised two measures of relief: first, reduction of interest by one per cent on the second consolidated bonds; second, the settlement of the floating debt. The first might be thought to have been the kernel of the plan, and the reduction in fixed charges the principal thing aimed at. That it was not is shown by the fact that so liberal were the new bond issues that the total fixed charges after reorganization were to be greater than those before. The floating debt which remained had arisen from lack of funds with which to make current and necessary improvements and repairs. This debt was the immediate cause of the failure of the company, and its cancellation was the real purpose of the plan. The method proposed was a forced levy upon bondholders, but the levy took, not the form of an assessment, but that of a subscription to new bonds on which payment of interest was to be as obligatory as any other charge. The operation differed, therefore, from an ordinary sale of securities in the more favorable selling price which it assured. It did little, however, to lighten the burden which had crushed the company. The only bright spot in the plan was the provision for future construction and improvement, which, though involving a still further increase in indebtedness, was justified because these improvements would serve not only to maintain but to make greater the earning powers of the company. Finally, it was the peculiar effect of this plan that it put the pressure imposed upon the wrong parties: the second consolidated and other junior bondholders were to be forced to subscribe to the new issue, when in fact it was the stockholders who should have been turned to, and whom it was consonant with no sound principle of finance to spare. Other matters come out in the objections raised by bondholders.

Opposition to the plan was vigorously headed by men like Kuhn, Loeb & Co., E. H. Harriman, August Belmont, Hallgarten, Peabody, Vermilye, and others.[2] In England a meeting of dissentients was held and a committee was elected;[3] in America the first

---

[1] R. R. Gaz. 26: 18, 1894.
[2] Ry. Times, 65: 120, 1894.   [3] Ibid. 65: 152, 1894.

formal action was the dispatch of a letter to the Erie managers by opposing bankers which is important enough to be quoted in full.

"Consultations and comparisons of views have recently taken place," said these gentlemen, "between the owners and representatives of the second consolidated mortgage bonds and other bonds of your company, to whom the proposition as detailed in your circular of January 2 is not satisfactory. . . . Your plan seems unjust, inasmuch as it demands a permanent reduction of interest on the bonded indebtedness for which no adequate equivalent is offered, and it levies a forced contribution upon the bondholders through the demand for a subscription to new bonds at a price considerably over and above the market value these new bonds are likely to command, while the fixed charges proposed to be created appear to be considerably larger than, in the light of past earnings and experience, the property of the company can carry with safety.

"Instead of 5 per cent bonds, as provided in the published plan, 4 per cent bonds, in our opinion, should be issued, while for the interest to be surrendered the bondholders should receive an equivalent in interminable non-cumulative 4 per cent debentures, interest payable if earned; the holders of the debentures to have sufficient representation in the management to protect them.

"The floating debt should be liquidated from the proceeds of an adequate amount of new 4 per cent bonds (and debentures if desirable), which shall be offered to the shareholders and bondholders at a price rather below than above the probable market value of the new securities, and under the guarantee of an underwriting syndicate.

"Provision should also be made to obtain the conversion on fair terms of the reorganization prior lien bonds into the new bonds, so that it shall become practicable to secure the new 4 per cent bonds at once by a lien second only to the 'Erie first consolidated 7 per cent bonds'; the new 4 per cent bonds to be issued under a general mortgage to an amount sufficient to provide for future additions and improvements, and with adequate provision for the taking up of the underlying bonds, and the issue of 4 per cent bonds in their stead. . . . Any plan now adopted for the readjustment of the finances of your company should seek, as its first object, to reduce the permanent charges so well within the earning capacity of the property as to make another default in the future an improbability. . . . We trust this communication will be received in the spirit in which it is submitted." [1]

The directors refused to modify their plan, and the bankers, therefore, notified them of the election of a protective committee.[2] On March 6 a meeting of stockholders approved the plan, and the same week Messrs. Drexel, Morgan & Co. gave notice that, having received deposits of a majority of each class of bonds, they had declared the plan operative as announced.[3]

Defeated in their appeal to the securityholders, the opposition turned to the courts. As a preliminary, they obtained an opinion from the well-known firm of Messrs. Evarts, Choate & Beaman, which held, first, that the Erie could not legally pay interest on the new bonds proposed until it had paid the interest on every one of the old second mortgage bonds, regardless of whether the latter was deposited with the reorganization committee; second, that if the old second mortgage bonds which were deposited as security for the new issue should be kept alive as proposed, the company would be increasing its obligations beyond the legal limit; [4] and third, that much of the stock voted at the special meeting at which the new mortgage had been authorized was not really owned by the persons who had issued the proxies thereon as the law provided.[5] Following the opinion, suit was commenced by Mr. Harriman in April for an injunction against the recording of the new mortgage, on the ground that the Drexel & Morgan proxies did not represent the actual stockholders, and in June by one John J. Emery to prevent the execution of the mortgage. Judge Ingraham in the Supreme Court Chambers denied an injunction, using in his opinion the following language: "While it is clear," said he, "that there are certain obligations resting upon the majority to refrain from infringing the legal right of the minority, and that a court of equity will enforce and protect the rights of the minority, still, when the holder of a very small number of bonds or shares of stock seeks to

---

[1] Chron. 58: 264, 1894.   [2] Ibid. 58: 383, 1894.   [3] Ibid. 58: 430, 1894.

[4] According to the law of 1892 the bonded indebtedness, including mortgages given as consideration for the purchase of real estate and mortgages authorized by contract prior to May, 1891, could not exceed the amount of the paid up capital stock.

[5] Ry. Rev. 34: 181, 1894.

enjoin a very large majority from carrying out a plan such majority deem to be for their benefit, I think the court should not interfere unless it plainly appears that some legal right of the minority is endangered." [1]

What could not be accomplished by the hostile bankers was nevertheless to happen from the inherent weakness of the plan itself. It has been said that the new scheme involved an increase instead of a decrease in fixed charges. How this was to be met was not demonstrated; and already in June, 1894, it was necessary to announce that the coupons then due would not be paid for the present. In December matters were even worse, and a circular from Drexel, Morgan & Co. confessed the company's inability to meet the coupons maturing. "Nevertheless," the firm continued, "it seems to us inexpedient to treat the inability of the company to pay interest as an occasion for present foreclosure without giving a further chance to the company, especially as payment of bond-holders' subscriptions to the new bonds has not yet been called to provide the company with money necessary to pay the floating debt. It is, therefore, now proposed that the new bonds be issued with the coupons of June 1, 1894, and December, 1894, attached, but stamped as subject to a contract with the company which shall provide that they shall be paid as soon as practical out of the first net earnings over and above the railroad company's requirements to meet interest and rentals accruing after December 1, 1894, except in case a default on later coupons shall give power of foreclosure, in which event the stamped coupons shall retain all their original rights." The modification was assented to,[2] but could not save the plan. Reluctantly the managers were forced to abandon it, and to consent to more radical propositions.

August 26, 1895, the new and final reorganization plan appeared. There were to be issued:

> $175,000,000 first consolidated mortgage 100-year gold bonds;
> 30,000,000 first preferred 4 per cent non-cumulative stock;
> 16,000,000 second preferred 4 per cent non-cumulative stock;
> 100,000,000 common stock.

The first consolidated mortgage bonds were to be divided into prior lien bonds to the amount of $35,000,000, and general lien

[1] R. R. Gaz. 26: 472, 1894.   [2] Ibid. 27: 554, 1895.

bonds to the amount of $140,000,000; the former to have priority of lien over the latter for both principal and interest. Both classes of bonds were to be secured by mortgage and pledge of all railroads and properties of every kind embraced in the reorganization as carried out and vested in the new company, and also all other properties which should be acquired thereafter by issue of any of the new bonds. Both issues were to bear interest at 4 per cent, except $29,435,000 of the general lien bonds, which were to bear 3 per cent for two years from July 1, 1896, and 4 per cent thereafter. The stock was to rank for dividends in the order given. Provision was made that no additional mortgage could be put upon the property to be acquired, and that no additional issue of first preferred stock could be made except with the consent in each instance of the holders of a majority of the whole amount of each class of preferred stock, given at a meeting of the stockholders called for that purpose; and with the consent of the stockholders of a majority of such part of the common stock as should be represented at such meeting, the holders of each class of stock voting separately; also that the amount of second preferred stock could not be increased except with like consent of the holders of a majority thereof, and a majority of such part of the common stock as should be represented at the meeting. All classes of stock were to be deposited in a voting trust until December 1, 1900, and until the expiration of such further period, if any, as should elapse before the Erie should in one year have paid 4 per cent cash dividends on the first preferred stock; though the voting trustees might terminate the trust earlier at their discretion.

Generally speaking, the prior lien bonds were relied on to pay the floating debt, to buy in the New York, Pennsylvania & Ohio, and to retire certain prior liens of the old company. The general lien bonds were reserved for undisturbed bonds, and, with the first preferred stock, exchanged for junior New York, Lake Erie & Western securities. The second preferred stock went for old preferred stock and income bonds, and the new common stock exchanged for old common.

The distribution was as follows: The old New York, Lake Erie & Western reorganization first lien and collateral bonds were paid off from the proceeds of the new prior lien bonds; the second consols received 75 per cent in new general lien bonds and 55 per cent in preferred stock; the funded coupon bonds of 1885 received 100 per cent in general lien bonds, 10 per cent in first preferred, and 10 per cent in second preferred stock; the income bonds 40 per cent in general liens and 60 per cent in first preferred stock; the New York, Lake Erie & Western preferred stock, on payment of assessment, 100 per cent in new common. For all other bonds included in the plan there were reserved general lien bonds in amounts usually equal to the par of the securities to be retired.

The cash requirements and the floating debt were as follows:

Floating debt, receivers' certificates, etc.,	$11,500,000
Collateral trust bonds (Erie), at 110,	3,678,400
Reorganization first lien bonds (Erie),	2,500,000
Early construction and expenditures,	5,337,288
Car trusts for three years,	2,000,000
	$25,015,688

The necessity for retirement of the first lien and collateral bonds arose from the early maturity of the former, and from the fact that stocks and bonds of various Erie properties which it was desirous to consolidate with the new company were pledged for the latter. The wisdom of allowing for early construction and expenditure could not be denied; car trust payments were required to preserve the rolling stock, and the floating debt and receivers' certificates called obviously for cash. Provision was made, first, by an assessment on the stock of $8 on preferred and $12 on common, with higher payments in case of delay, and estimated to yield $10,023,368; second, by a contribution from the New York, Pennsylvania & Ohio of $742,320; and third, by the sale of $15,000,000 prior lien bonds as indicated above. A syndicate of $25,000,000 was formed to subscribe to the prior liens, and to take the place of and succeed to all the rights of stockholders who should not deposit their stock and pay the assessment thereon.

With the settlement of cash requirements, unification of the Erie system was assured; "subject only to the undisturbed bonds and stock until retired by use of the bonds reserved for that purpose or the rentals corresponding thereto." "The new bonds and stock will," said the plan, "represent the ownership (either in fee or in possession of securities) approximately of:

N. Y., L. E. & W. proper,	538 miles
N. Y., P. & O.,	600
Chicago & Erie,	250
N. Y., L. E. & W. Auxiliary Companies,	550
Total,	1938 miles [1]

— with valuable terminal facilities at Jersey City, Weehawken, Buffalo, etc., and also one-fifth ownership in the stock of the Chicago & Western Indiana Railroad Company. Also all the Erie coal properties, . . . representing an aggregate of 10,000 acres of anthracite, of which about 9000 acres are held in fee, and 14,000 acres of bituminous, held under mining rights . . . also the Union Steamboat Company, with its terminals and other properties in Buffalo, and its fleet of five lake steamers on which the Erie mainly depends for the lake and railway traffic," etc.

Fixed charges under the plan were estimated at $7,850,000. Fixed charges in 1894 had been $9,400,000. For the first two years after reorganization, moreover, the charges were to be further reduced by $300,000 per annum, as the new general lien bonds were to bear only 3 per cent interest during that period; and an additional saving of $1,000,000 was looked for when the exchange of old bonds for new on the maturity of its existing prior issues should have been eventually completed. This sum of $7,850,000 the company was expected to have no difficulty in earning in view of the immediate expenditure of $5,337,208 for new construction, additions, and betterments, and the gradual distribution of the proceeds of $17,000,000 of general lien bonds to the same end. The compensation to Messrs. J. P. Morgan & Co. and Messrs. J. S. Morgan & Co. for their services as depositaries, and in carrying out the plan was put at $500,000 and expenses. Foreclosure was finally to take place and a new company was to be organized.

This plan differed from its abandoned predecessors in four important particulars, each of which was in its favor:

(1) It employed bonds and stock instead of bonds alone;

(2) It lowered instead of increased fixed charges;

(3) It procured cash from stockholders instead of from second consolidated mortgage bondholders; and

[1] New York, Pennsylvania & Ohio voting trustees agreed to foreclose and deliver the New York, Pennsylvania & Ohio property, subject only to the prior lien, equipment, and leased-line securities for which reservation was made.

(4) It absorbed the New York, Pennsylvania & Ohio into the Erie system instead of continuing the lease thereof.

In the employment of bonds and stock instead of a simple issue of bonds, the Erie managers adopted what experience has shown to be the best method of dealing with the complicated situation arising from a great railroad default. The use of securities on which return was optional side by side with those on which return was obligatory tended both to protect the railroad company when earnings were low, and to benefit the recipients of the new securities when earnings were high. As worked out, it gave to the second consols and funded coupons a less return in the one case, and an equal or greater return in the other, than did the plan of 1894, and to the income bonds, though it offered no chance of equal gain, it at least promised a minimum below which payments should not fall. It further made a far nicer recognition of the relative priorities of different classes of old bonds possible, and whereas the previous plan had made the same demands on, and had given the same return to the second consols, the funded coupon bonds of 1885, and the income bonds, the new plan gave, as has been pointed out, to the first 75 per cent in general lien bonds and 55 per cent in first preferred stock; to the second, 100 per cent in general lien bonds, 10 per cent in first preferred, and 10 per cent in second preferred; and to the third, 40 per cent in general liens and 60 per cent in first preferred stock. Income, coupon, and consolidated bonds benefited alike from the assessment upon the stock, which laid the burden of raising cash upon the owners of the road, where it most properly fell. No species of security was given for the assessment, not even common stock, with which the managers might well have been generous; although it must be remembered that the sale of $15,000,000 prior lien bonds for cash was part of the reorganization plan. It may be remarked that since, on July 2, 1895, the common stock was being offered at 10⅝, with no sales, and the preferred at 22½, and since the chance for dividends which the new stock was to enjoy was most remote, it was perhaps well that the syndicate guarantee of the payment of assessments had been obtained. Fixed charges by the new plan were lower, as a result of the liberal use of stock in the exchanges and the cancellation of floating debt as above; while the terms under which the outstanding

New York, Pennsylvania & Ohio bonds were retired were the most drastic part of the scheme. In all, the total mortgage indebtedness of the Erie Company and its leased or controlled lines of $234,680,180 for January, 1896, was reduced to $137,704,100 by June 30 of that year.[1]

A weak point in the plan was, nevertheless, the small reduction in bonded indebtedness which it occasioned. Although, to repeat, the bonded indebtedness of the system was reduced from $234,680,180 to $137,704,100, the shrinkage was more apparent than real, since it consisted chiefly in the exchange of stock for New York, Pennsylvania & Ohio mortgage bonds, on which interest had not been paid by the Erie, and but seldom by the New York, Pennsylvania, & Ohio itself. These securities were slashed in most drastic fashion, particularly such of them as were inferior to the first mortgage. The amount of the reduction in the volume outstanding is indicated by the fact that for $5000 first mortgage New York, Pennsylvania & Ohio bonds were given $1000 Erie prior lien bonds, $500 Erie first preferred, $100 Erie second preferred, and $750 Erie common stock; and for $500 second mortgage, or for $1000 third mortgage, were given $100 Erie common stock. If, now, we exclude the New York, Pennsylvania & Ohio bonds from our consideration of the funded debt, we find the indebtedness of the Erie system on January 1, 1896, excluding the non-assumed New York, Pennsylvania & Ohio bonds to have been $121,399,431; and on June 30, excluding the new prior lien bonds used to exchange for these securities, to have been $123,304,100; or an increase through the reorganization of $1,904,669.[2] Further, there was an accompanying increase in the capital stock of the combined companies, which did not, of course, involve an increase in fixed charges, but which

---

[1] Chron. 61: 368, 1895; R. R. Gaz. 27: 583-4, 1895.

[2] The following was the rate of exchange of Erie securities for New York, Pennsylvania & Ohio securities on payment by the latter of $12 per new share:

Old securities in amounts of	Prior Lien Bonds	1st Pref.	2d Pref.	Com. Stock
1st mortgage, $5,000	$1000	$500	$100	$750
2d mortgage, 500				100
3d mortgage, 1,000				100
Pref. Stock, 6,000				100
Com. Stock, 10,000				100

To be exchanged for

increased the volume of securities outstanding.[1] What the reduction in the capital of the New York, Pennsylvania & Ohio, joined with its amalgamation with the Erie system, did do was to lessen the burdens of that line to the parent company. For many years the Erie had engaged to operate the branch for 68 per cent and had paid 32 per cent of its gross earnings to the New York, Pennsylvania & Ohio, to be applied to payment or partial payment of interest on the excessive issues which were now retired. It was probably to be long before an operating ratio of 68 per cent could be successfully maintained; but the Erie after reorganization was obliged to turn over, not 32 per cent of gross earnings, but 4 per cent on the $14,400,000 prior lien bonds which had been given for New York, Pennsylvania & Ohio securities, or an amount of $576,000; which amounted to a reduction of the minimum rental of more than one-half, and of the sums actually paid of almost three-quarters.[2]

Turning again to fixed charges, we find them estimated, after the first two years, at $7,850,000. The average net earnings for the period 1887–94 had been $9,331,250. These earnings will not serve strictly as a basis for calculation, for from 1887 to 1892 they include an average of perhaps $750,000 derived from Lehigh Valley trackage payments and other sums now discontinued. With the deduction, therefore, of this amount from the net earnings of the period named, the average is reduced to $8,768,750; or $918,750 more than it was thought fixed charges would be. When it is considered that this $918,750 represented the sum available for dividends on $146,000,000 of outstanding Erie stock, it is plain that the over-capitalization of the company in 1895 was still very great.

With these comments it is necessary to leave the plan. It was far the best that had ever been applied to the rehabilitation of Erie's

---

[1] Capital Stock —

Before reorganization	Common	Preferred
Erie,	$77,837,000	$8,536,600
N. Y., P. & O.,	34,999,350	10,000,000
	$112,836,350	$18,536,600
After reorganization		
Erie,	$100,000,000	$46,000,000
Nypano,	20,000,000	
	$120,000,000	$46,000,000

[2] This real rental was increased somewhat by the assumption of New York, Pennsylvania & Ohio prior liens.

affairs; it was discriminating in its nature, and, thanks to the increasing prosperity of the last eleven years, it has been fortunate in its results. In August, 1895, a decree of foreclosure was signed in the city of New York, and the following November the property was sold under the second consolidated mortgage, and purchased by the reorganization committee for $20,000,000.[1]

Since 1895 the Erie has shared in the prosperity of the country. Its ton mileage has increased from 3,939,679,175 in 1897 to 6,275,-629,877 in 1907; its gross earnings have grown from $31,497,031 to $53,914,827; and its net earnings, which had hovered for so many years near or below the level of fixed charges, have now soared away above. Under these circumstances it is but natural that large sums should have been applied to improvements. Between December 1, 1895, and June 30, 1907, $12,732,486 were spent in the purchase of land, in yards, stations, and buildings, in reducing grades, relocating tracks, and in other ways, and charged to capital; $36,511,-046 were spent for new equipment, and charged to capital; and $8,625,307 were taken from income for equipment and improvements of various sorts. These expenditures have had a most gratifying result. The average train load has grown from 224.74 tons in 1895 to 471.67 in 1907, although coal now constitutes a smaller proportion of the freight; and the average revenue per train mile has more than doubled, in face of a revenue per ton mile which has only slightly increased. In 1907 the Erie's ton mileage was 59 per cent greater than in 1897, and its passenger mileage was 73 per cent greater, but the expense of conducting transportation had increased but 27 per cent. Instead of freight cars with an average capacity of 22½ tons the company now uses cars which average 34 tons. Instead of locomotives which on the average could exert a tractive force of only 24,500 pounds as late as 1901, it has now engines which average 31,000. Freight train mileage is 2,600,000 less than it was in 1896, and passenger train mileage has only slightly increased.

And yet, with all this prosperity, it cannot be said that the Erie enjoys an assured position. In 1907 it had to pay out 89 per cent of the largest income which it had ever received for operating expenses, fixed charges, and taxes. Of its net income of about $6,000,000 the modest dividends of 4 per cent on its first and second

[1] Chron. 61: 831, 1895.

preferred stock absorb some $2,500,000, and the widespread finan-
cial difficulties of 1907 have led its management to declare the dividends for that year payable in scrip and not in cash. And although
the present period of reaction dates back but a little way the company
has been already obliged to the issue of short term notes.

In matters of railroad policy the Erie has accordingly been conservative. In 1898 it acquired control of the New York, Susquehanna & Western, from New York City to Wilkesbarre in northeast Pennsylvania. Three years later it bought the entire stock of
the Pennsylvania Coal Company in order to protect its tonnage, and,
as the directors expressed it, for other reasons which seemed good;
and in 1901 also it bought an interest in the Lehigh Valley. The
most sensational episode which has occurred has been the purchase
and subsequent release of the Cincinnati, Hamilton & Dayton. It
seems that in 1905 Mr. J. P. Morgan bought a majority of a syndicate's holdings in Cincinnati, Hamilton & Dayton stock, amounting to a majority of the total issue; a purchase which carried control
of the Pere Marquette and of the Chicago, Cincinnati & Louisville, or of a total system of 3675 miles. This stock Mr. Morgan
turned over to the Erie at a price reported to be $160 a share. From
a traffic point of view the deal seemed likely to strengthen the Erie's
position in Ohio, Indiana, and Michigan, while more than doubling
the mileage of its system. Because of the financial condition of the
new companies, however, the purchase was decidedly unwise; and,
after an investigation, Mr. Morgan's offer to take the road off the
Erie's hands was gladly accepted. On December 4, 1905, Mr. Judson
Harmon was appointed receiver of the Cincinnati, Hamilton &
Dayton and of the Pere Marquette, and the reorganization of these
properties is just being completed.

At present the Erie is operating 2169 miles of road as against
2166 in 1896. Its earnings have greatly increased, its capitalization
has grown in less proportion,[1] but it has not yet a sufficient margin
of surplus earnings to meet a decline in prosperity without serious
misgivings. Dividends on its first preferred stock have been paid
since 1901, and on its second preferred since 1905. The common
stock cannot expect a dividend in any period which can be foreseen.

[1] Capital —

	Stock	*Bonds*
1896	$146,000,000	$137,704,100
1907	176,271,300	209,633,900

CHAPTER III

PHILADELPHIA & READING

Early history — Purchase of coal lands — Funding of floating debt — Failure — Struggles between Gowen and his opponents — Reorganization — Second failure and reorganization.

THE Philadelphia & Reading Railroad has been peculiarly unfortunate. Although serving a region of abundant traffic, it failed three times between 1880 and 1895, and was in the hands of receivers ten years. It was reorganized after each failure, and each reorganization was marked by bitter struggles between contending parties, due in part to divergence in financial interests, and in part to personal rivalries.

In 1833 the Philadelphia & Reading Railroad was chartered by the Legislature of Pennsylvania to build a road from Philadelphia to Reading, a distance of 58 miles. Its early history does not concern us. In 1862 it leased, owned, and operated 437.4 miles of track, equivalent, roughly, to 119.4 miles of line; and derived $2,879,419 out of its gross earnings of $3,911,830 from the carriage of coal. Its capitalization was extremely high, roughly, $193,417 per mile of line,[1] and the necessary payments each year, not including dividends, took up $1,454,635. At this time the road owned no coal lands, but, like the Lehigh Valley Railroad and the Schuylkill Canal, remained a common carrier, and relied upon the advantages of its position in respect to the Southern coal fields to secure the tonnage which it required.

From 1862 to 1865 inclusive the Reading enjoyed a period of extreme prosperity. The Navy Department, during the war, required large quantities of fuel, and in the revival of business after the conclusion of peace the Reading took its part. Merchandise earnings increased from $523,416 in 1862 to $1,165,277 in 1865; coal earnings from $2,879,419 to $8,627,292; and though expenses

---

[1] Calculated. Poor gives the figure of 340.3 miles of *track*. In 1867 the miles of track were reported as 418.1, and the miles of line as 147, the latter being 35.1 per cent of the former. Supposing the proportion to have been the same in 1862, to 340.3 miles of track there would have been 119.4 miles of line, which, divided into a capital of $23,094,829, gives $193,417.

also increased, yet net earnings grew from $2,375,247 to $5,236,655, and the balance of earnings, after all charges had been paid, from $920,612 to $2,632,566. Dividends meanwhile ranged from 14 per cent on the preferred stock in 1862 to 10 per cent on both preferred and common in 1866, though the majority of the distributions were made in stock. On the whole, during the Civil War and for a whole year afterwards, the Reading was able to carry without difficulty the burden of an enormous capitalization. What increase in capital occurred at this time was in stock, and did not add to the load, although the desire to pay dividends on the increased stock led to the piling up of new issues.

In 1869 an entirely new departure in Reading policy occurred. Whereas the road had previously owned no coal lands, with the advent of Mr. F. B. Gowen to the presidency it began to purchase on an enormous scale. "The repeated and serious interruptions of the business of the company," said the annual report for 1871, "caused by strikers in the coal regions during the last few years, and the many fluctuations in the coal trade, produced by alternate periods of expansion and depression resulting therefrom, have attracted the attention of the managers of the company to the necessity of exercising some control over the production of coal, so as to prevent a recurrence of the difficulties heretofore experienced; and it was believed that the best way to accomplish this result, without injuriously affecting individual interests, was for the company to become the owner of coal lands situate upon the line of its several branches." [1] Further, it was felt that some steps were necessary to retain for the Reading even the coal tonnage which it enjoyed. In 1871 every rival carrier had invested large sums in coal properties, and all the fields but the Schuylkill and Mahanoy (western middle) were occupied, while carriers had begun to enter the Mahanoy district, and it was reported to be their intention to build lines straight through to the Schuylkill fields.

The anthracite coal regions of Pennsylvania lie in four main districts: the Northern or Wyoming; the Southern or Schuylkill; and two smaller intermediate fields known respectively as the Eastern Middle or Lehigh region and the Western Middle or Mahanoy and Shamokin basins. The Northern field is the more easily worked,

[1] Annual Report, 1881, p. 63.

and the Southern field is the richer.[1] Between 1869 and 1881 the Reading Railroad and its alter ego, the Coal & Iron Company, formed for the purpose, spent $73,326,668 for lands in the Schuylkill and Western Middle districts, securing 142 square miles, or 60 per cent of all the anthracite lands of these districts, and 30 per cent of all in Pennsylvania. Of the purchase money $69,816,204 were supplied either by the Railroad Company or by sale of Coal & Iron Company bonds which the Railroad Company guaranteed. The Coal & Iron Company incurred non-guaranteed liabilities for the rest.[2] This gave ample resources for the permanent supply of coal tonnage to the railroad, and was sufficient also to give a considerable measure of control over production in the Southern district. Independent operators did continue, however, and the Reading coal was subject to the competition of coal from other fields. More important still, in attaining control, "all kinds of coal properties, good, bad, and indifferent, were purchased without regard to original cost, location, or revenue producing capacity."[3] In 1880 an engineer of reputation was appointed to evaluate the Reading coal lands, and

[1] Industrial Commission, vol. 19, p. 445. Area of fields as given in Annual Report for 1881 was: Schuylkill, 146 sq. miles; Western Middle, 91 sq. miles; Lehigh, 37 sq. miles; Wyoming, 198 sq. miles.

[2] An analysis of the Coal & Iron Company's operations in 1881 (Annual Report, 1881) showed that there had been expended:

For coal and timber lands and leasehold collieries, and for dead work, colliery equipments and improvements, real estate and miners' houses, etc.,	$39,385,080
For stocks and bonds and loans to secure the control of tributary properties,	5,672,394
For iron ore lands, iron furnaces, mills, and other properties,	1,720,566
For profit and loss account in working properties, including interest payments, etc.,	22,454,500
For supplies and miscellaneous accounts,	1,485,426
For bills and accounts receivable, cash, etc.,	2,608,702
	$73,326,668
Of which amount there was furnished by the Railroad Company,	54,886,647
And the Coal & Iron Company's obligations held by the public, for which the Railroad Company became responsible as guarantor, amounted to	14,929,557
Other direct liabilities of the Coal & Iron Company amounted to	3,510,464
	$73,326,668

[3] Annual Report, 1881.

recommended the surrender of five properties that originally cost $5,207,167, upon which there were encumbrances of $5,015,000. "But little weight," said he, "should be given to the fear that rivals will possess the surrendered property; most of it is not a tempting investment." Exorbitant prices were paid for the lands purchased. By 1881, as noted, there had been expended in all by the two Reading companies $73,326,668. This same report said that, "assuming the profit on the future coal product to be 30 cents per ton of coal shipped, that the company will be able to reduce the rate of interest on the money needed to hold and develop the property from 7 per cent to 6 per cent per annum, and that the development will be at the rate just stated [outlined earlier in the report], the whole estate has a value of $32,394,799: the company's interest in the estate is worth $30,630,648, and, including colliery improvements belonging to the company, but situate on lands owned by others, the whole of the company's property is worth $31,197,484." [1]

It is unquestionable that the Reading did acquire an enormously valuable property in the decade succeeding 1870. It seems just as clear that it paid more for this than was necessary; but what is perhaps more to the point is the fact that the Reading paid more than it could afford. Whatever the ultimate advantages to be gained by exclusive possession of any considerable section of the coal fields, the Reading was not large enough nor financially strong enough to make such vast purchases within so short a space of time. The prosperity of the Civil War had disappeared, net profits were fluctuating without marked tendency to increase, the figures for 1870 being actually less than those of 1863, while the interest on bonds had more than doubled since 1867, and the sum required for dividends had increased. To advance $54,886,647 to the Coal & Iron Company under these conditions, and to become responsible as guarantor for $14,929,557 more, would have been ill-advised even had the prices paid by the company been in strict accord with the commercial estimate of the time. Under the best of circumstances returns from much of the property acquired could not be secured for many years. The parts of the coal fields which were worked yielded an income, though it was seldom that the collieries were allowed to run to their full capacity; but those districts which

---

[1] Part of the difference was due to the inflation of the currency before 1879.

were bought for the sake of controlling the coal situation, or in order to secure a future reserve, and which in many cases could not be worked at existing prices, occasioned a drain upon the company to the amount of interest on the purchase money, with no return of any kind. Moreover, the purchase of the coal lands put the Reading in the anomalous position of a railroad corporation interested in industrial lines. It could no longer be content with encouraging the transportation of its main source of revenue (coal), but had to care as well for the price at which this coal was sold. When depression in the coal trade came, the Reading lost both as producer and as carrier, for less was transported, and that amount was sold at a lower price; but when good times came, from which as a simple carrier it might have profited largely, it struggled with conditions of over-production which should rightly have been none of its concern. There was, finally, a peculiar fatality in the time which the Reading chose for its expansion. The year 1873 will always be remembered as one of the most disastrous in the history of the United States. Commencing with the failure of Messrs. Jay Cooke & Co. on the 18th of September, the panic spread with such rapidity as to lead to the closing of the New York Stock Exchange on September 30. All railroad securities were exceedingly depressed, call loans were high, and it was nearly impossible to secure new capital. Business the next five years was very dull, and the Reading actually earned less gross in 1879 than in the year before the panic, and this at the very time that its liabilities were so largely extended. The natural result was the financial difficulty which can be detected as early as 1876. In June it appears that, owing "to the continued depression in the iron and coal trades and the consequent falling off in transportation," the road was obliged to reduce its working force. In July the usual dividend was passed; salaries were lowered in September, and still later a temporary loan was secured to tide over the floating debt, which then amounted to $8,272,359. By the next year the matter had become serious enough to necessitate a formal proposition to creditors for the postponement of interest payments and of payments on the floating debt. The company professed itself able to carry out the following:

(*a*) To pay the interest on prior liens in full.

(*b*) To pay one-half the interest on the general mortgage bonds and on the Perkiomen sterling mortgage bonds for three years in cash, and one-half in five-year interest-bearing scrip, with the option to the holder of receiving instead scrip for the three coupons first maturing and cash for the rest.

(c) To pay for five years in scrip the interest on the debenture bonds of both the Railroad and Coal & Iron Companies; the convertible bonds of the Railroad Company, the bonds due in 1885, 1902, and 1918 of the Tidewater & Susquehanna Canal Company, and so much of the rent due to the Schuylkill Navigation Company as was applicable to the payment of dividends to stockholders of the Company and to the interest upon its mortgage loan of 1895.

(d) To suspend the drawings for the payments of sinking funds and of the improvement and general mortgage bonds for a period not exceeding four years, if so long a time should be required for the payment of the floating debt.[1]

"The relief to be obtained from the above," said President Gowen, "will undoubtedly enable the managers, even with no improvement in traffic or increase of rates, to meet the fixed charges on all obligations of both companies other than those above named, and to pay off the entire floating debt within such time as will be satisfactory to the holders thereof." Certain modifications were suggested by the London securityholders, providing for trustees with some power to protect the creditors,[2] and the plan went quietly into effect.

From now on matters went from bad to worse. The year 1878 showed a falling off in almost every source of revenue, while expenses and charges remained very nearly the same. Depression in the coal trade and connection with the Coal & Iron Company, general dulness of business after 1873, troubles with employees, overcapitalization, all had their share in pushing the company still further into the mire. It became unable to keep its share of the existing business, and the percentages of the Schuylkill output carried by it steadily decreased from 83.49 in 1877 to 75.45 in 1881, while its percentage of the aggregate output from all the anthracite region diminished from 32.82 to 24.44. "It appears, therefore," said the annual report for 1881, "that while other companies have steadily increased their capacity of production by regular and judicious expenditures

[1] R. R. Gaz. 9: 225, 1877; Ibid. 9: 146, 1877.
[2] Ibid. 9: 284, 1877.

for new openings, breakers, machinery, and other facilities for mining and delivering coal, the Reading Company has apparently remained stationary. . . . For this policy the local officers in charge are not probably responsible, as it was undoubtedly forced upon them by the management, because of the impoverished and embarrassed condition of the company's finances." [1]

Throughout 1879 there was trouble over the payment of wages, perhaps as good a sign of financial difficulty as can be desired. Employees were paid in scrip, not cash, and even scrip wages were left overdue. President Gowen went to Europe toward the middle of the year, but not at all, as he carefully explained, in order to place a new loan, or to transact any business except a little in relation to some railroads for the company; in fact, the condition of the Reading was an open secret, and new loans were impossible to obtain. In May, 1880, the New York and Philadelphia banks began to refuse further accommodations. At the same time the period during which, according to the agreement of 1877, cash payment of general mortgage coupons was suspended, drew to a close, and on May 21 the Philadelphia & Reading announced its inability to meet its obligations. As was said at the time, the company did not fall with a crash because it had not far to fall.

The failure occurred on May 21, and on May 24 Messrs. F. B. Gowen (president of the company), Edwin A. Lewis, and Stephen A. Caldwell were appointed receivers. Their resources were scanty and they had to do with them as best they could. On the one hand they applied to the court for authority to borrow $1,000,000 to pay the wages of employees and interest falling due July 1, and on the other they cut down expenses by reducing the working force in the repair shops, by putting the shops on short time, by discontinuing many of the trains on different lines, and by ceasing all dead work at the collieries.

Before any plan could be proposed for the rehabilitation of the company the condition of its finances had to be known, and this again the receivers took in charge. Their report in June, 1880, showed a sufficiently serious state of affairs. The floating debt of the Railroad Company had mounted up to $10,254,766, besides $1,900,482 more for the Coal & Iron Company. This represented

---

[1] Annual Report, 1881, p. 28.

an increase of $3,604,000 as compared with November 30, 1879, and an English bondholders' committee declared that only $2,930,000 of it were represented by value.[1] The rest had apparently been incurred in desperate attempts to preserve the solvency of the company. The total liabilities of the Railroad and Coal & Iron Companies, including mortgage, debenture debt, floating debt, and miscellaneous items, but excluding stock, were $152,436,890. The deduction from these figures of the Coal & Iron bonds held by the Railroad Company, which would have constituted a duplication of indebtedness, left a total of $106,215,830.

The stock of the two companies amounted to $42,278,175, and the stock in the hands of the public to $39,278,175. The grand total of liabilities was thus the enormous sum of $145,494,005. The charges for interest and sinking funds were $7,542,094, and the annual payment of $5,629,764, due on $87,558,482 of railroad bonded indebtedness, shows that the rate of interest upon the bonds was high. The net revenue was $5,494,979, and there was therefore a deficit of $2,047,115. Meanwhile the Coal & Iron Company had reported a regular deficit up to 1880, which, though not significant in itself, because of close relations with the Railroad Company and the impossibility of determining how much the Coal Company's rightful profits were reduced by exorbitant transportation rates, yet made it very clear that from this source the Railroad Company could expect no aid toward the cancellation of the railroad deficit revealed.

The combined companies were unable to earn their fixed charges: the continuation of the struggle to do so was sure to mean, as it had in the past, merely a piling up of the floating debt. The coupon-funding scheme of 1877 had shown the inevitable result of temporary measures of relief; and though business in 1880 was rapidly improving, there was need for a radical reduction in the burden resting upon the company. Pending action, a bill for foreclosure was introduced under the general mortgage of 1874.[2] A valuation of the Reading coal properties, to which reference has already been made, was started. It was entrusted at first to Mr. S. B. Whitney,

---

[1] Chron. 31: 46, 1880, Report of the English Bondholders' Committee, June 18, 1880. This committee was in the interests of the Messrs. McCalmont.

[2] Ry. Age, 5: 365, 1880.

chief engineer of the Coal & Iron Company, and to Mr. Frank Carver, the land agent; but was later given over to Mr. Joseph S. Harris, chief engineer of the Lehigh Coal & Navigation Company, in order to have the opinion of an unprejudiced expert.[1]

The first suggestion for a plan of reorganization came from England. The consolidated mortgage, prior to the general mortgage, was to be foreclosed; general mortgage bonds were to be deprived of their right to sue or to foreclose; all unsecured bonds and junior mortgages were to be exchanged for preferred stock; and a $15 assessment was to be levied upon the stock, for which collateral trust 7 per cent bonds were to be given. This assessment was relied on to pay off the floating debt, and the new company was to start free, with but $33,564,000 of mortgage indebtedness.[2]

This plan was a step in the right direction. It recognized the validity of prior liens, followed a sound principle in providing for the floating debt by assessments upon the stock, and relieved the company from the likelihood of a future failure by its treatment of the general mortgage bonds; but it was weak in that it reduced the general mortgage to the anomalous position of a bond entitled to a fixed return without the power to enforce it. Stockholders, moreover, objected strenuously to the assessment, maintaining that business conditions were now such as to make milder measures sufficient.

In October, 1880, Mr. J. W. Jones, formerly vice-president of the Reading Company, urged that an assessment on the stock was not necessary, and proposed the following:

(1) To convert the income, debenture, and convertible bonds and scrip into second preferred stock bearing 5 per cent interest if earned;

(2) To issue $15,000,000 of first preferred stock, with which to retire the floating debt;

(3) To scale the Coal Company mortgage bonds $200,000 per annum, which could possibly be done by consent of holders, if not, then by foreclosure.[3]

The main difference between this and the English scheme lay in the treatment of the floating debt. It is improbable, however, that

[1] R. R. Gaz. 12: 363, 1880. [2] Ry. Age, 5: 351, 1880; R. R. Gaz. 12: 350, 1880.
[3] R. R. Gaz. 12: 542, 1880.

the substitute which this plan offered would have been sufficient, and that the preferred stock could have brought $66, at which price alone it would have covered the floating debt. Reading common stock was selling in the middle of the month at 16⅜; general mortgage 6s were bringing only 74¼, while debentures and convertible 7s were being quoted at 28 and 37 respectively.

In October a representative of the English bondholders arrived in Philadelphia for the purpose of examining into the condition of the company, and the following month agreed with the board of managers upon a reorganization committee to act in the United States. "The probabilities are," said this gentleman (Mr. Thomas Wilde Powell), "that it will be found that the bondholders in London will be willing to do as they did in the case of the Erie, that is, fund a reasonable number of coupons . . . for the purpose of setting at liberty a portion of the revenue to pay unfunded claims." [1] The next move in the reorganization of the company came, however, not from this committee but from President Gowen, the man who had led the Reading into the purchase of coal lands, and who still remained in office in spite of the hostility shown toward him. His scheme comprised two parts: the first an issue of income bonds with which to pay off the floating debt (together with $5,000,000 mortgage bonds); the second a grand general mortgage to retire existing indebtedness. The plan in more detail was as follows:

(1) The company was to create $34,300,000 deferred income bonds, on which interest was to be deferred to a dividend of 6 per cent on the common stock. After this amount had been paid the bonds were to take all revenue up to 6 per cent and were then to rank *pari passu* with the common shares for further dividends. The debentures were to be issued at 30 per cent of their par value, or $15 per bond; and before selling or disposing of said bonds in the market the option of taking a *pro rata* share was to be first offered to the stockholders of the company.[2]

(2) A more permanent relief for the company was to be obtained from the proposal to issue a new long time or perpetual 5 per cent funding mortgage of $150,000,000, divided into two classes, A and B, of $75,000,000 each: class A having priority of lien and interest charge over class B. With this issue it was proposed, by purchase

---

[1] R. R. Gaz. 12: 564, 1880.   [2] Chron. 31: 536, 1880.

or exchange, to retire all outstanding indebtedness, and to acquire by purchase the securities of the companies owning the leased lines. It was estimated that $140,000,000 of the new issue would provide for all of this, the total interest on which would be $7,000,000, as against fixed charges for interest, sinking funds, and rentals, of $10,657,116, making an annual saving of $3,657,116.[1] Mr. Gowen did not expect to secure so large an annual reduction, owing to the impossibility of purchasing the higher securities and the probable appreciation in value of the lower ones; but he did expect to realize in all a saving of some $2,700,000.

In part this plan was commendable; in part it was inadequate, and in part it relied on a mere juggling with words. The proposal to unify all classes of indebtedness by a grand consolidated 5 per cent mortgage was a good one, both in the simplification of accounts which was to be expected, and in the reduction in fixed charges so far as this reduction went; but on the one hand a reduction of $2,700,000 in charges was too little for a company which had reported for that very year a deficit of $2,000,000, and on the other hand too little allowance was made for the difficulty of forcing securityholders without a foreclosure sale to submit to a definitive scaling down of their holdings, with not even a preferred stock to show for the sacrifice. In its handling of the floating debt, the plan was a second edition of Mr. Jones's stock-selling scheme, with all the good points left out. What justification there could have been for calling securities, such as the deferred incomes, "bonds," which were to be issued for no definite time, ranked even after the common stock for dividends, and were of such doubtful character that Mr. Gowen himself proposed to sell them for one-third of their face value, does not appear; unless it be that the lack of voting power, itself a disadvantage, entitled them to the more respected name. The deferred income bonds were a device for saddling the holders of the unsecured debt with a worthless certificate which they might be induced to accept because of its name, and to which not even the Reading stockholders could object. Furthermore, even if the creditors had been eager for this new issue, in itself it would not have been sufficient. The issue, if taken up, would have yielded $10,200,000. It was proposed besides to sell $5,000,000 of unissued

[1] Chron. 31: 607, 1880.

general mortgage bonds, which, after the success of the deferred income bonds, it was presumed would sell at par. Income bonds and general mortgage together promised a total of $15,200,000, or more than $1,000,000 over cash requirements after commissions had been paid.[1]

However poor the prospect, there was no lack of syndicate guarantee. In November, 1880, a London syndicate agreed to deposit with an American bank, to be named by the company, the sum of $2,058,000, to be forfeited in case they failed to take at the issue price all deferred income bonds not taken by the shareholders. This syndicate further agreed that the company might retain, up to $1,000,000, out of the deposit money, whatever might be necessary to make up a second instalment of $4 on such neglected bonds.[2] Nothing was asked from the company in return except the chance to sell the bonds purchased at a premium. "As long as the bond- and shareholders find the money," remarked the London *Times*, "there is nothing to be said. In all probability, however, these deferred bonds will become a medium for the very worst kind of gambling, and their chances for a dividend appear to us to be very small."[3]

In December Mr. Gowen's plan received the approval of the American committee and of the board of managers of the company. Bondholders were in no way injured by the worthlessness of the deferred income bonds, and only the most far-sighted could be expected to have demanded a larger reduction in their claims. The same month a meeting of London bond- and shareholders passed unanimously a resolution expressing confidence in President Gowen, and adopting his scheme.[4] Opposition came from the influential London banking firm of McCalmont Bros., and the struggle centred about the annual election set for January 10, 1881. The last of November or first of December President Gowen issued a circular in which he said: "As I am about to visit Europe on business of the company, and as it is possible that I may not return until the first week in January, I think it proper to call your attention to the fact that it is highly important that all shareholders who can possibly do so should attend the annual meeting in Phil-

[1] R. R. Gaz. 12: 609, 1880.　　[2] Ibid.
[3] Ibid. 13: 11, 1881.　　[4] Ibid. 12: 704, 1880.

adelphia on the second Monday in January. An effort will undoubtedly be made at the next election to control the management of the company in the interest of rival lines, and if the effort is successful the future of the Philadelphia & Reading Railroad Company will be little, if any, better than that of the Philadelphia & Erie Railroad Company, or of the Northern Central Railroad Company." [1] In Europe, or, more strictly speaking, in London, Gowen busied himself in placing his deferred income bonds, with apparently a very considerable measure of success. As to the result of the coming election he professed absolute confidence. It made little difference, said he, which way the McCalmonts decided to vote their shares. He could be elected without any English votes at all, and with the backing of the English bondholders who had resolved to support him, the matter was not at all in doubt.[2] On January 4, six days before the date set for the election, Gowen actually issued a prospectus for his new income and mortgage loans, and cabled to Vice-President Keim that he was satisfied that he could dispose of the general mortgage A bonds at 110 and the general mortgage B bonds at par.[3]

Meanwhile in America both parties had recourse to the courts: the McCalmonts, to prevent the issue of the deferred income bonds, and the friends of Mr. Gowen to get the election postponed in order to give the president time to return from Europe. The latter suit was the first decided. Judge McKennan, of the United States Circuit Court, refused to grant an order, but unofficially advised postponement. The board of managers therefore withdrew the notice of the annual meeting, and on January 12 voted to postpone it indefinitely. Counsel for the McCalmonts then made application to the Court of Common Pleas in Philadelphia for a mandamus to compel the board to call a meeting. They obtained a peremptory mandamus on January 24, but accepted the date of March 14 as satisfactory, and forbore further proceedings.

The matter of the deferred income bonds was complicated by a full and complete authorization which Mr. Gowen had before obtained from the Circuit Court for the issue of his bonds. The request of the McCalmonts was twofold: the court was prayed to revoke the previous decree, and to enjoin any further action in the negotiation or consummation of the said scheme; or, failing this, to direct the

---

[1] R. R. Gaz. 12: 652, 1880.   [2] Ibid. 12: 704, 1880.   [3] Ibid. 13: 11, 1881.

officers of the company and the receivers to refrain from the issue
of the bonds until the form thereof should have been settled by the
said court, and also until deposit with the receivers should have
been made of the $2,058,000 provided as a guarantee.[1] The first
request sought a prohibition of the issue; the second attempted to
delay the negotiation of the bonds until the annual election should
have passed and the McCalmonts should have had a chance to
obtain control. The immediate result was the transference to Philadelphia of the $2,058,000 guaranteed, from its place of deposit in
London. In February the McCalmonts obtained a revocation of the
original grant of authority for the deferred income bonds, a continuance of the suit for a preliminary injunction, and an order re-
straining the respondents from "making any agreement or ordering
any act by which the Philadelphia & Reading Railroad Company
[might] be definitely bound touching the deferred bond plan or
the proposed mortgage loan of $150,000,000." [2]

In January the Coal & Iron Company quietly held its annual
election, and chose Mr. Gowen president. As the time for the postponed election of the Railroad Company came round, the activity
of both sides became intense. Both Gowen, who was still in London,
and the McCalmonts issued calls for proxies. The former appealed
to the shareholders to save the property from passing into the hands
of the Pennsylvania Central Railroad Company, which he said was
believed to be the ruling power behind the McCalmont litigation.
The latter objected vigorously to this charge, and pointed out that
the Reading managers held only 16,500 shares of the company's
stock, and that some of them had barely enough to qualify them for
the positions which they held.[3] The McCalmonts, furthermore,
applied to the courts for an injunction to prevent Gowen from voting
on the shares pledged as collateral for the floating debt. They
maintained with some justification that these shares could not
legally be voted, and that it was particularly illegal for the president to use them to elect himself.[4]

On March 12 the Court of Common Pleas issued a decree regu-
lating the conditions under which the election should be held, providing for the separate count of votes of shares transferred three

[1] R. R. Gaz. 13: 25, 1881.
[2] Chron. 32: 206, 1881.
[3] R. R. Gaz. 13: 43, 1881.
[4] R. R. Gaz. 13: 132, 1881.

months before the election, and for the ultimate reference of all disputed points to the Court. By this time Mr. Gowen had become alarmed at the apparent strength of the McCalmonts, and had come to realize that a possible disenfranchisement of a part of his own holdings on the ground of too recent transference might lessen his chances of retaining control. He recalled, however, that the annual meeting had been postponed from January 10 to March 7, and finally to March 14. This, it occurred to him, might transform it from a regular to a special meeting, and might, according to the terms of the company's charter, make necessary the presence and vote of a majority of all the shares outstanding, instead of a simple majority of all the shares on hand. If this should be true a disenfranchisement of his holdings would be of less importance; for whether disenfranchised or not, these would form part of the total shares outstanding, of which an absolute majority would be required.

On March 12, two days before the appointed date, Mr. Gowen issued a letter to the shareholders. "I hold," said he, "up to the present time, the proxies of 1921 shareholders of the company, owning 359,500 shares of the capital stock, being very considerably more than a majority of all the shares. . . . Of the shares for which I hold proxies, so large a proportion, however, may possibly be disenfranchised by failure to register, that if the legal meeting of the stockholders is held on Monday next, and it should subsequently be determined by the Court that three months' prior registry is essential to confer the right of voting, it may be possible that the wishes of the great majority of *bona fide* shareholders may be overruled by a minority. . . . I have determined to abstain from attending the meeting, and I earnestly request all shareholders who support the present management to absent themselves from the meeting on Monday, and thus to give legal effect to their wishes by making it impossible for the minority to secure the attendance of a quorum. . . ."[1]

Mr. Gowen's friends, English and American, followed his suggestion; and at the meeting on Monday but 211,095 out of 687,663 registered shares appeared to vote. The immediate result was the almost unanimous election of Mr. Bond, the candidate of the

[1] Chron. 32: 313, 1881.

McCalmonts, which was followed by litigation on the part of Mr. Gowen, disputing the legality of the election. By the terms of the decree under which the election had been held, the matter came first before the Court of Common Pleas, which, on April 9, decided that the meeting had been a legal one, and that the officers then voted for by the McCalmonts had been duly elected. With the above court ranged against him, Mr. Gowen took appeal to the Supreme Court of the state, and meanwhile declined to surrender his position. On April 11 the new board proceeded to the Reading offices in Philadelphia, made formal demand for admittance, and were refused. On April 22 President Bond issued formal notice of his election. An injunction was asked against Mr. Gowen, but was held back until the Supreme Court should have taken action. Meanwhile the old board of managers announced that if a decree supporting the decision of the Court of Common Pleas should be rendered they would make no further opposition; and the transfer agents of the company in Philadelphia and New York refused to transfer any stock until the dispute should have been settled. On April 19 an order of the United States Court interfered with Mr. Gowen's exclusive possession, and compelled him to furnish to Messrs. Frank S. Bond, etc., suitable accommodations in the offices of the Philadelphia & Reading Railroad Company, with free access to all books and papers. In May the Supreme Court rendered its decision, holding the meeting of March 14 to have been a regular meeting, and a majority of all the stock outstanding not to have been required for a quorum. Gowen asked for a rehearing, which was denied, and in June, nearly four months after the election, he grudgingly acknowledged Mr. Bond and his associates as the legally elected president and board of managers.

During all this time the deferred income bond scheme had not remained untouched. In April, 1881, on application of the McCalmonts, the United States Circuit Court at Philadelphia had granted a preliminary injunction against it. "Whatever power the defendant has in the premises can only be found in the general authority to borrow money," said Judge McKennan, and went on to state that the issue did not constitute a loan, because a loan implied reimbursement, and the income bonds were redeemable at no special time.[1]

[1] Chron. 32: 445, 1881.

Mr. Gowen promptly proposed to make them redeemable, and insisted that this made them still more desirable. A week later the $150,000,000 general mortgage was also enjoined.[1]

Once out of the presidency Mr. Gowen endeavored to induce the McCalmonts to accept his plan. If they would adopt the deferred income bond scheme, he said in an address to shareholders, he would resign the receivership of the road at once, give bonds never to stand for the presidency again, and further coöperate with them in selecting a new board of directors. As an alternative he offered to buy the McCalmont shares at $40 each, and threatened to beat that party at the next election if it refused.[2] In September he assured the stockholders that he could without difficulty put the road upon its feet. "If Bond and his colleagues will resign and reinstate the old management," he cabled from London, "and advise me by cable of the change, I can, before sailing on Saturday, procure sufficient advances against the proceeds of preferred [deferred?] income bonds and new 5 per cent consols to pay the floating debt, receivers' certificates, and all arrears of interest."[3] Finally, appealing to Mr. Bond direct, Gowen made formal application that the new board should adopt his plan after changing the form of the proposed obligations by making them payable in 100 or 200 years.[4] Bond refused. He pointed out that the deferred income bondholders would be in constant conflict with the management in their endeavor to secure dividends on their holdings, and would attempt to prevent proper and necessary expenditures upon the property from current net revenues. He declared that it was questionable whether the company had authority to sell its unsecured obligations below par, and that in any case the process would be enormously expensive; and, further, that the language of the obligation did not limit the payment of interest to the source of net revenue only, but might be construed to compel the declaration of 6 per cent on the income bonds whenever 6 per cent should be paid on the common stock.[5] Failing in his attempts to win over his opponents, Gowen turned his energies toward securing their defeat.

Meanwhile President Bond brought forward a plan of his own.

[1] Chron. 32: 469, 1881. [2] R. R. Gaz. 13: 446, 1881.
[3] Ry. Age, 6: 528, 1881. [4] Annual Report, 1881, p. 52.
[5] Annual Report, 1881, pp. 50 ff.

He had grasped three points of weakness in Gowen's scheme, namely, —

(1) The issue of a mass of worthless obligations in the deferred income bonds;

(2) The high level of fixed charges which a $150,000,000 5 per cent mortgage entailed;

(3) The lack of any security which had a right to interest only when earned, and which might be given to the bondholders in return for sacrifices which they would otherwise refuse to make.

He proposed, therefore, to create a general consolidated mortgage to cover all the property of the Reading Railroad and Coal & Iron Companies, together with the interest of both companies in all other corporations and property, whether owned or controlled by lease or otherwise. This mortgage was to be junior to the consolidated and to the improvement mortgages only, but was to contain a provision by which, as bonds under these senior mortgages should be retired, additional bonds might be issued under the new mortgage, which was eventually to become a first lien upon all the properties of both companies.[1] The total was to be $150,000,000, to be divided into two series: of which series A, for $90,000,000, was to run for fifty years, and was to have a prior lien over series B upon the revenues for interest at the rate of 4½ per cent, with a right to enforce foreclosure in case of a twelve months' default; and series B was to run sixty years, and was to carry interest at 3 per cent, with a right to enforce foreclosure in case of a three years' default. In prosperous years series B might receive more than 3 per cent: thus the mortgage provided that from current net revenue applicable to dividends it should get 1½ per cent additional interest before any dividend should be paid on the stock of the company; after that 3 per cent might be paid on the capital stock, and then 1½ per cent additional might be paid on series B; it being understood that the interest in excess of 3 per cent should not be cumulative, but was to be paid only from current net revenues of the company otherwise applicable to dividends. These two issues of unequal worth were to be used for different purposes. Series A was to be in part reserved to retire the senior obligations, and in part to be sold to pay off the general mortgage bonds, the general mortgage scrip, the income bonds, the floating

[1] Annual Report, 1881, pp. 50 ff.; see also Chron. 33: 177, 1881.

debt of the Railroad and Coal & Iron Companies secured by collateral, the receivers' obligations, and the mortgages on real estate that could be paid off. Series B was to be exchanged for the junior obligations, such as the debenture or convertible loans, or was to be held in reserve for subsequent acquisition of the guaranteed stock or obligations of affiliated corporations of the Railroad and Coal & Iron Companies.

What this meant for the immediate future was that all prior liens were to remain untouched, while everything from the general mortgage down was to be funded into the new obligations. In some ways this resembled the earlier scheme of Mr. Gowen, since in each case there was to be a $150,000,000 general mortgage in two parts, of which one part was to have priority over the other, and in each case this grand mortgage was to be used ultimately to retire all previously existing indebtedness. An innovation was now made, however, in the difference introduced between the two series. In Gowen's scheme the amount of each series was to be the same, and each was to fare alike, except for the priority of series A; in that of President Bond, series A was to be half again as large as series B, and was to bear a higher rate of compulsory interest; although, a point of extreme importance, the return upon series B was to run from a minimum of 3 per cent to a maximum of 6 per cent whenever the road should earn it. Thus President Bond gained two things: he reduced the rate of interest which his new bonds could claim in any year from 5 per cent (as under Gowen's scheme) to an average of something under 4 per cent, which would yet, in prosperous times, net them as much as the old bonds surrendered; and as a still further concession, he gave to the 3 per cent bonds a term of sixty instead of fifty years, raising their value to that extent. As the various existing issues of bonds had different market values, he thought it proper to equalize these values in the exchange by the grant of a bonus in stock, for which the capital stock of the company was to be increased one-third. Here were two of Gowen's problems in a fair way of solution: the reduction of fixed charges was accomplished, while some incentive was given to the junior bondholders to assent. Scarcely less from the point of view of sound finance was the gain from the abandonment of the anomalous deferred income bond scheme, with its $34,300,000 of worthless speculative securities. Instead, the floating debt, under President Bond's plan, was to be cared for by the sale of series A bonds, not at one-third their face value, but as near par as possible; by the best of the company's new securities, in other words, and not by the worst. And, finally, the acquisition of the securities of subsidiary roads was provided for rather ingeniously by the conversion into series B bonds of $10,527,900 convertible 7 per cent bonds, against which had perforce been reserved an equal amount of stock. Conversion released the stock, which became a free asset available for any uses to which the company saw fit to apply it.

Yet while the advance which the plan of President Bond marks over that of President Gowen may be recognized, its defects must also be observed. It was, in the first place, in common with all other schemes suggested, too mild, too little drastic in its operations. The condition of the Reading companies was desperate in the extreme. By President Bond's own figures the previous five years had shown a deficit of $11,479,217, or an average loss per annum of $2,295,853. The net earnings for 1881 by the same computation had been $8,418,009, and the fixed charges $11,265,666.[1] What was needed was a radical scaling down of indebtedness, to take effect not in the far distant future but at once. President Gowen, face to face with a similar situation, had evolved a reduction in fixed charges from about $11,000,000 to about $7,000,000, but had explained that, owing to the impossibility of retiring all of the prior liens at once, the actual figures would be approximately $7,957,000. President Bond, less optimistic, or more honest, stated that the ultimate charge under his plan would be about $6,000,000; but that the immediate reduction would be to about $8,339,000 only, scarcely more than $100,000 below the net earnings of the current year. Both estimates would probably have been under the mark; but the relief which President Bond proposed was utterly inadequate even on his own showing. A margin of surplus earnings which could be wiped out in a single month was no answer to the demand for a restoration of the Reading companies to solvency. In regard to the floating debt, too, Bond's plan left something to be desired, in that it provided for no assessment, but cared for the floating obligations by the sale of bonds. The danger in relying upon

[1] Ry. Age, 6: 486, 1881.

the sale of securities to supply the cash requirements of a bankrupt road has been mentioned in connection with Mr. Gowen's scheme, as indeed at other times before. At best it is advisable only in prosperous times, and when the bonds offered are of high grade; and though the series A bonds might perhaps have been considered high grade, the prosperity of 1880 was not repeated in 1881, and a year of bankruptcy and litigation had not improved the Reading's credit. That the plan failed, however, was due neither to its inadequacy nor to its method of dealing with the floating debt; but rather to the resolute and uncompromising opposition of Mr. Gowen and his friends, and to the determination of the junior securityholders to stand out for better terms. This twofold resistance caused a syndicate of bankers, which had been relied upon to place the new loan, ultimately to reject it, and the plan fell through.[1]

To return now to Mr. Gowen. This gentleman had been strengthening his following in every possible way, and had secured one ally of particular importance in the person of Mr. Vanderbilt, who in October, 1881, was reported to be buying largely of the company's stock. Early in November Mr. Gowen and President Bond both issued addresses to the shareholders. The former maintained that although the present management had been in power for over four months it had done nothing to extricate the company from its difficulties, and promised that if elected he would "retain the office long enough to place the company in a good financial condition, by completing the issue of deferred income bonds and by issuing and selling the 5 per cent consolidated mortgage bonds, the result of which will be the resumption of dividends upon the company's shares." [2] The business prospects of the company were never better, he continued, and the wisdom of the purchase of the great anthracite coal estate was being demonstrated. Bond, on the other hand, alluded to the failure of Mr. Gowen's many promises, to the wasteful expenditure of money, to the coal speculations in which the road had been engaged, to the payment of unearned dividends, and to other points of Gowen's policy, actual or alleged; [3] and his statements were repeated by the McCalmonts in spite of Mr. Gowen's vehement denials.[4]

[1] Chron. 33: 256, 1881.
[2] Ry. Age, 6: 628, 1881.
[3] R. R. Gaz. 13: 624, 1881.
[4] R. R. Gaz. 13: 672, 1881.

The election was held from January 9 to January 14, 1882. There were cast 493,601 votes, of which Gowen received 270,984 and Bond 222,617; a result mainly due to the 72,000 Vanderbilt shares voted for Mr. Gowen. The same meeting approved by resolution Gowen's financial plans, and called on the incoming board of managers to carry them into effect. To clear the way a test suit was brought in the Supreme Court of the state of Pennsylvania, and a close decision obtained favoring the issue.[1] Counsel for the McCalmont Bros. petitioned in the Circuit Court for leave to withdraw their complaint, stating that the McCalmonts had disposed of almost all their holdings, and the Circuit Court vacated the injunction which it had previously granted.[2]

Gowen's plan was now triumphantly brought forward, with the few alterations which time had suggested. There was to be as before a deferred income bond issue of $34,300,000, which was to retire the floating debt; the general mortgage was to be increased in amount from $150,000,000 to $160,000,000, but was still to be divided into two series, equal in amount, and differing in privileges only on the point of priority of lien; of which series A was ultimately to exchange for the senior, series B for the junior obligations of the company. $13,500,000 of the first series and $10,000,000 of the second series were to be put out at once, and $4,000,000 convertible adjustment scrip were to be issued to settle back coupons. Time had apparently made more modest Mr. Gowen's estimate of the saving to be secured; for instead of not more than $7,000,000 as before, he now hoped for fixed charges of not more than $8,000,000; but with undaunted optimism he made up for this admission by glowing pictures of what the company in the future was going to earn. "Net earnings last year" (1881), said he, "were over $10,000,000 — in 1882 they may be expected to reach $11,000,000, and they will before long be over $12,000,000. With net earnings of $12,000,000, and fixed charges of $8,000,000, there will remain a dividend fund of $4,000,000, equal to 6 per cent on the share capital, and 6 per cent upon the par, or 20 per cent upon the issue price, of the deferred income bonds. "In order to get the property out of the hands of the receivers an earnest effort was made fo sell the $13,500,000 series A

[1] Chron. 34: 265, 1882; R. R. Gaz. 26: 156, 1882.
[2] Chron. 34: 409, 1882.

bonds of which mention has been made, but at the minimum price of 98 subscriptions for but $723,500 were received, and the company was obliged to have recourse to the $5,000,000 unissued general mortgage 7 per cent bonds, which it fortunately had at its disposal. Even before this the management had been forced to abandon any immediate attempt to retire the old general mortgage bonds,[1] and had been compelled to answer inquiries as to the reasons for a decline in the price of the deferred income bonds. On February 28 the receivers of the Railroad and Coal & Iron Companies formally surrendered the control of the property to the officers of those corporations.

One of the first acts of the reconstructed company was the lease for 999 years of the Central Railroad of New Jersey. This road in many ways formed a natural complement to the Reading system. Like it, it was a coal road, carrying something less than half as great a tonnage as the Reading itself, and owning extensive coal lands in the Wyoming region; while in location it supplied the necessary connection between the Reading lines and New York. At a later date Mr. Joseph S. Harris testified that all the business of the Reading coming from the South or Southwest went to New York over the Central; while, on the other hand, business from the Northwest was carried by the Jersey Central from Scranton, where its lines began, to Bethlehem, and was there handed to the Reading for transportation to Philadelphia.[2] The advantages of the Central to the Reading were thus enumerated by General Traffic Manager Bell in 1885: "The joint traffic with the Central Railroad, outside of coal, and outside of passengers, adds $1,500,000 to the revenue of the old Reading system. By means of the Lehigh & Susquehanna division of the Central Road we extend from Phillipsburg to Scranton or Green Ridge through the entire Lehigh Valley; that system feeds our North Pennsylvania line; it is our connection for the Catawissa system by way of Tamanend and Tamaqua; it is the connecting link in the cross line or Allentown system; it creates the shortest line from interior Pennsylvania, and from Northwest Pennsylvania to New York waters. Through the operations of the lease we reach the largest slate territory in Pennsylvania, and the largest iron producing furnaces anywhere in this country, with the exception of Pitts-

[1] R. R. Gaz. 14: 354, 1882.   [2] Industrial Commission, vol. 9, p. 607.

burg." [1] In 1883 the Central was bankrupt with no immediate prospect of recovering from its difficulties, and had therefore an incentive to accept any arrangement by which interest on its obligations should be paid; while Mr. Gowen, with misplaced confidence in his scheme of reorganization, was ready to put fresh burdens on his road in the hope of future gain.

Rumors of a lease were abroad in 1882, and after the termination of the Reading receivership the operation was pushed tó a speedy conclusion. The Reading undertook to assume all the obligations of the Central, and to pay 6 per cent on its capital stock then outstanding, as well as $18,000 annually for maintaining the corporate organization of the lessor. In case any of the Central bonds should be retired, or rentals or interest reduced, the rental to be paid by the Reading was likewise to be reduced. The roadbed and rolling stock of the Central was to be maintained undiminished, but if the Reading should make any additions or improvements, or if from its own funds it should pay off any of the Central's obligations, it was to receive equivalent bonds with interest not exceeding 6 per cent from the Central Company. The lease was terminable on 60 days' notice in case the lessee should fail at any time to carry out its provisions. [2] This involved something more than a nominal obligation. The net earnings of the Jersey Central in 1882 had been $5,091,072, while the sum due for rentals, interest, 6 per cent dividends, etc., had mounted up to $5,898,087, not including payments on car trusts or certain contingent obligations. Broadly speaking, the Reading proposed to guarantee 6 per cent on the stock of a road which had failed because unable to meet its fixed charges; and however great the ultimate advantages, it is apparent that the prospect of a drain upon the Reading Company was real. In order to get the road out of receivers' hands, the Reading had further to take care of a floating debt of $2,062,000, and to compromise with certain creditors by settling back interest on their bonds. This was done, and on May 29, 1883, possession formally passed over. The same day was concluded another arrangement, whereby the Central of New Jersey leased the coal and railroad companies comprised in the Lehigh Coal & Navigation Company for one-third of their gross receipts, and the Philadelphia & Reading Railroad became liable for the

---

[1] Ry. Age, 10: 218, 1885.   [2] Annual Report, 1883, pp. 111 ff.

faithful execution of the contract. The Reading agreed that the Lehigh coal lands should be developed *pari passu* with its own, so that the product of the two estates should be constantly as 28 to 72 until the Lehigh production should reach 3,000,000 tons. The rental of the road was not in any year to be less than $1,414,400, nor more than a sum rising from $1,728,700 before 1887 to $1,885,800 from 1887 to 1892, and $2,043,000 after 1892, plus certain minor payments; and there was provision for arbitration of any disputes which might arise.[1]

The year 1883 now seemed to find the Reading imbued with new life. Earnings increased, both gross and net, fixed charges as reported rose less rapidly, and the net profits for the year, or balance on all operations, showed a threefold increase. "The company," said Mr. Gowen, "has now surmounted the difficulties of the last four eventful years."[2] The annual meeting in January was a genuine love-feast, marked by the presentation of resolutions highly flattering to Mr. Gowen. "We trust," said one, "we thankfully appreciate your herculean efforts in our behalf, in the face of unparalleled difficulties and obstacles, in rescuing our property from bankruptcy against the malignant and determined efforts of its enemies and conspirators to foreclose and wreck it." "As citizens of this great commonwealth," said another, "we beg to add our gratitude and admiration for your untiring, brave, honest, and able devotion, which has preserved the Philadelphia & Reading Company intact, and has fairly started it on a broader career of usefulness."[3] Not less extraordinary was the further action of this harmonious meeting. In the first place, it authorized the creation of a collateral trust loan of $12,000,000 for the purpose of paying the floating debt, the balance due upon the purchase of Central Railroad Company of New Jersey stock, and the retirement of the outstanding income mortgage bonds. What, may be inquired, had become of the deferred income bonds of which Mr. Gowen had been so proud, and the $5,000,000 additional first series consols which with them were to cover the floating debt, if a new collateral loan was needed for the purpose for which they had been considered ample? As for the purchase of Jersey Central shares, an account would require

---

[1] Annual Report, 1883, pp. 139 ff.   [2] Chron. 37: 563, 1883.
[3] Annual Report, 1883, pp. 25-7.

a chapter in itself. The intent had been to secure more complete control of this subsidiary road. The purchase had been made on margin in May. By January, 1884, more funds were necessary to carry the stock; and as the business depression grew acute, the Reading was obliged to seek a time loan from Mr. Vanderbilt, and to pledge the purchased securities as collateral therefor. When the loan matured Reading was no better off than it had been before, and Vanderbilt, who seldom mixed philanthropy with business, sold the stock. The original purchase had been at 78; the prices obtained when the stock was thrown on the market ranged from 57 to 50, and the Reading lost the difference, besides those advantages which it had expected to gain.

In the second place, the meeting proposed a dividend of 21 per cent on the preferred stock, representing arrears due, and of 3 per cent on the common; both cash, and to be paid in case the collateral loan should succeed.[1] In order to give shareholders time to consider, an adjournment was taken for two weeks, after which the dividend on the preferred stock was approved, though that on the common was not. It seems almost superfluous to insist upon the folly of this dividend. The Reading had not, in reality, "surmounted the difficulties of the last four eventful years." Scarcely any of the benefits promised by Mr. Gowen's plan of reorganization had been secured; fixed charges had not been reduced, because it had been found impossible to get creditors to take new securities in exchange for the old, and equally impossible to sell any considerable amount of the new securities for cash. While old charges had remained unabated, new charges had been added through the lease of the Jersey Central, new car trusts, and the like, and the very gain in earnings which might have been construed as favorable was due to increased mileage, and was not proportional to the growth of the system.[2] A fitting sequel to Mr. Gowen's words and acts was the scrip payment for labor and supplies which took place in May, 1884, and the accompanying fall in the prices of the company's securities. On June 2 the company again passed into receivers' hands. The same judges were applied to as in 1880, and the same receivers were ap-

---

[1] Annual Report, 1883. The proposition was made by Mr. Gowen.

[2] From November 30, 1883, to January 2, 1884, reliable figures subsequently showed a deficit of $2,000,000.

pointed, except that Mr. Gowen, who had given up the presidency of the company, was replaced by Mr. George de Keim, his successor.[1]

The various creditors had now to do what should have been done before, and, by lightening the charges upon the road, to put it in a position where its solvency could be maintained. The chances for obtaining radical action from the bondholders were somewhat brighter, since even the most obstinate were being forced to realize that no halfway measures would avail; and a reasonable solution was even thus early hinted at in the suggestion that some of the bonds under which the road was staggering should be replaced by stock. Nevertheless, we shall find in this reorganization a slow working out of the requirements for a plan, and a slow process of at least partial reconcilement to the inevitable.

The receivers' report was issued in October, but contained little not known or suspected before. From November 30, 1883, to June 2, 1884, there had been a net loss in operation for the Railroad Company of $2,322,282, and for the Coal & Iron Company of $1,049,702, showing conclusively the condition of the companies. The total bonded indebtedness was $94,613,042; a total to be compared with the $78,101,894 of four years previous. The total floating debt was $16,549,968 as compared with $10,254,766 at the beginning of the previous receivership. Including the Central of New Jersey, the total fixed charges for the Railroad and Coal & Iron Companies were $18,241,051; a sum which certain offsets, however, reduced to $16,584,732.[2]

The first suggestion for a reorganization came from a committee primarily representing the general mortgage bondholders, though including other interests as well. The chairman was Mr. Townsend Whelen, and the committee may be taken to represent the views of the management. "The present fixed charges of the company," said Mr. Whelen, "are in round numbers $16,650,000, while the earnings of the past fiscal year are, in round numbers and after proper deductions, $12,900,000. The objects sought to be accomplished by the committee are:

"(1) To reduce fixed charges to the limit of last year's earnings;

"(2) To preserve the proper order of priorities of each class of securities, so that no income applicable to any senior security that

[1] Chron. 38: 679, 1884.　　　　[2] Ibid. 39: 461, 1884.

remains unpaid can by any possibility be diverted to paying the interest on a junior security;

"(3) To provide a method of paying the floating debt."

The plan was, roughly, to leave the prior liens untouched, to fund one-half the coupons upon the general mortgage for three years, and to convert all of the other obligations into income bonds. Preferred stock was to be changed from cumulative to non-cumulative; rents of leased lines, including the Central of New Jersey, were to be reduced to the amounts which the properties had earned; the canal leases were to be reduced; the interest on some of the divisional coal land mortgages was to be reduced, and on some was to be paid in full. In regard to the floating debt the committee decided to postpone any attempt to raise money for its extinction. If the bondholders should accept the scaling down of their indebtedness, the company might have no difficulty in procuring cash by a collateral loan; if this should prove impossible, the duty of providing funds would devolve upon the junior securities.[1] The committee found it impossible to prepare within the short time at their disposal a complete plan of reorganization with exact figures of present and proposed fixed charges; and it is therefore impossible to ascertain how great was the saving which they expected to secure.

The plan marks sufficiently well the advance which had been made since the reorganization of 1880-3. The best that could then be imagined had been the creation of a grand general mortgage for which the old bondholders might, but mostly did not, exchange their holdings; while now the very first suggestion endeavored to retain for all bondholders a chance for the same return as before, and found the salvation of the company in the transformace of certain bonds from mortgage to debenture obligations. The general criticisms which may be made are three: first, that it was unwise to defer all provision for the floating debt; second, that the new income bonds might better have been replaced by stock; and third, that the probable reduction in fixed charges would have been insufficient. So far as the committee suggested any action in relation to the floating debt, it favored a funding of it. This funding might have been either into mortgage or into income bonds: if the former, the fixed charges of the company would have been increased, or else the other

[1] Annual Report, 1884, pp. 21-8.

mortgage bondholders would have been compelled to accept a lower rate of interest; if the latter, the volume of securities of slight value would have been increased, or the junior securities would have had to take less for their holdings. The action taken would have gone far to determine what classes of securities would assent, while in the absence of definite declaration it was on the whole likely that all classes would hold off. As for the income bonds, it is in general true that they are an unsatisfactory sort of security, and likely to hinder the legitimate increase of capital. Most important was the question of fixed charges. It will be remembered that of the first and second series 5s of the previous reorganization only $23,500,000 had been intended for immediate sale, and that of these but a portion had been disposed of; and yet these consols were the only securities the nature of which was really changed by the Whelen plan. Interest had been optional before on the income bonds, the convertible bonds, the convertible adjustment scrip, debenture and deferred income bonds; interest was not made optional on the general mortgage or prior liens. The result would not have been, in spite of the reduction in rents and the scaling of the divisional coal mortgages, any sufficient lessening of the fixed requirements. This fact was, moreover, perceived. The board of managers, to whom the scheme was reported, concluded a favorable opinion with the declaration, "to conclude, we are satisfied that the large economies already in operation, with those which are still being introduced, should be regarded as a margin to meet adverse contingencies. . . . That the revenue we reckon on, though reasonably certain under such reorganization, will surely not be realized in case the property should be torn asunder by foreclosure sale." [1] In other words they relied, much as Mr. Gowen had done two years before, on a subsequent increase in earnings to ensure the solvency of the company. A final objection made at the time was that the plan asked too little of the junior securities.

The Whelen plan was reported to the general managers' committee, and was approved by them. Some slight modifications were made, and a large number of signatures was secured. Opposition was not slow to spring up. In February a meeting of general mortgage bondholders elected a committee, known as the Bartol Committee, to prepare a plan more suited to their interests. This body

[1] R. R. Gaz. 17: 80, 1885.

conferred with the Whelen Committee, and two members from each were selected to construct a new reorganization plan.[1] In March it reported to its constituents that it had made all the concessions which were possible without sacrificing the interests of the general mortgage bondholders, and that in spite of this, the negotiations had not proved successful.[2]

In April, ten months after the beginning of the receivership, the Reading managers evolved a plan for dealing with the floating debt. Holders were to agree to accept renewals at intervals of three months for three years, with interest at the rate of 6 per cent, paid at the time of each renewal, and to hold the collateral pledged as security until the whole of the debt should have been discharged. In case the Philadelphia & Reading should fail at any time punctually to pay the interest on any of the obligations agreed to be renewed, or should fail to cause the same to be renewed, or in case nine-tenths of the floating-debt holders should not assent to the plan, or in case an adverse judicial sale should be made, the obligation to accept further renewals should immediately cease.[3] The scheme deservedly fell through. Creditors were asked to tie up their assets for three years, with no concession in return except the payment of interest quarterly in advance; while the unofficial suggestion that the Reading pay ¼ per cent commission on each renewal was felt to be too expensive for the company to entertain.

The following month the Whelen and Bartol committees came out with a new edition of the Whelen plan, which introduced an assessment on the junior bonds and stock, but preserved the same method of dealing with the old securities as before.[4] Assent to the plan was to be on the condition that sufficient money should be raised to pay off the floating debt. Interest on such debt was not to have priority of payment over interest on the general mortgage for longer than three years; and during those three years the preference was to be limited to that part of the floating debt secured by collateral yielding income to cover interest, or important for other reasons to be retained. There were to be seven reorganization trustees to receive the assents of parties in interest, and to receive

---

[1] R. R. Gaz. 17: 144, 1885.   [2] Ibid. 17: 160, 1885.
[3] Ibid. 17: 224, 1885.
[4] Collateral bonds were to be given for the assessment.

and hold the securities and assessments thereon pending reorganization, and when accomplished to return such securities duly
stamped to their respective owners.[1] The trustees were further to
decide whether the assents to the plan in question should be considered adequate, and if they should conclude on or before May 1,
1886, by a vote of six of their number, that the assents were not
sufficient, they were to call into a council the managers of the Philadelphia & Reading Railroad Company, the receivers of that company, and the committees of the general mortgage (Bartol) and
income mortgage bondholders; and this council, by a vote of four
of the five interests therein represented, was to formulate a plan of
reorganization adapted to the circumstances, and involving no larger
contribution in money to be paid than under the plan as then modified; and under such power the trustees were to proceed to foreclose under such mortgage or mortgages as they might deem advisable.[2] The plan was obviously a compromise whereby the Whelen
Committee clung to the main lines of its previous proposition, and
the Bartol Committee secured modifications which benefited the
general mortgage at the expense of the junior securities. Criticisms
which applied to the earlier plan largely apply to this also; but it is
to be noticed that at last the idea of funding the floating debt was
abandoned for the sounder scheme of paying it off in cash. The
reorganization trustees were an innovation, but were destined to be
a useful one. On the whole the compromise was a step forward; and
yet it was not more successful in obtaining assents than the scheme
which had preceded it. Although the directors approved it, as was
to have been expected, the bulk of the bondholders held off.

Matters now went on in much the same old way. The seven reorganization trustees, representing the principal interests concerned,
held meeting after meeting with no apparent result. The courts
became impatient; bondholders clamored for their interest; but after
the failure of the earlier plan the way out seemed harder and harder
to find. In September, 1885, Mr. E. Dunbar Lockwood addressed

---

[1] Chron. 40: 569, 1885. The trustees were to be appointed as follows: One by
foreign creditors, two by the general mortgage bondholders, one by the income
mortgage bondholders, one by holders of securities junior to the income mortgage,
and two by the shareholders.

[2] Ry. Age, 10: 314, 1885.

an open letter to Mr. John B. Garrett, one of the trustees, in which the following points were made:

(1) "The trustees should recognize promptly and unequivocally that the Reading Railroad is bankrupt, and has not sufficient available assets to meet its obligations.

(2) "Two dollars of obligations cannot be paid with one dollar and a half of assets, and the sooner all persons interested . . . recognize this fact, and agree to scale both principal and interest sufficient to meet the obligations of the company and put it upon a strong financial basis, with sufficient working capital to enable it to conduct its future business economically, the better it will be for all concerned.

(3) "The trustees should look only at the facts as they exist . . . and while endeavoring to rehabilitate the road, also bring it into harmonious relations with its adversaries.

(4) "The trustees should consider the problem . . . precisely as business men consider the matter of the settlement of a bankrupt firm. The question at once presents itself, is it best that the company should continue in business, or should it be wound up?" [1]

In his reply Mr. Garrett pointed out the difficulties to be overcome, and concluded by saying that in his judgment no reorganization would be final that did not ensure the establishment of credit, the entrusting of the management to an interest having an actual equity in the property, and just expectation of pecuniary return from it, and harmony with competing lines, coupled with due regard for the rights of the public.[2]

The reorganization trustees by this time appeared discouraged, and the following month called a conference of creditors at which a resolution was passed looking toward foreclosure. In November a suit was actually begun, supplementary to a similar suit instituted a year before. It was during the pendency of these proceedings that the plan of reorganization devised by the reorganization trustees themselves came out, and marked a third effort to rehabilitate the road. The first plan proposed, it will be remembered, had suggested the conversion of all of the junior securities into income bonds, plus a funding of one-half the general mortgage coupons for three years; and the second had introduced an assessment on the junior bonds and stock. This third plan, while preserving the

[1] R. R. Gaz. 17: 607, 1885.   [2] Chron. 41: 307, 1885.

assessment, and making it more severe, added a provision for the conversion of general mortgage liens into 3 per cent bonds, and of junior liens into preferred stock. For the ultimate retirement of the prior liens a new fifty-year 5 per cent mortgage was to be created; for both the prior and general mortgage liens the difference between the return from the old bonds and that from the new was to be adjusted by the use of 5 per cent preferred stock, so that bondholders in prosperous times would not find their incomes diminished. Preferred stock was to be of two kinds, of which the first was to go to satisfy the general mortgage bondholders and for assessments, while the second was to exchange at varying rates for the junior securities above the second series 5s. Everything below the second series 5s was to receive common stock instead. Under the scheme the company's obligations would have been reduced to $60,731,000, of which $33,400,000 prior liens and $24,686,000 new 3 per cents; while its stock would have been increased to the very considerable figure of $96,516,282. The total cash assessments, if all paid, would have amounted to $13,506,620; and, joined with the balance of stock, were expected to be sufficient to cover the floating debt. The new fixed charges were to be $7,064,830.[1]

Various points in the plan deserve mention. For the first time since the failure of 1880 it was proposed to use two kinds of securities, of which interest on one should be fixed, and interest on the other optional. For the retirement of senior bonds President Bond had suggested a bond on which half the interest should be fixed and the other half variable, but his plan had been inferior in flexibility to the one now proposed. The junior securities received less favorable treatment than before; but the general mortgage itself did not escape, and was required to accept 3 per cent plus preferred stock instead of a mere funding of its coupons. The increase in the amount of stock was very great, and naturally so, in view of the new uses to which it was put.[2] Assessments were made heavier, and for the first time the management frankly excluded from their calculations the Central of New Jersey, foreshadowing the abandonment of the lease. To repeat, the first two plans described had developed the idea of an assessment and the conversion of the junior bonds into

[1] Chron. 41: 654, 1885.
[2] Preferred from $846,950 to $36,381,820; common from $36,822,975 to $60,134,462.

income obligations. To this the reorganization trustees added the use of preferred stock, and, more important still, the combination of two securities, respectively with obligatory and optional liens, which were to be given for the general mortgage bonds. In principle the result was excellent, in practice the degree of reduction was somewhat too slight from the point of view of the company, although it seemed more than the creditors were willing to accept. The general mortgage bondholders in particular were loud in their protest. "The truth of the matter is this," said one of them, "while the plan of the trustees has much to commend it, and is based on an excellent theory, it fails to cover the whole ground, and falls terribly short of meeting our reasonable demands." Thus, although the Bartol and Whelen committees accepted the plan, matters again stood still for a while, while the financial powers talked and wrote and threshed the question out.

In February, 1886, the reorganization trustees received a letter signed by J. Pierpont Morgan and John Lowber Welsh, which is important enough to be quoted in full.

"A syndicate has been formed," said these gentlemen, "composed of leading bankers and capitalists here and in Europe, together with corporations or their representatives controlling large transportation and coal producing interests, who have agreed to subscribe in the aggregate $15,000,000 for the purpose of aiding in the reorganization of the Philadelphia & Reading Railroad Company and its affiliated lines. The syndicate has no commitment of any kind with any other railroads or corporations upon this subject beyond securing a management in harmony with the principle that capital invested in internal improvements should be so managed as to result in a fair return in the way of interest and dividends. Their object and purpose is to secure the reorganization on business principles for the Philadelphia & Reading bondholders, stockholders, and creditors without prejudice to the relative position of either, and in their interest only.

"To do this effectually there must be suitable arrangements made with the Pennsylvania Railroad and other kindred coal interests for harmonious relations, in order that suitable prices may be obtained for coal produced and shipped. These objects we shall endeavor to secure, and we now enclose you a copy of a correspondence with Mr. Roberts, president of the Pennsylvania Railroad, on these subjects, which seems to us sufficient to warrant the syndicate in placing reliance upon the assurance given by that company.

"As the reorganization shall proceed our effort and expectation will be to bring about satisfactory arrangements with all the anthracite coal roads, and also the trunk lines, which shall secure to the Philadelphia & Reading Railroad Company, when reorganized, its just share of the business at remunerative rates.

"The syndicate have believed that your plan was, in the main, suitable for the purpose of reorganization, and that your board was composed of gentlemen who would command the confidence of all parties in interest.

"They therefore prefer to make an arrangement with you and to aid you in working out a plan.

"But they also think that there should be certain modifications as to your organization, and also as to your plan, as follows:

"(1) The syndicate would wish two persons, to be named by them, added to your board.

"(2) Your plan should be made so flexible that it could be modified hereafter in such respects as may be found necessary to success.

"(3) There should be an executive committee of five to take charge of the foreclosure proceedings, the purchase of the property, the organization of the new company, and generally of whatever may properly appertain to reconstruction under the plan. There should be five voting trustees who should vote on the stock when deposited under the plan, and to whom the power of voting on the stock in the reorganized company should be confided for five years after reorganization. These two committees should be composed of parties satisfactory to the syndicate and the trustees, and shall fill their own vacancies. But in case the syndicate and trustees cannot agree upon the five, then, and in that case, three shall be named by the syndicate and two by the trustees, and each class shall fill any vacancy occurring in its own number.

"(4) The compensation to be allowed to the syndicate shall be 5 per cent on the amount of the syndicate capital.

"(5) The syndicate to be allowed interest at the rate of 6 per cent upon any amount they may advance the company in the course of the process of foreclosure and reorganization.

"(6) Proper provision must be made for securing to the syndicate the refunding of the money they may advance on account of interest not exceeding 4 per cent per annum on the general mortgage bonds during reconstruction, and also for the substitution of the syndicate in the place of any creditor or stockholder who may abandon his holding and refuse to pay his assessment, it being the purpose of the syndicate to pay 4 per cent per annum interest on the general mortgage bonds during reconstruction, and also to pay the assessments of such parties as may abandon their holdings or right to take the securities to which they may be entitled under the plan." [1]

The correspondence with Mr. Roberts referred to contained the assurance that the Pennsylvania Company would not hold aloof from an understanding with the Reading either in respect to the coal or transportation business, and would, moreover, "cordially unite in the arbitration of all differences." [2] This could not, of course, force distasteful terms upon the Reading bondholders, but it could and did supply sufficient capital to ensure the success of any plan adopted, and it infused confidence and vigor into the action of the nearly discouraged reorganization trustees. The executive committee which they were to name was perhaps a useful tool, but the suggestion of a voting trust was a genuine contribution, and aided powerfully in securing necessary backing for future schemes.

It is to be remarked that the syndicate appeared with no panacea, was without a plan of its own, and at first merely adopted that of the trustees, with a few modifications which it thought advisable; but that by March, 1886, it had so worked over the proposals of the reorganization trustees as to make in many respects a new plan; which retained the assessments, likewise the combination of fixed and optional charges and the use of preferred stock, but reserved 4 per cent bonds against prior liens, gave 4 per cent bonds with preferred stock in exchange for the general mortgage instead of 3 per cents, and created four classes of stock instead of three. Somewhat more in detail this plan was as follows: The Reading was to issue a new 4 per cent general mortgage for $100,000,000, and four kinds of stock: a preferred, income, consolidated, and common. Of the general mortgage $9,792,000 were to be for future use in the im-

---

[1] R. R. Gaz. 18: 138, 1886.   [2] Chron. 42: 216, 1886.

provement of the railway; of the remainder $38,422,000 were to be reserved against prior liens; $24,686,000 were to exchange for the general mortgage if such should not be paid off in cash; $15,000,000 were to take up shares or bonds of leased lines, and $10,000,000 were to exchange for or to redeem Coal & Iron Company divisional mortgages. The total amount issued was to be $90,208,000, and no mortgage in addition was to be placed on the Reading properties for five years after the reorganization without the consent of a majority of the preferred stockholders. Of the different classes of new stock the preferred was to be given dividends up to 5 per cent non-cumulative, and then the income and consolidated stocks were to have up to 5 per cent non-cumulative. Generally speaking, the preferred stock was to go for assessments; the income stock for the income mortgage and convertible adjustment scrip; the consolidated stock for the first series 5s and one-quarter of the principal of the second series 5s; the common stock for the rest of the second series 5s, for the convertible debentures, deferred income bonds, and for old preferred and common stock. New fixed charges were estimated at $6,971,687, which dividends on the preferred stock would raise to $8,198,636. There was to be a voting trust for five years, consisting of J. Lowber Welsh, J. P. Morgan, Henry Lewis, George F. Baer, and Robert H. Sayre; and a syndicate was to advance necessary expenditures and disbursements pending reorganization, including unpaid assessments. The syndicate compensation was to be 6 per cent on its advances, plus a commission of 5 per cent upon its $15,000,000 of subscribed capital. The property was to be sold at foreclosure sale, and a new company was to be organized.[1]

A comparison of this with the plan of the reorganization trustees at first announced will show the changes made. Nothing of value which previous reorganizations had worked out was cast aside. The fixed interest allowed the general mortgage bondholders was raised in the hope that they might support the plan, and more care was taken to follow the order of priority in the advantages offered to the various classes of junior securityholders; an end to which the four classes of stock were admirably adapted. The voting trust was altogether new, and was doubtless intended to ensure a policy in

---

[1] Chron. 42:365, 1896. Assessments ranged from 2½ per cent on the deferred income bonds to 15 per cent on certain junior securities and $10 on both classes of stock.

accord with the syndicate's wishes for a series of years, and to prevent a renewal of the vagaries of Mr. Gowen's administration. The provision for foreclosure was to be expected in view of the extreme difficulty of obtaining the assents of so many conflicting interests; but with a net revenue of $12,026,309 (both companies) and fixed charges of $6,971,687, the task of maintaining the solvency of the companies in future did not seem an impossible one.

In opposition to the plan the Lockwood Committee urged that the scheme was unjust to certain classes of bonds; that it was cumbersome, expensive, conferred power on the trustees which should have been reserved for the direction of the new company, and that the reserved powers to change any part of the plan, and the uncertainties connected with the settlements under it, involved risks which creditors should not accept.[1] The objections were not weighty. If the Lockwood or any other committee had proved itself able to formulate and carry through a plan, or if the syndicate arrangement had been proposed at the very beginning of the receivership, bondholders might fairly have criticised its expense. In point of fact numerous attempts to reconcile divergent interests had failed, and what with Messrs. Lockwood, Bartol, Whelen, Gowen, and their respective followings, the future offered no more promising result. Meanwhile bondholders were going without their interest, and costs of the receivership were mounting up; so that a greater expense than that of which Mr. Lockwood complained was being incurred by delay. As for the general mortgage bondholders, they were given a chance at their old interest whenever the road should earn it, and could fairly ask no more; while that it was inequitable to ask income bondholders to accept a reduction to $50 in their annual interest, or holders of the first series 5s to wait for their interest until liens before theirs had been satisfied, are conclusions to which few will agree.

In April Messrs. Whelen and William H. Kemble, representing the Reading consolidated mortgage bondholders, announced that they had determined not to accept the syndicate plan. Even before this Mr. Gowen announced that he was organizing a syndicate and would soon be able to pay off overdue coupons on the general mortgage bonds, and to prevent any foreclosure under that mortgage.[2] It is scarcely necessary to say that he had a plan of his own. He proposed

---

[1] R. R. Gaz. 18: 271, 1886.   [2] Ibid. 18: 138, 1886.

to issue $100,000,000 4 per cent 70-year consolidated mortgage bonds much as did the syndicate, part of which should go to redeem the general mortgage and the floating debt; but second to this he suggested a cumulative 4 per cent first preferred income bond, to take the place of the income and consolidated stock under the syndicate plan, and to be exchanged for the first series 5s, a portion of the second series 5s, and some of the leased canal securities; while finally he planned a second preferred cumulative 4 per cent income bond, to be exchanged for those securities down to the deferred income bonds, which under the syndicate scheme were to receive common stock. The surplus of income offered by the old general mortgage was to be made good by first preference bonds. The existing preferred and common stocks were to remain as they were, and the deferred income obligations were to remain untouched. Finally, the New Jersey Central was to be retained in friendly alliance, either under a modified lease at a rental equal to earnings, or under a special traffic contract.

A comparison of this with the syndicate plan shows that Mr. Gowen gave up the idea of an assessment; provided for the floating debt through first preference bonds; swept away three of the four classes of stock, replacing them by two kinds of income bonds; and retained the deferred income bonds which the syndicate proposed to retire. His plan was to be carried through without foreclosure, but outside of this its advantages are rather difficult to ascertain. The abandonment of the assessment was distinctly bad; the retention of the deferred income issue was also bad; the reduction in the number of kinds of securities tended towards simplicity, but made impossible the nice distinction of priority on which the syndicate had relied; while even the replacement of stock by income bonds must be condemned, substituting as it did an obligation without any very distinct character of its own for a stock which represented frankly only a share in the profits of the enterprise. These things were realized, and the plan received no serious support; but as every plan so far proposed contributed something to the final product, so Mr. Gowen's income bonds and his aversion to foreclosure were not without influence upon the scheme which ultimately attained success.

The next few months saw active hostilities between Mr. Gowen and the syndicate; the former taking the position that he would never consent to foreclosure, nor to the placing of the property for five years under the management of a board of trustees named by his adversaries.[1] To Mr. Garrett, chairman of the reconstruction trustees, he wrote suggesting that the board should substitute his plan for that of the syndicate, and that seven reconstruction trustees should be appointed by the managers of the company to carry it through. "Upon this being done," said he, "I will engage that the plan shall be underwritten by an association of capital sufficient for the purpose of paying off all the general mortgage bonds which do not voluntarily accept the new securities provided by the plan, and I will agree that the financial responsibility of these subscribers to this fund shall be determined by the presidents of the Bank of North America, the Farmers' & Mechanics' National Bank, the Pennsylvania Company for Insurance of Lives, etc., and the Union Trust Company. . . ."[2] Mr. Garrett naturally refused.

As in many cases before, the struggle ended in a compromise. The new agreement was as follows: The syndicate was to be enlarged by $4,000,000 additional subscriptions, and the reconstruction trustees increased to thirteen by the addition of certain friends of Mr. Gowen, one of whom was also to be given place upon the executive committee. The syndicate plan was to be carried through without foreclosure, providing sufficient assents could be obtained, and was to be modified by the substitution of first, second, and third 4 per cent income bonds for preferred, income, and consolidated 5 per cent stock. Dividends on the bonds, like those on the stock, were to be payable from net earnings only; but net earnings were defined as the profits derived from all sources after paying operating expenses, taxes, and existing rentals, guarantees and interest charges, *but not fixed charges of the same sort subsequently created.* All third preference bonds issued for convertible bonds were to have the right to be converted into common stock; and the company was to have the privilege of increasing the issue, subject for five years to the approval of the voting trustees. As finally worked out, the first preference bonds were to be given for assessments; the second preference for all securities which had been promised income or consolidated stock; and the third preference for the second series 5s, convertible and debenture bonds, and preferred stock to which common stock

[1] Ry. Age, 11: 376, 1886.　　　　[2] R. R. Gaz. 18: 502, 1886.

had before been allotted. Somewhat more emphasis was laid on the possibility of paying off the general mortgage. It was proposed to reduce the aggregate of rentals and guarantees (exclusive of the Central of New Jersey, the Schuylkill Navigation Company, and the Susquehanna Canal Company) to an annual charge of less than $2,350,000 by direct negotiation with the companies affected. And to deal directly with the three companies above named upon the basis of a continuance of their respective leases at rentals involving no fixed liability beyond the earning power of the leased line, or on the basis of a surrender of the said leases, and the cancellation of the traffic agreement with the Schuylkill Navigation Company for a consideration. The voting trust was to be composed of three representatives of the syndicate and one friend of Mr. Gowen, which four should elect a fifth who should be satisfactory both to the syndicate and to the reconstruction trustees. A united effort was to be made by the company, the reconstruction trustees, and the syndicate to secure the immediate appointment of Mr. Austin Corbin as an additional receiver; and, if Mr. Corbin would take the position and legally qualify himself to fill it, it was understood that the presidency of the company would be offered to him. The other provisions of the syndicate plan were to remain unchanged.[1]

The total capital and charges under the plan were to be as follows:

	Est'd Capital	*Fixed Charges*
Prior mortgage liens,	$85,807,920	$4,233,055
Annual rental of leased lines not to exceed		2,350,000
		$6,583,055
First preference income mortgage,	24,410,822	1,220,542
	$110,218,742	$7,803,597
Second preference income mortgage,	26,140,518	1,307,026
	$136,359,260	$9,110,623
Third preference income mortgage,	14,956,016	747,800
	$151,315,276	$9,858,423
Common stock,	38,369,076	
Deferred incomes, $20,751,090 at issue price,	6,225,327	
	$195,909,679	

We have now the reorganization in its final shape, and it will be interesting to review briefly the gradual way in which this shape was fashioned. With the company plunged anew into bankruptcy

[1] Chron. 43: 368, 1886; Ibid. 43: 747, 1886; Annual Report, 1887.

after a reorganization insufficient to afford any genuine relief; the proposal was made to fund one-half the general mortgage coupons for three years and to convert all junior claims into liens on income. This scheme failed because plainly inadequate to meet the needs of the situation, and a modified version was presented providing for an assessment with which to pay the floating debt. The assessment was approved, but not the plan, and an ensuing scheme supplied an altogether new method of treatment, whereby on the one hand the assessment was made more heavy, and on the other two classes of preferred stock were proposed, with one issue of bonds at 3 per cent. This plan failed, not so much because of its inadequacy, although it was inadequate, but because general mortgage bondholders felt that a 3 per cent bond was less than they could reasonably expect for their holdings, and insisted on a security with a higher obligatory rate of interest. The next plan took note of these objections: it raised the interest on the bonds which it proposed from 3 to 4 per cent; and in the endeavor to please the junior bondholders as well, created four classes of preferred stock, by means of which the relative priority of different issues was carefully and completely recognized. Assessments were retained, and a guarantee by a syndicate and a voting trust for five years was suggested. In the discussion that followed, a new scheme was introduced, which replaced the preferred stock by two classes of income bonds, and forced the managers to realize the desire of the old bondholders for some new security with at least the name of bond. As a result, the syndicate which had fathered the previous plan consented to substitute for three of their classes of stock first, second, and third preference bonds. Meanwhile the fixed charges estimated for the successive plans steadily decreased. The first looked for $12,911,000, or $14,266,051 as variously reckoned; the second for $14,143,384, or, deducting the Jersey Central, for $8,223,177; the third for $7,064,830; the fourth for $6,971,687; and the sixth for $6,583,055. Thus each plan took over what was most satisfactory in its predecessor; and there was on the one hand a steady decrease in the fixed charges proposed, and on the other a continuous effort to discover some plan which might be satisfactory to all concerned.

That the compromise plan last mentioned succeeded was in part due to the feeling of all contending parties that concessions must be made; it was due also to endorsement by the leaders of the more important interests; and, finally, to an appreciation that the plan was after all a good one, reducing largely the fixed charges which the company would have to pay, while depriving no one of a return which, under the circumstances, he could fairly expect to receive. Mr. Corbin proved willing to undertake the new responsibilities put upon him. He was therefore appointed receiver in October, and elected president in the January following.

Nevertheless, it would be a mistake to suppose that the plan was unanimously accepted from the start. The Lockwood Committee of general mortgage bondholders were prompt in their disapproval, pronouncing it "unjust, uncertain, and indefinite"; saying that reorganization under it would be unduly expensive, and that it was more objectionable than the plans which had preceded it.[1] Equally decided was a small group of capitalists which held a majority of the first series 5s outstanding, the members of which were said to have agreed to hold their bonds and to abide the result.[2] The original time limit for deposits expired on March 1, 1887; it was then extended to March 15, and again to March 31, and deposits of $110,409,464 out of a total of $117,972,859 were secured. By October certain other bondholders had been induced to come in, and the trustees declared the plan operative. Holders of $3,348,000 of first series 5s stayed out, and forced an arrangement by which they were practically paid off in cash.[3] Arrangements were made with some of the subsidiary Reading lines, but the lease of the Central of New Jersey was not renewed. Only odds and ends now remained to be cleared up, and all through the rest of the year the managers were busy paying off receivers' certificates, floating debt, overdue interest, etc. On January 1, 1888, without formalities, the Reading passed out of receivers' hands and into the control of the stockholders.

---

[1] R. R. Gaz. 18: 897, 1886.

[2] Ry. Age, 12: 692, 1887. These bondholders even proposed a plan of reorganization of their own, which it is not worth while going into.

[3] Ry. Age, 12: 746, 1887; Chron. 45: 539, 1887.

CHAPTER IV

PHILADELPHIA & READING

Difficulties of the Coal & Iron Company — McLeod's policy of extension — Collapse of this policy — Failure of company — Summary of subsequent history.

WITH the year 1888 a new period in the history of the Reading began. The long struggle to bring the company back to solvency was fairly over, and for the first time in seven years the road saw before it a chance for genuine prosperity. Unlike the reorganization of 1880–3, that of 1884–7 succeeded in accomplishing the greater part of the saving expected of it. According to the plan, interest charges were to be reduced to $4,233,055; — in 1888 they were $4,516,433, and in 1889 $4,058,139; rentals were not to exceed $2,350,000; — in 1888 they were $2,882,582, and in 1889 $2,842,-319. Other payments, it is true, the necessity for which was passed over by the advocates of the plan, raised the total which the road was obliged to meet, but did not prevent a comfortable balance of over $2,000,000 for the Railroad Company in 1888, and one of $1,444,000 for both Railroad and Coal Companies combined. During the next few years large sums were spent in improving the permanent way. By January, 1889, almost the entire line between New York and Philadelphia had been relaid with 85 and 90 pound rails; grades had been smoothed, bridges strengthened, and culverts strengthened or rebuilt.

Less satisfactory than the results for the Railroad Company, however, were those for the Coal & Iron Company. In this case profits of $654,211 for 1887 turned into a loss of $806,222 for 1888, and in the following year a weak demand for coal, combined with a high cost of mining, increased the loss to $974,373. President Corbin felt called upon to explain that prior to 1886 the deficits of the Coal Company had been habitually met by inflating the capital account of the Railroad Company; so that with allowance for this fact the showing of the companies under his management had been relatively good.[1] In November, 1889, a letter of Mr. Gowen's was issued, hopeful as ever, criticising the management for their refusal

[1] R. R. Gaz. 22: 370, 1890.

or neglect to give authoritative information about actual earnings, but pointing to the large expense for new coal cars, barges, and collieries, and explaining the benefit which these would confer.[1]

The weakened position of its allied company pulled the Reading down, and prevented it from attaining the secure position which had seemed in sight. The payment of dividends only increased the general dissatisfaction. In February, 1889, holders of a considerable amount of second preference bonds circulated a petition objecting to the official statement of net earnings applicable to these securities, and demanded an examination of the books. After an investigation their expert declared that a $7\frac{1}{2}$ per cent dividend had been earned, but the bondholders could not induce the company to increase its distribution. The next year preference bondholders fared even worse. The managers declared that the surplus over all fixed charges for the year was barely $100,000, and that no dividends at all upon their holdings could be paid. Again an investigation was demanded and accorded, and Mr. Howard Lewis, the expert appointed, reported that there was applicable to the payment of interest upon first preference bonds the sum of $90,101, or $\frac{3}{8}$ of one per cent; a sum which the company promptly agreed to pay. Meanwhile even the stockholders were becoming restless. In June, 1889, a suit was commenced in Philadelphia, praying that the company's voting trustees and the trust under which they acted should be set aside, on the ground that the trust was to be exercised by five voting trustees, whereas only four had ever been appointed. Later on the matter was taken up by London stockholders, and became serious enough to force a concession of two seats in the board of managers of the company.

There was no question but that the trouble was caused by depression in the anthracite coal business, for in the carriage of both passengers and freight the Reading in these years made steady and substantial gains. In the three years following 1887 the number of passengers transported increased by 2,400,000 and the earnings from them by $470,000; while the freight tons moved gained 1,500,000 and the freight earnings $1,000,000. Only in coal was there a decrease, which appeared for the Coal & Iron Company in the figures for sales and gross and net receipts, and for the Rail-

[1] Chron. 50: 37, 1890.

road Company in the earnings from anthracite transported. The result was an attempt to improve the situation: first, by a combination among coal producing roads which should raise the selling price of that commodity; and second, by extension of the railroad into new markets, whereby an outlet for increased production should be obtained. At the instigation of Mr. Gowen a syndicate was formed to purchase a majority of the stock of the Reading Company,[1] which bought much more than 50 per cent, even though Mr. Gowen, the prime mover, died in the mean time. The existing managers showed no desire to combat the movement, although the voting power lay entirely in their hands. In June, 1890, President Corbin resigned, and Mr. A. A. McLeod was elected in his place.

Mr. McLeod now began a vigorous policy of consolidation and expansion with the lease for the second time of the Central of New Jersey. He evaded a New Jersey law which forbade the lease of a domestic to a foreign corporation by incorporating the Port Reading Railroad Company and then executing a lease of the Central to this minor corporation.[2] The Port Reading promised 7 per cent on the Central stock or 999 years, plus one-half the surplus earnings above the dividend up to 10 per cent, and secured a guarantee of the fulfilment of these promises from the Reading Railroad proper. Finally, Mr. McLeod leased the Lehigh Valley to the Reading direct, on a guarantee of 5 per cent on the stock until May 31, 1892; 6 per cent from that time until November 30, and 7 per cent thereafter for the rest of the 999 years. So far as control over the coal supply was concerned this put the Reading in a very favorable position. The Lehigh Valley tapped the northern Wyoming field, and the Central of New Jersey the Mahanoy and Shamokin deposits, and both had access to New York through New Jersey. The Lehigh, moreover, extended to Buffalo; and with a line of steamers to Duluth, Milwaukee, and Chicago, promised to command a large proportion of east-bound traffic in other things than coal. Figures for the coal industry show that the Reading, Central, and Lehigh shipped in 1891 53.3 per cent of the total production of 40,448,000 tons; in 1890 55.5 per cent; and in 1889 57.75 per cent. In addition, control of the Delaware, Lackawanna & Western was said to have

---

[1] Chron. 53: 408, 1891.
[2] Chron. 54: 288, 1892; Industrial Commission, vol. 19, pp. 455-7.

been acquired by the purchase of a majority of its stock, which added 15.1 per cent more;[1] making a total of 68.4 per cent for the year 1891, or sufficient to give a considerable measure of control over prices. But the terms were severe; quite as severe as in the case of the leases earlier put through; and though the Reading was in better shape than it had been five years before, full interest on its preference bonds was not being paid, and so long as this continued no outside payments could properly be made. The subsidiary companies, on the other hand, were not earning the dividends promised on their stock by nearly one-third of a million dollars; and it seemed unlikely that sufficient economies could be secured to cover permanently the deficit. The question could fairly have been asked whether the Reading had not bought a chance to contribute an annual sum to the Lehigh Valley and Jersey Central stockholders; and whether these roads had not deliberately entered into a contract which was little likely to be carried out. The justification of the arrangement lay in the control of coal prices which it made possible, and in the advantages of close traffic arrangements and connection with both Philadelphia and New York. "The main reason why the combination failed," said Mr. I. L. Rice before the Industrial Commission, "was that there was not an understanding of the first principles of an operation of that kind, *i. e.* that it must reduce prices and not increase them. The anthracite coal combination was killed because prices were immediately put up. . . .

"Q. Mr. McLeod has testified before this commission that it was his intention to effect such economies as should be reflected in lower prices. Do we understand that you criticise the policy in that it did not so reduce the prices?

"A. He did not do it, no matter what his intention was."[2]

The situation was, however, as clearly understood by the public as by the managers themselves. Even before the combination had begun to carry out its policy, outcry was made, and as prices went up the agitation became intense. In New Jersey an act to legalize the combination which passed both houses was vetoed by Governor Abbot on the ground of the effect upon the price of anthracite coal;[3] and in June the Attorney-General applied for an injunction to

---

[1] R. R. Gaz. 24: 138, 1892.   [2] Industrial Commission, vol. 9, p. 738.
[3] Annual Report, 1892.

dissolve the lease of the New Jersey Central to the Philadelphia & Reading, alleging that the tripartite agreement between these companies and the Philadelphia & Reading was illegal. The court granted a temporary injunction,[1] which it continued in August to a final hearing, with conditions to make it more effective.

Prices did not go down, and in October Attorney-General Stockton of New Jersey again appeared before Chancellor McGill. He now charged the Philadelphia & Reading, the Central, and the Port Reading with having conspired to advance the price of coal in defiance of the order of the court, and asked for the appointment of a receiver to enforce the former decree, and to restrain the company from further using the New Jersey railroads for carrying any coal until the advanced price should have been reduced.[2] The officers denied the allegations, but the Chancellor sustained the Attorney-General on every point; and only the official announcement of the abrogation of the lease prevented the granting of the order.[3] The lease of the Lehigh Valley fared better. In a suit brought by M. H. Arnot, a stockholder in the Lehigh Valley, Judge Metzger of the Court of Common Pleas held that the Reading and Lehigh Valley were not parallel and competing lines in the sense contemplated by the law; and that mere incidental competition between branches or spurs of two systems would not prevent the consolidation of their main lines.[4] So much then of the original programme was allowed to stand.

Meanwhile, in the search for new markets, the Reading had stretched into New England, having chosen that territory in the hope of increasing its tonnage without a desperate struggle with its neighbors.[5] The most available subject for control was the Boston & Maine, which reached from Northampton and Boston, Massachusetts, to Portland, Maine, was independent of the large trunk lines, and had a profitable local business of its own. Purchases of this railroad's stock were quietly made; and in October, 1892, the public was surprised by the election of Mr. McLeod to the presidency, although, as it subsequently transpired, an actual majority of Boston & Maine stock was not secured.[6] It was obvious that nothing could be gained

---

[1] R. R. Gaz. 24: 420, 1892.

[2] Chron. 55: 680, 1892.

[3] Chron. 56: 82, 1893.

[4] R. R. Gaz. 25: 102, 1893.

[5] Industrial Commission, vol. 9, p. 567, testimony of A. A. McLeod.

[6] Ibid. vol. 9, p. 574.

from the new arrangement unless the gap between the Reading and the Boston & Maine should be filled; and so, even before the purchase of stock in the latter was begun, the lease of the Poughkeepsie Bridge across the Hudson was put through,[1] and a controlling interest was bought in the stock of the Central, New England & Western. The last-named road extended from Hartford, Connecticut across the Poughkeepsie Bridge to Campbell Hall, 145½ miles, and connected at this point with the Pennsylvania, Poughkeepsie & Boston, a road controlled in the interest of the Reading. This completed a through route from Philadelphia to Hartford. Later the Central, New England & Western Railroad Company and the Poughkeepsie Bridge Railroad Company were consolidated into the Philadelphia, Reading & New England, with Mr. McLeod as president;[2] and a controlling interest was purchased in the New York & New England Railroad, which ran from Poughkeepsie via Hartford and Providence to Boston,[3] and afforded another entrance into New England. All this involved a very great extension of the Reading system. The lease of the Lehigh Valley had connected it with Buffalo; the subsequent consolidations brought it into every New England state, and gave it a total mileage of, roughly, 5000 miles.

Danger lay in two directions. First, it was possible that even the union of the Lehigh, Jersey Central, and the Reading might fail to secure a profit for the mining end of the business, and second, the financing of the New England deals might be so conducted as to put the parent road into a very difficult situation.

Both these contingencies occurred. The early termination of the Jersey Central lease weakened the control of the Reading over prices, while the severity of the winter of 1893, though assisting to maintain prices, so increased the expense of operating the mines that earnings fell below fixed charges for the three months ending February 28, 1893, by the amounts of $933,443 for the Railroad Company and $468,362 for the Coal & Iron Company. Moreover, losses of $616,351 accrued during the same time under the Lehigh Valley lease, and were met by the Reading, contrary to expectation, and contrary to the express provisions of the mortgage by which its income bonds were secured. In order to accomplish

---

[1] Ry. Age, 17: 109, 1892.　　[2] Ry. Rev. 32: 507, 1892.　　[3] Chron. 55: 723, 1892.

the New England extensions shares were bought on margin by President McLeod personally with collateral in part supplied by himself, in part taken from the treasury of the company, and consisting of general mortgage, collateral trust, and income bonds. "On or about September 22," said Mr. I. L. Rice, a representative of the bondholders, who had been examining the books, "Mr. McLeod entered into certain individual stock transactions which resulted in the purchase of 24,036 shares of the stock of the Boston & Maine Railroad Company and 32,000 shares of the stock of the New York & New England Railroad Company. On October 15, 1892, he withdrew from the control of the company, without having previously obtained the authority of the board of managers therefor, and without expressing the purpose for which he intended to use the securities, 30,000 general mortgage bonds of the company, which as afterwards appeared were used at that time as margins in the transaction. He subsequently withdrew from the control of the company in the same manner and for the same purpose, between October 28 and December 1, 1892, $713,000 of collateral trust bonds, and $99,000 third preference bonds. No reference whatever is made to these stock transactions on the books of the company except the mention of the withdrawal of securities against the personal receipt of the president, nor are they referred to on the minutes of the board of managers prior to December 24, 1892. On the latter date the board of managers in a resolution approved the transaction, calling for the use of $613,000 of the company's collateral, and indemnifying Mr. McLeod for advances made for the same purpose to the extent of $400,000. On January 17, 1893, Mr. McLeod deposited $250,000 additional collateral trust bonds as margin, making a total of $963,000. On February 15 Mr. McLeod directed that the account be transferred from his individual name to that of the company's." [1]

Leaving aside the matter of the propriety of Mr. McLeod's action, it is plain that the method which he employed was an extremely expensive one, in that it raised the necessary cash by temporary loans at high rates from brokers in New York and Philadelphia instead of by the sale of stocks or bonds, or by the use of funds which the company might have had on hand. According to President Harris, the average charges paid on the floating debt in

---

[1] R. R. Gaz. 25: 386, 1893.

1892, a large portion of which had been accumulated in these operations, was 9 per cent. If the control over the corporations acquired had been desired for temporary reasons the operation would have been a stock speculation pure and simple, and the Reading would have trusted to the possible rise in price of the securities purchased to cancel the expense of advances to the brokers who did the buying; but in this case the control was designed to be permanent, not temporary, and Mr. McLeod expected results which could be obtained only after a series of years.

This brings us to the beginning of 1893. Mr. McLeod had succeeded in carrying out his plans for a combination of coal producing roads and for the extension of the Reading into New England, but had seen his first project bitterly attacked, and his second scheme become a burden because of the insufficient funds behind it. Matters came to a head in February with an attempt to borrow on $10,000,000 collateral trust bonds. Speyer & Co. accepted the issue, but the Drexels refused to handle it, and began to sell the company's securities at any price.[1] Quotations dropped from 46¾ to 40⅝ on February 17, and continued to fall the two succeeding days, reaching 28 on February 20. On this last day application was made to the United States Circuit Court in Philadelphia, and Messrs. McLeod, Wilbur, and Paxon were appointed receivers. "I am very sorry," said President McLeod, "that we were driven to the necessity for a receivership, but it was the only thing to do. Our credit was attacked in a way which made it impossible for us to meet our obligations, and we had the receivership established before the property was further injured. . . . The trouble was brought about by the fact that we were doing an enormous business on a small capital, and when this attack was made . . . it hurt our credit so that we could not borrow money."[2] Lack of capital was the repeated cry of the management. At a later date Mr. McLeod again said, "When I leased the Lehigh Valley and the Jersey Central and took over their coal operations . . . I found that I had $13,000,000 invested in coal and in carrying the customers of the companies. The Reading did not have that much capital, and I had to borrow $8,000,000 of that $13,000,000. Then the panic of 1893 came on. I had arranged to fund that $8,000,000 of floating debt by selling

---

[1] Ry. Age, 18: 314, 1893. [2] Ibid. 18: 164, 1893.

securities, etc., giving me a working capital of $17,500,000, but the parties who were to furnish the money had six months in which to do it, and on account of that panic coming on before I could get the money, there was nothing in the world for me to do except to put the Reading in the hands of the receivers to save its securities."[1] The statements concerning the lack of capital were a true explanation though not an excuse. Money had been tied up in unsalable coal, acquired not only by the leases of the Lehigh and Central, but also by purchases from independent operators[2] and by production during the current year;[3] while whatever spare funds the Reading had been able to provide had been put into New England securities at high prices to carry out the road's ambitious plans. In the mean time the large purchases on margin made a fall in the price of Reading securities of especial moment; and, as Mr. McLeod explained, it proved impossible to liquidate the floating debt. The failure of 1893, then, was caused less by a continued inability to meet fixed charges than by an undue expansion of operations such as has ruined many a solvent firm. Reading's venture in the coal fields had not proved a success, but the loss had not been sufficient to ruin it within a year; its New England extensions had not brought all the results desired, but they had not had a fair trial; the true cause for the failure was the attempt to accomplish by means of stock speculation and temporary loans at high rates more than the road could do out of its legitimate resources, with the intent on the one hand to raise the price of coal and on the other to secure fresh markets for the sale thereof.

After the failure the first impulse of the bondholders was to denounce Mr. McLeod. A meeting of European creditors in London chose a committee to represent them and solicited McLeod's removal from the receivership on the "serious ground" that the administration of their property should not any longer be jeopardized by remaining under the control of an official who had already brought it into its existing difficulties. A New York general mortgage bondholders' committee decided to act in a similar direction, and Mr. Drexel represented to the president that he should resign for the sake of the future of the company.[4] Mr. McLeod

---

[1] Industrial Commission, vol. 9, p. 573.   [2] Ibid.
[3] Ry. Times, 63: 265, 1893.   [4] Ry. Age, 18: 314, 1893.

unwillingly gave way. For successor the board of managers chose Mr. Joseph S. Harris, a man of long experience in railroad affairs. Mr. Harris had been for many years connected with the Lehigh Valley system, and was the same man who, it will be remembered, had evaluated the Reading coal properties in 1880. Following his election as president he was appointed receiver in the place of Mr. McLeod.

The receivers' statement came out in March and announced a floating debt of $18,472,828, against which were held reported assets to the amount of $15,779,784; but of these last $4,985,276 were in the shape of coal, and $8,861,065 consisted of the items "due for freight," "tolls due from connecting roads," "bills receivable," "cash," etc., a large part of which was probably of little worth. Both the current liabilities and the current assets are instructive, and show that on the one hand Mr. McLeod's stock operations had involved the company in heavy obligations to his brokers, and that on the other losses in the coal business had necessitated current advances to branch lines from which it was impossible to get return. It appears, for instance, that the Coal & Iron Company had been unable to pay the sums charged it for freight, and while the full amounts had been nevertheless included in reported earnings, the actual result had been a swelling of bills receivable by debts which the Railroad Company was quite unable to collect.[1]

The general lines of the policy to be pursued were now sufficiently clear; the more pressing claims were to be met by the issue of receivers' certificates, expenses were to be cut down, payments under leases were to be amicably reduced where possible, holdings of Boston & Maine stock were to be sold, and on the side of the bondholders the various interests were to agree on some scheme for raising cash and for improving the general condition of the property. There was need for some reduction of fixed charges, but not for such radical cuts as in 1880 or in 1884.

The receivers and managers carried out their part of the work first. Application was made in March, and again in June, for permission to issue certificates in settlement of the most urgent claims. In May Mr. McLeod resigned the presidency of the Boston & Maine

---

[1] Industrial Commission, vol. 9, p. 739, testimony of I. L. Rice.

after a large part of the Reading's holdings had been sold, and the same month President Harris inaugurated a policy of retrenchment by the retirement of four out of the five vice-presidents which the Reading had been accustomed to maintain. In July the receivers obtained permission to dissolve the agreement with the Pennsylvania, Poughkeepsie & Boston Railroad, and in August the appointment of a separate receiver for the Philadelphia, Reading & New England marked, except for the minor matter of the Poughkeepsie Bridge, the final abandonment of New England extension. Meanwhile an arrangement had been made with the Lehigh Valley, whereby the payments under the lease were reduced for two years from 7 per cent to 5 per cent, on condition that the Reading should make extra payments at the end of that time if the Lehigh proved to have earned more than 10 per cent in the interval; and permission had been obtained from the Circuit Court to surrender the possession and operation of the Eastern & Amboy Railroad and the Lehigh Valley Terminal Railroad, both lines belonging to the Lehigh Valley in the state of New Jersey. The Lehigh lease, even as modified, aroused much opposition from bondholders, who rightly maintained that payments under it constituted a diversion of funds which should have gone to the creditors of the Reading proper. Suit was begun before the Circuit Court, and on August 8, 1893, a formal abrogation was obtained. This incidentally caused the resignation of Mr. Wilbur, president of the Lehigh Valley, from his position as receiver of the Reading, and the appointment of Mr. J. Lowber Welsh in his place.

The more complicated task of the bondholders was at first undertaken by two committees: one for the general mortgage bondholders, of which Mr. J. Edward Simmons was chairman; and one for the income bondholders, led by Mr. George Coppell. Three demands were at once made: first, that Mr. McLeod retire from the receivership; second, that the lease of the Lehigh Valley be abrogated; and third, that the books of the company be examined by a railroad accountant. The first and second points were complied with, though not altogether because of the insistence of the committees, and in the end the third was also granted, and Mr. Stephen Little was set to work.[1]

[1] Chron. 57: 105, 1893; Ibid. 57: 423, 1893.

On May 27, 1893, the managers of the company brought forward a reorganization plan, which estimated the floating debt at $19,991,941, and proposed to cover it by the issue of $22,000,000 collateral trust bonds at 95. These bonds were to be redeemable any time before maturity at 110, and the trustee was authorized "to apply the surplus income or the proceeds of sales . . . of any of the securities pledged until 1898, and thereafter so much as might be determined from time to time by the Railroad Company, to the purchase of the said bonds at the best price obtainable, or, if necessary, to draw the same for redemption." General mortgage and first, second, and third preference bonds were to be entitled to subscribe to the amount of 10 per cent of their holdings; deferred income bonds to 4 per cent; and stockholders to 24 per cent; while besides the $22,000,000 mentioned, $2,000,000 additional bonds were to be issued each year for working capital and for the acquisition of real and personal property. General mortgage bondholders were to fund their coupons to and including January 1, 1898, and to receive an equivalent amount of coupon trust certificates. The rental under the Lehigh Valley lease was to be reduced, and the Reading stock was to be transferred for seven years to a voting trust composed of Joseph S. Harris, E. P. Wilbur, Thomas McKean, and two others to be afterwards named.[1] Assents of 90 per cent of the general mortgage bondholders and of 60 per cent of the stockholders were required by the 21st of June to make the plan effective, and a syndicate was pledged to carry out the provisions if such assents should be obtained.[2]

An issue of collateral bonds, a reduction in the Lehigh rental, a funding of coupons, and a voting trust: these were the propositions which President Harris and his associates presented for the consideration of the bondholders. There was to be no disturbance of existing securities, no assessment, not even a reduction of fixed charges except as these were lightened by the lowering of rentals and by the payment of the floating debt. It is to be presumed that the attempt to extend the Reading into New England was not to be continued, for no provision was made for the purchase of the shares of the New England roads hitherto held on margin, and in fact large sales of Boston & Maine stock had already taken place; but

[1] New York *Herald*, May 29, 1893.   [2] Ry. Times, 63: 783, 1893.

no formal mention of the deal was made. The lease of the Lehigh Valley was to be continued in the hope of better times, while the reduction of rental which the plan required had already taken place. Under ordinary circumstances any plan such as the one outlined would have been quite futile. Where the failure of a road is due to deep-seated causes the remedy must be fundamental; and when a piling up of indebtedness is due to inability to pay fixed charges the situation must be met by a reduction of those charges even though a foreclosure sale be a necessary preliminary. In the present case matters were somewhat different: bankruptcy had come, not from a long-continued drain, but from a rapid diffusion of resources in an attempt to accomplish more than the finances of the road would permit; and a change of policy was the thing most urgently required. But this again was not a question with which a reorganization plan had to deal, except in so far as such a plan might smooth the difficulties which lay in the way; and any scheme which should restore to the company the collateral imperilled in its rash campaign, fund the floating debt at a reasonable rate of interest, and give the management a chance to start again, was worthy of serious consideration. It may be observed, however, that granting all of the above, the plan before us did not go far enough. The extensions due to President McLeod had been in the heart of the coal regions, as well as in New England, and one of the most important of these, the Lehigh Valley, the managers proposed to retain. This policy, it may be said, was of very doubtful wisdom. The attempt to monopolize the production of anthracite coal had already been fruitful of disaster, and the possession of the Lehigh would have constituted a continual temptation to future purchases; while it was far from certain that even under the reduced rental the road could have been made to pay. What the Reading needed was a period of quiet attention to its own business, undisturbed by meddling in the business of other people; an attention which would be sure to result in increased economies, and was the true remedy for the lack of prosperity in the coal industry which had driven Mr. McLeod on his wild career. It is to this latter judgment that we must in the end conform. The plan of President Harris was not so inadequate as might at first appear; it accomplished much that needed to be accomplished, and it gave an opportunity to the management of the road to retrace many of the steps of the previous two years; but on the other hand, it did not embrace the chance to free the Reading from all its mistaken enterprises, and passed by an occasion which could only again occur after much suffering and loss.

Discussion turned, however, on other features. In a circular to securityholders in June, President Harris said: "My deliberate opinion is that the assistance asked for by the proposed plan . . . is none too great, and that there is a good probability that if it is afforded and the plan is carried out prudent and careful management may prevent the recurrence of such a crisis. My judgment is that the securityholders will make a very serious mistake if they do not accept the relief offered them, for I see no probability that the necessary assistance can hereafter be obtained except upon much more onerous terms. I strongly advise that the plan shall be promptly accepted." [1] "We cannot but regard these terms as very easy," said the *Financial Chronicle.* "To be sure a new collateral trust mortgage for $30,000,000, bearing 6 per cent, is to be created, but the greater part of this goes to take up floating debt and other existing obligations, and will involve no increase in fixed charges. . . ." [2] On the other hand, it was objected that the plan was formed entirely in the interest of the floating debt holders, income bondholders, and stockholders; and that the management under the arrangement would have the power to pay dividends upon the income bonds, while at the same time the coupons on the 4 per cent mortgage bonds were being funded. [3] In an editorial urging foreclosure proceedings the London *Standard* said: "That [foreclosure] will prevent holders of pledged collaterals from getting a market for their securities, and, at the same time, bring a good many doubtful matters connected with the finances of the company into the light of day. It should also tend to make the 'floating debt' swindle less popular with eminent American financiers. At present they pile these debts up in the full assurance that they can easily arrange matters so as to put them, when funded, before existing mortgages. It is for the Reading general mortgage bondholders to act promptly for their own interests." [4] Finally, it was objected that the plan

[1] Ry. Age, 18: 501, 1893.   [2] Chron. 56: 905, 1893.
[3] Ry. Times, 63: 751, 1893.   [4] Ry. Times, 63: 783, 1893.

was in the interest of the McLeod management, and that the voting trust was to be a McLeod organization, which would either white-wash the ex-president's operations, or by keeping them in the background would virtually outlaw them.

The plan failed because the time allowed for deposits was too short. In spite of the objections raised 31,356 general mortgage bonds and 411,218 shares of stock were deposited in twenty-five days, and it was maintained that additional securities would surely be obtained to make up the percentages required. The managers alleged, however, that extension was impracticable, and announced that the scheme could not go through.[1]

The year following this attempt at rehabilitation was full of the struggles of different interests, each jealous of any concession and working devotedly for its own hand. Prominent at this time was Mr. I. L. Rice, the same gentleman who has before been quoted in connection with Mr. McLeod's operations in New England stocks. Mr. Rice had been a member of the syndicate which had put Mr. McLeod into the presidency, and had served as foreign representative of the company during his régime. He had been instrumental in forming the anthracite coal combination, and at the time of the Reading failure had been in England raising money to finance the coal holdings then acquired.[2] Returning from Europe upon the appointment of receivers, he examined the Reading books with the results which have been noticed, and now appeared as the active enemy of everything connected with Mr. McLeod, even to the receivers who had succeeded him. In May, 1893, he resigned the seat which he had held on the Reading board, on the ground that the management had condoned the use by Mr. McLeod of the company's securities in carrying on his private and personal specula-tions; in September he resigned from the income bondholders' committee, and attacked in a circular the McLeod régime and the succeeding receivership;[3] and in December he applied for the removal of the receivers, alleging that they had grossly neglected their duties to the stockholders, and had ignored the financial trans-actions of Mr. McLeod prior to their appointment.[4]

[1] R. R. Gaz. 25: 496, 1893. The deposits required were: general mortgage, $41,828,000; stock, 480,424 shares.
[2] Industrial Commission, vol. 9, p. 737, testimony of I. L. Rice.
[3] Ry. Times, 64: 369, 1893.   [4] Ry. Age, 18: 897, 1893.

In spite of his hostility to the existing régime, Mr. Rice hoped to rehabilitate the company without foreclosure or, indeed, formal reorganization. The action of others was inspired by a less optimistic view. The original suit on which receivers had been appointed had been brought by one Thomas C. Platt; but as early as March Alfred Sully and A. B. Rand of New York, and John Lowrie of London, holders of first and second preference income bonds, petitioned to intervene. In July Judge Dallas dismissed the Lowrie suit, but the petition was renewed in September, alleging that Mr. Platt "did not file his bill in good faith on his own behalf, and on behalf of all other holders of bonds, but at the request and for the benefit and protection of the men who were then managers of the Philadelphia & Reading Railroad Company and the Philadelphia & Reading Coal & Iron Company, and that the suit was not being pressed with due diligence." [1]

All this time the receivers had been busy on a plan, which they presented in January, 1894. By leaving out of consideration some $5,000,000 of car trusts they arrived at the figure of $12,500,000 for the floating debt. This they proposed to cover by the issue of $6,000,000 in 6 per cent ten-year trust certificates, based on the stock of coal on hand, and by $10,000,000 in 5 per cent collateral trust bonds then in the treasury of the Reading Company. They hoped that a balance of $2,500,000 would then remain available for working capital or other purposes. General mortgage coupons were to be funded for five years, although the receivers planned to have a syndicate formed to purchase at par for cash the coupons as they matured, giving to the bondholders in each case the choice between receiving money or coupon trust certificates for the interest due. There was to be no formal reorganization, no cuts in charges, nothing but a provision for the floating debt and for a temporary funding of interest payments; and this was the more feasible because the Lehigh Valley lease had been by this time abrogated and the New England extensions definitely abandoned. [2] It will be remembered that to the plan of May, 1893, it had been objected that the provisions contrived to bring in the floating debt ahead of previously existing liens, and were a premium on a kind of financial juggling too common among American railroads. This plan, therefore,

---

[1] Ry. Age, 18: 735, 1893.   [2] Ry. Rev. 34: 55, 1894; Ry. Times, 65: 87, 1894.

avoided a new issue of bonds, and used only what the treasury already possessed. The coal notes were obviously unobjectionable, and served at the same time to utilize the unsalable stock which the management had earlier accumulated. If their value should prove small the loss would fall on the holders of the floating debt and not on the owners of the general mortgage bonds; while the return to the company was assured by arrangement with Drexel & Co., Brown Bros. & Co., and J. Lowber Welsh on the one hand, and the Finance Company of Pennsylvania on the other. On the whole this plan was gentle even to tenderness with the creditors of the road, and its failure revealed clearly the bondholders' state of mind. The holders of the general mortgage refused to fund their coupons for five years, they refused to fund them for two years, and they insisted that foreclosure proceedings should be instituted unless they should receive immediate payment of their interest. "In view of this," the receivers were forced to remark, "it would be idle for [us] to continue the efforts to readjust the affairs of the company. . . ." [1] The trouble with the receivers' scheme was not that it demanded large concessions, — much larger had been asked and granted in 1887, — but that the general mortgage bondholders felt that on the one hand the road was very nearly earning fixed charges, so that in the contingency of a foreclosure sale their interests would be reasonably safe; and on the other that a demand for concessions so soon after a complete reorganization of the property was an irritant which might well be resented even at the risk of some pecuniary loss. Fortunately the assent of the bondholders was not necessary to the issue of the coal trust notes, and the receivers executed them under the authority of the court, practically as proposed.

In April, 1894, Mr. Simmons, chairman of the old general mortgage bondholders' committee, resigned his position, and Mr. Fitzgerald, president of the Mercantile Trust Company, was chosen to succeed him. The committee presently issued a notice which, after reviewing its early activity, went on to say that it had believed it prudent to give the receivers every opportunity to familiarize themselves with the affairs of the company, but that in its judgment the time had come for action to enforce the rights of the bondholders

[1] Chron. 58: 774, 1894.

under the mortgage.[1] In May, 1894, a new general mortgage committee was organized, with Mr. F. P. Olcott as chairman, designed not directly to oppose the Fitzgerald Committee, but to hasten the rehabilitation of the property. The committee prepared a bondholders' agreement calling for the deposit of general mortgage bonds, and in a statement of their position said: "Difficulties in the way of a foreclosure and reorganization thereafter are exaggerated; if any danger is wrought by such foreclosure it will fall upon the junior securities and not upon us." [2] Lastly, at this time, there was a committee headed by Mr. Earle, president of the Finance Company of Pennsylvania.

The first matured suggestion after the failure of the receivers' plan appeared in what was known as the Olcott-Earle Agreement, published on September 25, 1894, which seems to have been in many respects a revival of that scheme. It proposed to cover the floating debt by the sale to securityholders of $10,000,000 collateral trust bonds, heretofore held in the treasury, and to fund coupons on the general mortgage 4s for five years. A syndicate agreed to advance $9,000,000, or as much thereof as might be needed, to buy the coupons as they should mature. The stock was to be held and voted by the reorganization committee until all the money advanced by the syndicate should have been repaid; that is, till June, 1898; a second syndicate guaranteed the sale of the collateral bonds at 70; and the preferred bondholders were asked to forego any claims for interest until all the general mortgage coupons should have been retired and cancelled. Certain other details are of interest. The collateral bond issue was to be taken up by the preferred bondholders and stockholders, each individual subscribing to 10 per cent of the par value of his holdings; but the bondholder might, if he preferred, pay 3 per cent of the par value of the securities he owned and receive nothing, instead of paying 10 per cent and getting a collateral bond. Securityholders were given 60 days in which to assent, and if at the end of that time the number of assents did not amount to practically all the interests involved, the committee proposed to reorganize by foreclosure for the benefit only of those who had assented to the

---

[1] Ry. Times, 65: 623, 1894. See also the report of the company's comptroller to the receivers in Annual Report, 1893.

[2] Ry. Rev. 34: 307, 1894.

plan; while for the future the committee was to provide by agreement with the railroad company that the latter should call an annual meeting of general and income mortgage bondholders and stockholders, at which bondholders as well as stockholders should vote in proportion to the par value of their holdings.[1]

It will be observed that the source of relief sought by this plan was precisely that of the receivers' plan earlier described. Certain changes, however, of considerable importance were introduced. The subscriptions to the collateral issue were made distinctly obligatory, and an alternate assessment was provided; greater use was made of syndicate assistance; some voting power was given to the bonds; and a voting trust was added to ensure permanency of control to the designers of the reorganization till their work should be complete. On the whole there were still few concessions to creditors, and indeed could be few. Ten coupons of the general mortgage were to be funded, though it was made easy for the bondholder to get cash if he preferred it; the provisions concerning subscriptions to the collateral bonds were rather more burdensome than before; and the voting trust, while redounding to the ultimate advantage of creditors, was only indirectly a concession to their demands. The grant of voting power to the bondholders would have been a great concession, but the wording of the clause was vague and probably little practical effect would have ensued. As in the previous plans, no particular attention was paid to the reduction of fixed charges.

So much for the provisions of the plan. It was a hopeful innovation for the suggestions it contained to come from holders of general mortgage bonds, and seemed to give some evidence of a change of heart; especially since the Olcott Committee did secure the assent of a larger proportion of the issue than had accepted either of the propositions before brought forward. The Fitzgerald Committee strenuously protested, still insisting on the advisability of foreclosure; and further objections came from Mr. Rice and from the Hartshorne Committee. Nevertheless, the general mortgage as a whole gave its consent, and ultimate shipwreck was due only to the

---

[1] Chron. 59: 515, 1894; Ry. Age, 19: 557, 1894; Ry. Rev. 34: 561, 1894; Ry. Times, 66: 571, 1894.

abstention of the income mortgage bonds.[1] It is not surprising that the income bondholders should have felt that the plan had little in it for them. They had been given no voice in its making, — their wishes had at no time been regarded. During the whole reorganization the question had been of the terms to which the general mortgage bondholders would consent, and the only sign of the existence of junior liens had been an occasional fearful inquiry as to what would become of them under foreclosure; until now the combination of a voting trust with the expenses of a syndicate reorganization, and an assessment upon them and upon the stock, touched the limit which they would stand. There was, moreover, at this time no question of the wiping out of the value of their holdings. The preamble to the Olcott-Earle plan stated that the annual charges were $10,477,560 and that the net earnings for 1891 had been $10,977,398; thus showing that something was left for the junior securities even after the payment of interest on all prior and general mortgage liens. It seemed also barely possible that the difficulties of a foreclosure, with the danger under the laws of Pennsylvania of losing the coal properties of the company, might secure better terms for the holders of junior obligations in case they should withhold their assent.

Early in January, 1895, the following official notice was issued: "The plan of readjustment, dated October 1, 1894, has not been assented to by a sufficient number of income bondholders and stockholders to make the same effective. The committee now hold over a majority of the general mortgage bonds, and have, in accordance with the bondholders' agreement of May 7, 1894, and their circular of October 1, 1894, notified the trustees of the general mortgage to bring suit for the foreclosure thereof . . . as expeditiously as possible." [2] Suit for foreclosure was brought March 2 in accordance with the announcement, and the Junior Securities Protective Committee, an organization with purposes indicated by its name, was allowed to intervene.

[1] Deposits of bonds were up to the last of January (R. R. Gaz. 27: 78, 1895):

	Total Issue	Deposits
General Mortgage	$44,663,000	$33,099,000
1st preferred	23,948,133	12,182,300
2d preferred	16,176,326	6,261,600
3d preferred	18,591,099	8,631,400

[2] Chron. 60: 43, 1895.

Meanwhile the Fitzgerald and Olcott committees together prepared and brought forward the final reorganization scheme. The conditions now differed from those with which any previous plan had been confronted, in that it was no longer necessary to seek for as little change as possible, and a broader, more radical reorganization was in point. "Unless," began the scheme, "the managers shall decide to proceed without foreclosure or sale, the properties of the existing Reading companies will be sold and successor companies will be organized under the laws of Pennsylvania, and the stock and securities of these successor companies will be vested in a new company formed, or to be formed, under the laws of Pennsylvania or of some other state."

There were to be issued:

General mortgage 100-year 4 per cent gold bonds,	$114,000,000
Non-cumulative, 4 per cent first preferred stock (subject to an increase of $21,000,000),	28,000,000
Non-cumulative 4 per cent second preferred stock,	42,000,000
Common stock (subject to an increase of $21,000,000),	70,000,000

If at any time dividends of 4 per cent should have been paid on the first preferred stock for two successive years the company might convert the second preferred stock at par, one-half into first preferred and one-half into common stock. These new issues were ultimately to retire all outstanding securities, to provide for expenses of reorganization, and to go for new construction, additions, betterments, etc., in the succeeding years. Since, however, it was obviously impossible to cancel prior liens before maturity, sufficient general mortgage bonds ($44,550,000) were reserved from immediate issue to retire these when they should fall due. This left new general mortgage bonds with four classes of stock against old general mortgage bonds with three classes of preferred bonds, common stock, and deferred incomes; and, as might be expected, new general mortgage 4s were given for the old general mortgage, second preferred and common stock went for preference bonds, and new common stock for old common stock and deferred income bonds. Certain cash payments were made on the general mortgage, and $4,000,000 of the new issue were sold to a syndicate; but on the whole we may say that the prior liens and general mortgage bondholders occupied the same position in the new company which they had occupied in the old; that the income bondholders exchanged a bond with a lien on income for a stock with a right to dividends; and that the floating debt, syndicate, and other expenses were given equal rights with the general mortgage.

No additional mortgage was to be put upon the property, nor was the amount of the first preferred stock to be increased, except with the consent, in each instance, of the holders of a majority of the whole amount of each class of preferred stock, given at a meeting of the stockholders called for that purpose, and with the consent of the holders of a majority of such part of the common stock as should be represented at such meeting, the holders of each class of stock voting separately; neither was the amount of the second preferred stock to be increased, except in a similar way. These careful clauses made some provision for future capital requirements necessary which should be independent of the consent of the stockholders at any time; and $20,000,000 general mortgage bonds were accordingly set aside, to be issued in amounts not greater than $1,500,000 in any one year for future construction, equipment, and the like. Additional general mortgage bonds were provided to retire Philadelphia & Reading Terminal and Coal & Iron Company bonds up to the sum of $21,000,000.

The floating debt, estimated at $25,150,000, was provided for in part by assessment, and in part by the sale of securities to the syndicate for cash; 20 per cent being levied on first, second, and third preference income bonds, 20 per cent on the stock, and 4 per cent on the deferred incomes; while the syndicate agreed to take $4,000,000 of the new general mortgage bonds and $8,000,000 of the new first preferred stock. The assessment was expected to yield $20,862,289, and the syndicate to contribute in cash $7,300,000; leaving an estimated cash balance of $3,000,000. In addition, the syndicate (Messrs. J. P. Morgan & Co., J. Kennedy Tod & Co., Hallgarten & Co., and A. Iselin & Co.) undertook to underwrite the payment of the assessments on the income bonds and stock, and to guarantee the extension or payment of the improvement mortgage and Coal & Iron Company bonds, most of which were to mature in the following two years. No great reduction of fixed charges was of course to be expected. The cancellation of the floating debt effected, nevertheless, a certain saving, so that charges for the future were estimated at $9,300,000 as against net earnings of $9,839,971 in 1894; while the refunding or extension of maturing bonds was looked to for a reduction of $500,000.[1]

It is plain that this plan favored the general mortgage bond-holders to the last degree, and admitted them to the reorganized company with absolutely no sacrifice save that of the addition of $4,000,000 to the total general mortgage issue. They funded no coupons, they suffered no diminution of interest and no shaving of principal; they paid no assessment; and as an additional protection to them, the provision was inserted that all classes of stock of the new company, except such number as might be disposed of to qualify directors, were to be voted by three voting trustees, of whom J. P. Morgan and F. P. Olcott were designated in the plan. It has seldom happened in any reorganization that a mortgage similar to the general mortgage in this case has been able to take and hold so strong a position.[2] The secret lay in the fact that the road had been earning the interest on the general mortgage bonds; and that under these circumstances no interest or combination of interests could force the holders to accept less than payment in full of all their claims. The situation could never have arisen in the earlier reorganization; it could never have occurred where a reduction in annual payments was required for the salvation of the property, or even where the amount of cash to be raised to pay the floating debt was so large that junior securityholders would have relinquished their holdings rather than pay the necessary assessments. In this case none of these conditions existed, and all the burden was thrown on the holders of junior mortgages and stock. It must be remembered, also, that though in ordinary cases the difference between the income bonds which the old first and second preference bondholders surrendered and the preferred stock which they received would not have been very great, yet here the provisions of the old income mortgage, which forbade the deduction from net earnings of any interest on bonds subsequently created until its interest should have been paid, rendered the loss more serious.

To sum up, the holders of junior securities and stock paid the expenses of reorganization, paid the floating debt, lost what right they had to interest before the settlement of interest on subsequently

---

[1] Ry. Times, 68: 802, 1895; Chron. 61: 1109, 1895.   [2] Ry. Age, 20: 625, 1895.

created claims, and got only stock, and for the most part second preferred or common stock at that. The general mortgage bond-holders got new 4 per cent bonds, plus 12 per cent, or 2 per cent in cash, had no greater interest charges ahead of them, and without paying any assessment or making any concession, except to allow the immediate increase of the amount of their issue by $4,000,000, and thereafter by $1,500,000 per year, secured a lien on the assets of the company; a privilege which was, moreover, extended to un-deposited as well as to deposited bonds. The company itself was dissolved, but the new corporation which took over its assets en-joyed, with slightly decreased charges, freedom from the old float-ing debt and from the extensions and combinations which had caused the floating debt of the old management, and seemed besides a strong financial backing.

In May, 1896, Judge Atchison of Philadelphia signed the decree for the foreclosure and sale of the property of both the Railroad and the Coal & Iron Companies, and on September 23 the sale took place, C. H. Coster, of J. P. Morgan & Co., and Francis Lynde Stetson paying an aggregate of $20,500,000 for the whole estate.[1] The sale ended the life of the old Reading charter; and in view of the constitution adopted for the state of Pennsylvania in 1871, which forbade any railroad owning more than 30,000 acres of coal land, some device had to be sought whereby the Philadelphia & Reading Railroad and the Philadelphia & Reading Coal & Iron Companies could hold together. Diligent search revealed the exist-ence of the "National Company," a corporation chartered in 1871 by special act of the legislature of Pennsylvania at the very time when the new constitution was under consideration. This company, originally the Excelsior Enterprise Company, had power "to pur-chase, improve, use, and dispose of property to contractors and others and for other purposes," with privileges fully as broad, it was said, as those enjoyed by the Reading before foreclosure.[2] The National Company now changed its name to the Reading Company, called a special meeting, increased its stock to the amount required by the plan of reorganization, and, jointly with the Coal & Iron Com-pany, authorized a mortgage to secure bonds up to a possible amount of $135,000,000; to be secured on the property of both companies,

[1] Chron. 63: 560, 1896. [2] Chron. 64: 84, 1897.

including the stock and bonds of the Railway Company. Meanwhile the Philadelphia & Reading Railway Company had been organized to succeed to the property and franchises of the old Philadelphia & Reading Railroad Company,[1] with a capital stock of $20,000,000 in $50 shares. The charter of the Coal & Iron Company was preserved in spite of the foreclosure sale.[2] The next step was for the Reading Company to exchange its bonds and stock for the general mortgage bonds and stock of the two minor companies in the proportions already agreed upon, and to deposit the securities so obtained in its treasury; leaving the prior liens the only direct obligations of either company in the hands of the public. This meant, of course, absolute control of both companies by the Reading Company; and in the future, when the prior liens should mature, it was to mean the replacement of all outstanding obligations by the obligations of the holding company. Both the Railway and the Coal & Iron Companies retained their separate organizations; the belief was that there was no merger which might be attacked before the courts; that it only happened that one corporate individual had invested in both Railroad and Coal Company shares and proposed to vote this stock, as was lawful, to further the policies of which it approved.[3]

---

[1] Chron. 63: 923, 1896.

[2] See testimony of Mr. Baer before the Interstate Commerce Commission, 1904, "Synopsis of Stenographers' Minutes, etc., in the case of W. R. Hearst against the Philadelphia & Reading Railway Company," p. 55. The managers wished to take no chances.

[3] Organization and scope of the three Reading Companies. The Reading Company owns practically the whole of the capital stock of the Philadelphia & Reading Railway Company and the Philadelphia & Reading Coal & Iron Company, and all of the other stocks and securities which were acquired by the purchases under the sale made by the Trustees and the Receivers. It also owns the $20,000,000 purchase money mortgage bonds issued by the Philadelphia & Reading Railway Company, the locomotives, cars, steam collieries, tugs, and barges constituting the railway and marine equipment, and all the real estate of the old Philadelphia & Reading Railroad Company which was not appurtenant to the railroad itself. This, of course, does not include the depots, rights of way, etc., which belong to the Railway Company. The Philadelphia & Reading Railway Company owns all the roads formerly belonging to the Philadelphia & Reading Railroad Company, and it controls the roads hitherto leased to that company, either by transfer of the old leases or by new leases made since November 30, 1896. It leases from the Reading Company the railway and marine equipment which it uses in the conduct of its business and a number of wharves and warehouses on the Delaware River. Annual Report, 1898.

Representatives of the reorganization managers laid an elaborate defence of the legality of these operations before Attorney-General McCormick of Pennsylvania, and on January 2 secured an opinion confirming the validity of the charter of the Reading Company. "After due consideration," said Mr. McCormick, "I reach the conclusion, most reluctantly, that the Commonwealth of Pennsylvania cannot now successfully attack the chartered rights of the Reading Company. . . . My view of the whole matter is that the charter of the company authorized it to do the kind of business in which it engaged prior to January 1, 1874, which business was of the same general character as that in which it proposes to engage for the purpose of controlling the stocks of the Railway Company and the Coal & Iron Company." [1]

Like the Baltimore & Ohio and the Erie, the Reading has benefited largely from the favorable business conditions of the last decade. The combined income of the three Reading companies has grown from $48,422,971 in 1898 to $95,715,088 in 1907:[2] Earnings on the Philadelphia & Reading Railway alone are now nearly as great as the combined income of the three companies at the earlier date. Net receipts were $13,586,710 in 1898 and $29,190,316 in 1907; and the surplus over all payments rose from $1,376,420 to $8,741,454 between those years. It is important to notice that this showing does not depend primarily upon the anthracite business. Not only has the carriage of general merchandise increased until it affords to the railway a return almost equal to the earnings on coal, but in the coal business itself bituminous has assumed an importance nearly as great as that of its harder rival. The Coal & Iron Company still concerns itself almost entirely with anthracite, and has accordingly been more affected by special causes. The strike of the miners in September and October, 1900, and again from May to October, 1902, checked the growth in production for a time; but the increased demand for domestic consumption has made possible an increase in output from 4,849,002 tons in 1897 to 10,034,713 in 1907. Increasing business has stimulated improvements. Over $15,300,000 have been withdrawn from income by the Philadelphia

[1] Chron. 64: 84, 1897.
[2] There are certain duplications in both of these figures, but the same duplications appear in each.

& Reading Railway Company for this purpose between 1896 and
1907; and over $10,000,000 have been invested from earnings by
the Coal & Iron Company during the same time in colliery improvements alone. Maintenance charges have been ample. Whereas
$1300 to $1500 per mile of single main track are sufficient for normal
repairs upon a trunk line, the Philadelphia & Reading Railway has
spent over $2600 per mile of line for the last seven years, and over
$1700 for the three years preceding. As much as $73 has been spent
in a single year for average maintenance per freight car, $609 in
maintenance per passenger car, and $3244 in maintenance per loco-
motive. In consequence of these repairs and of renewals upon a
considerable scale, the average value of all locomotives has increased
between December 1, 1896, and June 30, 1906, from $4906 to $8393;
the average value of freight cars producing revenue from $383 to
$622; the average value of steam colliers and tugs from $41,533 to
$55,451; and the average value of barges from $7930 to $21,074.
The average freight train load was 194 tons in 1897 and 403 tons
in 1907. Ton-mileage has increased during the period 159 per cent
and freight train mileage only 27 per cent.

It is true that no great sums have been spent from capital account.
$5,137,825 in car trust certificates were outstanding on June 30,
1907, and $5,608,000 in general mortgage bonds have been sold and
the proceeds invested principally in new equipment, but this is all.
Improvements have been made mainly from earnings, and fixed
charges have not had to be increased. In fact, the voting trustees
stated at the expiration of their trusteeship in 1904 that, eliminating
the fixed charges created since December 1, 1896, on account of the
acquisition of additional properties and interest upon the additional
mortgage bonds issued for the purchase of equipment, the fixed
charges of the Reading system were $1,018,065 less for the fiscal
year ended June 30, 1904, than they were for the fiscal year ended
November 30, 1896.[1]

It thus comes about that the finances of the Reading, while not as
secure as could be desired, are yet in better shape than they have
been for thirty years. Fixed charges, taxes, and operating expenses [2]

[1] Chron. 79: 2087, 1904.
[2] See the nineteenth volume of the Industrial Commission's report for a brief de-
scription of the renewed attempt at consolidation in the anthracite coal fields; also
testimony in the case of W. R. Hearst against the Philadelphia & Reading Railway
Company.

took 86 per cent of gross income in 1907, but a decline of nearly $12,000,000 in net earnings must precede a default on any bonds outstanding. To this margin should be added the considerable amount by which maintenance expenses now surpass normal figures. An initial dividend was declared on the Reading Company first preferred stock in August, 1900; on its second preferred in October, 1903; and on its common in February, 1905. Four per cent is now being paid upon all classes of stock.

Large amounts of Reading stock are held by the Baltimore & Ohio and by the Lake Shore. The Reading has again bought control of the Central of New Jersey, and owns besides a steamship line and something under 500 miles in other subsidiary roads. Its large earnings, its troubles with its mine employees, its influence over the supply of a necessity of life, and the possibility of discrimination which its control of both railroad and coal properties affords, have made it a target for legislative attack from state and national governments. Action was begun by the Department of Justice in 1907 to dissolve the merger between the Reading and the Central of New Jersey. In June of the previous year the so-called "commodity clause" of the Hepburn Act forbade any railroad company to transport in interstate commerce any article except timber and the manufactured products thereof which it should have produced, or in which it should have any interest, except those products necessary and intended for its own use in its business as common carrier. The legality of the Reading's position in these matters is yet to be decided by the courts. The student may well doubt whether legislative action will ever succeed in preventing the common ownership of the Reading railroad and mining interests. What is more probable is that a strict governmental control will come to be imposed. Against this proper development no appeal to legal technicalities will avail.

CHAPTER V

THE SOUTHERN

Richmond & Danville — East Tennessee, Virginia & Georgia — Formation of the Southern Railway Security Company — Growth and Combinations — Failure and reorganization of the East Tennessee — Reversal of position between the Richmond & Danville and the Richmond & West Point Terminal — Acquisition of the Central of Georgia — Failure and reorganization of the whole system — Subsequent development.

At the present time there are in the South five great railway systems: the Atlantic Coast Line; the Seaboard Air Line; the Southern Railway; the Louisville & Nashville Railroad; and the Illinois Central Railroad, which cover, in the order named, the territory between the Atlantic Ocean and the Mississippi River.

The backbone of the Southern Railway is formed by the old Richmond & Danville and East Tennessee, Virginia & Georgia companies: of which the first formerly stretched with its subsidiary lines from Washington and Richmond on the north to Atlanta, Georgia, and Greenville, Mississippi, on the south and west; and the second reached from Bristol, Tennessee, in a great half circle to the ocean at Brunswick, Georgia, and by means of the Mobile & Birmingham straight to the Gulf at Mobile.

The Richmond & Danville was opened in 1856 between Richmond and Danville, Virginia. It was largely aided by the state of Virginia. Three-fifths of its stock were owned by the state in 1867, there was a state loan of $400,000, and a state guarantee of $200,000 besides.[1] In natural consequence the state elected three of the six directors. It was not long, however, before the state was able to relieve itself of a large part of its investment. On the 31st of August, 1871, all of the state shares were taken over by the

[1] The Virginia state bonds were redeemable in 34 years from April 8, 1853, to September 30, 1854, by the payment of an annuity of 7 per cent. Of this rate 6 per cent covered the interest and 1 per cent, by continuous reinvestment at 6 per cent, was expected to yield the principal sum in the 34 years agreed upon. Annual Report, 1867. Like most new companies, the Richmond & Danville found difficulty at first in meeting its obligations, and was obliged to issue bonds to provide for overdue interest to the state and to keep its floating debt within bounds. R. R. Gaz. 5: 499, 1873, and Ibid. 5: 507, 1873.

Pennsylvania Railroad Company.[1] The money sunk in the company's bonds still remained. From Danville the Richmond & Danville steadily pushed south in the years following 1856. Under the leadership of the Pennsylvania it became its ambition to open direct rail communication from the great Northern cities to the heart of North and South Carolina and Georgia. To obtain a ninety-mile extension to Charlotte the company leased the North Carolina Railroad, 223 miles in length.[1] To get into Atlanta it allied itself with the Atlanta & Richmond Air Line Company, projected to construct a line between Atlanta and Charlotte.[2] In 1878 it bought a controlling interest in the Charlotte, Columbia & Augusta Railroad and secured entrance to the latter city.[3] The Pennsylvania aided the new enterprise by advances from time to time, and when the current liabilities became unmanageable took $1,000,000 of a new refunding mortgage.[4]

Meanwhile the East Tennessee, Virginia & Georgia Railroad had been established to the west of the Richmond & Danville, in the heart of the southern Appalachians.[5] This company was a consolidation in 1869 of the East Tennessee & Virginia Railroad, from Bristol, on the boundary between Virginia and Tennessee, to Knoxville, Tennessee; and the East Tennessee & Georgia Railroad, from Knoxville, Tennessee, to Dalton, Georgia. Both roads were aided by the state of Tennessee. In 1870, however, the new company extinguished its debt to the state by the payment of $4,117,761 in state bonds. Not long after the completion of its line from Bristol to Dalton, the East Tennessee fell under the control of the Pennsylvania Railroad, which already dominated its neighbor

[1] R. R. Gaz. 3: 279, 1871. This road stretched from Goldsboro in the eastern part of North Carolina to Charlotte in the southwestern part, via Greensboro. It was principally owned by the state of North Carolina. By the terms of the lease the Richmond & Danville agreed to pay $260,000 per annum for thirty years.

[2] The whole road was opened for traffic in September, 1873. It went into the hands of a receiver in 1874, and was sold in foreclosure in 1876; but the Pennsylvania Railroad relieved the Richmond & Danville from all collateral liabilities incurred on its account. The reorganized line was leased by the Richmond & Danville in 1881. Chron. 32: 367, 1881.

[3] Annual Report, 1878.

[4] Ibid. 1874.

[5] Ulrich B. Phillips, A History of Transportation in the Eastern Cotton Belt to 1860. New York: The Columbia University Press, 1908, pp. 372 ff.

to the east. To facilitate the control and to unify the interests of the Pennsylvania south of Washington a "Southern Railway Security Company" was formed, with a capital of $5,000,000. This company was entrusted with a majority of the stock of the Richmond & Danville and of the East Tennessee. It also controlled the Coast Line railroads from Richmond to Charleston, and the Memphis & Charleston from Chattanooga to Memphis.[1] Unfortunately the financial results of the combination were disappointing. Of the subsidiary roads the East Tennessee managed to pay at least 3 per cent on its capital stock from 1872 to 1876; but the Richmond & Danville paid nothing, the Coast Lines nothing, and the Memphis & Charleston barely earned the 3 per cent guaranteed under its lease. In 1873, therefore, a special meeting was held at the office of the Southern Railway Security Company to consider the propriety of making sale of certain properties of the company.[2] In 1874 the lease of the Memphis & Charleston was surrendered,[3] and in 1876 the bulk of the securities held, outside of the Richmond & Danville stock, were disposed of.[4]

The retirement of the Southern Railway Security Company marked the beginning of the withdrawal of the Pennsylvania from investment in the South. For the rest, it left the lines north of South Carolina in three main competing groups. There were the Coast Lines from Richmond south, the Richmond & Danville, and the East Tennessee, Virginia & Georgia properties. And stretching from west to east was the Memphis & Charleston, which was already in financial difficulties of a serious nature. All three of these groups were now thrown upon their own resources; and two of them, at least, took vigorous measures in self-protection. The policy of the East Tennessee was the most aggressive. Shut up in the narrow valley between the Clinch and the Great Smoky Mountains, and flanked by hostile roads, it conceived it to be necessary for it to acquire connections to the south, to the east, and to the west. Accordingly, it leased the Memphis & Charleston in 1877 and obtained an outlet upon the Mississippi River.[5] In

[1] Including 37 miles of running rights over the N., C. & St. L.
[2] R. R. Gaz. 5: 475, 1873.   [3] Ibid. 6: 178, 1874.   [4] Ibid. 8: 540, 1876.
[5] The Memphis & Charleston stockholders agreed to the lease in order to avoid bankruptcy. At a meeting in May, 1877, it was pointed out to them that the net

1878 it bought the Georgia Southern and the Selma, Rome & Dalton and provided itself with a line as far south as the Flint River in Alabama.[1] In 1881 it bought the Alabama Central, extending some 96 miles west from Selma. The same year it secured control of the Macon & Brunswick in Georgia, and began construction from Macon to Rome to complete a line to the South Atlantic coast.[2] In the north it made an alliance with the Norfolk & Western, which opened that company's line from Bristol to Norfolk,[3] and arranged with the Louisville & Nashville and the Kentucky Central for construction to a connection at the Kentucky-Tennessee state line which should open to it the business of the Central West.[4]

The Richmond & Danville fell under the control of a group of capitalists who already controlled the Atlantic Coast lines and held an interest in the East Tennessee, and who now bought the 24,000 shares of Danville stock still held by the Pennsylvania Railroad.[5] Like its rival, it enlarged its system. It leased the Atlanta & Charlotte Air Line in 1881,[6] with certain minor roads in the Carolinas and in Georgia. In 1882, under the charter of the Georgia Pacific, it began construction westward from Atlanta to the Mississippi. It did not stretch out, as did the East Tennessee, but it secured a very complete control of the territory between

earnings of the road had not been enough to pay the interest on its bonds, and that a large amount was due to the state of Tennessee which the company had no present means of paying. Either an assessment on the stock or a lease to the East Tennessee was declared to be necessary. Accordingly, a lease was concluded. The East Tennessee agreed so to discharge the principal of the company's indebtedness to the state as to reduce the annual interest account from $360,000 to $310,000 as a maximum, and upon the fulfilment of this and of certain other minor conditions took over the operation of the road. Two years later the lease was extended for twenty years at a definite rental amounting to 7 per cent on $4,225,000 or a yearly payment of $295,750. See R. R. Gaz. 9: 421, 1877, and Ibid. 11: 672, 1879.

[1] The Selma, Rome & Dalton was bought from the purchasers at foreclosure sale for $2,600,000. The Georgia Southern cost $367,369. Outstanding debts were assumed. To provide for these and other outlays $10,000,000 new 5 per cent bonds were authorized. R. R. Gaz. 12: 622, 1880.

[2] This line was completed in 1882. Chron. 35: 430, 1882; R. R. Gaz. 13: 420, 1881.

[3] Chron. 33: 357, 1881.

[4] R. R. Gaz. 13: 420, 1881.

[5] Prominent among them were Messrs. Clyde, of the Coast Line railroads, Wilson and McGhee of the East Tennessee, Stewart, Plant, Logan, and others.

[6] This had been the Atlanta & Richmond Air Line.

Richmond in the north and Augusta, Savannah, and Atlanta in the south. In 1881, also, the Richmond & Danville took a step destined to have important consequences. Since it desired to acquire certain railroads, and since its charter allowed it to hold stock in none but connecting lines, it caused to be incorporated a so-called Richmond & West Point Terminal Railway & Warehouse Company, with authority to acquire stocks and bonds of railroad companies in North Carolina, South Carolina, Tennessee, Kentucky, Georgia, Alabama, Mississippi, and other states. This company increased its stock by October, 1881, to $3,000,000; of which the Richmond & Danville then owned $1,510,000. The most important acquisition which it made at the time was the Virginia Midland Railway, from Alexandria, Virginia, to Danville; but other additions were to follow.

The independent action of the Danville and East Tennessee companies was followed by a new consolidation which reunited most of the lines dominated by the old Security Company. In response to queries in August, 1883, Mr. Calvin S. Brice admitted that a syndicate in which he was interested had bought control of the Richmond & Danville.

"We have secured," said he, "about 28,000 of the 50,000 shares of stock issued by the Richmond & Danville Company. Our syndicate controls, besides our new purchase, the East Tennessee, Virginia & Georgia Railway and the Chesapeake & York River line of steamers that ply between West Point, on the Chesapeake, and Baltimore, and has close traffic arrangements with the Clyde steamers, which run between New York and Philadelphia and all Southern points. Our purpose is to confine all our railroad and steamship lines under one management, and to equip and operate the system in the best possible manner." [1]

It appears from this statement that the capitalists who controlled the East Tennessee now again consolidated with the leading interests of the Richmond & Danville and lines east, albeit changes in personnel and transfers of holdings occurred. Return to the old combination was made desirable by the more intimate connection of the two groups of roads. The Western North Carolina had been opened across the mountains of North Carolina in 1882. This had

[1] Chron. 37: 128, 1883.

made practicable the diversion of the western traffic of the East Tennessee from the Norfolk & Western to the Richmond & Danville; a traffic which the northern connections of the East Tennessee promised largely to increase. Consolidation was doubtless also prompted by the desire to save the East Tennessee from serious financial difficulty which threatened it. It had become apparent that this company, at least, had severely taxed its strength in the rapid extension of mileage which had followed 1876. Before that time its position had been secure. It had possessed a monopoly of the somewhat limited local traffic between Chattanooga and Bristol, and had formed part of the most direct route between New York, Philadelphia, Baltimore, and Washington, and towns in Tennessee, Northern Alabama, and Mississippi. Its extensions had changed the situation. They had brought it into touch with the Mississippi River and the Atlantic Ocean, and had increased its fighting power; but they had also endowed it at large cost with a group of poorly equipped, unprofitable lines located in a keenly competitive territory. The Selma, Rome & Dalton had been purchased just after a foreclosure sale. The Macon & Brunswick had never been able to earn much more than working expenses. The Alabama Central had not seen fit to publish its financial figures after 1878, while the Memphis & Charleston, as we have seen, had turned to the East Tennessee only to escape bankruptcy.

The East Tennessee had hoped to make profitable the lines which it had so rapidly acquired. Unfortunately the company was poorly equipped for such a task. Its finance had been extravagant. In 1875, on 269 miles of lines there had been $7317 in stock and $15,-620 in bonds per mile. In 1883 the mortgage bonds and car trusts outstanding per mile owned amounted to $23,444, the income bonds to $15,404, and the capital stock to $41,079. A grand total of $79,927 as compared with the $22,937 of eight years earlier, and an average of almost $100,000 in securities per mile of new line acquired! Ninety-nine per cent of net income was being absorbed in paying interest on all classes of securities, although maintenance figures were kept as low as $630 per mile of line. This large volume of stocks and bonds made improvement from earnings impossible, and prevented conservative management by taking from the stockholders any chance of dividends, and by reducing the quotations of common

stock to less than $5 per share. And though in some respects the
location of the system was good, the route which it offered to much
of its business was indirect, the competition which it had to meet
was severe, and its Atlantic terminal, Brunswick, was of small importance compared with the thriving cities of Savannah and Norfolk.
The result was a failure to secure the gains from consolidation which
had been expected. Surplus earnings were continuously small, and
current bills were left to run; until by 1883 the floating debt had
become so large that an issue of $1,200,000 in debenture bonds
was required to take care of it.

The failure of the East Tennessee to weld its connections into an
efficient transportation system left it helpless in face of the panic
of 1884. Earnings fell off in that year, a directors' committee was
appointed,[1] and the resulting report revealed a plain inability on
the part of the company to meet its charges.

"The interest charges proper for the calendar year 1885 are," said
the committee, $1,476,505.85

"To this must be added the principal due on car trusts and
debentures in 1885,   280,954.11

"Or a total of $1,757,459.96

"The payments on similar account will be —
in 1886, $1,739,196.28
in 1887,   1,720,932.60
gradually decreasing until the debentures and car trusts
being paid off in 1894, the total fixed charges for the year
1895 will be $1,295,970.00

"The net revenue for the year 1883-4 was   1,699,925.84

"The net revenue for 1885 and 1886, allowing for the decrease
in earnings following the panic, and supposing the road to be
operated for 60 per cent, may be estimated at $1,400,000.00

"This will leave," said the committee, "an annual deficit of
$350,000, to which must be added a total of $1,000,000 required
by the general manager for steel rails, iron bridges, and other
needed improvements.

"The sums for covering these expenses should not be raised by
temporary loans, as this would not relieve the company of its embar-
rassments nor place its finances upon a sound footing. It cannot
be raised by an additional mortgage, on account of the provisions
of the mortgage securing the income bonds. It must and can be

[1] Chron. 39: 733, 1884.

raised from a funding of coupons which shall leave the earnings of the company sufficiently free to meet the demands upon them. The committee therefore recommends:

(1) "That the holders of the consolidated 5 per cent bonds be asked to fund four coupons, being those maturing January and July 1, 1885, and January and July 1, 1886, by depositing said four coupons with the Central Trust Company of New York, as trustee, and receiving instead the company's funded coupon bond dated July 1, 1885, and bearing 6 per cent interest per annum from that date, . . . which bond shall run ten years from its date and be redeemable at the pleasure of the company at par and accrued interest after three years, on three months' notice; such funded coupon bond to be secured by the coupons so deposited, the lien of which will be in all respects preserved.

"The total extensions under this clause would be $1,467,400.

(2) "That the holders of the $2,000,000 of the Cincinnati & Georgia Division first mortgage 6 per cent bonds be asked to fund four coupons, . . . being those maturing March and September 1, 1885, and March and September 1, 1886, . . . and accepting in lieu thereof a funded coupon bond . . . dated September 1, 1885.

"The total amount extended under this clause would be $240,000.

(3) "That the holders of the debentures be asked to extend for ten years such of the debentures as fall due during the years 1885 and 1886, and to accept similar debentures running from five to ten years, for the interest. . . .

"The total amount extended under this clause would be $373,200.

(4) "That an arrangement be made with the holders of the car trust certificates of the company, series A, for an extension for ten years of all the payments of principal falling due in 1885 and 1886, being $100,000 in each year.

"The total amount extended under this clause would be $200,000." [1]

The committee had an apology to offer for the state in which the company was placed. "The actual cost of the 190 miles of the new roads constructed by the company has largely exceeded," said they, "the estimated cost. The physical condition of the roads purchased by the company necessitated the expenditure of large sums in the

[1] Chron. 40: 29, 1885.

improvement of roadway and track; the construction and reconstruction of bridge masonry and bridge superstructure. The facilities for the conduct of the company's business were entirely inadequate to the requirements of its increasing traffic and had to be enlarged. Unfortunately the company did not fully provide for these expenditures, and the shrinkage of the value of its securities greatly aggravated the evil." This much was very true. In its criticism of existing facilities the committee was on sure ground. In its suggestions for relief it was less well advised. It seems to have felt that the East Tennessee's difficulties were due to a temporary inability to raise cash for the improvement of its roadbed and equipment, and that the suspension of certain charges for a few years would allow the expenditure of liberal sums from income, ensure the improvement of the road, and bring about a condition of permanent prosperity. The truth was that the East Tennessee was in too bad a shape to be reëstablished by such means. The heavily burdened and physically defective lines which made up the system were past being restored from income even with the aid of a funding of a few years' coupons. They required a definitive surrender of portions of the claims against them, extensive new charges to capital account, and a correspondingly complete reconstruction of their whole operating plant.[1] The practical service which the committee rendered was not in suggesting an adequate remedy for existing troubles, but in making plain how serious these troubles were. So imminent, in fact, did they show collapse to be, that the management determined to forestall hostile action by themselves asking for the appointment of a receiver; and on January 7 the Circuit Court appointed Henry Fink to that position.[2] The committee's funding scheme fell of its own weight.

---

[1] The committee overestimated the net earnings of the next few years. Instead of $1,400,000 each year these proved to be $1,288,343 in 1885 and $1,382,749 in 1886.

[2] Chron. 40: 60, 1885. There was some dispute as to the jurisdiction of the different courts in this connection. The Circuit Court appointed Mr. Fink receiver for the whole line on January 7. The next day a state court appointed R. T. Dorsey and E. P. Alexander receivers for the lines in Georgia under another mortgage. This suit was removed to the Federal Court and Dorsey, who had meantime been appointed sole receiver in Georgia, was displaced. Subsequently the Georgia Supreme Court held that the transfer was illegal, and Dorsey vainly endeavored to regain his position. The dispute was ended by the withdrawal of the suit upon which the Georgia application was based.

The decrease in the earnings of the company, a truer appreciation of its condition, and, it may be surmised, the influence of New York banking houses, forced it to make room for a thorough plan of financial reconstruction.

Action looking toward reorganization of the East Tennessee, Virginia & Georgia began with the year 1886. In January Mr. Nelson Robinson,[1] who had held proxies for a controlling stock interest at the previous election, returned from Europe; and after a conference with certain large bondholders agreed with them to draft a plan for the reorganization of the property. A reorganization committee was chosen from members of large banking firms,[2] meetings were held, and in the first part of February, 1886, a scheme was put forth. This plan comprised the following points:

(1) Reduction of fixed charges;
(2) Exchange of new bonds and preferred stock for old bonds;
(3) Assessment on the junior securities;
(4) Foreclosure.

Foreclosure was to take place under the consolidated mortgage. A new 5 per cent seventy-year consolidated mortgage was then to be created. Enough of the bonds under this mortgage were to be reserved to retire the liens prior to the existing consolidated mortgage as they should mature, and the balance was to be used for taking up the outstanding consolidated mortgage bonds, the Cincinnati & Georgia division bonds, and the ten-year debentures. It was estimated that the exchanges would reduce the annual interest charge from $1,757,460 to $994,737.[3] This necessitated considerable demands upon old securityholders. Thus the old consolidated mortgage bonds bearing 5 per cent received only 60 per cent of their face value in new consolidated bonds with the same rate of interest; and the old 6 per cent Cincinnati & Georgia division

---

[1] Son-in-law of George Seney.

[2] This committee was chosen by the consolidated bondholders. Its membership consisted of Robert Fleming, a representative of the foreign holders; Charles McGhee, president of the Memphis & Charleston; G. W. Smith, of Kountze Bros.; Frederic D. Tappan, president of the Gallatin National Bank; E. W. Corlies, vice-president of the Bank of America; and Frederick P. Olcott, president of the Central Trust Company, which was trustee of the mortgages of the company. Chron. 42: 155, 1886.

[3] As might have been expected, this estimate was too optimistic. The actual reduction was to $1,167,000. Even this constituted a cut of about one-third.

bonds received only 48 per cent in consols, besides suffering a
decrease in interest rate from 6 to 5 per cent. The difference was
made up by the allowance of preferred stock, to which, moreover,
was given the right for five years to elect a majority of the board
of directors, unless before that time the new company should have
paid out of its net earnings 5 per cent dividends on such preferred
stock for two full successive years. To the Cincinnati & Georgia
division bonds were given 62 per cent in new first preferred besides
the 48 per cent in bonds, — a total of 110 per cent; upon which the
yield in prosperous times might exactly equal the yield on the
securities which they surrendered. To the consolidated bonds were
given 50 per cent in new first preferred, making possible a total
return greater than that which they had formerly enjoyed. For
the debentures was made the same provision as for the divisional
bonds. In order that net earnings might go first of all to the prior
liens and to the above securities, new second preferred and common
stock was issued for the benefit of the old income bonds and stock.
Of these the income bonds received 100 per cent in new second
preferred; while the old preferred received 100 per cent and the
old common stock 40 per cent in new common. Only in return for
their assessments did the income bonds receive first preferred stock,
and even for their assessment the common stock took second
preferred. Cash assessments were 5 per cent on the income mortgage and 6 per cent on the new common stock. This was expected
to yield $2,475,000, which, with a surplus of new securities in the
treasury of $1,534,000, was thought sufficient to liquidate out-
standing car trusts and to provide the company with a fund available for future use.[1]

The plan may be criticised in some respects. It made no adequate provision for future capital requirements. Two millions and
a half of cash and two millions of securities were considerable sums
in hand, but of these over half a million was in the form of stock,
and from the rest had to be deducted at least a million and a half
for the liquidation of car trusts. This left, it is true, enough for
existing needs,[2] but it did not allow for constantly recurring

---

[1] Chron. 42: 186–7, 1886. See also Poor's Manual for 1886.

[2] The reader will remember that that same year the general manager had estimated
the sum required for steel rails, iron bridges, and other improvements at $1,000,000.

and legitimate demands for improvements out of capital in future years. Moreover, the securities given for the consolidated, the Cincinnati & Georgia division, and the debenture bonds exceeded by 10 per cent the nominal value of the bonds retired by them. But on the whole the reorganization plan was an excellent attempt to solve a difficult problem. It proceeded on a sound principle, it laid the burden on the proper parties, it avoided a funding of current liabilities, and even in respect to the volume of securities outstanding it accomplished a much needed reform by wiping out 60 per cent of the almost worthless common stock.[1] It was accordingly accepted by the securityholders. On March 18, the reorganization committee obtained a decree of sale.[2] By May 1, practically all the consolidated and income bonds, with a majority of the preferred stock, had assented;[3] and on May 25, 1886, the East Tennessee, Virginia & Georgia Railroad was sold for $10,250,000 to a representative of the reorganization committee. Previous to this the opposition committee, which had been formed by the minority stockholders, had disbanded.[4] The final step was the organization of the East Tennessee, Virginia & Georgia Rail-

---

[1] It is true that the severity of the treatment of the junior securities caused sharp protest. A number of the stockholders met in New York February 23, and appointed a committee to prepare a plan of assessment and to oppose foreclosure. Under the auspices of this committee, Messrs. William H. Sistare and Harold Clemens filed a suit against the reorganization committee of the East Tennessee Company. The capitalization of the company, said they, had been fraudulently inflated by the members of the Thompson-Seney-Brice syndicate. By false reports these financiers had unloaded upon the public securities which they had previously distributed among themselves, and then had entered upon a scheme for wrecking the property. The suits made specific charges of irregularity, and prayed for relief. Ry. Age, 11: 192, 1886.

[2] Chron. 42: 364, 1886.   [3] Ibid. 42: 575, 1886.

[4] Ibid. 42: 663, 1886. In a circular to their constituents this committee said: "That after a full and satisfactory presentation of the case by very able counsel it appeared that the committee had been misinformed as to the material facts upon which their case was predicated. It especially appeared to the Court that there was no ground for the charge of fraud against the directors of the Company or the Central Trust Company. It further appeared that the litigation must be a protracted one, without substantial benefit to either party. Your committee were not willing to assume the responsibility of such a contest, in view of the expressed willingness of the majority to give to the minority the same terms which they had accepted for themselves. It was deemed wise to harmonize all interests, and join hands to promote the future of the property."

way, which on July 1 took over the title to the East Tennessee, Virginia & Georgia Railroad and branches, a controlling interest in the stock of the Knoxville & Ohio, and a controlling interest in the stock of the Memphis & Charleston Railroad Company.[1]

During this time the Richmond & Danville had not been standing still. It will be remembered that in 1883 the capitalists who dominated the East Tennessee and the Coast Lines had purchased a controlling interest in this company, with the purpose, according to Mr. Brice, of confining all their railroad and steamship lines under one management and of operating the system in the best possible manner. These gentlemen had found the earnings of the Richmond & Danville sufficiently unsatisfactory and the need for improvements sufficiently great to lead them to pass the interest on its debenture bonds in October, 1883. The net earnings for 1882, out of which this dividend would have been paid, they found had been fully taken up by the fixed charges and the expenses for new equipment and betterments. The net earnings for 1883 they believed sure to show large gains, but still not likely to be equal to necessary expenditures.[2] Strict economy was to be the order of the day. In the three previous years the company had accumulated a large floating debt. This the new management reduced more than one-half by the end of 1885. The funded debt it allowed to increase largely, but the earnings it managed somewhat to improve. In general, however, it secured no very striking gains. Union in interest with the East Tennessee and the Coast Lines modified the severity of competition, but the panic of 1884 checked business, and the real saving in operating cost was very slight.[3]

In their search for means to reduce expenses the owners of the Richmond & Danville came across the Richmond & West Point Terminal Company. By 1884 this company was in peaceful pos-

[1] Annual Report, East Tennessee, Virginia & Georgia, 1887.

[2] Chron. 37: 344, 1883. The debentures were cumulative income bonds entitled to 6 per cent out of earnings after payment of interest, rentals, and operating expenses, including expenditures made for the repair, renewal, and improvement of existing property and equipment necessary for the proper conduct of the business of the railroad. Certain provisions of the mortgage protected them against the insertion of new mortgage bonds before them. Chron. 37: 373, 1883.

[3] Curiously enough the chief saving seems to have been in maintenance of cars, an expenditure which one would expect to be least affected by the syndicate control.

session of 1815.8 miles of railroad, which included all the important branches of the Richmond & Danville except the North
Carolina Railroad, from Goldsboro to Charlotte, and the Atlanta
& Charlotte Air Line, from Charlotte to Atlanta. It had been
obliged to issue notes to retire its floating debt in 1883,[1] but had
no earnings apart from dividends on the stock which it held, and
no expenses other than its cost of administration and the interest
on the notes above mentioned and on its floating debt. There
was a possibility, nevertheless, that the maintenance of the company involved the Richmond & Danville in unnecessary outlay,
and caused a certain loss of efficiency through indirectness of control. The Terminal Company had originally been necessary because the Richmond & Danville could by its charter hold stock
in none but connecting lines. By 1885 this prohibition had been
removed, and there was open an opportunity to consolidate the
system.

Early in 1886 the directors of the Richmond & Danville appointed a committee to report a plan of union with the Richmond
& West Point Terminal.[2] Apparently this committee recommended the elimination of the Terminal Company; for in April
it was known that the Richmond & Danville was trying to buy
from the Terminal the stock of certain of the more important
branches which it had formerly controlled.[3] In that month the
Richmond & Danville leased the Virginia Midland Railway [4]
and the Western North Carolina; in May it took over the Charlotte,
Columbia & Augusta and the Columbia & Greenville; in June
the Northeastern of Georgia; and in October the Washington,
Ohio & Western, or a total of 1483 miles out of the 1839 held by
the central corporation.[5] At the same time the Richmond & Danville transferred into its own treasury $13,617,400 in stock and
bonds of subsidiary companies, giving in return 25,000 shares of
the Terminal's own stock, and a guarantee of the Virginia Midland's general mortgage bonds. This done, the Danville Railroad
threw the rest of its holdings of Terminal stock upon the market;

---

[1] Chron. 36: 56, 1883.   [2] R. R. Gaz. 18: 138, 1886.   [3] Chron. 42: 575, 1886.
[4] The Richmond & Danville guaranteed interest on some $12,500,000 of Virginia
Midland bonds.
[5] Cf. Poor's Manual for 1887.

where they were bought by investors who knew nothing of the above transactions. The operation left the Terminal high and dry. It was of no further use to the Richmond & Danville, for that company had made arrangements with its branch lines direct; and it could not launch upon an independent existence, because the greater part of its mileage was in its rival's hands.

Fortunately for the small Terminal holders it so happened that men of large wealth and resourcefulness were interested with them. Under the leadership of these capitalists the Terminal Company began in its turn the purchase of Danville stock. It may have been that the East Tennessee group who had acquired a majority in 1883 had meantime parted with their holdings, or members of that syndicate may have sold in 1886 to take advantage of a favorable price.[1] At any rate, 25,000 shares were rapidly acquired, and the control of the company obtained. This done the new Terminal interests turned to the East Tennessee, Virginia & Georgia. Negotiations were at once begun, and culminated in an agreement in 1887 by which the Brice-Thomas group sold 65,000 shares of East Tennessee first preferred for $4,000,000 in cash and 50,000 shares of new Terminal common. Since the Tennessee first preferred elected a majority of the directors this ensured control. At the same time the Richmond Terminal provided for its floating debt, and for the purchase of the balance of the Richmond & Danville shares outstanding.[2]

[1] The very high average price of $200 per share was reported to have been paid. R. R. Gaz. 18: 825, 1886; cf. R. R. Gaz. 19: 162-3, 1887. The Terminal Company issued $5,000,000 new preferred and $9,000,000 common stock. Of this it sold the preferred and $7,500,000 of the common, giving to every holder of 100 of its shares the right to subscribe to the extent of one-third of the par value of his stock, and to receive for his subscription 33⅓ shares of the new preferred and 50 shares of common. Then to the $5,000,000 cash thus secured the Terminal Company added the $1,500,000 common stock left from its $9,000,000 issue, and turned the whole over to the Richmond & Danville in payment for the securities which it had purchased. R. R. Gaz. 18: 825, 1886.

[2] The floating debt amounted to $3,161,325 when Mr. Sully assumed the presidency, and $1,708,700 of it matured January 1. Chron. 44: 401, 1887. To provide for it, and for the Richmond & Danville shares, $5,500,000 6 per cent collateral trust bonds were issued, secured by East Tennessee first preferred, Richmond & Danville stock, Columbia & Greenville stock, Virginia Midland stock, and Western North Carolina bonds; and also $16,000,000 common stock. The bonds were sold for cash and the returns applied to the East Tennessee purchase and to the floating

Thus was the Richmond & West Point Terminal Company saved, and the principal railroads east and west of the southern Appalachians still kept under common control. The new grouping was weaker than the old, however, in that it did not include the Coast Line railroads. It was also imperfect as regards the nature of the control possessed over the East Tennessee, Virginia & Georgia. It has been said that the Richmond Terminal held a majority of the first preferred stock of this latter road.[1] By the terms of the Tennessee reorganization of 1886 this stock was to have the right for five years to elect a majority of the directors, unless before that time it should have received 5 per cent dividends for two successive years. This gave control to the Terminal Company; but it plainly made a control precarious which rested, as this did, on ownership of first preferred alone. In 1887 4 per cent was paid in dividends, and in 1888 5 per cent. In 1888, accordingly, a lease was drawn up, and the Richmond & Danville took the operation of the road for ninety nine years. For four years it agreed to pay over 33⅓ per cent of the gross earnings; for five years more 35 per cent; and so on until 37 per cent should be reached. And, further, it guaranteed that the percentage allowed should be sufficient to pay all the East Tennessee's fixed charges, including 5 per cent annually on the first preferred shares outstanding.[2]

It cannot be denied that the ethics of the Tennessee's lease were questionable. The East Tennessee reorganization had invested the first preferred stock of that company with temporary authority. To use this to bind the property for years to come was neither fair to the other stockholders, nor in accordance with the spirit of the reorganization plan. We need not, therefore, be surprised at the prompt application for an injunction and for the appointment of a receiver which occurred.[3] In a circular to the second preferred and junior stockholders the opponents of the lease urged that its consummation would constitute an abuse of power on the

debt; $5,000,000 of the stock went for East Tennessee first preferred; and the rest for Richmond & Danville common, Washington, Ohio & Western stock and income bonds, and for other purposes. Chron. 44: 149, 1887. Also Poor's Manual, 1890.

[1] It was reported that the East Tennessee first preferred stock had been offered to the Norfolk & Western before the Richmond Terminal acquired it.

[2] Chron. 47: 410, 1888.   [3] Chron. 47: 532, 1888.

part of the existing board; that it was entirely in the interests of the first preferred stockholders; that under no circumstances could the junior stockholders derive any income from the lease; that it failed to provide other safeguards and was in many respects improvident and imperfect. In one suit before State Chancellor Gibson at Knoxville, Tennessee, emphasis was laid on the statutory prohibition of the consolidation of competing lines. In another, petition was even made that the holders of the first preferred stock be enjoined from electing a majority of the board of directors at the approaching meeting.[1] Chancellor Gibson handed down two vigorous opinions. He refused to enjoin the voting of the first preferred stock, on the ground that the plaintiffs had been in possession for two years of stock certificates which bore on their face the conditions and agreements under which they were issued, and that the complaint was not justified, either in law or equity.[2] But he held that the East Tennessee had no power under its charter to lease its road as it had done; that the combination of the East Tennessee and the Richmond & Danville was forbidden by the law of Tennessee against the consolidation of competing lines; and that similar prohibitions in the laws and constitution of Georgia were so stringent as to imperil the East Tennessee's charter in case the lease should be carried through.[3] This effectually checked the lease. After Chancellor Gibson's first opinion the East Tennessee election had been held and the arrangement with the Richmond & Danville approved.[4] After his second the lease was cancelled, and the management of the East Tennessee restored to its own officers.[5] The Richmond Terminal was still left in control of the property. It was forced, however, to secure a majority of all the East Tennessee stock outstanding if it wished to make its control permanent, and it was prevented from using the power temporarily given a section of the stock to bring about a ninety-nine-year arrangement distasteful to the majority.

Master of the Richmond & Danville, the East Tennessee, and their allied lines, the Richmond Terminal now took one step further; it acquired the Central Railroad & Banking Company of

---

[1] Chron. 47: 532, 1888; Ry. Rev. 28: 663, 1888; R. R. Gaz. 20: 778, 1888.
[2] Chron. 47: 625, 1888. [3] Chron. 47: 663, 1888.
[4] Ry. Rev. 28: 679, 1888. [5] Ry. Age, 13: 788, 1888.

Georgia. The importance of this was very great. The Central Company owned the most considerable of the lines in Georgia and Eastern Alabama. It stretched from Savannah and Port Royal on the Atlantic coast to Spartanburg, South Carolina, on the north; to Atlanta, Birmingham, and Montgomery on the west; and to Albany, Georgia, and to Columbia on the south. Its system had been formed by a consolidation in 1872 of the Central Railroad from Savannah to Macon with the Macon & Western from Macon to Atlanta,[1] and was compact, ably managed, and profitable. Previous to June, 1847, the Central Railroad Company had paid seven dividends aggregating 10.68 per cent. From June, 1847, to June, 1889, the Central Railroad and the Central Railroad & Banking Company which succeeded it, had paid seventy-five dividends aggregating 337.5 per cent,[2] besides stock dividends of 8 per cent in 1854 and 12 per cent in 1861, and a dividend of 40 per cent in certificates of indebtedness in 1881. It was paying 8 per cent in 1888 when the Richmond & Danville was paying 5, and the East Tennessee was congratulating itself on the 5 per cent which it was able to turn over to its first preferred stock.[3]

So fruitful a piece of railroad property was naturally looked on as desirable, especially since its acquisition was to free the East Tennessee from one of its most dangerous competitors. From a traffic point of view, nevertheless, the advantages of a consolidation were doubtful. The local business of the Central was likely to be little increased by a merger. The through business was in danger of being decreased. The Central lines ran on the whole east and west. It was to their interest to carry freight from Georgia, Alabama, and the West to Savannah, and thence to send it north by way of the Ocean Steamship Company which they controlled, and from which they obtained in 1889 one-fifth of their total net earnings; while the Richmond Terminal's interest was to send

---

[1] Cf. Central Railroad Company *vs.* Georgia, 2 Otto, 665. The Central Railroad was granted certain exemptions from taxation, and the question came up in 1874 whether the right to these exemptions was surrendered by consolidation with the Macon & Western, and whether, if not, they extended to the Macon & Western as well as to the original company.

[2] Including 67 per cent paid in Confederate notes during the war.

[3] See Ulrich B. Phillips, *op. cit.*, chap. vi, for the early history of the Central of Georgia Railroad System.

this traffic north by land so as to secure for its own railroads the long haul. The advantages to the Terminal of a union depended on the price at which the Central Railroad could be acquired. The purchase was made, and the price was a high one. And this price was paid, it was freely charged, not in pursuance of an honest though mistaken judgment, but in order to allow a large personal gain to individual capitalists who were interested in both the Central and the Terminal Companies.

Among the most prominent owners of Central of Georgia stock at this time were members of the Logan-Rice group of financiers, who had begun to accumulate holdings at least as early as 1886. The average price which these parties paid was later estimated at 130, and their holdings were apparently secured with a view to resale at a higher figure. At any rate, when 40,000 shares had been purchased, a double operation was put through. The shares bought were turned over, with $400,000 cash, to a newly formed "Georgia Company," and for them $4,000,000 in 5 per cent trust bonds and $12,000,000 in Georgia Company stock were received in exchange. And, second, a vigorous campaign was entered upon to secure control of the Richmond Terminal. Sully resigned the Terminal presidency in April. For his vacant place the Logan-Rice people offered General Alexander of the Central of Georgia, and the Terminal management supported John H. Inman. The struggle which ensued was most extraordinary. The existing board of directors charged the Central group with trying to unload their Georgia Company's stock upon the Terminal system; and the Logan-Rice party insinuated that the purchase of the East Tennessee Railroad had been the occasion of fraudulent profits to the Terminal directors.[1]

---

[1] The following is representative from a pamphlet issued by the Rice Committee:

"The matter of the purchase of sixty-five thousand shares of the first preferred stock of the East Tennessee Railroad Company and the circumstances attendant thereon.

" 1st. Why did the directors of the Terminal Company purchase sixty-five thousand shares of that stock at par, when fifty-five thousand and one shares would have been sufficient to have given the Terminal Company a majority of that stock, the minority stock at that time selling at about eighty?

" 2d Why was the minority stock of the Danville Railroad Company purchased at the same time at a price which then amounted to about two hundred dollars per share, being a premium of one hundred per cent?

" 3d. Is it true that the majority of the committee appointed for the purpose of

"We understand," declared the directors, "that a majority of the names thus far proposed by the parties soliciting proxies to be cast for directors and president of this company are gentlemen who are well known to be the owners of a majority of the stock of the Georgia Company, which owns railroads whose business and interests are at all points of our system in competition with and antagonistic to the business and interests of this Company; any diversion of traffic, or exercise of influence favorable to the Georgia Company at the numerous competitive points would work incalculable injury to your prosperity. . . . If on the other hand the preponderance of the Georgia Company's interest in this Company should result in a sale to and purchase by your Company of the Georgia Company stock owned by these gentlemen, it would necessitate the issue of many millions of your common stock, or some kind of obligation taking precedence of that stock, the effect of which upon the value of your property you are fully competent to judge." [1]

The general election of the Terminal was held on May 31, and Mr. Inman was elected president for the remainder of the unexpired term.[2] The Rice party was apparently overwhelmingly defeated. In reality its activity and the presence of its friends in the councils of the victors resulted in the successful sale of the Georgia Company securities. In October, 1888, little over five months after the directors' circular of April 6, the Richmond Terminal took over the Georgia Company stock at $35 a share and allowed its owners to withdraw successfully from their speculation. Subsequently it also took the Georgia Company bonds from the bankers who had purchased them.[3] This left Inman, Hollins, and the rest a profit of $60 a share on their original investment. It meant for the Richmond Terminal a direct annual loss which there was very little prospect

negotiating the purchase of the stock of the East Tennessee Company consisted of directors of the Terminal Company largely interested in the minority stock of the Danville Company?" Chron. 46: 579, 1888.

[1] Chron. 46: 449, 1888. The opposition pamphlet is reprinted in Chron. 46: 579, 1888. It contained thirteen heads, each of which charged or insinuated fraud on the part of the existing board of directors.

[2] Chron. 46: 699, 1888. The vote was 298,006 to 94,645. For resolutions condemning the action of the minority see Ry. Rev. 28: 332, 1888.

[3] Chron. 47: 499, 1888.

of making good. To provide for the $4,000,000 in bonds and the 120,000 shares of stock acquired, this latter issued approximately $8,200,000 of 5 per cent collateral bonds bearing an annual interest charge of $410,000. Now both the stock and the $4,000,000 of bonds were a lien on 40,000 shares of Central of Georgia stock and depended altogether upon the dividends declared on these by the Central Company. The Central never paid over 8 per cent, or a total of $320,000 on 40,000 shares. The difference between this and $410,000, or $90,000, constituted a direct loss which the Terminal pledged itself to meet each year. If the victory of the friends of the company in May is to be considered a genuine one, one wonders what price the owners of the Georgia Company would have charged had the election gone the other way.

With the Central of Georgia, the East Tennessee, and the Richmond & Danville under its control the Richmond Terminal could look for still further extension. In 1890 it acquired control of the Erlanger group of roads from Cincinnati in the north to Chattanooga, thence to Meridian, Mississippi, thence to Vicksburg, Mississippi, and to Shreveport, Louisiana. At the same time it took in the Louisville Southern, which joined Louisville with the Cincinnati lines.[1] In 1888 the Richmond & Danville had concluded a close alliance with the Atlantic Coast Line,[2] and arrangements had been made for terminal facilities at Norfolk.[3] In 1889 it leased the Georgia Pacific, and two years later, when this road reached Arkansas City, it executed a traffic agreement with the Missouri Pacific.[4] In 1891 the Georgia Pacific leased the Central Railroad & Banking Company

---

[1] The Erlanger or Queen & Crescent system comprised the following roads: Cincinnati Southern (336 miles); Vicksburg & Meridian (142 miles); Vicksburg, Shreveport & Pacific (189 miles); New Orleans & Northwestern (195 miles); Alabama Great Southern (295 miles). Total mileage, 1157. The road actually acquired was that of the Cincinnati Southern and Alabama Great Southern between Cincinnati and Meridian (about 631 miles); a close working contract being concluded with the rest. *Ry. Age*, 15: 230, 1890. The East Tennessee made payment by the issue of $6,000,000 5 per cent collateral trust bonds, put out jointly by the East Tennessee and Richmond & Danville Companies and secured by deposit of the shares purchased. *Chron.* 50: 560, 1890. For a monograph on the Cincinnati Southern Railway the reader is referred to a study by J. H. Hollander in the Johns Hopkins University Studies for January–February, 1894.

[2] *Chron.* 46: 828, 1888. [3] *Ry. Rev.* 28: 386, 1888; *Ibid.* 397, 1888.

[4] *Ry. Age*, 16: 76, 1891.

of Georgia for ninety-nine years at 7 per cent on its capital stock.[1] This immensely improved the connection of the East Tennessee with the North and West, did away with the competition of a parallel line, and afforded another outlet upon the Mississippi.

Here, then, was the Richmond Terminal system in 1890. Three great north and south lines: one from Cincinnati through Birmingham to York, over the Erlanger system; one from Bristol through Rome to Selma, over the East Tennessee, Virginia & Georgia; and one from Alexandria and West Point through Danville, Charlotte, and Atlanta to Montgomery. One of these took business from Indiana, Illinois, and the North and Central West; one from Baltimore, Philadelphia, and the East; one from both West and East; and all three opened upon the Gulf over the Mobile & Birmingham to Mobile. In addition, three parallel east and west lines: from Chattanooga to Memphis, from Birmingham to Arkansas City, and from Meridian to Shreveport in Alabama; outlets on the Atlantic coast at Charleston, Port Royal, Savannah, and Brunswick; and dominance of the local traffic of the whole territory east of Alabama, south of Kentucky and Tennessee, and north of Florida. It was by all odds the leading system in the South. It had a mileage of 8558.5 as compared with the 2383.4 of the Louisville & Nashville, and gross earnings, exclusive of the Erlanger lines, of $41,361,095, or more than twice those of its greatest competitor.

And yet, for all its size, the Terminal group was perilously near collapse. Its physical condition was poor and much of its mileage was unprofitable; its capitalization was tainted with dishonesty; and the legality of its recent combinations had not been tested in the courts. Let us quote from the results of an examination made by a well-known banking firm three years later.

"While in a general way the *main lines* of the Richmond & Danville [West Point and Alexandria to Atlanta]," said this firm in its report, "are in fair condition — better than those of the East Tennessee, excepting parts of its main line between Bristol and Chattanooga, the Cincinnati, New Orleans & Texas Pacific, and the Alabama Great Southern — nearly all the rail in both systems is too light (50 to 60 lbs. while on the main lines it should be 70 to 75 lbs.), many of the trestles need renewing, and a large number of the

[1] Chron. 52: 862, 1891.

bridges, principally on the East Tennessee system, are not sufficiently strong to warrant the use of heavy engines, which are essential to hauling long trains and operating with economy. To a very
large extent ballast is altogether lacking or insufficient in quantity.
Excepting that portion of the equipment represented by equipment
bonds or notes, the engines and cars are generally small and weak
and unsuitable for main-line service, and are also insufficient in
quantity for any considerable enlargement of business. Other appointments, such as shops, yards, etc., are, with but few exceptions,
crude and uneconomical.

"On the branches and secondary lines, especially those of the
Richmond & Danville system, the condition is even worse, little or
no effort having been made to maintain them at proper standard,
even for a moderate traffic. About 700 miles of the Richmond &
Danville secondary lines and branches (including about 200 miles
of narrow-gauge lines) are still laid with *iron rails*. On July 1st,
1892, there were 72 miles of iron rails in the *main* lines of the East
Tennessee.

"An expenditure of several million dollars should be promptly
made on these properties for equipment alone, but it is no use to do
so, even if it were possible, unless additional track and yard facilities are also provided, nor unless such enlargements of engine and
car shops be made as will permit of the equipment being kept in
order." [1]

This verdict was only reinforced by the characterization in detail
of a number of the subsidiary lines. Thus the Columbia & Greenville was termed "a collection of weak lines of constantly decreasing
value"; the Mobile & Birmingham "of no value whatever to the
East Tennessee"; and the Memphis & Charleston "valuable, but
in a condition totally unsuited to modern requirements." How the
capitalization of the system was tainted with fraud has already been
pointed out. The legality of the recent combinations had not been
tested in the courts. In January, 1889, counsel for certain unnamed
parties had a plea for a *quo warranto* presented to the Attorney-
General of Virginia.[2] The petition alleged that the purchase of the

---

[1] From the reorganization plan prepared by Drexel, Morgan & Co., dated May 1,
1893. Chron. 56: 874 ff., 1893.
[2] Ry. Age, 14: 78, 1889.

control of the East Tennessee, Virginia & Georgia Railway and of the Virginia Midland was an abuse of the powers of the Richmond & West Point Terminal . . . a violation of public policy, and an usurpation to the great damage and prejudice of the constitution and laws of Virginia. This petition the Attorney-General dismissed on technical grounds. The legality of the various mergers was soon, however, to be attacked again, and in 1889 the question was decidedly unsettled.[1]

The storm broke in August, 1891. On the eighth of that month the New York *Herald* published a vigorous onslaught upon the company. It maintained that the Richmond & Danville system had failed to earn its fixed charges by $526,560 in the year ending 1890; that this fact had been concealed by deceptive or false entries on the books which made a fictitious profit emerge by covering up the losses on auxiliary lines; that the 8 per cent dividends which had been paid on the Central of Georgia had not of late years been earned, and that the price paid for the Georgia Central stock had been grossly excessive; that the East Tennessee was just about paying its way ; and, finally, that the other recent acquisitions were either just paying their way or were showing annual deficits.[2] Color was given to the charges by the trouble caused by the floating debt. Though denied by the officials of the company, the sale of 2000 shares of Baltimore & Ohio stock held in the Terminal treasury;[3] the negotiation of a short time loan at 6 per cent and 2½ per cent commission for the Central of Georgia and the extension of another

[1] The failure of this initial suit encouraged the Richmond Terminal to take steps to make its position more secure. In February, 1889, a collateral trust mortgage of $24,300,000 was announced, intended not only to pay off the floating debt and several classes of bonds, but also to purchase the balance of common stock of the Central of Georgia and Richmond & Danville and of the first preferred stock of East Tennessee outstanding. See Poor's Manual for 1890; also Chron. 48: 764, 1889. Subsequently the company issued common shares of its own instead of bonds in exchange for the East Tennessee first preferred, and succeeded in securing nearly $2,000,000 of the outstanding issue. Chron. 49: 374, 1889. The rate of exchange was 3⅓ to 1. The Richmond & Danville shares were retired by new collateral bonds at 85, plus $26 per share in cash, and in connection with the operation more stock and $5,700,000 collateral bonds were sold on favorable terms to stockholders to provide for the floating debt.

[2] For replies by Alexander and Inman, see New York *Herald*, August 10, 1891, and Chron. 53: 224, 1891.

[3] At 97½. See R. R. Gaz. 23: 718, 1891.

loan;[1] the placing of $500,000 at 6 per cent for the Richmond & Danville; and the active financial support which General Thomas felt obliged to render the East Tennessee showed the anxiety which it occasioned.

On November 25 the directors held a meeting and appointed Messrs. Eckstein Norton, late president of the Louisville & Nashville; Wm. Solomon, of Speyer & Co.; Jacob H. Schiff, of Kuhn, Loeb & Co.; Chas. S. Fairchild, president of the New York Security & Trust Company; and Louis Fitzgerald, president of the Mercantile Trust Company, a committee to carefully inquire into and examine the condition of the Terminal properties and to aid the company in perfecting a plan of readjustment. Owing to the financial depression, they explained, "the company has been unable to sell securities based upon engagements they had made prior to the period of depression and to pay for necessary equipment and improvements. A large floating debt has in this way been accumulated, but each of our important railroad systems is solvent. . . . After maturely considering the whole situation, we felt it wise to invite the gentlemen whose names appear . . . to aid us in perfecting the best plan for a permanent adjustment of our affairs." [2]

The committee reported provisionally on December 8. It then stated that it was essential to the proposed plan of relief that the elections of all the subordinate companies in the Richmond Terminal system should be postponed till after the Richmond Terminal affairs were settled, and requested that financial provision be made for the employment of an expert or experts in the examination of the properties and accounts. It was understood that the committee's plan was to make a considerable assessment on the stockholders. The board of directors refused to respond and the committee therefore withdrew.[3]

[1] Chron. 53: 674, 1891.

[2] R. R. Gaz. 23:870, 1891. The composition of this committee was severely criticised, partly on the ground of the relations of Norton and Schiff to the Louisville & Nashville and to the Norfolk & Western respectively, and partly on the ground that the other members were creditors only and had no interest other than the repayment of their loans. It would seem, however, that the property was likely to have fared better in the hands of reputable New York bankers than in the hands in which it had formerly reposed.

[3] Chron. 53: 922, 1891.

The next day the stockholders selected Mr. F. P. Olcott to appoint a new committee to take up the work.[1] They were not in favor of radical action, and Mr. Olcott expressed the opinion that there was no necessity for measures so stringent as those which the Schiff-Norton Committee had had in mind. It was but natural that at this point there should have been some delay. Meetings were held, expedients for raising cash discussed, and a reorganization plan was gradually whipped into shape. It was not, therefore, until March 19, 1892, that the public were informed what Mr. Olcott and his backers did consider that the situation required. The main points of the elaborate scheme which was then proposed were as follows:

First, a consolidation of the Richmond Terminal, Richmond & Danville, and East Tennessee properties. The Central of Georgia and the Erlanger systems were not to be included in the reorganization, but the interest of the Richmond Terminal and the East Tennessee in their stock was to be made subject to a new mortgage.

Second, a reduction in fixed charges.

Third, the sale of securities to pay off the floating debt.

Consolidation of properties was found advisable for several reasons. "While some of the companies show a surplus of earnings," said the committee, "in many instances it has been impossible to apply such surplus earnings to make up deficiencies arising from the operations of other companies. The committee finds that the various systems have not been operated throughout for the common benefit of the controlling interest, but that they have competed among themselves for business, each system maintaining separate organizations for obtaining business. . . . In the judgment of the committee the only adequate remedy which can be adopted is to unite the several corporations, as far as practicable, in one system under one management, and to consolidate their obligations."

In order to unify the system the committee proposed three great issues of new securities as follows:

$170,000,000 four per cent first mortgage 35-year gold bonds, to be issued by a new corporation representing the consolidation of the

[1] Chron. 53: 969, 1891. The members were: F. P. Olcott; Col. Oliver H. Payne; F. D. Tappan, president of the Gallatin National Bank; W. H. Perkins, president of the Bank of America; and Henry Budge, of Hallgarten & Co. These gentlemen appointed Messrs. Olcott, Budge, and Perkins a sub-committee to prepare a plan. Ry. Rev. 32: 14, 1892.

Richmond & Danville Railroad Company and the Richmond & West Point Terminal Railway & Warehouse Company.

$70,000,000 five per cent non-cumulative preferred stock.

$110,000,000 common stock.

In general, the new bonds were to exchange for old bonds and the new common stock for old common and preferred, while the new preferred stock was to be joined in varying proportions with each of the other issues to make the exchanges look attractive. Thus, for the Richmond & Danville consolidated 6s were offered 120 per cent in new bonds and 45 per cent in new preferred; for the East Tennessee first mortgage 7s 120 per cent in new bonds and 45 per cent in new preferred stock; for the Richmond Terminal common stock 100 per cent in new common and 50 per cent in new preferred. This arrangement was not rigidly adhered to. Some of the poorer of the outstanding stocks received new common only, and the Richmond Terminal preferred was given par in new bonds besides a bonus in preferred. These were, however, exceptions. The principle which determined the various ratios of exchange is more difficult to discover. It was not that of equivalence of return. The plan did not attempt to allow to each holder a chance at the same receipts which he had formerly enjoyed while reducing the amount which he could demand, but gave sometimes more than this and sometimes less. And the variations from what might be called a normal ratio did not always correspond with the relative security of different issues as indicated by their market quotations. For instance, the East Tennessee first 7s sold in December, 1891, at 113½ and the Richmond Terminal collateral 6s at 83; yet the former received 120 per cent and 35 per cent and the latter 120 per cent and 40 per cent in new bonds and preferred stock respectively. Again, the Atlanta & Charlotte first 7s sold in October, 1891, at 118½ and received under the plan 120 per cent in bonds and 40 per cent in preferred stock; the Richmond & Danville consolidated 6s sold at 109 and received 120 per cent and 45 per cent. It is clear that the committee desired to reduce the interest which the various classes of bonds should have a right to demand, and that it expected to make compensation by means of preferred stock on which payments should be made if earned. So much of its scheme was commendable. On the other hand, the rates of exchange of old securities for new were in many cases ill-advised. The reduction in fixed charges was to be $1,819,837, although by the exchanges alone the capitalization was to be increased by over $50,000,000. The charges on the system had amounted in 1891 to $9,474,837.[1] Net earnings had been $8,744,736. Fixed charges under the plan were to amount to $7,666,000. As a matter of fact they would have been greater than this, for some of the old bonds would have remained outstanding, and the estimate did not include interest on any bonds issued for improvements. The floating debt was to be retired by the sale of new securities, namely, $18,235,800 new first mortgage bonds and $6,382,530 preferred stock. These were to net $14,588,640, or sufficient to cancel a debt of $6,310,000 and car trusts of $2,369,564 and to provide a balance for miscellaneous uses. A syndicate guaranteed the sale, but holders of stock or of collateral trust 5 per cent bonds were to be allowed to subscribe up to 16 per cent of their holdings at the rate of $800 for one new mortgage bond and $350 in new stock. New bonds to a maximum of $10,000,000 were to be issued only for the acquisition of additional property, while beyond this the vote of a majority of preferred stock was to be required to authorize any additional mortgage on property covered by the first mortgage.[2]

Such was the plan laid before securityholders. It proposed a considerable reduction in fixed charges, though probably not enough to put the company out of danger, and a large increase in new securities. It failed because it imposed losses upon the wrong parties. As between the various classes of bonds its terms were frequently inequitable. As between the bonds and the stock it altogether favored the latter. It levied no assessment, it compelled no subscription to new securities, and in three cases only did it announce an intention of reducing the nominal value of the stockholders' holdings.[3] The original time limit for deposits was set at April 14,

[1] This excluded the Central of Georgia and the Alabama Great Southern. The figure was based on existing bonded debt, floating debt, and rentals. It included car trust payments, but excluded taxes, which were included in operating expenses, and excluded also the interest on securities owned by the system or the various corporations composing the system.

[2] The plan in full is reprinted in Chron. 54: 487, 1892.

[3] Consider for instance the treatment of the Richmond Terminal preferred stock. This was quoted in December, 1891, as low as 45. The plan accorded it 100 per

1892. This was subsequently extended, but without effect, and on May 16 the Olcott Committee announced that the plan had failed.[1]

The collapse of this attempt at readjustment was a blow to those who had hoped for a speedy and amicable reorganization of the Richmond Terminal system. On the same day that failure was confessed the stockholders met and appointed Messrs. W. E. Strong, Samuel Thomas, and W. P. Clyde a committee to confer with the Olcott Committee to ascertain what had best be done. A week later General Thomas reported a plan for the reorganization of the Richmond & Danville alone. The Richmond Terminal Company, he said, should be wound up and be succeeded by a new company with $43,000,000 of preferred stock and $70,000,000 of common. The present 6 per cent bonds should be given 170 in new preferred stock; the present 5 per cent bonds and preferred stock par in new preferred stock; and the present common should receive par in new common and be compelled to subscribe for $8,000,000 collateral trust two-year 6 per cent notes at 92½.[2] This amounted to an assessment of 10 per cent upon the common. It was not proposed to pay off the floating debt with the proceeds of this assessment, but to buy the claims held by bankers, and, if necessary, foreclose these claims and take possession for the stockholders. If the full amount should not be subscribed by the stockholders the preferred stock was to have the right to make subscription for the balance, and to take the securities that would have gone to the non-paying common stock; and the common stock not subscribing was to have no rights to the common stock of the new company.[3]

That this scheme was much more radical as well as more limited than the Olcott plan appears upon its face. No serious attempt was

cent in new bonds and 20 per cent in new preferred stock. *Per contra*, the Richmond & Danville consolidated 5s were quoted the same months at 75 and received 100 per cent in new bonds and 40 per cent in new preferred. Was it any wonder that the holders of prior liens refused to come in?

[1] Chron. 54: 846, 1892.

[2] These notes were to be secured by the same securities that were then pledged to secure the floating debt and were to be exchanged for $170 in new preferred stock if the plan should prove successful.

[3] Ry. Age, 17: 414, 1892. It was not proposed to retain control of the Central of Georgia, but instead certificates of aliquot parts in the holdings of the Georgia stocks were to be issued to each stockholder, making him the actual owner of his proportionate share.

mâde to carry it into effect. On suggestion of General Thomas the stockholders' meeting voted that a consulting committee of fifteen be appointed by the chair to confer with the committee of three, and then adjourned subject to call.[1] The enlarged committee found that application had been already made to Messrs Drexel, Morgan & Co. by a number of prominent banking firms, asking that they enter upon the work of reorganization. It therefore dropped the Thomas plan and joined in the petition. Drexel, Morgan & Co. on their part agreed to undertake an examination of the Terminal property,[2] but four weeks later replied that while in their opinion a reorganization was feasible, the lack of assurance of support from Mr. Clyde made them unwilling to undertake the task.[3]

At this point efforts at reorganization were checked. One plan had failed, one had been formulated but not pushed forward, and the task of creating a third had been refused by the banking firm which was apparently best able to carry a plan to a successful conclusion. For a time now the field was left to the disputes between members of the Richmond Terminal family, which made up in bitterness for what they lacked in the matter of valuable result. Mention will be made only of the wrangles between the Central of Georgia and the other parts of the system.

The Central of Georgia had been placed under a receiver of its

[1] This committee was subsequently enlarged and became known as the "Independent Committee of Seventeen."

[2] Chron. 54: 888, 1892.

[3] Ibid. 55: 23, 1892. On July 6, Chairman Strong, of the Advisory Committee of Seventeen, appointed Messrs. George F. Stone, J. C. Maben, and W. E. Strong a sub-committee to further consider reorganization. Chron. 55: 59, 1892. Subsequently Mr. Strong appointed Messrs. Coppell, Manson, and Plant a committee to look after the Terminal 5s, and Messrs. Bull, Goadby, and Cyrus J. Lawrence a committee to look after the 6s. Mr. Strong, as chairman of the Advisory Committee, was ex-officio member of each. The first of August Messrs. Thompson Dean, Albert B. Boardman, and Charles P. Huntington were appointed a committee by the holders of between 50,000 and 60,000 shares of stock and other securities of the Richmond Terminal system, "for the purpose of removing the obstacles which now stand in the way of a fair and equitable reorganization of the Richmond & West Point Terminal Railway & Warehouse Company and its constituent corporations, and to this end to employ attorneys and to take all necessary steps to secure the appointment of permanent receivers, who will be in the interest of no clique or faction in said companies." Chron. 55: 216, 1892. See in this connection Ry. Rev. 32: 521, 1892.

own some two weeks before the publication of the Olcott plan. Some months later this receivership was made permanent, and the Richmond Terminal was enjoined from voting the 42,200 shares of Central stock which it held. It can scarcely be said that the withdrawal of the Central of Georgia from the Terminal system was unwelcome to the latter. Already the Richmond & Danville had refused to carry out its guarantee on the Central's stock unless that company should deposit bonds to cover an alleged sum due from it,[1] and President Oakman had hastened to inform General Alexander, the temporary Central receiver, that the Richmond & Danville would not operate the Central of Georgia after the end of the temporary receivership.[2] When, however, the Central not only insisted on withdrawal, but asked Judge Speer, of the District Court of Macon, Georgia, to appoint a receiver for the Richmond & Danville Railroad on the ground that that company was insolvent and was indebted to the Central in the sum of $2,459,670,[3] prompt action was made necessary. Application was made to Judge Bond of the Circuit Court for the Eastern District of Virginia, and on June 16 this magistrate appointed Messrs. F. W. Huidekoper and Reuben Foster receivers of the Danville road.[4]

"This appointment of receivers by Judge Bond," explained the parties responsible,[5] "is not only not inimical to nor in opposition to any plan for the financial reorganization and rehabilitation of the Danville system, but will be found to greatly facilitate and aid any plan of reorganization, while if the Georgia court had obtained possession of and jurisdiction over the Danville system this would have been rendered practically impossible. . . . The necessity for such action," they continued, with a touch of pathos, "will be further appreciated when it is known that for some weeks past the Richmond & Danville Company has not been able to keep either a dollar in bank or in its safes within the state of Georgia, because every such dollar has been attached or garnished by parties alleging claims

---

[1] R. R. Gaz. 24: 33, 1892. The deposit was made and the dividend paid.

[2] Ibid. 24: 237, 1892.   [3] Chron. 54: 965, 1892.

[4] It will be observed that although the minority stockholders of the Central of Georgia objected to the Terminal's stock control they were not averse to having the precise terms of the lease to the Georgia Pacific carried out: that is, to being guaranteed 7 per cent upon their stock.

[5] W. P. Clyde, etc.

against the company, and even the money sent by express for the liquidation of pay-rolls has been attached in the hands of the express company, and in every instance enormous bonds have been required to release such moneys. . . ." [1]

The temporary securing of their position by the receivership allowed the Danville people to hit back at the Central in its weakest point — the details of the sale to the Terminal of the Georgia Central Company. On August 19 the Advisory Committee of Seventeen of the Terminal securityholders declared that the investigations of their sub-committee showed that certain trustees of the company, with their friends, had profited to the extent of between three and four million dollars in this operation. [2] Toward the end of the year tender of the Georgia Company stock and bonds was made back to the original vendors and was refused. [3] In December suit was begun to set aside the purchase on the ground that there had been no ratification sufficient in law or equity to bar the stockholders from cancelling the transaction. The plaintiff charged that "the said combination and plan so formed by and between its president and divers of its directors [referring to the purchase of the Georgia stock], confederating with the other syndicate defendants for the purpose of selling their unsalable and discredited securities to the plaintiff at such prices as yielded them an enormous profit and necessarily imposed on plaintiff a heavy yearly loss, was contrary to equity and good conscience, and that the pretended contract dated October 26, 1888, . . . and all the acts done in pretended purchase of the stocks and bonds of said Georgia Company . . . and the taking from the assets and money of the plaintiff of over $7,000,000 cash . . . to put into the pockets of the said faithless directors, the syndicate defendants, and their confederates, were all acts planned . . . and per-

[1] Chron. 54: 1010, 1892. Messrs. Huidekoper and Foster were also appointed receivers by courts in Virginia, North Carolina, and South Carolina. For reply by President and Receiver Comer, of the Central, to Clyde's statement, see Chron. 55: 22, 1892.

[2] Ry. Rev. 32: 549, 1892. The committee also stated that the Terminal Company had been made to purchase $1,800,000 Georgia state bonds at par and interest, which paid only 3½ per cent a year, although the company was unable to borrow money at less than 6 per cent; that the drafts of the directors to a large amount were paid by the company, and that no vouchers were on file to show how this money was expended.

[3] Chron. 55: 938, 1892.

formed by said Inman, or under his direction, in the execution of such original fraudulent scheme, combination, purpose, and confederacy. . . ." And so the plaintiff prayed the court to decree the contract of purchase void.[1]

These accusations and counter-accusations, justified though many of them were, had little direct bearing on reorganization. In this progress had completely ceased. At the same time some progress was urgently required. The Richmond Terminal, the Richmond & Danville, and the Central of Georgia were in the hands each of a different set of receivers, unpaid interest was piling up, and the year 1893 was to show a marked decline in earnings. Necessity and mutual distrust dictated a second appeal to Drexel, Morgan & Co. to undertake the rehabilitation of the property. On February 2, 1893, the following letter was addressed to the firm in question:

Messrs. Drexel, Morgan & Co.,

Gentlemen: Since the time you were previously requested to take up the reorganization of the Richmond Terminal system much time and thought have been devoted to its affairs, and we realize that adverse financial conditions and also the present general distrust of all plans for the restoration of this system require that, to be successful, its reorganization must be undertaken by parties possessing the confidence of both the securityholders and the public, and also the financial strength sufficient for its accomplishment. We therefore ask you to take up this reorganization of the Richmond Terminal and its allied properties, each pledging you our personal support and aid in full confidence that the securityholders will support us in this request.

We appreciate the labor and responsibility connected with this undertaking, and are therefore willing to do all in our power to give you full control of the reorganization, as suggested in your letter of June 28,[2] and to advise our friends and the securityholders generally to deposit their securities, without requiring the assurances customary in such cases.

Very respectfully,

WM. P. CLYDE,
GEO. F. STONE,
WM. E. STRONG,
J. C. MABEN,
THOMAS F. RYAN.

---

[1] Chron. 55: 1078, 1892. For replies of defendants see Chron. 56: 414, 1893, and Ibid. 972, 1893.

[2] This was the letter finally declining to undertake the reorganization in 1892 because of lack of assurances of support.

This letter was accompanied by a letter from F. P. Olcott, president of the Central Trust Company, pledging his support. Inasmuch as lack of the assurances contained in this correspondence had alone prevented Drexel, Morgan & Co. from undertaking the task proposed the previous year, their prompt though conditional acceptance was not surprising. A definitive engagement to attempt the work followed on April 12.[1] The enlistment of Drexel, Morgan & Co. in the reorganization provoked general satisfaction. Mr. Hollins, of the Central of Georgia reorganization committee, expressed his pleasure in having responsible parties to deal with not connected with any past differences.[2] The directors of the Richmond Terminal urged all classes of securityholders to deposit, and the Clyde Committee was emphatic in its recommendation. It was recognized that the situation was the most favorable which could be hoped for. No group of Southern railroad financiers seemed capable of producing a fair reorganization plan, and it was also probable that no plan from such a source, however fair, would have received a sympathetic welcome. Drexel, Morgan & Co., on the other hand, were both capable and sure of a hearing.

There was remarkably little delay in making public the Drexel-Morgan plan. Less than three weeks after their final acceptance of responsibility, though about three months after the correspondence of February 2, the firm published a comprehensive plan, to the examination of which the next few pages may be devoted. The principles of this plan of May 1, 1893, were simple, and were clearly and convincingly set forth. The property to be considered was to be that of the Richmond Terminal, the Richmond & Danville, and the East Tennessee. The Central of Georgia was to be omitted. The imperative needs of these properties the plan declared to be two:

First, the provision of a large sum for the physical improvement of the system;

Second, the reduction of fixed charges to an amount which the companies could earn.[3]

---

[1] The correspondence appears in full in Chron. 56: 207, 1893, and Ibid. 56: 622, 1893.

[2] Ry. Rev. 33: 95, 1893.

[3] These needs had already been emphasized by the Olcott plan.

The physical condition of the above roads in 1893 was extremely bad. "One obvious trouble . . . is," said the plan, "that their maintenance and repairs have been neglected. Another is that, while nearly all the lines in the United States have been steadily substituting solid roadbeds, heavy equipment, and other modern facilities for the light and ineffective appliances formerly in use, these lines, because of the constant drain to which they were subject for the obligations assumed, and from the necessities of the Terminal Company for the payment to it, as dividends, of every available dollar with which to meet its own obligations, have not been in a financial condition to keep up to the times in this respect, and now they find themselves so far behind as to be, to a considerable extent, unqualified to handle business with economy, or to compete successfully with other lines." [1] The financial condition was little better. The absolute fixed charges of the Richmond Terminal, the Richmond & Danville, and the East Tennessee systems, viz., interest on bonds held by the public, rentals, equipment notes, and sinking funds, and interest on floating debts, receivers' certificates, etc., the plan declared to amount annually to about $9,900,000. The entire net earnings for the fiscal year ending June 30, 1893, were estimated at $7,000,000. The result was a deficit for the year of about $2,900,000. This state of affairs required serious sacrifices from somebody. The Olcott plan had illustrated the folly of laying the burden largely on well-secured senior bonds. The Drexel plan proposed to demand the necessary concessions from the junior bonds and from the stock. "About $74,000,000 of the bonds and guaranteed stocks of the Richmond & Danville and the East Tennessee systems held by the public," it continued, " are on

---

[1] Lack of space forbids a full statement of the criticisms which the Drexel plan had to make upon the physical condition and financial practice of the Richmond Terminal properties. The following is from the plan, section 9: "As an example of the manner in which accounts have been kept, it may be mentioned that in the operating expenses of the entire Richmond & Danville system only $20,000 were charged for renewal of rails in the fiscal year ending June 30, 1890, and not a dollar in the fiscal years ending June 30, 1891 and 1892, respectively. In seven months under the receivership (July, 1892, to January, 1893, inclusive) about $600 were charged. Since that date, it is understood, about $18,000 have been charged. With these exceptions all renewals of rails were charged to construction accounts. Renewals, properly to be included in operating expenses, would be at least $100,000 to $150,000 per annum." Other instances, almost as bad, could be stated.

properties which are believed for the most part to afford adequate security, and for this or other reasons this plan has not sought to disturb them. About $50,000,000 (mostly recent issues) are junior liens, inadequately secured, or else are on new or branch lines of uncertain earning capacity, and the holders, in self-preservation, must make such reasonable concessions as the situation necessitates, taking compensation therefor in preferred or common stock of the new company. . . ."

The tools of the reorganization were to be the following new issues:

$140,000,000 first consolidated mortgage and collateral trust 100-year 5 per cent bonds, secured by mortgage and pledge of all the property of the new company. This total might be subsequently increased to acquire the whole or part of the Georgia Central system, or to acquire the ownership of the Cincinnati Southern Railway or any other line as a substitute therefor.

$75,000,000 5 per cent non-cumulative preferred stock.

$160,000,000 common stock.

"The general theory of adjustment of disturbed bonds," said the plan, "is to substitute for them the new 5 per cent bonds to such an extent as is warranted by earnings and situtation of the properties covered by the present mortgages, and the new preferred stock for the remainder of the principal. In some cases, where the bonds are on properties of no actual and little prospective earning capacity, a more severe reduction is necessary. In several instances, where the bonds are on properties which are likely to improve more rapidly than other disturbed parts of the system, this fact is recognized, and an extra allowance is made in compensation. Finally, in one or two cases, where the bonds are on properties the loss of which would adversely affect the rest of the system, a proper recognition is made of this fact." In practice not only bonds and preferred stock, but preferred and common stock, or even common stock alone were exchanged for old securities of little value.

This provided for old securities but not for cash requirements. To raise cash three devices were resorted to, all of which bore entirely on the junior securityholders or on the stock. The most direct was the levying of an assessment. Terminal common stock was assessed $12.50 per share, East Tennessee first preferred $3, second preferred $6, and common stock $9; new preferred stock being in each case given in return. This distribution was based on the idea that the stockholders of each railroad should provide for its floating debt. The floating debt of the Richmond & Danville was about $7,000,000, that of the East Tennessee about $3,000,000, and that of the Richmond Terminal about $100,000. But since the last named held practically all of the Richmond stock and a considerable proportion of the East Tennessee, its stockholders were saddled with a total of $8,300,000 or an equivalent of $12.50 per share, while the East Tennessee was taxed proportionately. The rest of the cash requirements were covered by the sale of $8,000,000 new bonds at 85, and $33,333,000 new common stock at 15. Depositors of all classes of Terminal securities and of all classes of readjusted securities of the other systems were allowed to subscribe to the extent of $1000 in a new bond and $4000 in new stock trust certificates for each $22,000 par value of stocks or bonds deposited. The balance of the issues was looked after by an underwriting syndicate.[1]

Future capital requirements were provided for mainly by new bonds. $35,383,000 in new 5 per cents were set aside to be used only for new construction, betterments, purchase of rolling stock, and extensions and additions to the system. Not over $2,500,000 of these were to be used in any one calendar year; except that, in addition to this annual appropriation, a total of $3,000,000 in bonds might be specifically appropriated with the unanimous consent of the stock trustees, for the building of branches or extensions, if undertaken within three years after the creation of the new mortgage. All property acquired with these bonds was to be brought under the lien of the new mortgage. $8,000,000 of the cash raised by assessment and sale of securities, moreover, were to be available

---

[1] Total cash requirements, as estimated, were:

Floating debt, including equipment notes	$12,900,000
New construction and equipment during two years	8,000,000
Expenses of reorganization and contingencies	2,350,000
	$23,250,000

To be provided from:

Assessments on Terminal stock	$8,750,000
Assessments on East Tennessee stocks	2,700,000
Sale of $33,333,000 new common stock	5,000,000
Sale of $8,000,000 new bonds	6,800,000
	$23,250,000

for new construction and equipment on the Richmond & Danville and the East Tennessee. And, finally, there was provision for the limitation of new bond issues, for a voting trust and for the consolidation of the Terminal system.

"The ultimate object of the reorganization," said the plan ("excluding the Georgia Central Company from consideration), is to have the new company acquire, so far as practicable, the ownership of the Richmond & Danville and East Tennessee systems, including the various securities now owned by the Terminal Company . . . and the securities pledged for the Richmond & Danville and East Tennessee floating debt. . . .

"Both classes of stock of the new company . . . are to be issued to three Stock Trustees, who shall be appointed, on or before completion of reorganization, by Messrs. Drexel, Morgan & Co. The stock shall be held by the Stock Trustees and their successors, jointly, for five years, and for such further period (if any) as shall elapse before the preferred stock shall have paid 5 per cent cash dividend in one year, although the Stock Trustees may, in their discretion, deliver the stock at an earlier date. . . .

"No additional mortgage shall be put upon the property to be acquired hereunder by the new company, nor shall the authorized amount of the preferred stock be increased without the consent in each case of the majority in amount of the preferred stockholders."[1]

The result of all these provisions was to be a cancellation of the floating debt, a reduction in fixed charges, and a decrease in mortgage bonds; though inevitably also an increase in stock outstanding. The plan proposed to disturb $49,117,900 of outstanding bonds, or, including the Richmond Terminal 5s and 6s, a total of $65,617,900. But the new bonds which it offered in exchange amounted to $19,806,700 only. On the other hand it took $111,819,550 in stock from the hands of the public, and offered $165,559,514 new stock in the course of the exchanges.[2] This was very conservative, since the increase in total capitalization through these exchanges was less than 4½ per cent; and less too than the cash assessment for which preferred stock was allowed. Somewhat greater increase in securities

---

[1] The new company reserved the right at any time to redeem its preferred stock in cash at par.

[2] Of which $104,303,894 for stock and the rest for bonds outstanding.

appears if we consider, not only the exchanges, but the provisions of the plan as a whole; for here we must include $33,300,000 new common stock and $8,000,000 new bonds issued to retire in part the $12,900,000 of floating debt and for other purposes. Even so the net increase was only 6 per cent.[1] The natural result was a considerable reduction in fixed charges. The absolute fixed charges of the system in 1893 the plan stated to be $9,900,000. The fixed charges under the plan were to be $6,789,000. This was certainly a step in the right direction. It was the point, nevertheless, at which the plan was weakest. The clauses which have been outlined made abundant and conservative provision for cash requirements; and the sums which they allowed for future development were not on their face inadequate; but the reduction in fixed charges was less than should have been ensured. The net earnings for the year ending June 30, 1892, were $7,725,000, and those for 1893 were estimated by the plan itself as not likely to exceed $7,000,000. This would have left $936,000 over the proposed fixed charges in 1892 and $211,000 in 1893: — or a surplus of some 3 per cent in the latter year. This was altogether insufficient. It not only put out of the question dividends on the $200,000,000 of stock, but it precluded the partial improvement of the road from earnings, and left the system at the mercy of the slightest decrease in the annual returns. Compared with previous fixed charges the plan proposed noteworthy reductions; compared with the earnings of the lines involved it did not go far enough.[2]

The reception of the Drexel-Morgan plan was, nevertheless, satisfactory. Certain concessions were made to various classes of bonds, and by June 17, over 95 per cent of the securityholders had given their assent.[3] Unfortunately the earnings of the property now steadily decreased. The gross receipts of the Richmond & Danville proper were 15 per cent less in 1893 than in 1892; and Terminal system lines which had earned $6,100,000 in 1892 earned $5,300,000 in 1893, and promised to earn some $4,250,000 only in 1894. This decrease was common to the country at large. It was of peculiar

[1] The reorganization plan estimated the capitalization under its provisions at about $20,000 per mile of road owned and controlled; about $10,000 preferred stock per mile owned and controlled; about $25,000 common stock per mile owned and controlled.

[2] The plan is published in full in Chron. 56: 874, 1893.

[3] Ry. Rev. 33: 388, 1893.

importance, however, in emphasizing the weak point in the Drexel plan. From January 1 to July 1, 1893, the Terminal floating debt, exclusive of car trusts, increased $2,600,000. From July 1 to March 1 it increased at least a million more. The reorganization plan had been prepared "on the assumption that, during reorganization, the receivers of the various properties could provide for the interest charges on the undisturbed securities, as well as accumulate a sum sufficient for the interest accruing on the 'disturbed securities' as readjusted." [1] As it turned out, the receivers were obliged to make many defaults among the undisturbed securities, and saved nothing for the disturbed. Some modification of the published plan had perforce to be arranged.

These modifications were detailed in a pamphlet dated February 20, 1894. They comprised three proposals:

(1) To exclude from the reorganization certain unprofitable properties which had previously been included. Certain alterations had already been made toward this end in the exclusion of the Erlanger line, the Memphis & Charleston, and the Mobile & Birmingham. Further modification was to exclude the Northeastern Railroad of Georgia, the Macon & Northern, and five other subsidiary lines.

(2) To fund for a year or two the coupons on new bonds given for certain securities, and to provide in other cases that the new bonds should not bear interest till 1895 or 1896.

(3) To lighten the assessment on Richmond Terminal and East Tennessee common stock, and to allow to all assessed securities one-quarter of their assessment in bonds and three-quarters in preferred stock instead of all in preferred stock.

At the same time a few other modifications allowed to some bonds a more liberal grant of new securities than they had obtained in May. It was hoped by these means to raise the average earning ability of the system, while reducing the new securities to be issued. [2]

[1] Modified reorganization plan. Chron. 58: 385, 1894. Some information concerning traffic conditions in the South in 1894 is to be found in the Eighth Annual Report of the Interstate Commerce Commission, pp. 20–24.

[2] From $140,000,000 5 per cent bonds, $75,000,000 preferred and $160,000,000 common stock to $120,000,000 bonds, $60,000,000 preferred and $125,000,000 common stock. Since, however, some of the poorer properties were cut off and the terms granted to others were made more liberal, the smaller absolute amount of new securities represented a greater relative increase than before.

The temporary funding of coupons further lightened fixed charges until business should have had time to revive. "Under the plan as now modified," stated Drexel, Morgan & Co., "and assuming that one-half of the new bonds to be sold are used in 1894 and the other half in 1895, the fixed charges are estimated at about

$4,100,000 in 1894,
4,700,000 in 1895,
5,400,000 in 1896.[1]

"The depression in the South began in 1890–91. There would appear to be no reason why in a comparatively short time these properties should not very easily earn, *gross*, as much as and more than they earned in that fiscal year, viz., over $21,000,000. Operated at 70 per cent . . . there would remain, say $6,600,000 net against an interest charge of $5,400,000."[1]

The reduction in assessments was made possible by the decrease in mileage. Although the floating debt had increased $2,600,000 from January 1, 1893, and the equipment notes recorded were greater by $1,048,000,[2] yet the debt to be provided for by the modified plan of 1894 was estimated at only $12,200,000. Besides this the cash to be reserved for new construction was reduced $3,000,000, and the surplus for expenses and contingencies $1,380,000. Assessments were therefore set at $10 a share on Richmond Terminal common instead of $12.50; $7.20 on East Tennessee common instead of $9; and $3 and $6 on East Tennessee first and second preferred as before. The new securities to be sold were reduced correspondingly to $8,000,000 of bonds and $25,000,000 of common stock. Finally, the bonds to provide for new construction, betterments, and additions were reduced from $35,383,000 to about $19,000,000, of which not over $2,000,000 (instead of $2,500,000) were to be used in any calendar year. Other provisions of the earlier plan were to remain unchanged.

It was this modified plan which was carried to a successful conclusion. In principle it did not mend the weak spot in its predeces-

---

[1] The actual charges in 1895 were $4,195,000.

[2] "The increase in car trusts is due to the existence of about $1,200,000 of such obligations on the Richmond & Danville system, *which, up to the date of the plan of reorganization, had not been entered on the ledger of either the Railway Company or its Receivers, although, as it appears, they were well known.*" Modified reorganization plan.

sor of May. That plan had contemplated a surplus of $211,000 over fixed charges for 1893. This estimated charges at $4,100,000 for 1894 and net earnings at $4,250,000 on a somewhat reduced mileage. There was not to be more left for dividends and improvements than there had been before, while the cash and bond provisions for improvements were notably reduced. The concession of bonds to stockholders for one-quarter of their assessments was unsound financiering, as was, on the whole, the funding of coupons on the new mortgage bonds. The success which the modification had, nevertheless, in restoring the company to solvency, was due to the improvement in earnings which soon took place. The original plan had based its calculations on the first year of depression; the amended plan kept charges down till three years had elapsed. By that time business had begun to mend, and all danger of bankruptcy was past. Other points in either plan leave little to criticise.

The modifications to the original plan were issued on February 20, 1894. Over 75 per cent of the system bonds had assented by March 24. At one foreclosure sale after another the reorganization committee now bought in the portions of the old system covered by the plan. Suits against the Richmond Terminal had been brought under the two collateral mortgages, and on July 13, 1893, the reorganization committee bid in the pledged securities. On February 6, 1894, it bought the remaining assets of the Terminal Company; on June 15 it bought the Richmond & Danville, and on July 7 the East Tennessee, Virginia & Georgia. Two trustees' sales, one receivers' sale, ten foreclosure sales, and six conveyances without foreclosure had occurred by September, 1894, and more minor sales were in progress.[1] On June 15 the Southern Railway Company was organized with a charter from the state of Virginia, and took over in succession properties to the extent of 4607 miles.[2] Samuel Spencer was elected president. Some thirty corporations were swept away and thirty boards of directors abolished; for the Southern Railway was an operating company, and, unlike the Richmond Terminal and the Richmond & Danville, controlled but an inappreciable fraction of

[1] R. R. Gaz. 26: 613, 1894.
[2] Statement compiled by the reorganization committee. Chron. 59: 515, 1894. The mileage controlled by the Richmond Terminal system on November 30, 1892, had been 9053.3.

its mileage through the ownership of stock. The new securities were issued at the proper times, and according to the plan the common and preferred stock was turned over to three voting trustees,[1] who issued trust certificates in their stead.

This completed the reorganization of the Richmond Terminal Company so far as the principal part of its mileage was concerned. The portions of the system excluded from the plan have been to some extent bought back in later years. Control of the Alabama Great Southern was bought in 1895; the Memphis & Charleston was acquired in 1898; the Richmond & Mecklenburg was leased in 1898 and the Mobile & Birmingham in 1899; and the Northeastern of Georgia was bought in 1899. The system has not yet, however, fully regained its old position. The most important loss has undoubtedly been that of the Central of Georgia. We left this company engaged in active disputes with the Terminal management. During 1892 and 1893 efforts to reorganize it were made under the leadership of Hollins & Co. The principal difficulties were the large floating debt and the money required to put the property into good physical condition.[2] A plan was actually prepared at the beginning of 1893 and submitted to securityholders, but failed because of that same decline in earnings which had caused the modification of the Terminal reorganization plan. A second plan, prepared in 1894, had a better fate,[3] and in modified form was put into effect. The *Railroad* was sold at auction in 1895, the Central of Georgia *Railway* was organized to take its place,[4] and the corporation entered upon a new career which we have not space to follow.[5]

As for the Southern Railway, the years from 1895 to 1907 have brought it prosperity. It has extended considerably in mileage. Besides reacquiring lines which formerly were part of the Rich-

[1] J. P. Morgan, Charles Lanier, and George F. Baker. See Chron 59: 836, 1894, and Ibid. 880, 1894.

[2] See statement by Receiver Comer Chron. 55: 805, 1892.

[3] Chron. 60: 1008, 1895.

[4] With a charter from the state of Georgia.

[5] The capital stock of the Central of Georgia Railway was held by the Richmond Terminal Reorganization Committee until the spring of 1907. It was then sold to Oakleigh Thorne, president of the Trust Company of America, and Marsden J. Perry. Later the same year these gentlemen resold this stock to E. H. Harriman and his associates.

mond Terminal system, it has grown south to Jacksonville and Palatka, east to Charleston and to a more direct connection with Norfolk, and west from Louisville to East St. Louis. It has further joined its Louisville-East St. Louis line to Chicago by acquiring a half-interest in the Monon, and to the rest of its system by a half-interest in the Cincinnati, New Orleans & Texas Pacific; and it has bought control of the Mobile & Ohio, which stretches through four states from East St. Louis to Mobile. Instead of 4392 miles as operated on June 30, 1895, it now reports 7546. The earnings of the system have increased more rapidly than its mileage. The revival of business after 1897 occurred with singular force in the South, and seems to have introduced there a new industrial era. As a result, the Southern's gross earnings have trebled and its net earnings have been multiplied by two. Passenger receipts, which were $4,329,499 in 1895, have become $14,683,006 in 1907. Freight receipts have increased from $10,816,024 to $37,368,095.

It has been this increase in earnings which has at last allowed some of that margin for improvements which the reorganization plans weakly attempted to secure. And accordingly, large sums have been expended. Maintenance of way charges are now over $1000 per mile instead of $630. Expenses per locomotive mile have increased from 4.19 cents in 1895 to 7.54 cents in 1907; expenses per passenger car mile from .83 to 1.03 cents; and expenses per freight car mile from .47 to 2.18 cents. It is true that locomotives and cars are larger to-day and that rails are heavier, but this fact is far from accounting for the difference. Not only has the existing plant been kept in good repair from earnings alone, but distinct improvements have been made. New rail has been laid, additional ballast put in, wooden trestles filled or replaced with steel. It was estimated in 1906 that $5,000,000 had been spent in betterments and charged against income up to that time, besides some $15,000,000 more paid for equipment out of earnings. Meanwhile considerable sums had been spent from capital account. The reorganization plan allowed for some $19,000,000 of new bonds to be sold at the rate of $2,000,000 per year.[1] Of these the company had sold $13,000,000 for improvement of the property by February 1, 1906, besides disposing of some $23,000,000 of equipment obligations.

[1] The original estimate was $19,000,000. The amount available seems to have been finally $20,000,000.

The appreciation of the need for still more liberal expenditure led in 1906 to a comprehensive plan for the issue of new capital. Under date of February 1, the company submitted to its voting trustees [1] a scheme for a $200,000,000 mortgage, of which $15,000,-000 were to be issued at once and the rest were to be reserved. Of the immediate issue $4,962,774 were to refund payments for equipment hitherto made and charged to capital; $3,501,000 were to refund investments in securities of, and advances to, subordinate companies, as well as to be used for the acquisition of property not heretofore funded; and $6,536,226 were for double track, revision of grades, new yards, shops, etc. Of the securities reserved, $65,164,000 were for refunding purposes: $20,000,000 for certain subsidiary lines: and $99,834,000 to go, first, for betterments and improvements on the entire system and for new equipment in amounts not exceeding $5,000,000 in each year; and second, in exchange for first mortgage bonds not exceeding in amount the actual cost of railroads and terminals hereafter to be acquired. In other words, about one-half of the total issue is to go, sooner or later, for improvements, and the rest for refundings and for new acquisitions.[2] It was believed that the Southern could readily pay the interest on the increased immediate issue without endangering dividends on its preferred stock, and that the subsequent increases in earnings would more than provide for whatever additions to charges might occur. Negotiations for the placing of the new securities were concluded with J. P. Morgan & Co. at a reported price of 96½.

The results of the expenditures for improvements have been remarkable. In 1895 the Southern Railway had in use 623 locomotives; in 1907 the number was 1536. In the former year there were 487 passenger cars and 18,924 freight cars; in the latter there were respectively 995 and 56,225.[3] Only 370 miles of track in 1895 were over 65 pounds in weight per yard; more than 3100

[1] The voting trust was extended in 1902, in respect to a majority of the stock, for a period of five years. See Chron. 75: 442, 1902, and R. R. Gaz. 34: 826, 1902.

[2] Annual Report, 1906.

[3] The narrow-gauge equipment included in these figures is as follows:

	1895	1907
Locomotives	9	4
Passenger cars	9	4
Freight cars	86	106

surpassed that limit in 1907. It is nevertheless in its inability to handle the business offered it that the Southern has provoked sharpest criticism. Over 3600 miles of its system still have rails weighing 62 pounds or less to the yard; — that is, rails incapable of meeting modern operating conditions. Only 206 miles of double and 1981 of side track exist. Equipment appears to be still inadequate. Signals are imperfect, and speed and promptness seemingly impossible to attain. The late tragic death of Mr. Spencer was a forcible illustration of the deficiencies of the road which he had done so much to improve.

The earning power of the system cannot yet, therefore, be said to be secure. Moreover, the capitalization of almost $72,000 per mile,[1] as well as the less dense railroad business in the South, the slight construction of many of the Southern Railway lines, the lack of adequate facilities which compels an operating ratio of 76 per cent, and the absorption of minor roads less prosperous than the main stem, — all these factors have kept down the net surplus from operation. On the other hand, the management is making an earnest attempt to raise the standard of the property. Bonds and notes to the par value of over $32,000,000 have been sold to provide for additions and improvements during the past year, and a very great change for the better has taken place. Dividends on the preferred stock have been paid since 1897. As the country develops, and as the sums spent upon improvements come more and more to have their effects, a dividend upon the common stock will be paid. The near future is more likely to witness the cessation of dividends upon the preferred.

---

[1] "It will hardly be claimed," said the Interstate Commerce Commission, of the Southern Railway in 1900 (8 I. C. C. Rep. 583), "that the cost of reproducing that property in its present state would equal $40,000 a mile."

CHAPTER VI

ATCHISON, TOPEKA & SANTA FE

Charter — Strategic extensions — Competitive extensions — Effect on finances — Raise in rate of dividend — Reorganization of 1889 — Acquisition of the St. Louis & San Francisco and of the Colorado Midland — Income bond conversion — Receivership — English reorganization plan — Mr. Little's report— Final reorganization plan — Sale — Subsequent history.

THE Atchison, Topeka & Santa Fe Railroad has been reorganized twice, in 1889 and in 1893–5; the first time without, but the second time after a foreclosure sale. The keynote of its history has been extension. It was the enterprise of the men in control before 1889 which gave it the position and power it holds to-day, but it was also that enterprise which necessitated its first reorganization by imposing upon it heavier burdens than it could bear.

Chartered in Kansas in 1863, the Atchison spread west, southwest, south, and northeast. It received some aid from the state of Kansas in the shape of a grant of lands, but depended primarily on the investment of private capital. Kansas itself was not, in 1870, a very encouraging field for railroad building. It had been admitted as a state only in 1861, and could boast for the most part of less than two inhabitants to the square mile; — although settlement was pushing westward with considerable rapidity, and stores of mineral wealth had been discovered in Colorado. The railroad in those days had to create its own traffic, and population followed the means of transportation. The peculiarity of Kansas was a central position, which lent itself to schemes of the most far-reaching nature. A railroad reaching from one end of the state to the other might almost equally well have been extended to California, to Chicago, or to the Gulf; and could be sure in time, if it survived, of the carriage of a vast volume of traffic out in every direction from the Central West. The Atchison managers saw this opportunity, and courageously and persistently endeavored to realize it; — part of the project they announced, and part they kept back till the fitting time should come.

The systematic extension of the Atchison Railroad may be divided into four parts:

(1) The construction through Kansas to Colorado, to save the charter, then down the valley of the Rio Grande to Albuquerque.

(2) The securing of a connection with the Pacific Coast by construction, lease, or traffic agreement.

(3) The connection with the Gulf.

(4) The connection with Chicago.

As the system neared completion, and its territory came to be invaded by other roads, there were added to this systematic extension what may be called competitive extensions, consisting largely in the construction of branch lines, and multiplied beyond anything which the country could need for years to come. This sort of building was most prominent from 1884 to 1888 and will be considered in its place.

The first stretch of road was built with few difficulties or complications. It was commenced in 1869, and, after numerous delays, it reached the western border of the state of Kansas on December 28 of the same year; from this point it went on more leisurely, first west and then southwest, to Albuquerque.[1] These early miles were paid for from the proceeds of both stocks and bonds. From Albuquerque a variety of routes presented themselves. The Southern Pacific had by that time built to El Paso, and it was feasible to extend the Atchison to that point and to rely on a traffic agreement for the handling of the western business. Or, building to Deming near El Paso, Atchison might have extended its line down the river valleys in the northwestern part of Mexico to Guaymas on the Gulf of California. Or, Atchison might have built directly west from Albuquerque. All three of these routes were considered, and all three were eventually carried out.[2]

The connection with the Southern Pacific was not a very difficult one to make, and the Atchison reached Deming in March, 1881. By the traffic agreement then concluded the Atchison secured the use of the Southern Pacific tracks from Deming to Benson, Arizona, and arranged to build south into Mexico from this point; while the Southern Pacific was allotted 51 per cent of the through rate on traffic passing over Southern Pacific lines.[3] This formed the second through route from the East, and in September, 1881, it

---

[1] This route followed roughly the old Santa Fe Trail.

[2] Chron. 29: 583, 1879.   [3] Ibid. 33: 23, 1881.

took one-quarter as much business as the Central Pacific. It was also the first of Atchison's projected routes to be completed. The line to Guaymas was added by purchase. Instead of building, Atchison exchanged its stock for the stock of the already existing Sonora Railroad in the proportion of one to two, and guaranteed the interest on the Sonora first mortgage 7 per cent bonds.[1] This made up for the lack of an independent line to the coast further north. The total of Sonora stock was $5,400,000, requiring $2,700,000 Atchison stock in exchange. The total first mortgage 7 per cent bond issue was $4,050,000. With the railroad came a subsidy of $2,608,200 (American gold), equal to $11,270 (Mexican) per mile. This subsidy kept cropping up in Atchison finance for some time, and was finally adjusted in 1896 by the transfer to the company of $1,159,800 in 3 per cent bonds of the Mexican Interior Consolidated Debt.

For the direct route President Strong sought the help of the St. Louis & San Francisco, and the use of the charter of the Atlantic & Pacific which it owned. The Atlantic & Pacific was a road incorporated in 1886, with a charter to build from St. Louis to California. In spite both of its charter and of its name it had never gone further west than Vinita, in the northeast corner of Indian Territory.[2] President Strong and the Frisco now agreed to continue construction under the name of the Atlantic & Pacific, both from Vinita and from Albuquerque. The Atchison was to be given a half-interest in the charter, directors were to be chosen equally from the two companies, and the cost was to be met by a $25,000,000 loan, which the Atchison and the Frisco were to guarantee jointly but not severally.[3] Before the new construction neared completion, however, the St. Louis & San Francisco fell under the control of Messrs. Gould and Huntington, who, as owners of the Texas & Pacific and the Southern Pacific respectively, naturally disapproved of the plan to extend the Atlantic & Pacific to the coast. The Atchison, therefore, agreed to build no further west than the Colorado River. At that point the Southern Pacific was to meet it with a line from Mojave. The Southern Pacific gave to the Atlantic

---

[1] Chron. 34: 315, 1882, Circular of Sonora Railroad Company to stockholders.
[2] Chron. 29: 630, 1879. Statement by Vice-President Baker.
[3] Ibid. 29: 630, 1879.

& Pacific an interest guarantee on its bonds to the extent of 25 per cent of the gross earnings derived from Atlantic & Pacific through business, and the latter road retained all its rights for a line in California.[1] This proved unprofitable, for the Southern Pacific persistently diverted traffic to Ogden and El Paso, and in 1884 still another arrangement was made. By this —

(*a*) The Atlantic & Pacific bought the Southern Pacific division between the Needles (the Colorado River) and Mojave, 242 miles, for $30,000 per mile, and, until such time as title could be given by the discharge of the mortgage upon it, took a lease at an annual rental of 6 per cent on the purchase price.

(*b*) The Atlantic & Pacific secured trackage and traffic rights and facilities between Mojave and Oakland and San Francisco, as well as the use of terminals at the latter point.

(*c*) The Atchison (and the St. Louis & San Francisco likewise) agreed to buy from the Pacific Improvement Company first mortgage bonds and other securities of the Atlantic & Pacific of the par value of $3,096,768, at the actual cost to the Improvement Company, to wit, $1,524,356.

To complete the connection to the coast the Atchison built from Waterman, some seventy miles east of Mojave on the Atlantic & Pacific, to Colton on the Southern Pacific, and secured control of the California Southern from Colton to San Diego.[2] In 1885 entrance was obtained to Los Angeles by lease of the Southern Pacific track between Colton and that city.[3]

The money for this rapid progress was obtained by the sale of both stocks and bonds, but on the whole stock predominated. The directors rightly considered it much more conservative to issue stock and sell it at par than to load the road down with a heavy debt in the shape of bonds; and what is more, they were able to make good their word, and to sell stock at or near par in spite of the risk incident to operations such as the Atchison was conducting and the frequent bonuses or stock dividends declared.

By 1884, then, Atchison had reached the Pacific coast. The next great steps were the extensions to Galveston and to Chicago. The

[1] Chron. 34: 243, 1882.   [2] Chron. 41: 444, 1885.
[3] Annual Report, 1885, contains a discussion of the Atlantic & Pacific and of the California Southern projects.

year of entrance to Los Angeles the Atchison did not cross the southern boundary of Kansas. Certain of its stockholders were, however, unofficially interested in the Gulf, Colorado & Santa Fe, which ran from Galveston on the south to the Indian Territory on the north, roughly 200 miles. In 1884 a charter was obtained for the Southern Kansas Railway Company, a corporation organized solely to build south from Arkansas City. The same year the Gulf, Colorado & Santa Fe obtained permission to stretch north. The two roads met at Purcell in the summer of 1887.[1] In 1886 the Gulf, Colorado & Santa Fe was formally brought in. Gulf stock then amounted to $4,560,000 and bonds had been issued to a limit of $17,000 per mile. For the entire capital stock, subject to the above encumbrance, Atchison agreed to pay $8000 a mile in Atchison stock, par value.[2] The final move was to get into Chicago. "The Atchison Company has been much too conservative during the last few years," said the *Chronicle*, "and thus has allowed its territory to be invaded." The first intent was to build direct. There were incorporated, in Illinois the Chicago, Santa Fe & California Railway Company, and in Iowa the Chicago, Santa Fe & California Railway Company of Iowa. In 1887 the Atchison was able to purchase the Chicago & St. Louis Railroad, between Chicago and Streator, with a branch to Pekin,[3] and to save itself construction between these points. The whole line was opened for traffic in May, 1888.[4]

This completed Atchison's systematic extensions before 1889. From a local road in Kansas it had become a through route, taking freight over its own rails from Chicago to Galveston and to the Pacific coast. But especially in the latter eighties competition had become keen; and to its strategic extensions Atchison was obliged to add competitive building on an enormous scale. Of the 7000 miles in 1888, over 2700 had been added since January, 1886, and had been built, not to tap new sources of traffic, but to defend what was thought to be Atchison's rightful territory by means of a desperate war of rates. "About three or four years ago," said a competent observer, "a mania seized three great corporations (Atchison, Missouri Pacific, and Rock Island) to gridiron Kansas with railroad

---

[1] Chron. 42: 462, 1886; Annual Report, 1887.   [2] Ibid. 42: 518, 1886.
[3] Annual Reports, 1886 and 1887.   [4] Annual Report, 1888.

iron, and each tried hard to see which could cover the most ground, without regard to the character of the ground, the result [being that] railroads were built where they would not be required for ten years to come." [1] Such roads could not be expected to pay, and in fact did not. Even in the case of better planned extensions, the lines had to be built in an unopened territory, the traffic of which had yet to be developed. In Indian Territory, Oklahoma, and Arizona, the bulk of the country had less than two inhabitants to the square mile; in New Mexico and Lower California only one-half of the area was more thickly settled; and it was largely from this southwestern corner that local traffic for the Atchison had to be built up.

The method of financiering these competitive extensions varied: sometimes the parent company guaranteed the principal and interest of the branch-line bonds; sometimes it took these into its treasury and issued collateral bonds against them; sometimes, perhaps more frequently still, it leased new roads for a rental equivalent to the annual interest on their bonds. If the branches could have earned their fixed charges the burden on the Atchison would have been nominal, but as in large part they could not it was real and serious. In 1888 there were actually paid in rentals, interest on Sonora Railway bonds, and on sundry railway bonds, $2,361,300. Large sums were carried to capital account. In 1888 there was an accumulated account of "due from sundry leased, controlled, and auxiliary roads in construction and general account" (net) $13,558,678, including various cash current construction and other charges, which was carried as an asset, but which in reality consisted of advances from which there was little or no hope of return. Besides the claims for interest the parent company had in practice other claims to meet. Where a branch failed to earn operating expenses, as often happened, sums had to be advanced to keep the road and rolling stock in repair. Thus the item "due from auxiliary roads in current traffic and operation accounts" amounted in 1888 to $1,008,554. Bills and accounts payable the same year were $6,553,775, and accrued interest, taxes, and sinking funds totalled $915,337. The following table shows vividly the effect upon the system of the rapid extension of the years 1884 to 1888:

[1] Ry. Rev. 29: 511, 1889.

Total System

	1884	1888
Mileage	2,799	7,010
Bonds	48,258,500	163,694,000
Stock (Atchison)	60,673,150	75,000,000
Gross earnings	16,699,662	28,265,339
Operating expenses	9,410,424	21,958,195
Net earnings from operation	7,289,237	6,307,145
Net profits, excluding dividends	5,147,883	def. 2,933,197
Net profits, including payments for dividends and interest on floating debt		def. 5,557,323

Whatever may be said as to the necessity of extension, it is evident that the position of the system by 1888 had changed for the worse. This last-named year was a bad one, it is true, but certain evils of which the directors then complained were permanent, and should have been permanently allowed for. Some realization of the fact that the Atchison might be going too fast appeared in the financial journals of the time. "Were these undertakings less solidly backed," said the *Railway Age*, "there might be apprehension that enterprise was being pushed too far and too fast."[1] But on the whole the rapid growth and enormous extent of the system seem to dazzle beholders. "The career of this company," said the *Railway Age* again, "has been one of the marvels of railway enterprise, and it would be unsafe now to attempt to fix a limit to its extension or to the ambition of its Napoleonic president and its bold and enterprising directors."[2]

In 1887 the directors increased the rate of dividend from 6 to 7 per cent.[3] The action was thoroughly unjustifiable, and the rate

[1] Ry. Age, 12: 107, 1887.   [2] Ibid. 12: 325, 1887.

[3] This increase in dividend gave rise to sharp and well-merited criticism. The directors defended their action as follows:

"In forming a just opinion of this matter," said they, "it is necessary to recall to the stockholders the statement made in the circular of July 30, 1887. . . . It was stated in the circular referred to that for the six months ending July 1, 1887, the net earnings exceeded by more than $1,200,000 the net earnings for the first six months of the year 1886, that the earnings were still increasing, and what has always been true in the past may be expected this year also; namely, that the revenue of the second six months of the year will be considerably in excess of that of the first six months. . . . It will . . . be seen that . . . the year 1887 formed a remarkable exception to what had hitherto been the regular course of Atchison's earnings; the second half of that year showing an increase over the first half of only $278,096 gross, and $204,144 net. . . . Drouths, failure of crops, excessive competition,

was speedily again reduced. By the end of 1888 the main company was liable to be called on any year to the extent of $8,625,365, which was the amount of interest on auxiliary roads either guaranteed or payable as rentals. In four years the mileage of the Atchison system had increased 150 per cent; its bonded indebtedness 239 per cent; its fixed charges 216 per cent; and its gross earnings only 69 per cent; while the deficits on its branch lines were obviously not matters of bookkeeping, and the value of interchanged business was not equal to the increased burdens which the subsidiary lines imposed. The floating debt mounted up, as is usual in times of trouble. From a total of $3,317,446 in 1884 it increased to $8,076,059 in 1888. To offset it the directors secured in October, 1888, subscriptions to a $10,000,000 issue of "guarantee fund," three-year notes. Not all of the amount authorized was to be sold at once, but from time to time Atchison was to call on subscribers to take part of their subscription, and the notes were to bear 6 per cent from the time they were put forth.[1] For the rest, the directors economized as much as possible. Salaries were cut 10 per cent in every branch of the service, beginning with the president, and the unlucky 7 per cent rate of dividend was reduced to 6 per cent, to 2 per cent, and then to nothing at all in successive quarters. None of these expedients proved sufficient. In fact, the situation was so critical that nothing short of a general reorganization could probably have secured the radical reduction in fixed charges which the company required.

In September, 1889, accordingly, Messrs. Libby, Abbott, Pea-

continually decreasing rates, unwise legislation, strikes, and other calamities have befallen us as they have other Western roads; but your directors could not know in advance that any of these unfavorable conditions would have to be met, much less that they would all have to be met at one and the same time." Annual Report, 1888.

This defence was altogether unsatisfactory. An increase in the dividend rate is too important to be justified by anything but earnings actually in hand. Moreover, the conditions which the directors held responsible for the decline in Atchison earnings were either well known at the time when the dividend was declared, or could easily have been anticipated. It was even alleged that the decrease in business which the annual report for 1888 disclosed was due to lessened carriage of company material to the West for construction of new track, and not to crop failure or other decline in general business. See R. R. Gaz. 21: 327, 1889.

[1] Chron. 47: 472, 1888. The use of $3,000,000 of the notes was specifically deferred.

body, and Baring were appointed a committee to consider the broad question of financial and general reorganization,[1] and in October a plan for the complete rehabilitation of the company was brought forward. The obligations with which the plan had to deal are indicated in the following table:

Obligations of the Atchison Company in 1889

	Principal	Interest
Bonds, guarantee fund notes	$160,786,000	$9,203,620.00
Contingent issue of additional bonds	775,000	38,750.00
Car trusts	1,445,660	86,739.60
	$163,006,660	$9,329,109.60
Less interest on bonds and guarantee fund notes owned by the Company		253,340.00
		$9,075,769.60
Sinking Fund		359,000.00
Taxes		1,221,000.00
Rentals		502,000.00
		$11,157,769.60

Of the bonds outstanding $56,498,000 were direct loans upon the Atchison's main lines, bearing anywhere from $4\frac{1}{2}$ to 7 per cent, and $104,288,000 were bonds upon some of the thirty-two subsidiary corporations for whose obligations the Atchison was responsible.

The dealing of the Libby Committee with this situation was intelligent and comprehensive. It proposed an increase and simplification of securities, a decrease in fixed charges, and a cancellation of the floating debt. In place of the forty-one classes of bonds outstanding it suggested that two grand issues be put forth, one of 4 per cent general mortgage bonds to the amount of $150,000,000, and one of 5 per cent income bonds to a total of $80,000,000. From these issues $13,750,000 should be used to provide for cash requirements,[2] and the remainder should be employed in direct

---

[1] Ry. Age, 14: 644, 1889.

[2] Cash requirements were (Circular No. 63, Oct. 15, 1889):

To retire outstanding lease warrants	$1,445,660
To expend on incomplete construction of existing lines, and for new equipment as required	5,000,000
To pay floating debt	3,554,340
	$10,000,000

And the provision for cash subscription was

General mortgage 4s	$12,500,000
Income 5s	1,250,000
	$13,750,000

retirement of old obligations. The exchange of some $216,000,000 of new bonds for $163,000,000 of old was to mean an increase in securities outstanding, but since interest on only part of the new bonds was to be obligatory fixed charges were to be less than they had been before. The managers figured on what the property could earn, good times or bad, and capitalized this sum into 4 per cent general mortgage bonds. They then calculated the difference between this and the former return to bondholders, and capitalized the difference into income bonds.[1] Each individual bondholder, therefore, was offered a chance to receive the same return which he had previously enjoyed, although his right to demand an annual payment was limited to an amount which the road could earn.

A few points deserve to be specially noticed. The reduction in interest was sufficient to have transformed the deficit for the whole Atchison system for 1888 into a respectable surplus, providing that no dividends had been paid; but this reduction was dependent on the retention of the income bonds as optional obligations. There was no cash assessment. Had the reorganization taken place in a time of general depression, the sale of securities for cash would probably have been impossible, but the days of depression had not yet arrived. The stockholder suffered in the introduction of the principal of some $67,000,000 additional indebtedness between him and his property, although he was not called upon directly; but it should not be forgotten that for a long while the Atchison stockholders had received very liberal dividends, both in stock and in cash, and could not well complain of the moderate loss now necessary. There was no voting trust, although one was proposed, and the bonds were not even temporarily given voting power. The situation seems to have been that the securityholders thought it more to their advantage to reduce voluntarily the rate of interest than to force a foreclosure sale and take their chances; for the directors, in submitting the plan, said that they felt it necessary "to state in the strongest terms that the non-success of this proposal will inevitably result in foreclosure, with all its attendant misfortunes."[2]

---

[1] The income bond certificate is printed in full in W. A. Wood, Modern Business Corporations, pp. 237-9.

[2] Ry. Age, 14: 682, 1889.

By the end of November, although the plan had not been pro-
mulgated until well into October, more than one-half of the outstanding bonds had assented, and the directors were enabled to
announce success. Certain changes in the management had already
taken place. President Strong had resigned in September, and had
been succeeded by Mr. Allen Manville, general manager of the St.
Paul, Minneapolis & Manitoba Railway.[1] Mr. Reinhart was
credited with a large part in the construction of the new plan of
1889, and his later promotion may have been connected therewith.

After the reorganization Atchison resumed its policy of expansion, its new directors being apparently as "bold and enterprising"
as the old. In 1890 it took in the St. Louis & San Francisco, a road
running from St. Louis west and southwest through Missouri, Kansas, Arkansas, and Indian Territory, connecting at Paris, Texas, with
the Gulf, Colorado & Santa Fe, and through half-ownership of the
Atlantic & Pacific connecting Albuquerque in New Mexico with
Barstow in Southern California. The total length of the Frisco
system, exclusive of jointly owned roads, was 1329 miles, and this
constituted the largest single acquisition that the Atchison had
ever made. The terms of the purchase were highly favorable to
the Frisco shareholders, but the benefits to the Atchison were less
than was expected. Although the consolidation removed certain
difficulties experienced from the joint ownership of the Atlantic
& Pacific, and although the united roads were in a better position
to compete for transcontinental and Gulf traffic than either of them
had been before, the Atchison directors were forced to announce
in 1891 that, " with every opportunity given it to work with advantage, the property (Frisco) has failed to demonstrate its ability to
carry itself financially and to liquidate its debts; nor could it hope
to obtain such results without the provision of New Capital. . . .
This is due largely to the absence of complete and proper facilities
and machinery with which to conduct operations in the nature of
Round Houses, Machine Shops, Stations and other buildings, improved Bridges and Equipment."[2] A bond issue was needed, and
was in fact put forth, — the Atchison taking a goodly share.

---

[1] Annual Report, 1890. Economies were secured at this time through consolidation of branch lines with the main stem and in other ways.

[2] Annual Report, 1891.

Less important than this was the purchase, in 1890, of the Colorado Midland, a road 346 miles long in Colorado, valued chiefly for its ore traffic. In August, 1890, the Mexican Government resumed payment of the Sonora subsidy, on which nothing had been paid for eight years.[1] It does not seem as if at any time after 1889 the Atchison enjoyed unalloyed prosperity. The year 1890 showed an increase in net earnings of 48 per cent according to the figures given, and the directors were unhappy until they had increased the fixed charges to match, but the year 1891 recorded a falling off, and 1892 showed a comparatively slight gain over the figures of 1891. There was obviously nothing in the reported figures to cause alarm, but there was nothing which justified the payment of more than $2\frac{3}{4}$ per cent any year on the income bonds, or of any dividends on the stock.

Toward the end of 1891 the guarantee fund notes fell due. They had been issued, it will be remembered, to protect the property in 1888, and were secured by an equal amount of general mortgage 4s; but now the directors, disliking to put these 4s on the market at $83\frac{1}{4}$, decided to extend the notes for two years at par with a cash commission of one per cent.[2]

Extension of the guarantee fund notes did not increase the fixed obligations, it merely postponed a reduction; but the conversion of the income bonds of 1889 acted as a positive increase. There were $80,000,000 of these incomes, and it was in the optional character of payments upon them that the saving of fixed charges by the reorganization of 1889 had consisted. They had been issued instead of preferred stock probably because more acceptable to the bondholders; but it was early found that their use involved difficulties which had not been sufficiently regarded. By the conditions of their indenture no bonds could be inserted between them and the general mortgage 4s; they held a second lien for all time. But similarly it was difficult to put bonds after them. Their lien was on income, — interest was payable only when earned; any regular mortgage would of necessity have taken precedence. The hindrance to new issues was real and serious, and although some check on an aggressive management was salutary, yet the system required additions and improvements from time to time which could not

[1] Chron. 51: 171, 1890. [2] Ibid. 53: 474, 1891.

be supplied from current income. Under these circumstances the Atchison directors decided within three years to sacrifice the reduction in fixed charges secured in 1889 in order to obtain new capital with greater ease. "It is the opinion of the Management," said the annual report for 1892, "that the time has now arrived when all the obligations of the Company can be returned to a Fixed Basis, sufficient funds provided to take care of all Improvements . . . required for at least four years, and at the same time the junior Bonds and Capital Stock be restored to a more permanent market value with assured returns on the first, and probable balances for the latter."[1] "The Atchison plan of conversion," said Mr. Reinhart, ". . . is the completion of the reorganization plan put in effect October 18, 1889, and returns the obligations of the company . . . to a fixed and stable basis. . . ."[2]

The plan so cordially referred to provided for the issue of a new, second mortgage, 4 per cent bond, and the exchange of this security for the outstanding income bonds. The second mortgage was to be issued in two classes:

(*a*) $80,000,000. These were to exchange for income 5s, par for par, and bore a rate of interest which increased from 2½ per cent in 1892 to 4 per cent in 1896, and then remained at 4 per cent until maturity.

(*b*) $20,000,000. These bore 4 per cent and were to be issued in no greater sum in any year than $5,000,000 for specific improvements on the Atchison exclusive of the Colorado Midland or the St. Louis & San Francisco. There was reserved to the company the right, when all the above should have been exhausted, to issue more bonds of the same sort as in class B for the same purposes and on the same mileage, up to a limit of $50,000,000.[3]

The conversion plan was approved at the annual meeting in 1892, and was put into effect. The result was most unfortunate. The annual burden on the company was increased at the very time when the panic of 1893 was about to reduce railroad earnings, while the advantages of freer issues of new bonds were of little account in a year when the sale of new securities was practically impossible. Moreover, a new light was soon to be thrown on the whole opera-

---

[1] Annual Report, 1892. [2] Ry. Age, 17: 413, 1892.
[3] Annual Report, 1892.

tion by disclosures of dishonest manipulation of figures in the Atchison reports.

In 1892 and 1893 rumors of trouble were afloat, and were repeatedly and vigorously denied by Mr. Reinhart, president of the Atchison Company. Thus in June, 1893, this officer declared that "the Atchison, Topeka & Santa Fe Railroad Company, strictly speaking, has no floating debt. Its current liabilities are more than equalled by its current cash assets." In December Mr. Reinhart said again: "The interest on the General Mortgage Bonds of the Atchison Company, due January 1, will be paid. It seems hardly necessary to make this statement, because doubts as to its payment have, in my judgment, been created solely by speculators who have no substantial interest in the property." These official denials did not carry conviction, but opinions varied as to the seriousness of the situation. The *Boston News Bureau* cheerily insisted that all the Atchison needed was "days of grace" during the existing depression,[2] while in England it was thought that the rumors of a receivership were at most but premature.[3]

At the end of the year President Reinhart went to Europe to float a loan. On his return, after a failure to obtain subscriptions, a receivership was applied for and granted. It had been hoped up to the very last moment that the January interest could be met; but the refusal of English bondholders to subscribe additional capital, the failure to place a third mortgage loan in the United States, and the death of Director Magoun, one of the strong influences in Atchison's affairs, made a crash inevitable. Current obligations had mounted to over $10,000,000, credit had disappeared, and the railroad necessarily succumbed. The Atlantic & Pacific, the Colorado Midland, the Gulf, Colorado & Santa Fe, and the Southern California lines were not included in the Atchison receivership, though the Atchison receivers were given like office in respect to the Atlantic & Pacific.[4] The Gulf, Colorado & Santa Fe announced that it would continue to operate its own line, and was prepared to pay its current obligations as before.[5]

---

[1] Chron. 56: 1014, 1893; Ibid. 57: 1038, 1893.   [2] Ry. Rev. 34: 68, 1894.

[3] Ry. Times, 64: 533, 1893.

[4] See Chron. 58: 42, 1894, for an official statement of the reasons for the application to the courts.

[5] Ibid. 57: 1121, 1893. Some information concerning subsequent railroad competition during the Atchison receivership is to be found in 7 I. C. C. Rep. 61.

No sooner was failure announced than committees of bond-holders sprang up. In Boston a committee was formed with six members, including J. L. Thorndike and H. L. Higginson. In New York the Union Trust Company, the Mercantile Trust Company, the New York Life Insurance Company, Baring, Magoun & Co., and Giddes & Smith got together in a committee, with Edward King as chairman. A second New York committee, R. Somers Hayes, chairman, was formed by express invitation of the road. A directors' committee was organized, of which E. B. Cheney, Jr., was chairman. The London holders of the second mortgage class A bonds themselves formed a committee. Even before 1888 Eng-lishmen had invested heavily in Atchison, attracted perhaps by glowing stories of the business to spring up across the western plains. It was said that not only had they been influential in shaping the reorganization of 1889, but that from that date to 1893 the manage-ment had been controlled by a board elected by proxies entrusted to representatives of English interest. In particular Englishmen had become interested in the second mortgage bonds of 1892, suc-cessors to the income bonds of 1889, holding about one-half of the total issue, and they now fought for the protection of this issue as against the stock.

A plan of reorganization was early matured after the English influence substantially as follows: Either the general mortgage or the second mortgage bonds were to be foreclosed and a new company was to be formed. If the foreclosure should be under the general mortgage, overdue interest on that mortgage was not to be paid, and new securities, similar to the existing bonds, were to be issued, bond for bond. If the foreclosure should be under the second mort-gage, the company was to provide for past due interest, and was to assume the payment of principal and interest on the general mortgage bonds. The capital stock was to remain as before. There was to be a new income mortgage to the amount of $115,000,000, of which $84,000,000 were to go for the existing second mortgage A bonds, and $5,600,000 for the existing B bonds; the surplus to be given for assessments, or for the securities of such auxiliary com-panies as it should be thought advisable to acquire. These income bonds were to bear 5 per cent and were to have voting power. There was to be a second mortgage, to amount eventually to

$35,000,000; of which $5,000,000 were to be used at once to retire the floating debt and for other purposes, and $3,000,000 were to be used each year for improvements. The new stock was to be held in trust until 5 per cent per annum should have been paid in cash on the new income bonds for three consecutive years. Finally there was to be an assessment of $12 per share upon the stockholders, the proceeds of which were to go as far as necessary to pay the debts of the old company, including interest on the general mortgage.[1]

On the whole, the scheme was to put the Atchison back to the condition of 1889, and to regain the margin of safety afforded by the income bonds. So far it was acceptable enough. Conservative officers had looked askance at the income bond conversion in 1892, and this was a simple acknowledgment of the mistake. The old difficulty as to future capital requirements, moreover, was evaded by a provision for an annual increment of second mortgage bonds to take precedence of the incomes. The notable part of the scheme was the anxious care of the bondholders to protect themselves. Since their bonds had been converted from income bonds less than two years before they could not claim a large allowance for the reconversion; but as a condition of their assent to this and to the introduction of a second mortgage for $35,000,000 before their lien they demanded not only a bonus of 5 per cent in the new incomes for their holdings, but the grant of voting power to the income bonds, a stock assessment of $12 per share, and the interposition of an additional $5,000,000 of bonds between the stock and the property of which it was nominally the possessor. "It is true," said the *Railway Review*, "that the scheme contemplates the issue of income bonds which shall be given to assenting stockholders at par in return for the cash assessment, but it is a little difficult to see wherein such bonds are of very much more value than the stock of the company except that they are not subject to assessment."[2] The reception of the plan was what might have been expected. On July 30, in London, the London bondholders' committee met and passed a resolution in its favor. Having now secured, they said in substance, the substantial features for which they had contended, and although the plan was not altogether what they could have desired, they considered, after very prolonged and anxious

[1] R. R. Gaz. 26: 465, 1894.   [2] Ry. Rev. 34: 358, 1894.

negotiations, that a plan had been arrived at which was the best obtainable in the interests of bondholders.[1] Meanwhile meetings of stockholders were held in New York in protest. Resolutions were adopted condemning the plan, and a stockholders' committee was chosen.[2]

Debate was stopped by the publication in August of the report of an expert who had been selected to examine the books of the Atchison Company. Few more disgraceful instances of the juggling of figures have been brought to light in the history of American railroad finance. Whereas the reports of the company had shown net earnings steadily increasing from $7,600,000 in 1890 to $12,100,000 in 1893, being ample to meet existing charges and to pay from 2 to $2\frac{3}{4}$ per cent on the income bonds besides to the time of their conversion, Mr. Little, the expert, reported that the net earnings had never exceeded $8,085,608; and maintained that an annual deficit had occurred each year from 1894, which reached the portentous amount of $3,000,000 for 1891 alone. The condition of the company was far worse than had been imagined, and all plans had to be thoroughly recast. The following is an abstract of the report in question:

"I have already advised you verbally," said Mr. Little, "that income was, in my judgment, overstated in these several years (since '89), to the extent of $7,000,000 or more, and I now confirm this specifically. These overstatements may be classified as follows:

"(1) *Rebates.* For the four years ending June 30, 1894, the debits for rebates to shippers on the Atchison system aggregated $3,700,776, and on the St. Louis & San Francisco system $205,879, or a total of $3,906,656.

"This sum was charged, not to the earnings from whence it came, as it should have been, but to an account entitled, '*Auditor's Suspended Account-Special,*' and was reported from year to year as a good and available asset, while in fact it had no value whatsoever.

"(2) *Additions to Earnings and Deductions from Expenses.* Next in order of importance to the rebate account comes an aggregate of $2,791,000, which, on instructions from the East, was credited from time to time to the earnings and expenses respectively, but which credit has no foundation in fact. Of this aggregate $2,010,000 was added to earnings and $781,000 deducted from operating expenses, the sum of the two being debited to '*Auditor's Suspended Account.*'

" (3) *Improvements.* The sum of $488,000 was in the period under consideration transferred, improperly as I contend, from Operating Expenses to Improvements or Capital Account, these Improvements being finally closed into the account of Franchises and Property, which represents the cost of the road and property.

" (4) *Traffic Balances.* It further appears that a traffic agreement for a division of business was formed in November, 1890 (running to July, 1891), between the Atchison Company and certain other companies, whereby such other companies were charged with a balance of $305,843, which the Atchison Company was unable to collect, and which is absolutely uncollectable, and should have been heretofore written off, though it still stands as an asset, and hence must be written to the debit of profit and loss." [1]

Two facts appear from these charges on which emphasis was laid from different points of view: (1) That for four years the Atchison had been persistently violating the law by the granting of rebates. (2) That to conceal these rebates, and for other purposes, the books had been so systematically falsified as to defy detection, and to deceive not only the investing public but the whole railroad world. The report was handed to Mr. Reinhart, and an answer was requested by the following day. The answer was made, and proved inadequate; for though Mr. Reinhart pointed out some half-dozen items which he argued that Mr. Little had wrongly excluded, he explained no one of the charges directly brought against him.[2] There is no doubt at the present time that Mr. Reinhart was guilty, though perhaps because of the difficulty of fixing legal responsibility he was never prosecuted for falsification of the books. He resigned, of course, and Major Aldace F. Walker was appointed receiver in his stead. Two months later he was indicted with other officers of the company and certain shippers, not for falsifying the books, but for the illegal granting of rebates. His defence was that he had been, at the time the rebates were given, only the general auditor at Boston, and had had no part in the fiscal or executive

---

[1] Report of Mr. Stephen Little to the New York, London, and Amsterdam Committees of Reorganization, 1894.

[2] Chron. 59: 233, 1894.

business of the road.[1] The Government failed to prove connection, and the case fell through.

All this completely altered the requirements to be met by a reorganization plan. A more sweeping reduction in charges, and a more general distribution of losses was needed than before had been the case. Old proposals were laid aside once and for all, and a new scheme was built up from the beginning. The mortgage indebtedness of the Atchison in 1895 was $233,595,247, of which the first and second mortgage bonds comprised $217,258,276. The reorganization of 1889 had done its work in one respect at least, and the reorganization managers were able to concentrate their attention on two issues. The annual net earnings, according to the company's reports had been:

1890	$7,632,348
1891	7,631,598
1892	10,953,896
1893	12,126,866

but as corrected in Mr. Little's report were:

1891	$5,204,880
1892	7,853,173
1893	8,085,608
1894	5,956,615

Inasmuch as Mr. Little had discovered annual deficits of

1891	$1,964,285
1892	60,938
1893	134,825
1894	3,008,242

it was very evident that a reduction in interest charges was called for. As in 1889 the salvation of the company was sought in the substitution of securities on which payment was optional for securities bearing an obligatory charge.

Soon after Mr. Little's final report in November three of the existing committees, namely, the General Reorganization Committee, the London Committee, and Messrs. Hope & Co. of Amsterdam, joined in a Joint Executive Reorganization Committee, with Edward King as chairman.[2] With these now worked a committee chosen by the directors themselves. The result was a re-

---

[1] Ry. Times, 66: 543, 1894.   [2] Chron. 59: 878, 1894; Ibid. 59: 919, 1894.

organization plan under date of March 14, 1895. The purposes announced were:

(*a*) To reduce fixed charges to a safe limit;

(*b*) To make adequate provision for future capital requirements, subject to proper restrictions as to issue of bonds for this purpose;

(*c*) To liquidate the floating debt, and to make adequate provision for existing prior lien indebtedness shortly to mature;

(*d*) To reinstate existing securities upon equitable terms in their order of priority;

(*e*) To consolidate and unify the system (so far as practicable) and thus to save large annual expense.

It was proposed to foreclose the Atchison general mortgage . . . and to vest in a railway company the bonds, stocks, and other properties of the existing company, acquired at foreclosure sale or otherwise. The new company was to issue:

(*a*) Common Stock	$102,000,000
(*b*) Five per cent non-cumulative preferred stock	111,486,000
(*c*) General mortgage 4 per cent bonds	96,990,582
(*d*) Adjustment 4 per cent bonds	51,728,310[1]

Of the above the interest on only the general mortgage bonds was to be a fixed charge; — the stock obviously got a return only when earned, and the adjustment bonds were income bonds in fact if not in name. Additional issues to a comparatively small aggregate were provided for, but no mortgage, other than the general and adjustment mortgages, was to be executed by the company, nor was the amount of preferred stock to be increased, unless the execution of such mortgage, or such increase of preferred stock, should have received the consent of the holders of a majority of the whole amount of preferred stock at the time outstanding, given at a meeting of the stockholders called for that purpose, and the consent of the holders of a majority of such part of the common stock as should be represented at said meeting. The securities mentioned were to retire all previously existing issues. Old common stockholders were to receive share for share in the common stock of the

---

[1] In addition, prior lien bonds were authorized to a maximum of $17,000,000, of which $12,000,000 might be used if desirable in place of general mortgage bonds in the retirement of guarantee fund notes, equipment bonds, etc., and $5,000,000 for necessary improvements within five years.

new company. They were to be assessed $10 per share, and to receive for the assessment $10 in new preferred stock, while a syndicate guaranteed payment of assessments by engaging to take the place of non-assenting or defaulting stockholders. The general mortgage bondholders were to get 75 per cent of their holdings in new general mortgage 4s and 40 per cent in adjustment 4s. The second mortgage and income bondholders were to be assessed 4 per cent and were to get new preferred stock.[1] The prior lien bondholders were dealt with separately, and were to be paid either in general mortgage 4s of the additional issues (over the $96,-990,582) mentioned, or in the new prior lien bonds. If in the latter, the general mortgage bonds which would otherwise have been issued were to be held for the ultimate retirement of these bonds. Provision was made for future construction and additions by the allowance of $3,000,000 general mortgage bonds, to be issued each year to a limit of $30,000,000, and then of $2,000,000 adjustment bonds, to be issued each year to a limit of $20,000,000. Additional new general mortgage bonds, up to $20,000,000, might be issued and used in such amounts respectively and in such proportions as the Joint Executive Committee might determine, for the acquisition of the Atlantic & Pacific, the St. Louis & San Francisco, and the Colorado Midland; and for like purposes $20,000,000 preferred stock. The lien of the new general mortgage was to cover all properties which should be vested in the new company, and also any other property which might be acquired by use of any of the new bonds, but the Joint Executive Committee might, in its discretion, except from the new general mortgage the stocks and bonds deposited under the existing general mortgage, representing branch lines, the operation of which should be found to be unprofitable and an unnecessary burden to the system. A voting trust was considered, but was rejected as unsatisfactory; and the

---

[1] Second mortgage A bonds received 113 per cent in new preferred stock. Second mortgage B bonds received 118 per cent. "After careful consideration," said the plan, "it was decided to be best for the interest of those [the second mortgage] securities that they should now be converted into 5 per cent preferred stock, possessing full voting powers and preferential rights as to principal as well as interest, rather than revert to their original form of 'Income Bonds.' It was not thought that a greater assessment than $10 could be raised from the stock, and the remainder had to come from the junior bonds."

committee confined its efforts to the securing of the best possible management.

The proposed fixed charges amounted to	$4,528,547
Net earnings according to Mr. Little had been in 1891	5,204,880
1892	7,853,173
1893	8,085,608
1894	5,956,615

Thus the new charges appeared well within the earning power of the road. The plan made the following provision for cash requirements:

Assessment on Atchison stock at $10 per share	$10,000,000
Assessment on second mortgage and on income bonds at 4 per cent	3,567,644
	$13,567,644

The estimated cash requirements were:

For receiver's debt, preferred or secured floating debt of the Atchison Company, estimated as of January 1, 1895	$7,793,875
Leaving for receivers and floating debt, accrued interest and undisturbed securities, etc.,	5,773,769
	$13,567,644 [1]

This reorganization had certain interesting features. As before remarked, it sought, as did the reorganization of 1889, to replace securities, the interest on which was a fixed charge, by securities on which payment of interest or dividends should be optional. But whereas the earlier reorganization had depended on income bonds, this plan included both income bonds and preferred stock. There are several reasons why preferred stock is preferable to income bonds, and it will be remembered that a peculiar difficulty experienced from the income bonds of 1889 had arisen from the impossibility of putting other mortgages ahead of them; yet that this was not the chief obstacle sought to be avoided by the use of preferred stock at this later date appears from the current use of adjustment bonds. Provision for future capital requirements was in fact made in another way, and the question was not here involved. So far as the acceptability of the income bonds and the preferred stock respectively to the old bondholders was concerned, it should be noted that the men who received the greater part of the new issue were the holders of the old income and second mort-

---

[1] The plan of reorganization was published separately, but was reprinted in Chron. 60: 658, 1895.

gage bonds; that is, Englishmen who had already shown their preference for income bonds as opposed to stock. The chief reason for the new expedient seems to have been the desire to retain for the general mortgage holders a priority of lien, while reducing part of their holdings to the level of an optional obligation. If income bonds or preferred stock alone had been used, these would necessarily have been given to the owners both of general mortgage and of second mortgage or old income bonds; so that the former might have received a larger amount, but not any lien different in kind. By the scheme proposed, all possible interest on the securities given for old mortgage 4s was to be met before anything was to be paid on the equivalent of issues which had been inferior before the reorganization took place. Abundant provision was made for future capital requirements. That lesson had been learned once for all. Cash requirements were met by an assessment. In speaking of the reorganization of 1889 the rule was laid down that the disposal of securities for cash is impossible except at an enormous sacrifice in a time of general depression. There was widespread depression in 1895, and the reorganization managers wisely made no attempt to negotiate a sale. The amount of the assessment on the common stock was very considerably above the quoted price of the shares, but it was correctly figured that the hope of future increase in value would be sufficient to induce stockholders to furnish the sums required. Not to tax them too heavily call was made also on the junior securities. On the whole, the decrease of $5,000,000 in fixed charges more than compensated the stockholders for the additional obligations put between them and their property; their claim on the road itself was made more remote, but their chances for dividends were improved. Examination of the plan shows clearly that nothing was taken from either bonds or stock which those securities had a right to retain. The bondholders could not, in any case, have received more than the earnings of the road; and an amount equal to the return previously due them was assured, whenever the road should earn it, by the new combination of mortgage and income bonds and preferred stock. As it was, in return for an assessment they retained the right to participate in any future prosperity, a right which has proved of extreme value.

The plan was underwritten by Messrs. Baring Bros. & Co. and other strong foreign and American bankers, who assumed the liability of paying the assessment and of taking the stock.[1] The comment at the time was favorable. "On the whole," said the *Railway Age*, "we do not believe that any one who is acquainted with the properties could have expected a more satisfactory plan than that which the committee has evolved." [2] The London bondholders promptly accepted the plan. "We are disposed," said the *Railway Times* of London, "to regard the latest of Atchison reorganization schemes as a praiseworthy attempt to grapple with a very thorny problem." [3] Such opposition as there was came from a minority of the stockholders, and was directed at two points: the prevention of foreclosure, and the inauguration of an entirely new administration. It was asserted that certain old members of the board of directors who had been forced to resign by the earlier disclosures, had nevertheless secured the election of successors to perpetuate their policy and to protect their interest. With a directory so constituted, it was maintained that the stockholders would have no guarantee of important changes in the executive offices, financial policies, or business methods of the company.[4] Sharp criticism was directed to a statement of the existing board which referred to the "mistakes and misfortunes of the previous management." "Only those who believe," said the Stockholders' Protective Committee, "that gross irregularities, if not worse, have been perpetrated . . . may be relied upon to probe to the bottom the acts of the former officers of the Atchison." [5] On the other hand, the accusations of the committee were asserted by the directors to be unqualifiedly false.[6] It soon became apparent that the opposition could not muster enough votes to control an election, and although their fight had been begun in August, they had proxies by November for only 250,000 out of the 1,020,000 shares of stock. Recourse was had to the courts, and an attempt was made to secure at least a minority representation on the coming board by the enforcement of a provision for cumulative voting embodied in a Kansas law of 1879. This failed in November, 1894, and no further obstacle to reorganization was encountered.

[1] Ry. Rev. 35: 208–9, 1895.
[3] Ry. Times, 67: 482, 1895.
[5] Ry. Times, 66: 506, 1894.
[2] Ry. Age, 20: 199, 1895.
[4] R. R. Gaz. 26: 675, 1894.
[6] Ry. Rev. 34: 589, 1894.

Practically all of the assessments were paid in by September 21. On November 25 Mr. E. P. Ripley was elected president, and in the first week of December, 1895, Mr. Aldace F. Walker was elected chairman of the board of directors of the new company. On December 10, 1895, the property and franchises of the Atchison were sold at foreclosure, and were purchased for $60,000,000 by Edward King, Charles C. Beaman, and Victor Morawetz, representing the reorganization committee.[1] The Atchison, Topeka & Santa Fe Railroad Company was then organized by the purchasers pursuant to the laws of Kansas, under a certificate of incorporation dated December 12, 1895. A board of directors was elected, and by-laws were adopted. The entire estate embraced in the foreclosure sale was duly conveyed by deed of the same date as the incorporation of the company, in consideration of which the company executed a delivery to the Joint Executive Reorganization Committee of the securities acquired under the plan of reorganization. Certain subsidiary roads were subsequently foreclosed and bought in, notably the Atlantic & Pacific and the Chicago, Santa Fe & California. The St. Louis & San Francisco was not so bought in. "The question of retaining the St. Louis & San Francisco as a part of the Atchison system," said the annual report of 1896, "received very careful consideration from the Directors. . . . A series of conferences was held, which resulted in the matter ultimately presenting the alternative of the sale of our existing interest upon favorable terms, or the purchase by us of all other outstanding interests upon terms involving the outlay of a very large amount of both cash and securities. While the future control of that road was regarded as important, the financial considerations affecting the situation prevailed, and the sale was decided on the whole to be more prudent than the purchase." "With the acquisition of the Frisco," said Mr. Fleming of the Joint Executive Committee, "the fixed charges on the Atchison system of 7780 miles would have been increased from $7000 to $9000 per mile. Atchison is financially much stronger without Frisco."

This ends that part of the history of the Atchison Company which can be connected with either of its reorganizations. From 1895 to the present time the Atchison has enjoyed a rapidly increasing prosperity, due in part to the lightening of the charges upon it, in part

[1] Chron. 61: 1064, 1895.

to able management, and in part to the great increase in volume of business which has been a characteristic of the time. One or two things may be noted. A final settlement has been made of the relations between the Southern Pacific and the Atchison in the Southwest. It will be remembered that the final result of the negotiations in 1882 had been the purchase of the former Mojave division from the Needles to Mojave, but that since title could not be acquired until the maturity of the outstanding mortgages, Atchison had leased this track at an annual rental of 6 per cent on the purchase price. In 1897 this rental was cancelled. The Southern Pacific could not even then give a clear title, but exchanged a long time lease of the Mojave division against a similar lease of the Sonora Railway, the Atchison branch which reached from Deming to Guaymas. The rentals cancelled each other, and the actual transfer is eventually to take place.[1] The arrangement is mutually advantageous. On the one hand the Mojave division formed a spur of the Southern Pacific, and on the other the Sonora Railway was totally disconnected from the Atchison, so that the latter company was obliged to use the Southern Pacific's tracks to reach the property at all. In 1898 Chairman Walker of the Executive Committee was able to announce the substantial completion of negotiations for the purchase of the San Francisco & San Joaquin Valley Railroad, running from Bakersfield to Stockton, California; the former town being sixty-eight miles from Mojave and the latter something less than that from San Francisco.[2] Atchison at once began building at the Stockton end, and reached San Francisco the following year. The Santa Fe Terminal Company was then incorporated with a capital stock of $1,000,000, Atchison secured a traffic contract with the Southern Pacific, and through freight trains were run from Chicago to San Francisco on May 1, 1900, through passenger trains following two months later. Besides this there have been important extensions in Arizona and New Mexico. In 1901 the Atchison purchased two-thirds of the bonds, and practically all of the capital stock of the Pecos Valley & Northeastern Railway Company, stretching 370 miles from Texico through the southeastern corner of New Mexico to Pecos City, Texas. In July of the same year it bought the Santa Fe, Prescott & Phoenix Railroad, from Ash Fork, Arizona, to Phoenix, Arizona,

[1] Chron. 64: 609, 1897.   [2] Ibid. 67: 841, 1898.

some 195 miles. Construction has been practically completed between Belen, New Mexico, a few miles south of Albuquerque, and Amarillo, Texas, to afford an alternative and somewhat shorter route from California to Eastern Kansas. A still more noteworthy project is under consideration for a road to join the Gulf, Colorado & Santa Fe at Brownwood with the Belen line at Texico, and to open direct connection over the Atchison from California to the Gulf.

Briefly stated, the Atchison's mileage has increased from 6479 miles in 1897, to 9273 in 1907. Its gross earnings have grown from $30,621,230 to $93,683,407; its net earnings from $7,754,041 to $32,153,692; and its surplus above all charges from $1,452,446 to $21,168,724. This marvellous showing has been accompanied by heavy expenditures for improvements, so that the physical condition of the system is much better than before. Operating expenses, fixed charges, and taxes took less than 77 per cent of gross income in 1907, and a decline of over $21,000,000 can be suffered in net before interest on even the adjustment bonds becomes imperilled. It is not to be wondered at that Mr. Harriman saw fit to invest $10,395,000 of Union Pacific money in Atchison preferred stock in 1906,[1] nor that dividends of 5 per cent on preferred, and 5 per cent on common stock are being paid. The Atchison owns 1791 locomotives instead of 953 as in 1897; 1135 passenger cars instead of 622; 49,770 freight cars instead of 26,776. There has been a large increase in the capacity and power of rolling stock. The average freight train load has increased from 131 to 320 tons. Freight train mileage has grown but 35 per cent, while ton mileage has more than tripled. Thus, although the average length of haul has increased and the average receipts per ton mile have diminished, the earnings per freight train mile are actually more than double in 1907 what they were in 1897. And, finally, the Atchison is not dependent for its revenue upon any single kind of business. Coal, ore, and other mineral products yielded but 30.87 per cent of its tonnage in 1907; products of agriculture 25.34 per cent; manufactures 17.37 per cent; and products of the forest 12.12 per cent.

[1] This was not all the Atchison stock which Union Pacific interests acquired. President Ripley testified before the Interstate Commerce Commission on January 8, 1907, that two years before E. H. Harriman and his associates had secured $30,000,-000 of Atchison stock, and had caused the election of Messrs. H. C. Frick and H. H. Rogers to the Atchison directorate to represent them.

The capital account, meanwhile, has been kept from undue expansion. The funded debt has increased from $174,196,750 in 1897 to $284,171,550 in 1907, but the capital stock has decreased somewhat, and the greater part of the new bond issues have been convertible serial debenture bonds, which occasion no permanent increase in charges. It is within the last two years only that Atchison stockholders have authorized the issue of new capital on a scale commensurate with the growth of their property. In 1906 $26,060,000 in 4 per cent convertible bonds were offered to them at par, and this last year they have authorized the issue of $98,000,000 of common stock for improvements, extensions, and the like. This provides ample facilities for the future without endangering the solvency of the road.

CHAPTER VII

UNION PACIFIC

Acts of 1862 and 1864 — High cost of construction — Forced combination with the Kansas Pacific and the Denver Pacific — Unprofitable branches — Adams's administration — Financial difficulties — Debt to the Government — Receivership and reorganization — Later history.

THE construction of the Union Pacific was made possible by direct grants of lands and government bonds by Congress. The motive for the project was military and political as well as economic; on the one hand California was to be cemented to the Union, and aggression on the part of England was to be forestalled; on the other a great and fertile territory was to be opened and an additional market provided for the products of the East.

In 1862 the first act "to aid in the construction of a Railroad and Telegraph Line from the Missouri River to the Pacific Ocean, and to secure to the Government the Use of the same for Postal, Military, and Other Purposes" was passed.[1] It created a corporation to be known as the Union Pacific Railroad Company, with a capital of 100,000 shares of $1000 each, and authorized it to construct a railroad from the one hundredth meridian of longitude west from Greenwich at a point within the territory of Nebraska westward to the western boundary of the territory of Nevada. It granted the right of way, and in addition five additional sections per mile on each side of the track, plus a varying amount of United States bonds per mile, the use and delivery of which was to constitute a first mortgage on the property of the company. All compensation for services rendered to the Government was to be applied to the payment of these bonds and interest thereon; and after the road was completed, until the bonds and interest should have been paid, at least 5 per cent of the net earnings of the road was to be annually applied to the payment thereof. The directors were to be not less than fifteen in number, of whom two were to be appointed by the President of the United States. It was hoped that the offer would be sufficient to attract private capital to the un-

[1] Statutes at Large, 37th Congress, 2d Session, chap. 120.

dertaking, and when it failed in this, the inducements were increased. The Act of 1864 amended that of 1862. It reduced the par value of the shares of stock from $1000 to $100, and increased their number from 100,000 to 1,000,000. It increased the land grant from five to ten alternate sections per mile, and subordinated the government lien to the rank of a second mortgage. Only one-half the compensation for services rendered for the Government was required to be applied to the payment of the bonds issued by the Government. The directors were to be twenty in number, of whom five were to be appointed by the Federal President.[1]

It was under these main provisions that the Union Pacific Railroad was constructed. In their final shape they were intended to provide for the greater part of the cost of construction, while allowing the company to supply deficiencies by the issue of its own first mortgage bonds. Capitalization under these conditions would not have been excessive; the Government's investment would have redounded unmistakably to its own benefit, as well as to that of the country, and the corporation would have looked forward to a long and prosperous career. Three things interfered to swell the cost of the construction of the road, and with that its capitalization: First, construction was carried on during a time of high prices, swollen not only by depreciation of the currency, but by artificial conditions occasioned by the war; second, the normal level of the prices paid was raised by the speed with which the road was completed; third, construction was entrusted to a construction company, the famous Crédit Mobilier.

In its comparison of the prices of the years 1864–9, with those of 1860, the Aldrich Committee arrived, in 1893, at the following result:

Year	Food	Bar Iron Rolled	Rails, Iron	Metals & Implements exc. Pocket Knives	All Articles
1864	165.8	249.3	262.5	198.0	190.5
1865	216.5	181.1	205.5	218.7	216.8
1866	173.8	167.0	180.7	192.7	191.0
1867	163.9	148.2	173.2	178.9	172.2
1868	164.2	145.8	164.3	167.1	160.5
1869	162.9	139.0	160.9	157.9	153.5

[1] Statutes at Large, 38th Congress, 1st Session, chap. 216.

These figures may be divided by the premium on gold, in order roughly to ascertain gold prices. The index numbers then become:

Year	Food	Bar Iron Rolled	Rails, Iron	Metals & Implements exc. Pocket Knives	All Articles
1864	106.6	160.3	168.8	127.3	122.5
1865	100.1	83.7	95.0	101.1	100.3
1866	124.1	119.2	128.9	137.5	136.3
1867	121.8	110.1	128.6	132.9	127.9
1868	118.6	105.2	118.6	120.6	115.9
1869	120.1	102.5	118.6	116.4	113.2 [1]

The tables show that both currency and gold prices were much higher in 1866 than before the war, and that both remained high while the Union Pacific was being built. Wages were also above the normal, and for similar reasons. During the war the demand for men and goods of all kinds was great. After 1865 the country turned with tremendous energy to industry; and the upward swing, which was unchecked until the panic of 1873, and which was especially directed toward railroad building, maintained both wages and prices at an unusual height. Besides this, American rails were at the time in a period of transition from iron to steel; and much of the work carried through at such expense had completely to be done over within the next ten years.

The high prices were made higher by the speed of construction. The Union Pacific built west from the Missouri River, but at the same time the Central Pacific was building east from Sacramento, under similar conditions as to government aid. The two roads were expected to meet at the western boundary of Nevada; but to encourage their early completion, the Act of 1862 authorized the road which first reached the designated point to continue construction, east or west as the case might be, until junction with the second road should be made. Since the amount of land granted depended on the mileage completed, the haste of the companies was feverish. "The Union Pacific Company," says Davis,[2] "had its parties of graders working 200 miles in advance of its com-

[1] Aldrich Committee Report. The value of gold used is that given in the American Almanac for 1878, and varied from year to year as follows:

1864	155.5	1866	140.1	1868	138.5
1865	216.2	1867	134.6	1869	135.6

[2] John P. Davis, History of the Union Pacific Railroad, p. 151.

pleted line in places as far west as Humboldt Wells." The Central Pacific had completed 105 miles east of Sacramento by the autumn of 1867, hauling iron and supplies over the mountains without waiting for the piercing of its tunnels. No less than 1038 miles of the Union Pacific, including the difficult stretch over the Rocky Mountains, were completed by 1869, four years after construction was commenced. The prize of additional land was thereby secured, but this land was long unsalable, and the cost of construction was largely increased.

Finally, large sums were misapplied through a construction company. The story of the Crédit Mobilier has been so often told that only brief mention need be made of it here.[1] In 1864 T. C. Durant, vice-president of the Union Pacific, induced one H. M. Hoxie to bid for a contract to build from Omaha to the one hundredth meridian. Hoxie was financially irresponsible, and four days later assigned the contract to a company composed of Durant and other stockholders of the Union Pacific. Meanwhile Durant had purchased the charter of the Pennsylvania Fiscal Agency, a corporation which possessed convenient powers. Later in 1864 the members of Durant's construction company were given stock in the Fiscal Agency, now called the Crédit Mobilier of America, for the amounts they had paid in, and stockholders of the Union Pacific were allowed to receive Crédit Mobilier stock for the amounts they had paid in on their Union Pacific shares. Stockholders of the Union Pacific thus became also stockholders of the Crédit Mobilier, and in their former capacity were enabled to vote lucrative contracts to themselves as constructors of the railroad. Durant's company assigned its contract to the Crédit Mobilier. Subsequently it was found more convenient to assign contracts to certain individuals, who transferred them to seven trustees, who built the required road with funds furnished by the Crédit Mobilier, and turned over the profits to that organization, but the practical result was the same.[2] These various devices removed all incentive to economy on the

---

[1] Useful accounts of the Crédit Mobilier may be found in Davis, Union Pacific Railroad; Crawford, Crédit Mobilier of America; Hazard, The Crédit Mobilier of America; White, History of the Union Pacific Railroad; Poland Committee, Report and Testimony, 42d Congress, 3d Session, House Reports, No. 77.

[2] Davis, pp. 163–70.

part of the Union Pacific stockholders. Instead of gaining by cheap construction, they profited by dear; instead of aiming to reduce the cost in every possible way, they schemed at making the construction contracts as lucrative as possible to the persons to whom they were assigned. The advantages to them as stockholders of the Crédit Mobilier outweighed the disadvantages to them as stockholders of the Union Pacific. The profits realized by the Crédit Mobilier are still a subject of dispute. H. K. White figures them as $27\frac{1}{2}$ per cent, or $16,700,000; Davis says that the profit was safely over $20,000,000; but whereas White calculates the percentage of profits to the total cost of construction, Davis insists that a large part of the capital invested was replaced on the completion of each section of twenty miles by the proceeds of the government bonds and railway bonds and stock, and that though from $50,000,000 to $70,000,000 were expended, in all probability not more than $10,000,000 were sunk at any one time; in which case a profit of $20,000,000, spread over four years, represents $5,000,000 per year, or 50 per cent annually on the capital employed. Finally, the Union Pacific Railway Commission estimated the actual cash profits at $23,366,320, and remarked that the obligations incurred by the railroad company represented a very much larger sum, being measured by the bonds and stock at their par values.[1]

The result of the three factors was a corporation bonded at an extremely high rate. The cost of road in 1870 was reported to be $106,245,978, or $102,951 per mile, against which was a capitalization of $107,907,300, or $104,561 per mile, of which $32,715 per mile was stock, $26,080 government bonds, and $45,765 first mortgage, land grant, and income bonds. In 1873 the net earnings were $4,092,032, and the interest on the funded debt, not including the government interest, was $3,403,660. In 1874 the figures were $5,291,243 and $3,431,720; in other words, the corporation started with a heavy handicap, which its monopoly of transcontinental business at first helped to overcome, but which grew heavier and

---

[1] Union Pacific Railway Commission Report, 1887, p. 52. The Government endeavored to force the cancellation of the above mentioned construction contracts and the restoration of unlawful profits, but was held by the Supreme Court to have no standing in the case which would entitle it to demand relief. U. S. *vs.* Union Pacific Railroad Company, 98 U. S. 569.

heavier as the years went on. During the seventies, to repeat, the Union Pacific enjoyed generally large prosperity. The volume of stock outstanding remained the same, the bonded indebtedness but slightly increased, and the ratio of operating expenses to receipts declined. The first dividend was paid in 1875; in 1876 and 1877 8 per cent was declared, in 1878 5½ per cent, and in 1879 6 per cent. In 1880, however, a consolidation took place with the Kansas Pacific and Denver Pacific railroads, and this operation may well receive somewhat detailed consideration.

The Kansas Pacific, as well as the Union Pacific, was a creation of the Acts of 1862 and 1864, which required it to be constructed from Kansas City westwardly to form a junction with the Union Pacific at a point on the one hundredth meridian. Later, an Act of July 3, 1866, authorized it to change its route, and to connect with the Union Pacific at a point not more than fifty miles westwardly from the meridian of Denver in Colorado.[1] Like the Union Pacific the Kansas Pacific was built by means of construction contracts, which resulted in a total capitalization on its 638 miles of line of $9,437,950 in stock and $22,651,000 in bonds, or $14,793 and $33,455 respectively per mile, — high figures in view of the comparatively level character of the country traversed.[2] The road was not a paying one. It was poorly built and poorly managed, and running parallel with the Union Pacific, it had to meet competition of a very bitter kind. The report of Mr. Calhoun, expert accountant for the United States Pacific Railway Commission of 1887, showed that the total receipts of the road from 1867 to 1879 had aggregated $9,220,-218, while the bond and interest account, exclusive of United States interest, had amounted to $15,745,287; leaving a deficit of $6,525,-069, or, including the United States accrued interest, of $11,330,772.[3] That is, the Kansas Pacific was in a state of chronic insolvency. In 1874 it was placed in the hands of receivers, and the following year, by an arrangement with its creditors, it funded a considerable amount of overdue interest.[4]

---

[1] Statutes at Large, 39th Congress, 1st Session, chap. 159.
[2] United States Pacific Railway Commission Report, 1887, p. 55.
[3] Ibid. vol. 8, p. 4975.
[4] Records in Union Pacific Railway Foreclosure Cases, 55th Congress, 1st Session, Senate Document 10, Part 3.

In 1878 a number of securityholders of the Kansas Pacific got together in an attempt to reorganize that property, to take it out of receivers' hands, and to "unite in interest the Kansas Pacific and Union Pacific Railway Companies." Twelve large security-holders consented to contribute to a common pool or fund holdings of securities taken at a fixed valuation, their interests in the pool to be proportional to the amounts of said securities and stock taken at the value referred to.[1] For the securities deposited they were to receive stock at a reduced rate : thus for eight shares of old stock they were to receive one share of new; for $2000 unsubordinated income bonds they were to get ten shares, and for $10,000 subordinated income bonds thirty shares of new stock.[2] The final result would have been to replace securities with a par value of $17,330,-350 by stock with a par of $4,855,300, and greatly to lighten the burdens upon the road; though it must be remembered that the $17,330,350 were less than half of the total volume of securities outstanding, that the payment of interest on much of these had been optional only, and that no provision was made for the floating debt.

The scheme fell through, according to Mr. Gould, who was a party to the agreement, because securityholders outside of the pool refused to consent to so drastic a reduction of their holdings; and at his suggestion a consolidated mortgage was substituted for the issues of stock. This mortgage was for forty years at 6 per cent. The total issue was to be for $30,000,000, of which $24,000,000 were to be issued at once for the retirement of earlier bond issues and for payment of arrears of interest.[3] Like the previous proposition the scheme contemplated a scaling in the principal of the junior securities, and the same rates of commutation were retained; but in this case the old Kansas Pacific stock was withdrawn from the operation of the plan, and certain reservations were made for other purposes, so that an actual increase in indebtedness was finally to

---

[1] Parties to agreement were: Sidney Dillon, Fred L. Ames, Jay Gould, C. S. Greeley, John D. Perry, Robert E. Carr, Adolphus Meier, B. W. Lewis, Jr., Henry Villard, John P. Usher, D. M. Edgerton, Artemas H. Holmes.

[2] United States Pacific Railway Commission Report, 1887, testimony of A. H. Holmes, p. 165.

[3] Ibid. Testimony of Jay Gould, pp. 454–6. The change to a mortgage was made between April, 1878, and May, 1879.

result, and even the interest charges were certain to increase.[1] For the time being, however, by force of the reduction of interest on the funding mortgage in January, 1879, from 10 to 7 per cent, and by the disallowance of some claims for overdue interest, relief was obtained, while the consolidated mortgage was duly issued.

The Kansas Pacific ran west to Denver. Between Denver and Cheyenne the Denver Pacific, 106 miles long, served as a connecting link between the larger systems. The Denver Pacific stock was held by the Kansas Pacific, and 29,979 shares of it were pledged in 1877 as part security for an issue of 10 per cent funding mortgage bonds.[2] The total earnings of the Denver Pacific from 1870 to 1879 had been $3,122,141; the expenses had been $1,709,477, and the net earnings from operation $1,412,664, or an average per annum of $141,266; while for the first eight years of that time the annual interest charge had been about $185,000. The only value of the Denver Pacific stock lay in the control which it secured over a connecting link between Denver and Cheyenne.[3]

Under the conditions of competition existing between the Union Pacific, Kansas Pacific, and Denver Pacific, some sort of agreement or consolidation was both desirable and likely. The Kansas Pacific was entirely dependent on its competitor for access to western business, and this was soon perceived to be equivalent to continuous bankruptcy. Extension to Ogden would have removed the dependence; but this, while to be dreaded by the Union Pacific, was beyond the power of the Kansas Pacific for financial reasons, and no capitalist or group of capitalists before 1878 or 1879 seemed interested in the undertaking. On the other hand, rates were low, and the very success of its exclusive policy forced the Union Pacific to meet the competition of a road which, with no interest charges to pay, was able to cut all rates to the very verge of the cost of operation.

As early as 1875 there was talk of an agreement whereby the Kansas Pacific was to give up its claims for a pro rate on its Pacific business in return for a monopoly of the local business of Colorado,

[1] Records in Union Pacific Railway Foreclosure Cases, 55th Congress, 1st Session, Senate Document 10, part 3 (contains text of mortgage).

[2] United States Pacific Railway Commission Report, 1887, testimony of A. H. Holmes, pp. 130 and 133.

[3] Ibid. vol. 8, p. 4987, Report of William Calhoun, Accountant.

and in connection with the deal was to acquire the Colorado Central Railroad on issue of $10,000,000 Kansas Pacific stock to parties designated by the Union Pacific Company; but this was never carried out. In 1878, when Gould began to be interested in the property, a union by means of stock control seemed feasible. Gould's first purchases were of bonds, and it was as a bondholder that he entered the pool of 1878; but with the purchase of the holdings of the "St. Louis parties," he and his friends obtained control of a majority of Kansas Pacific stock. In fact one of the provisions of the pool was that if on the first day of June, 1878, it should be found that Messrs. Gould, Dillon, and Ames, all large stockholders in the Union Pacific, had not a majority interest in said pool, then they should have an option on such an amount of other interest ratably and for cash as on the basis of the schedule should give them such an interest; and though this majority did not necessarily involve a majority of stock, the operations of the pool aided Gould in the acquisition of control. The union between the Union Pacific and. the Kansas Pacific thus secured was, however, of the frailest kind; for Mr. Gould at no time had the permanent interest of either road at heart, and looked for his personal profit rather in their struggles than in agreement between them. For this reason, as he bought Kansas Pacific, Gould sold Union Pacific stock, reducing his holdings from about 200,000 to about 27,000 shares.[1] In 1879 the situation of the two roads was thus much the same as before, and the harmony apparent was of the most superficial kind. One change, how-ever, had taken place to the serious disadvantage of the Union Pacific; for the Kansas Pacific, although still badly built and dependent upon its rival for an adjustment of rates sufficiently favorable to let it into the western business, had now interested in it a group of capitalists quite capable of financing an extension to Ogden, and even of securing connections from Kansas City to the East.

In 1879, doubtless relying upon the strength of Kansas Pacific's new backing, Gould proposed to the Union Pacific a consolidation of the Union, Kansas, and Denver Pacific roads, in which the shares of each were to figure equally at par. The terms were absurd

---

[1] United States Pacific Railway Commission Report, 1887, testimony of Jay Gould, p. 463.

by every test of productive capacity which could have been applied. The relative earning power and annual interest per mile of the three roads at this time were given by a government accountant as follows:

	Annual Net Earnings per mile	*Annual Interest per mile*
Union Pacific	$5617	$3185
Kansas Pacific	1602	2295
Denver Pacific	1333	1750 [1]

The Union Pacific had reported an annual surplus, the other two roads an annual deficit; the Union Pacific had not defaulted, the Kansas and Denver Pacific had done little else; the highest mark which the Kansas Pacific stock had touched in January, 1879, had been 13, that of the Union Pacific had been 68½. But the question, as Gould well knew, was not one of productive but one of destructive capacity, and the means of coercion which he employed was a demonstration of the ease with which the Kansas Pacific could be made formidable as a competing line. In November, 1879, he purchased the Missouri Pacific from Kansas City to St. Louis; about the same time he bought two minor roads between the Kansas Pacific and the Union Pacific in Kansas, and announced his intention of extending the Kansas Pacific to Salt Lake City, there to connect with the Central Pacific and to form a third transcontinental route. The story is clearly told in the report of the United States Pacific Railway Commission.[2] The result was the consent of the Union Pacific directors to the terms imposed, and the execution of an agreement dated January 14, 1880, whereby the Union and the Kansas Pacific, with all their respective assets and liabilities, were put together at par of their respective capitals, — $36,762,300 and $10,000,000, — to which was added the capital of the Denver Pacific, $4,000,000, forming a new company called the Union Pacific Railway Company, with a capital of $50,762,300, and a bonded indebtedness of $92,984,624.[3] This corporation was larger in every way than the old Union Pacific Railroad, except in one particular — earnings above fixed charges. It had 1821 miles of line instead of

[1] United States Pacific Railway Commission Report, 1887, p. 58.
[2] Ibid. pp. 59 to 65.
[3] Ibid. Testimony of F. L. Ames, p. 668. The combined capital is given in the agreements as $51,762,300, but this is apparently a mistake.

1042; $22,455,134 gross earnings instead of $13,201,077; $10,545,119 operating expenses instead of $5,475,503; and yet, since the consolidation was a union of some strength with a vast deal of weakness, there were few who profited by it save the holders of Kansas Pacific or Denver Pacific stocks. Those lucky and skilful individuals saw the quotations of Kansas Pacific common rise from a high level of 13 in January, 1879, to one of 59 in June, and of 92½ in December; and the stock which had been a football in the market thus become of such value that in 1887 Gould was able to lay before a committee of Congress, in justification of the terms described, a table which showed for 1880· market prices of Kansas and Union Pacific stock which were approximately the same.[1]

It was to Gould, as chief owner of Kansas Pacific and holder of practically all of the Denver Pacific stock outstanding, that the lion's share of the profits went; but Mr. Gould was not satisfied with a harvest on these stocks alone. In the course of his operations he had become possessed of certain branch and minor roads in whole or in part. Thus he held $945,887 in bonds of a company known as the St. Joseph & Western Railroad Company, and 5013 shares of its stock; $634,000 in bonds of the St. Joseph Bridge Company; and $59,000 in St. Joseph & Denver Pacific Railroad receivers' certificates; while to convince the Union Pacific directors of the wisdom of accepting his plan of consolidation he had acquired the Missouri Pacific, the Kansas Central, and the Central Branch Union Pacific railroads.[2] The earning capacity of none of these lines was large, that of the Missouri Pacific being the greatest. The St. Joseph & Western had been sold in foreclosure in 1875, and had continued to be managed thereafter by a receiver. What value it had was due

---

[1] Quotations of Kansas Pacific common during 1879 (Chron. 1880):

January		February		March		April	
Low	High	Low	High	Low	High	Low	High
9⅝	13	11½	22¼	17	22½	20½	60

May		June		July		August	
Low	High	Low	High	Low	High	Low	High
50	59¾	54	59	56	60	53⅝	59½

September		October		November		December	
Low	High	Low	High	Low	High	Low	High
55	73½	70	85¼	83½	92	85	92½

[2] United States Pacific Railway Commission Report, testimony of Jay Gould.

to the fact that, as extended to Grand Island, it gave to the Union Pacific an outlet to the East other than the one at Omaha. The value of the Bridge Company bonds and of the receivers' certificates was dependent upon this same property. The Kansas Central was a narrow-gauge road and had been sold under foreclosure in April, 1879. The Central Branch Union Pacific had been designed to join with the Kansas Pacific, but had been left without western connection when this latter road had failed to meet the Union Pacific at the hundredth meridian. At the time of the consolidation, according to the United States Pacific Railway Commission, "the coupons for six years were in default, and were retained uncancelled as security for the income mortgage. The company had never earned sufficient to pay its own coupons, without taking into account the accruing interest to the United States in any form." [1] The Missouri Pacific was more prosperous, but need not here concern us. Mr. Gould had paid various prices for the above, ranging from $40 for the St. Joseph & Denver bonds to $238 for the stock of the Central Branch Union Pacific. In the case of each road he turned over his purchase to the Union Pacific for the same or a greater price.[2] Thus for the St. Joseph & Western bonds, for which he had paid 40, he received par in Union Pacific stock selling as high as 94 in January, 1880; for $634,000 bonds and 4000 shares of stock of the St. Joseph Bridge Company, costing $480,440, he received 6340 shares of Union Pacific stock; for $479,000 in bonds and 2521 shares of stock of the Kansas Central, he received 4790 shares of Union Pacific; and for 7616 shares of Central Branch Union Pacific, costing $1,826,500, he received $913,500 in Union Pacific six per cent bonds and $913,500 in Kansas Pacific six per cent bonds.[3] The result was the issue of considerable amounts of stock of the consolidated and bonds of the consolidating companies, without equivalent value received.

The Union Pacific Railway Company, therefore, began its career in 1880 in worse shape than the Union Pacific Railroad Company, which had preceded it, for it suffered not only from an initial watering of stocks and bonds, but from a watering of assets which had

[1] United States Pacific Railway Commission Report, 1887, p. 100.
[2] Except the Missouri Pacific, which Gould retained.
[3] United States Pacific Railway Commission Report, 1887, testimony of Jay Gould, pp. 467–9, 523, 524.

followed. Including the government subsidy and accrued interest thereon, the total bonds and stocks of the company in 1880 were $179,058,902, or $98,329 per mile, of which $27,876 were stock, $45,372 mortgage bonds, and $25,081 government subsidy and interest. The figures per mile were slightly lower than in 1870, and yet the water in the capitalization was more abundant, for the average value of the assets had declined still more. A dividend-paying road had been combined with non-dividend payers, with the result of large profits to the promoters of the consolidations, but of serious harm to the solvent party.

Between 1880 and 1883 a number of branches were constructed, to provide funds for which the capital stock of the Railway Company was increased $10,000,000. Of these the Denver & South Park was constructed in the years 1881 to 1883, and was the last of Mr. Gould's gifts to the parent line. This road was handled by several construction companies, in the last of which Gould took a quarter interest, receiving stock of the Denver & South Park Railroad Company as a dividend on his investment.[1] In November, 1880, acting in behalf of the Union Pacific Railway Company, he bought the stock of the Denver road at par for cash, benefiting in his capacity as quarter owner by his action as representative and stockholder of the Union Pacific.[2] In relation to the road Mr. Charles F. Adams, Jr., subsequently said: "The chief source of revenue . . . was in carrying men and material into Colorado to dig holes in the ground called mines, and until it was discovered that there was nothing in those mines the business was immense." [3] A more important and genuinely beneficial project was the organization in 1881 of the Oregon Short Line Railway Company to construct and operate a railway from Granger on the Union Pacific to and into the state of Oregon, a distance of 610 miles, with the intention of securing the Washington and Oregon business. The Northern Pacific was in financial difficulties at the time, and it was not expected that it could anticipate the new road; but even though this expectation was disappointed, and the Oregon Short Line was second in reaching the

---

[1] United States Pacific Railway Commission Report, 1887, testimony of Charles Wheeler, pp. 1735-6. Amount, $571,000.

[2] Ibid. Testimony of John Evans, pp. 1853-4.

[3] Ibid. Testimony of C. F. Adams, p. 47.

disputed territory, its value was great and steadily grew.[1] The road was built by the construction department of the Union Pacific, and was financed by the organization of a subsidiary corporation which issued stock and bonds to an amount of $25,000 per mile, one-half of the stock being reserved in the Union Pacific treasury for the purpose of control, and the Union Pacific guaranteeing the payment of interest on the bonds. This branch at least was not unloaded on the main line by interested parties, and forms an essential part of the system to-day. Other branches were bought or constructed at the time, but do not require detailed mention.

Gould for the time had obtained from the Union Pacific all that he thought possible, and quietly unloaded his stock, while keeping up the payment of dividends. By 1883 he was substantially clear, but he had left his mark; the consolidation of 1880, with the forced purchase of worthless branches, aided as it was by the high capitalization caused by extravagant original construction, and accompanied by a steadily increasing intensity of competition between transcontinental lines, had diminished the surplus to a dangerous extent. At the same time the prosperity of the country as a whole was declining; the wheat crop of 1881 was only three-quarters as large as the crop of 1880, and the corn crop was the smallest since 1874; though the decline was not so marked in Kansas and the far West as in the states east and south of Omaha and Kansas. By 1882, says Noyes, all the markets were moving downward, and after the reaction of that year, the volume of internal trade decreased continuously until after the panic of 1884.[2]

The evidence of distress on the part of the Union Pacific was the mounting up of the floating debt. In November, 1882, President Dillon stated that it then amounted to $3,400,000, and that a loan of $5,000,000 was to be negotiated to take care of it.[3] The annual report at the end of the year stated the net debt to be only $842,743, but included in the assets used to offset the gross debt $2,768,437 in fuel and material on hand, and $927,648 in balances due from auxiliary roads; so that early the following year it was again a subject of discussion, and the stockholders recommended to the directors the issue of collateral bonds in order to wipe it out. Pur-

---

[1] United States Pacific Railway Commission Report, 1887, pp. 91 ff.
[2] Thirty Years of American Finance, pp. 86 to 98.   [3] Chron. 35: 578, 1882.

suant to the recommendation the directors executed to the New England Trust Company of Boston an indenture under which it proposed to issue trust bonds to an amount equal to 90 per cent of the securities deposited. By 1884 the gross floating debt amounted, nevertheless, to $11,306,595, as against $9,852,325 gross in 1882, and the quick assets, exclusive of fuel and material, counted up to $8,068,898, instead of to $6,241,145. The chief increase in liabilities, as always, had taken place in bills payable, meaning that the road had been giving its notes for the payment of current indebtedness, with the consequent necessity of paying a high rate of interest, and of making frequent renewals. Meanwhile dividends had been stopped and salaries cut down.

At this juncture Mr. Sidney Dillon resigned the presidency, and Mr. Charles Francis Adams, Jr., was elected his successor. Mr. Dillon was well along in years, was said to be in poor health, and doubtless missed the support which Mr. Gould had been accustomed to render him. Mr. Adams was a younger man, only forty-nine years of age as against the sixty-nine of Mr. Dillon. He had been a member of the Massachusetts Railway Commission from 1869 to 1879, had served as government director of the Union Pacific in 1878, and now brought to his position as president an inexhaustible fund of energy, large resourcefulness, and more important still, a nice sense of his obligations towards the bondholders and shareholders of his road. Under his régime the economies earlier initiated were continued and extended; employees were discharged until, by June 28, 1884, the company had only about 10,000 men in its employ instead of the 20,000 who had been on the rolls at one time; and rolling mills, etc., were closed wherever the company found it cheaper to purchase rails and equipment at current prices. This, with the cessation of dividends, left a considerable surplus revenue applicable to the payment of the floating debt. In addition, bonds and stock from the company's treasury were sold between January 1, 1884, and January 1, 1887, for which $6,550,000 were obtained; and the aggregate of resources made available was $16,200,000, of which $8,251,368 were applied to the floating debt, $6,708,632 to betterment of the road and branch-line construction, and $1,240,000 to increase of equipment.[1] In addition the proceeds

---

[1] United States Pacific Railway Commission Report, 1887, p. 67.

from land sales were used to the same general end. In August, to reassure investors, President Adams stated that no part of the floating debt was pressing, and in November he repeated the statement; the truth of which was made evident by the payment of the last bit of net unfunded indebtedness on August 22, two years later. The result was highly creditable, although the continued cessation of dividends provoked some protest.

Much could be done at this time by able and energetic management; there was, however, much that could not be done; and it is to this that we must attribute Mr. Adams's failure to put the road in a permanently stable position. For first, the competition which the Union Pacific was obliged to meet was constantly increasing in severity. In 1881 the Atchison, Topeka & Santa Fe was extended to a junction with the Southern Pacific at Deming; in 1883, in the language of the annual report, "Not only was the Rio Grande completed to Ogden, making, in connection with the Atchison, Topeka & Santa Fe and the Burlington & Missouri extension of the Chicago, Burlington & Quincy, a direct competing route with the Union Pacific from Chicago and all eastern points to a common western terminus, but the Northern Pacific also was connected through, making a third transcontinental route."[1] In 1887 the Atchison built 450 miles of line and the Chicago, Rock Island & Pacific was scarcely behind, so that Kansas and Nebraska were covered with a network of lines, which transformed the natural local traffic of the Union Pacific into competitive business of the most uncertain kind. At the same time the profitable high grade business was giving way to a larger volume of mineral traffic, and the average length of haul was increasing, all of which resulted in a decrease of about 45 per cent in the average receipts per ton mile between 1881 and 1890, a slow increase in gross earnings which bore little relation to the greatly increased volume of business done, and a fluctuating progress of net earnings, which were actually over $3,000,000 less in 1889 than they had been eight years before.

And second, during this time the fixed charges of the Union Pacific did not materially decrease. They were $7,626,626 when Mr. Adams assumed the presidency, and $7,309,142 five years

[1] Annual Report, 1884, p. 5.

later; and the necessity for further decrease was shown by the fact that the total net income of the road was $11,402,199 in 1884, $10,339,402 in 1889, and $9,561,673 in 1890. What Mr. Adams could do he did, and the funded debt under his régime decreased from $90,760,582 in 1884 to $82,090,585 in 1889, and to $73,968,885 in 1890; the company steadily buying up its own indebtedness: but the conditions which he had to face were too exacting, and the saving made here was offset in other ways.

To save itself the Union Pacific was driven to a rapid extension of its branch mileage, which Mr. Adams held to be the only means by which fixed charges could be paid.[1] Between 1884 and 1890 3132.45 miles were built or acquired, all under separate organizations, but with their accounts and management under the supervision and control of the officers of the parent line; and the amount invested in branch-line securities was raised from about $28,000,000 in 1881 to $41,879,724 in 1892. These roads reported annual deficits, which were either paid out of earnings or carried as floating debt. The report of the Government Directors in 1891 declared that $15,000,000 out of $21,400,000 of floating debt were the result of expenditures and advances in the construction of branch and tributary lines and the purchase of stock in such lines for the purpose of control.[2] But speaking in 1887, Mr. Adams declared the branches to be worth $5,000,000 a year to the main line, entirely apart from anything which appeared in the accounts of the branches themselves, and in a letter to the Government Directors in 1884 he said: "The branches and auxiliary lines of the Union Pacific should be considered the only real security the Government has for the repayment of its indebtedness. . . . Were it not for these branches the Union Pacific would be confined to such small local traffic as it could pick up at points directly upon its main line; and to its share of the through transcontinental business which has recently been subdivided by four through the construction of competing routes."[3] The most important of the branches remained the Oregon Short Line, with the connecting line of the Oregon Railway & Navigation

[1] United States Pacific Railway Commission Report, 1887, testimony of C. F. Adams, pp. 45–6.
[2] Chron. 53: 436, 1891.   [3] Annual Report, 1884, p. 165.

Company, of which the Union Pacific became finally possessed in 1889. This last road had been long considered the natural outlet of the Northern Pacific to the Pacific coast, but had been leased by the Union Pacific in 1887 through the Oregon Short Line with a guarantee of 6 per cent dividends upon its stock as well as interest upon its bonds for 999 years. In 1889 negotiations with the Northern Pacific resulted finally in the sale of the Oregon Railway & Navigation stock held by Mr. Villard and his friends. Pending the issue of a collateral trust mortgage the stock was deposited with a trust company, a note was given for the amount, and the sum was carried as floating debt. Whatever the value of the property to the Northern Pacific, it proved of great worth to the Union Pacific, providing it with an independent outlet to the coast, and giving it a haul on its main line of over 800 miles on all interchanged traffic. The method of payment proved a dangerous one, however, in that it so largely swelled the volume of the Union Pacific's quick liabilities.

In 1891 Mr. Gould again began buying Union Pacific stock. Mr. Adams therefore resigned late in the year, and Mr. Dillon was elected to his position. The time was not ripe for expansion of any kind, and Mr. Gould's death the following year put an effectual check on any schemes which he might have entertained. The immediate problem was the floating debt, swollen to unwieldy proportions by the acquisition of branch lines, and in particular by the purchase of the Oregon Railway & Navigation Company. During 1890 a block of collateral bonds was issued and sold, but the remainder of the proposed issue was kept back in the hope of a better price. While waiting, Mr. Gould devised a scheme for the postponement of the payment of these and of other quick liabilities by the issue of three-year collateral notes, to be underwritten by a syndicate composed of himself and of other gentlemen interested in the property. These notes were to bear 6 per cent, and were to be issued at $92\frac{1}{2}$ to such holders of the floating debt as would accept them, the syndicate taking care of the balance. The authorized amount was to be $24,000,000, of which $5,500,000 were to be issued at once. The plan was declared operative on September 28, 1891. If, now, the Union Pacific had been a moderately capitalized corporation, with fixed charges normally well below its earning capacity, and if, in 1894, when the notes were to mature, the market conditions had been more favorable than in 1891, it is probable that this scheme, temporary as it was, would have met the needs of the situation. Since neither of these contingencies occurred the insufficiency of the plan may be said to be in part the misfortune of the Union Pacific and in part its fault. It was a particular misfortune that the severest panic since 1873 should occur when the road was staggering under a load which it could scarcely bear; but it was altogether a fault that the railroad should have been so burdened as to be able to lay by no reserve in good times for the hard times which were bound to come.

In 1892, therefore, the Union Pacific was in a difficult position. Its capitalization was high; its earnings had shown scarcely any increase for five years; its surplus had not been sufficient to prevent the accumulation of a large floating debt; it had to prepare to raise a large sum of money in two years for the payment of its short time notes; and, in addition, there was ahead a fact of which little has been said so far, — the maturing of the government indebtedness.

Briefly sketched, the history of this indebtedness was as follows: The Acts of 1862 and 1864 had provided for the issue of government bonds for stated amounts per mile on the subsidized portions of the system in aid of construction, which bonds were to mature thirty years from date of issue, and to have a lien on the property covered second only to the first mortgage of the company. The rate of interest was 6 per cent, payable to the bondholders by the Government; and in 1875 the Supreme Court decided that the company was not obliged to repay to the Government the accruing interest before the maturity of the bonds.[1] This ruling was regarded as a victory for the company, but meant the steady piling up of arrears of interest, lessened only by the retention by the Government of one-half the amounts due for government transportation, and, under the Thurman Act, of such additional sum not in excess of $850,000 as, added to the whole compensation for government services and to the 5 per cent of net earnings set aside under the Act of 1862, should make the annual contribution equal to 25 per

[1] 91 U. S. 72.

cent of the net earnings of the company, unless the remaining 75 per cent should be insufficient to pay the interest on the first mortgage bonds; in which case the Secretary of the Treasury was authorized to remit a portion of the 25 per cent of net earnings required.[1] The Thurman Act did not fulfil expectations. The Supreme Court in 1891 held that expenditures for new construction and new equipment could not be deducted from gross earnings in ascertaining net earnings,[2] but the road met hard times and the maximum limit of the contributions to the sinking fund was not attained, and in investing the fund in government bonds the Secretary of the Treasury was compelled to pay high premiums, thus reducing the net interest; so that from the beginning to 1892 the question of indebtedness to the Government occasioned constant dispute and litigation, introduced uncertainty into the affairs of the railroad, and caused hard feelings between it and the Government. In 1892 the necessity for some settlement was near at hand. The principal of the government debt matured as follows:

November	1, 1895	$640,000
January	1, 1896	1,440,000
February	1, 1896	4,320,000
January	1, 1897	6,640,000
January	1, 1898	17,342,512
January	1, 1899	3,157,000
		$33,539,512

Deducting from this amount the sums paid to the Government and the company's credits for mail and carriage, and adding arrears of interest, the sum due the Government at the last of 1893 was approximately $52,000,000.[3] It was obviously highly difficult for the company to pay this sum in 1892 or 1898 or any other time, and for some years both the company and the Government had been earnestly discussing schemes for refunding, and the advantages and

[1] Statutes at Large, 45th Congress, 2d Session, chap. 96.

[2] The Court held that while up to the passage of the Thurman Act expenditures for improvements could be deducted from gross earnings in calculating net, the language of that Act seemed to preclude the deduction of any charges for improvements or betterments, or increase of permanent value of the works in any manner whatever. See 99 U. S. 402; 99 U. S. 455; 138 U. S. 84.

[3] Report of the Government Directors for 1893.

disadvantages of the ownership and operation of the road by the United States. Thus in 1892 an overwhelming obligation was hanging over the Union Pacific; and did not crush it only because the inability of the road to pay was so evident, and the inadvisability of government ownership was so strongly believed in, that every one felt that the necessary concessions would be made.

In 1893 the sinking-fund 8 per cent bonds matured to the amount of $5,176,000, and were partially extended and partially paid off through the medium of an underwriting syndicate; but this was the last attempt to meet indebtedness coming due. During the year both gross and net earnings fell off enormously, owing to the general depression of business, and particularly to the stagnation upon the Pacific coast. Freight rates were said to be in a state of chaos; and the Union Pacific served notice that it would withdraw from the Western Passenger Association on October 10. As the year wore on the continued decrease in earnings made the situation desperate. "The company for the year ending December 31, 1892," said Mr. John F. Dillon, counsel for the Union Pacific, in November, "had a surplus of $2,000,000. In the month of September (1893) there was a loss of net revenue of $1,500,000 as compared with the preceding year, and from January 1 to August 31 there has been a falling off in net revenue of over $2,500,000. The company is indebted for labor and materials on October 1 to the amount of $1,500,000; and its sinking-fund and interest charges for September would be more than $1,000,000; for October $750,000, for November $850,000, for December $1,000,000, and for January $1,000,000. There will be a deficit for the year 1893 of at least $3,000,000 and the company is without money or means to meet these obligations. . . ." [1]

Under these conditions a receivership was the only device which could prevent the dismemberment of the system and protect the interests of all the creditors; and accordingly, on application of parties friendly to the company, Messrs. S. H. Clark (president of the Union Pacific), O. W. Mink (comptroller), and E. E. Anderson (government director), were appointed in October;[2] Mr. Clark taking charge of the operation of the road, and Messrs. Mink and Anderson of the financial and legal business.[1] One month later, on application of the Attorney-General, Messrs. John W. Doane and Frederick R. Coudert were appointed additional receivers to safeguard the government interests and to assist the other receivers in the general administration of the property.[2] These gentlemen remained in office until the reorganization was complete, though various portions of the system passed from their jurisdiction from time to time.

The appointment of receivers closed a long struggle to maintain the solvency of the road. A reorganization was now in order, and in this it was to be possible to do what Mr. Adams had not been able to do, — namely, to rearrange the capitalization of the road, thereby permanently lessening the fixed charges and securing a reserve of earning capacity sufficient to avoid bankruptcy when receipts for any cause should show a considerable decrease. This was the fundamental condition of future prosperity. Besides, the debt to the Government had to be settled, cash raised to pay the floating debt, including the three-year notes of 1891, and the system held together so that its earning capacity should not be destroyed.

As might be expected, it was the debt to the Government which was most publicly and persistently discussed. There seemed to be four ways in which this might be handled:

First, the Government might have cancelled the obligation and have remained satisfied with the enormous economies which it had secured in the transportation of mails and other government business. In the seven years between 1867 and 1873 alone the Quartermaster-General estimated that the Union Pacific had saved the Government $6,507,283 in the cost of moving troops and supplies,[3] and there was no doubt that by 1896 the investment of the Government, with interest, had been many times regained. But it was pointed out not only that the Union Pacific deserved little considera-

[1] Sen. Com. 1896, 54th Congress, 1st Session, Doc. No. 314, p. 42, testimony of E. E. Anderson. For bill of complaint see Report of the Commissioner of Railroads, 1894, pp. 99–120.
[2] Ibid. pp. 391–2, testimony of O. W. Mink. This gave to the Government three out of the five receivers. For petition of the Attorney-General see Report of the Commissioner of Railroads for 1894.
[3] Chron. 16: 292, 1873.

tion, in that its earnings had been wrongfully diverted from the payments demanded by the Thurman Act by the manipulations of Gould and others, but that the precedent of renouncing a just claim would be an extremely bad one for the Government to set.

Second, the Government might have exacted larger payments to the sinking fund, and have extended the debt at an unchanged rate of interest until it should be automatically discharged. This was the proposal of Mr. Hampton, Commissioner of Railroads, who suggested the amendment of the Thurman Act as follows: it should embrace all the United States bond-aided Pacific railroads; it should compel the contribution of 50 per cent of net earnings to a sinking fund instead of 25 per cent, and should extend the indebtedness to the Government until discharged as provided. If any company should abandon a portion of a subsidized line or divert its business from a subsidized to an unsubsidized line, that company should transfer the conditions which were attached to the former to the latter, in order to protect the interests of the United States Government.[1] The weak points in this scheme were many. Among them may be pointed out the fact that contributions to the sinking fund under the Thurman Act had been necessarily invested in government bonds, which, in view of the premium at which they were necessarily purchased, yielded a very small return. To double the contributions would have been to double the amount of the railroad's funds sunk in but slightly remunerative investments; and the Government did not seem inclined to permit the company to adopt the only practicable alternative, that of investing its sinking fund in its own securities. Also, Mr. Hampton's amendment would have continued to an enhanced degree the constant suspicious supervision of the company by the Government which had been, perhaps, the chief evil result of the Thurman Act.

Third, the Government might have consented to a refunding of the indebtedness to it at a lower rate of interest. This was most urgently pressed by representatives of the road. Mr. A. A. H. Boissevain, representing the Dutch bondholders, proposed to redeem the first mortgage by the securities in the sinking fund so far as possible, and to renew the rest at a lower rate of interest; — after

[1] Report of the Commissioner of Railroads, 1895, p. 14.

which the Government was to be given a 100-year 2 per cent bond
for the principal and interest of its claim.[1] Attorney-General Olney
similarly suggested a renewal of the first mortgage bonds at a rate
of not over 5 per cent, and an exchange of 100-year 2 per cent bonds
for the government claim; though he differed somewhat from Mr.
Boissevain as to the lien which these bonds should have.[2] Congress
and the Government Directors in 1894 were inclined to insist on
harder terms. The latter, in their annual report, proposed that the
first mortgage bonds be paid off in cash, and that a 100-year 3 per
cent instead of a 2 per cent bond be given to the Government, with
elaborate provision for a sinking fund; and the former had before
it in the Reilly Bill a very similar suggestion.[3] As a counter-proposition the railway company offered to pay off the first mortgage
bonds in cash if the Government would take a 50-year 2 per cent
instead of a 3 per cent bond for its claim. "The petitioners further
represent," it said, "that it will be utterly impossible to obtain the
very large sums referred to from the stockholders unless it be possible to offer to them in satisfaction of their assessments reasonable
security for the moneys so advanced. At a meeting recently held,
at which were present representatives of a large amount of the stock
of the said company, the conclusion was reached that if the debt to
the Government could be funded substantially on the terms of the
Reilly Bill, but at a rate of interest of 2 per cent per annum instead
of 3 per cent, the said stockholders would endeavor to raise the
funds needed for the purpose of meeting the requirements of the
Reilly Bill."[4] Finally, Mr. Pierce, on behalf of the Fitzgerald Reorganization Committee, proposed that the Government either take
4 per cent bonds for the principal of its debt, and preferred stock
for the interest, carrying into the settlement with the Government
the scheme which was found best adapted to the satisfaction of
other creditors; or that it take a 3 per cent first mortgage bond for
its principal, and a second mortgage non-interest-bearing bond for its
interest; or that it accept a lump sum of money equal to the value of
its lien, which he informally estimated as 50 per cent of the total

[1] Ry. Rev. 34: 335, 1894.
[2] Chron. 58: 775, 1894.   [3] Ibid. 60: 132, 1895.
[4] Report of the Commissioner of Railroads, 1895, pp. 9-10.

amount due.[1] The plan of refunding was the most obvious as well as the most practicable of all suggestions. It had, however, the disadvantage from the point of view of the Government of surrendering some part of the government claim, and from that of the company of continuing the relations of the Government with the road.

Fourth and last, the Government might have demanded payment in cash. The sum which the company would have had to obtain was extremely large, but the accumulated sinking fund reduced it considerably, and many thought that the balance could be raised. In March, 1896, before a Senate committee, Mr. John Rooney, for the first mortgage bondholders, proposed that the Government, through a commission, should buy in the Union Pacific at foreclosure sale, should issue a new general mortgage at a lower rate of interest than the existing prior liens, and should pay off both the first and the government mortgage with the proceeds; — the road to be turned over to the subscribers.[2] This suggestion took place among many others which were in the nature of a compromise. Thus the reorganization committee, in 1895, offered to pay the principal of the government debt provided that the interest were cancelled;[3] and Receiver Anderson proposed in 1896 that the company pay the principal of the debt by adding funds raised by it to the amount of the sinking fund, and settle the arrears of interest with a 50-year 2 per cent bond. Full payment in cash was, of course, what the Government desired, and everything short of that it hesitated to accept; but equally, of course, full payment was what the bondholders of the road were most unwilling to concede; and hearing after hearing took place before committees of the Senate and of the House without definite result.

Meanwhile the general reorganization of the company was going on. In November, 1893, the various interests and factions of the road held a conference in New York, which resulted in the choice of a reorganization committee as follows: Senator Brice, chairman; Mr. A. H. Boissevain, for the foreign holders; General Louis Fitz-

---

[1] Senate Commission, 54th Congress, 1st Session, Document 314, testimony of W. S. Pierce. See generally the report of this committee for a discussion of alternatives from the government point of view.

[2] Ibid. Testimony, pp. 451-2.   [3] Chron. 60: 303, 1895.

gerald, president of the Mercantile Trust Company, for the Gould interests; Mr. Carr, for the estate of F. L. Ames; General Dodge, for the Denver and Gulf roads' interests; and Colonel H. L. Higginson, for the Oregon Railway & Navigation interests.[1] Subsequently Mr. J. P. Morgan accepted a place.[2] This committee was the only comprehensive one appointed until 1895; but numerous other committees sprang up to represent special interests of one kind or another, appearing frequently as interest on new classes of bonds was defaulted, and having, with the main reorganization committee, to deal specifically with the payment of the floating debt and the reduction of fixed charges. Upon the ability of the committees to agree depended the retention of the Union Pacific in something like its existing shape.

Aside from the question of the government debt there seemed to be a general agreement as to what was needed to be done. Every suggestion contemplated the payment of the first mortgage in full and the reduction of the interest upon the junior securities; most included with this an assessment on the stock, and one at least proposed the cancellation of the guarantee on the stock of the Oregon Railway & Navigation Company.[3] The principles were obvious. A large sum of money had to be raised with which to pay the floating debt and to meet possible demands by the Government. This had to come from the junior securities or from the stock, and preferably from the stock, which represented ownership in the enterprise. On the other hand, reductions in fixed charges had to come from the junior securities as the youngest interests which had a mortgage lien. Differences of opinion occurred upon the details. Should there or should there not be a foreclosure? How large an assessment was required? How great must the reduction in interest charges be, and should bonds or stock or both be given to the junior securities in exchange for their holdings? Should the system as it stood be preserved, or should certain parts of it be let go?

In June, 1894, Mr. Boissevain stated that the reorganization committee thought that they should be in a position to formulate a

---

[1] Ry. Times, 64: 732, 1893. Mr. Brice was also a member of the Senate Committee on Pacific Railroads.

[2] Ry. Age, 18: 883, 1893.   [3] Ry. Times, 65: 336, 1894.

complete plan of reorganization speedily after the terms of the adjustment of the debt to the United States had been approved by Congress. "It is our opinion that the fixed charges of the reorganized company . . . should not exceed $8,500,000 per annum. Certain classes of existing bonds secured by mortgage on portions of the system cannot be and should not be disturbed, as they are amply secured by property earning the interest which is payable thereon. Other bonds, however, must be converted in whole or in part into securities not imposing a fixed charge upon the reorganized company. While the reorganization committee has not approved of any definite plan, we believe that holders of bonds which must be disturbed and creditors and stockholders interested in the system can be provided for upon an equitable basis by the creation of the following securities:

(*a*) An issue of general mortgage bonds (at 4 per cent), secured by a general mortgage covering the entire system, subject to such mortgages as cannot be disturbed, and to the lien of the United States upon the main line and Kansas Pacific division for the adjusted debt.

(*b*) An issue of 5 per cent preferred stock.

(*c*) An issue of common stock.

The plan of reorganization would require provision to be made to take up the trust notes secured by valuable collaterals. The funds required for this purpose and for the other cash requirements of the reorganization would be met in part by a reasonable assessment upon the stockholders, and in part by the sale of new securities." [1]

A not dissimilar suggestion was made by the Government Directors in 1894. They proposed to ascertain the minimum net earning power of the railroad or railroads to be reorganized, and to issue a blanket mortgage of 3 per cent 100-year bonds to an amount such that the accruing interest would not exceed the net earning power. By sale of a portion of these bonds, together with a $10 assessment on the stock, and the use of the moneys and securities in the sinking fund, they would have paid off the prior liens, and then, after ex-

---

[1] *Ry. Times*, 65: 750, 1894. The reorganization committee stated that this plan was not final. They concurred, however, with Mr. Boissevain in his recommendation of the above scheme.

changing the new 3 per cent bonds for the government claim, they would have used the balance to retire the junior securities, adding preferred stock, so much as necessary, to compensate for the difference in yield between the old securities and the new ones received. The amount of securities required they estimated at $150,000,000 3 per cent bonds, $20,000,000 preferred stock, and $61,000,000 common stock; the latter exchanging for old common stock at par.

Both of these plans contained excellent features, chief among which were their provisions for the raising of cash and their use of preferred stock. The cash which Mr. Boissevain proposed to raise was to meet the floating debt, for he hoped to refund the government indebtedness; and while he may scarcely seem to deserve commendation for not attempting to fund the quick liabilities as well, this is not the case, as the history of the Union Pacific itself can demonstrate. The Government Directors intended to use the cash procured not only for settling the floating debt, but also for partially retiring the prior liens, so under their scheme an assessment was quite inevitable; and having made that as large as they dared they are not to be criticised for resorting to the sale of securities for the additional funds required, especially since these securities were to have a first lien on the road. As regards the preferred stock it is not clear from his statement at the time whether Mr. Boissevain had in mind the exchange of junior securities for bonds and stock or some for bonds and some for stock alone, but subsequent developments show that his intention was the former. Thus his idea was the same as that of the Government Directors, viz., to give the junior bondholders a right to a low rate of interest well within the earning capacity of the road, and to join with this the right to a higher return whenever the road should earn it. Mr. Boissevain's estimate of the maximum fixed charges which the road could safely stand was, however, high, and the plan of the Government Directors, if conservatively carried out, would have been better. Finally, the Government Directors contemplated foreclosure, while Mr. Boissevain did not; the relative merits of the plans on this point depending largely on the terms which the bondholders could be induced voluntarily to accept.

During 1894 and 1895 discussion was active, both in Congress and out, while the reorganization committee worked over the scheme which Mr. Boissevain had put forward, without making any formal announcement of a plan. Everything depended on the terms upon which the United States should insist. The reorganization committee hoped for a refunding of the government debt at 2 per cent. It had suggested that it would raise the funds to pay off the prior liens if Congress would take a 2 per cent 50-year bond in satisfaction of the government claim, would extend the provisions contained in the Reilly Bill to a committee charged with the duty of purchasing the property of the Union Pacific, and would grant the committee the power to form a successor corporation for the general purpose stated in the Acts of 1862 and of 1864, and with the general powers given in those Acts, together with the same rights, privileges, and freedom of action that were exercised and enjoyed by other railroads.[1] Subsequently it had offered to pay the principal of the government indebtedness in cash, providing that the Government would relinquish all claims to interest.[2] If either of these propositions was accepted it was willing to go ahead; while if both were refused, and no official counter-proposition was made by the United States, it seemed idle for the general reorganization committee or any other committee to promulgate a plan.

But meanwhile the Union Pacific system was disintegrating; partly from the efforts of the receivers to rid themselves of branches and contracts which had become burdensome, and partly through the action of bondholders of subsidiary roads who refused to wait for the slow action of Congress, and insisted on foreclosure of their liens. As early as August, 1893, ex-Governor Evans, a prominent stockholder of the Union Pacific, Denver & Gulf, had petitioned for an accounting from the Union Pacific, alleging that the branch was being bled for the advantage of the main line. When receivers for the Union Pacific system were appointed Mr. Evans petitioned for a separate receiver, and was granted his request. Litigation followed, and an attempt was made to get Mr. E. E. Anderson appointed as co-receiver; but the machinery of foreclosure and sale were duly put in motion and the line became separated from the parent company. In October, 1893, in view of an impending default, the Fort Worth & Denver City Railway Company was placed

---

[1] Chron. 60: 132, 1895. [2] Ibid. 60: 303, 1895.

in the hands of receivers, as was the same month the Denver, Leadville & Gunnison and the St. Joseph & Grand Island. In April, 1894, a receiver was appointed for the Leavenworth, Topeka & Southwestern; in June one for the Oregon Railway & Navigation Company. Foreclosure proceedings against these and other branches were instituted, and were attended by a very considerable measure of success.[1] On the other hand, the receivers were anxious to get rid of onerous contracts and unprofitable branches. On the 16th of March, 1894, they formally abandoned the Leavenworth, Topeka & Southwestern. In July, 1894, they petitioned to be relieved from certain guarantees and contracts, and asked instructions concerning the operation of certain lines. Judge Sanborn, in the United States Court at St. Paul, set November 15 for a hearing, and appointed a special master to take testimony. The master reported in October. He recommended the continuance of operation of most of the lines in question, but found that the receivers were not bound by the disputed contracts; and in November Judge Sanborn confirmed the bulk of his report. The net result was a reduction in the mileage of the Union Pacific from 8167 in the latter part of 1893 to 4469 in May, 1895; at which time proceedings against the Oregon Short Line Railroad Company threatened to withdraw 1424 miles besides.

With matters in this state the reorganization committee was genuinely discouraged by the refusal of Congress to pass the Reilly Bill, providing for a refunding of the government debt; although this had been reported to the House with the alternative amendment proposed by the committee accepting the payment in cash of the principal of the government debt in full satisfaction of claims against the company.[2] Since Congress had earlier refused a proposition to pay off the prior liens in full on condition that the government debt be refunded at 2 per cent,[3] it was felt that nothing but cash payment of principal and interest would be acceptable, and this the committee refused to undertake. On March 8 the announcement was made that the reorganization committee of the Union

---

[1] For a summary of the foreclosure suit pending in 1895 see the Report of the Government Directors for that year.

[2] Chron. 60: 303, 1895.   [3] Chron. 60: 132, 1895.

Pacific road had abandoned its task and would return the securities deposited with it, and a few days later the actual disbandment took place.[1]

Between March, 1895, and the following October little progress was made. With the dissolution of the general reorganization committee disappeared the one body capable of formulating a comprehensive scheme and of securing its widespread acceptance. The committees which remained represented each some one or two mortgages, and were thus confined too narrowly in their sympathies to command much confidence from bondholders as a whole. Late in 1895, however, new interests undertook the reorganization of the property, and another general committee was formed, comprising General Louis Fitzgerald; Marvin Hughitt, president of the Chicago & Northwestern; Chauncey M. Depew, president of the New York Central; Jacob H. Schiff of Kuhn, Loeb & Co.; Oliver Ames, director of the Union Pacific; and T. Jefferson Coolidge, Jr., president of the Old Colony Trust Company.[2] This committee's plan of action was noteworthy in three particulars. First, it contemplated a foreclosure sale. This, it is true, was but resignation to the inevitable, for foreclosure suits were already under way, and an attempt to check them would have had scarcely a possibility of success. Second, it made no definite provision for the government debt. A certain amount of bonds and stock were reserved from the securities proposed to be issued for the purpose of settling the government claim, but the exact method in which that indebtedness should be treated was left for future arrangement. Third, it did not attempt to meet the collateral trust notes of 1891, which constituted so large a portion of the floating debt. "The securities embraced in these trusts," it declared, "are largely those of companies which have already, by orders of court made in the original general receivership, or in independent foreclosure proceedings, lost in part or in whole their character as parts of what has been known as the Union Pacific system. Independent reorganization of many of these properties are pending. The purposes which brought into existence guarantees of the obligations of many of these auxiliary companies have been accomplished by construction or otherwise, and

[1] Ry. Rev. 35: 153, 1895.   [2] Chron. 61: 663, 1895.

considerations will not exist, upon reorganization, for continued relations with (them) upon the basis of any assumption of their fixed charges." [1] Thus, at the very outset, this new committee removed the three matters which had given its predecessors the most trouble. The proposed foreclosure made it both easier to get assents to a plan and more difficult to block its operation; the postponement of the question of the government debt allowed the committee to go ahead without waiting for Congress; and the refusal to provide for the collateral notes relieved it of many difficulties, and threw the holders of these notes back upon the collateral which they had exacted as security.

The plan of the Fitzgerald Committee followed, for the rest, the general lines earlier laid down by the Brice Committee. To retire all existing mortgage indebtedness it proposed to issue:

First mortgage railway land grant 50-year 4 per cent gold bonds	$100,000,000
4 per cent preferred stock	75,000,000
Common stock	61,000,000

The reasoning by which these sums were arrived at was as follows:

The lowest net earnings the Union Pacific Railway had ever recorded had been those of 1894	$4,315,077
The committee planned to issue $100,000,000 4 per cent 50-year bonds, on which the interest would be	4,000,000

This would be all the company would have to pay in any one year.

The average net earnings for the 10 years before 1894 had been	$7,563,669
To the $100,000,000 bonds the committee proposed to add $75,000,000 preferred stock. The annual dividend on this would be	3,000,000

Payment on bonds and preferred stock together thus equalled the average earnings.

Net earnings between 1885 and 1894 had gone in some years as high as	$9,000,000

To the above bonds and stock the committee wished to add $61,000,000 common stock, on which dividends might be paid if it seemed advisable.

---

[1] Chron. 61: 705, 1895. (Reorganization plan in full.)

New common stock exchanged at par for old; new bonds and preferred stock exchanged for old bonds, with a residue which was to be set off against the government debt and to be used for cash requirements. The cardinal principle of the reorganization was that no new 4 per cent bonds should be issued in exchange where the old mortgage did not contribute the full value; or, to put it more accurately, that no securityholders were to be given the right to claim a sum greater than their property could earn as judged from past experience. At the same time enough preferred stock was distributed to give bondholders the same returns as before when the road should earn it. A $15 assessment was levied upon stockholders. This was several times the quoted price of the stock early in 1896, but was not more than the stock would probably soon sell for after reorganization. A syndicate agreed to advance $10,000,000 to $15,-000,000, for payment of coupons as they fell due and for expenses, in return for which they received $5,000,000 in preferred stock quoted at 59, or 19 per cent on a capital of $15,000,000 at current prices. In addition the bankers who managed the syndicate received $1,000,-000 in preferred stock; making a total expenditure of $6,000,000, a not exorbitant commission. Besides the bonds and stock for strictly reorganization purposes, there was reserved to dispose of equipment obligations, and for reorganization and corporate uses, $13,000,000 in 4 per cent bonds and $7,000,000 in preferred stock. Reorganization uses, as defined by Mr. Pierce, were those which might arise unprovided for and of an extraordinary character, all of which could not be foreseen. Corporate uses were those which would be proper to the corporation thereafter, such, for instance, as the issue of securities in extension of the property.[1]

After all the securities of the old corporation had been accounted for there remained $35,755,280 of the first mortgage bonds and $20,864,000 of preferred stock as a fund or resource for the settlement of the government debt; or, in round numbers, an amount of 4 per cent bonds equal to the principal of that debt and an amount of preferred stock equal to the accrued interest. Just how this was to be used the committee did not pretend absolutely to say. "We

[1] See testimony of W. S. Pierce, Senate Commission, 1896, 54th Congress, 1st Session, Document 314.

desire to meet any proposition of the Government," said Mr. Pierce, "or to suggest any proposition which, after investigation, we believe will meet the approval of the Government within the limits of the financial possibilities of the property based upon this plan. In other words, we have made no sort of a hard and fast rule." In case the Government should prove obstinate and should refuse settlement on reasonable terms, it was the idea of the committee that it would be entitled on foreclosure to its share as a second mortgage bondholder only, and that the property would pass under the sale free from all liens, including that of the United States. "Our view upon that point," said Mr. Pierce, "is that when the Government subordinated its lien to that of the first mortgage bondholders, it did so deliberately and in terms effective for that purpose. The Government then consented to all remedies that were necessary for the protection of this prior lien; and an indispensable element of such priority would be the right of foreclosure. And unless there was a concealed purpose on the part of the Government, that right of effective foreclosure was undoubtedly impliedly granted." [1]

Subsequent negotiations with the bondholders brought a reduction in the proposed issue of mortgage bonds from $100,000,000 to $75,000,000, affecting the Kansas Pacific consols and the Union Pacific Sinking Fund 8s. Thus the former were allotted 50 per cent in first mortgage 4s and 110 per cent in preferred stock, instead of 80 per cent in 4s and 50 per cent in preferred as before; and the latter 75 per cent in 4s and 100 per cent in preferred stock, instead of 100 per cent and 50 per cent respectively. This reduced the proposed charges $1,000,000, and proportionately strengthened the scheme.

On the whole, the plan was a strong one. It reduced fixed charges from over $7,000,000 to under $4,000,000, with an eventual lower limit of $3,000,000, and this amount such good authorities as Messrs. Mink and Clark pronounced the road safely able to earn in spite of the reduction in its mileage.[2] During the receivership, moreover, the system had become purged by the cancellation of onerous contracts and the lopping off of unprofitable branches, and though some lines were lost which it was desirable to retain, the Union Pacific was not precluded from the repurchase of these, and did in fact regain

---

[1] Testimony, Senate Commission, 1896, p. 23.   [2] Ibid.

the most important. The bondholders were put in no worse position than before, for they could never permanently get more than the earnings of the road, and this the new distribution of securities generally assured them. The position of the common stockholders was improved, for whereas between 1883 and 1893 fixed charges had only once fallen below $7,300,000, now less than $7,000,000 were to be taken before their claims were heard, while both the gross and the net earnings of the road promptly regained their old level. Finally, the general principle was sound, as has been emphasized several times before. It gave to each class of securities a claim to interest strictly proportional to the earning capacity of the road, and added to this a preferred stock on which no payment was to be made unless earned; while it provided for a liberal assessment upon stockholders, and attempted no funding of the current liabilities incurred during the past troubled years.

The time limit for deposits under the plan was originally set at December 31, 1895. It was then extended to January 15, 1896, and later to January 29 of that year. By January 8 the reorganization committee was able to announce that it had secured majorities of all of the first mortgage bonds outstanding except an inconsiderable shortage in one class. This was followed, in spite of some opposition among London brokers, by the deposit of a majority of the shares of the company, and by the assent of other securities. In January, 1896, in a letter to the chairman of the House Committee on Pacific Railways, Mr. Fitzgerald stated that his committee embraced a substantially single representation of all Union Pacific mortgage bonds in circulation except those held by the United States.[1]

Foreclosure proceedings had been long under way. In January, 1897, the Government agreed to join in them in consideration of a guarantee of a bid at least equal to the original amount of government bonds, less payments made by the company to the Government, with interest at $3\frac{1}{2}$ per cent per annum.[2] The guarantee was

---

[1] Chron. 62: 187, 1896.

[2] Report of Commissioner of Railroads, 1897, p. 8. The Government's dealings with the reorganization committee followed upon the defeat in the House of a renewed proposition for refunding the Government's loan.

to be of cash, so that the Government's relations with the property would terminate completely upon confirmation of the sale. This was the first affirmative action which the Government had taken, and the reorganization committee accepted it, despairing of better terms. The guaranteed payment was in part offset by sinking-fund assets of $17,062,664, leaving a net amount to be provided of $28,-691,336.[1] By August, 1897, foreclosure of the main line had been ordered by the courts in all the states through which the Union Pacific passed, both under the first and the government mortgages. Previous to this the plan of reorganization had been declared operative, and articles of incorporation for the new company had been filed; while the first instalment of the assessment on the stock was called by the middle of the month. An unexpected development now occurred. Although willing to join in foreclosure proceedings, the Government found the decrees of foreclosure to some extent unsatisfactory, and prepared the papers for an appeal. Objection was particularly made to the fact that the Omaha Bridge mortgage, amounting to about $1,200,000, was adjudged superior to the lien of the Government on that part of the road between Omaha and Council Bluffs, and that the money and assets in the hands of the receivers accruing from the operation of the roads were ordered to be sold instead of being reserved to meet a deficiency judgment expected to be obtained. Learning this, the reorganization committee increased its guarantee by over $4,000,000, making the total guaranteed bid $50,000,000 instead of $45,754,060. "This increase," said the Attorney-General, "removed the objections to the decrees so far as the money contents were concerned. In all else the decrees were just and satisfactory."[2] Even so, perhaps partly for political reasons, the Government was not ready to allow a sale, and later in the year gave notice that it would apply for a postponement to December 15, in order to give Congress an opportunity to consider the matter. The prospect of renewed congressional agitation stimulated the reorganization committee to prompt action. "The Committee," it declared, "has reached the conclusion that the interests

[1] The guarantee was provided by a syndicate with the same personnel as that which had agreed to advance the money for reorganization expenses.
[2] Chron. 65: 730, 1897; Report of Commissioner of Railroads, 1897, p. 9.

256 RAILROAD REORGANIZATION

of the securityholders represented by it and of the syndicate furnishing the funds to finance the reorganization demand reorganization without any further delay. In this situation the committee contemplates . . . to oppose any adjournment of the sale of the main line and to bid it in, if need be, for the full amount of the Government's claim, the additional sum involved in this being $8,000,000." [1] Postponement of the sale of the Kansas Pacific was to be allowed, the committee meanwhile making up its mind on what terms to bid it in. This proposition was telegraphed to Washington and quickly accepted. It constituted a complete surrender on the part of the committee, so far as the Union Pacific proper was concerned. Instead of being refunded, the government debt was paid off in cash; instead of compromising for the principal alone, both principal and interest were paid in full. The result reflects credit on the sharpness of the Attorney-General, but the method was scarcely worthy of the Government which he represented.

November 1st and 2d, 1897, the property was sold under foreclosure of the government and first mortgage liens, and the prices were:

For the Union Pacific main line,	$40,253,605
For bonds in the government sinking fund,	13,645,250
	$53,898,855
In addition the Government received in cash in the sinking fund as of November 1st,	4,549,368
	$58,448,224
In addition to this sum the committee was obliged, under its agreement with the Government, to buy up the first mortgage, amounting to	$27,637,436
The total of the first and second mortgages was	67,891,041
Adding	13,645,250
Of securities purchased for cash, the total payment aggregated over	81,500,000[2]

On February 12, 1898, the reorganization committee bought in the Kansas Pacific, guaranteeing for the Government a bid at the sale which should equal the principal of the government debt, *i. e.* $6,303,000.[3] Other minor roads were also bought back on fore-

---

[1] Ry. Age, 24: 897, 1897.

[2] Report of the Commissioner of Railroads, 1898, p. 9.

[3] The entire indebtedness of the Kansas Pacific to the Government was $12,891,-900. After the sale the Government brought suit for the balance, but received a decree for $821,898 only.

closure sales, and from time to time as the mortgage committee sold the collateral back of the trust notes of 1891 the Union Pacific Railroad Company bought portions of the same. In 1899 the Union Pacific stock was increased $27,460,000, and the new issue was exchanged share for share with Oregon Short Line stock, thus regaining control of that important property. Later the same year a further increase was effected to retire $14,000,000 Oregon Short Line bonds and $11,000,000 Oregon Railway & Navigation Company preferred stock. The net result was to avoid any considerable dismemberment of the system. Whereas 7673.59 miles had been reported for 1892, 5399.01 were reported for 1899. The main line from Portland, Oregon, to Omaha and Kansas City, via Ogden, Cheyenne, and Denver, was kept intact, the principal losses being of branch lines in Nebraska and Kansas.[1]

A detailed account of the later financial operations of the Union Pacific divides the company's recent development into three parts:[2] First, the regaining of control of the principal auxiliary systems and branch lines which the receivership had temporarily separated from the parent stem; second, the purchase of large amounts of stock in the Southern Pacific and the attempt to share in the control of the Burlington, which latter involved the purchase of Northern Pacific stock and the formation of the Northern Securities Company; and third, the sale of the stock acquired in the fight over the Burlington, and the subsequent purchase of Alton, Atchison, Baltimore & Ohio, Illinois Central, and other stocks. The repurchase of auxiliary lines has just been alluded to; and into the history of the Burlington struggle there is no need to go at length.

On June 30, 1900, the Union Pacific, Oregon Short Line, and

[1] Cf. H. R. Meyer, The Settlements with the Pacific Railways, Quarterly Journal of Economics, July, 1899. The receivership records have been published in fourteen volumes.

At its final meeting in 1898 the reorganization committee nominated a proxy committee of five members "to permanently represent, at the annual and other meetings, such holders of common and preferred stock as (should) desire to entrust their proxies to the said committee for the purpose of maintaining the management and general policies inaugurated by the reorganization committee." This took the place of a compulsory voting trust.

[2] Thomas Warner Mitchell, The Growth of the Union Pacific and its Financial Operations, Quarterly Journal of Economics, vol. 21, p. 569, 1907.

Oregon Railroad & Navigation Companies operated 5427.89 miles of line. The system stretched from Kansas City and Council Bluffs to Ogden, and reached the Pacific coast in the Northwest at Portland. It had no rails of its own in California, but was dependent on the Southern Pacific tracks for connections both at Ogden and at Portland. The Southern Pacific extended from New Orleans through Texas, New Mexico, and Arizona to California, and thence up the coast to Sacramento. At Sacramento it divided; one line continued north to Portland, and one turned northeast through Nevada to Ogden, Utah. Now, in 1901 it so happened that the Southern Pacific was for sale. Crocker, Stanford, and Huntington, who had controlled it, were dead, and their successors were not eager to retain the railroad as an independent line. Mr. Harriman seized the opportunity. In 1901 he bought for the Union Pacific 750,000 shares out of a little less than 2,000,000, and the following year he increased his holdings to 900,000. The Union Pacific financed the purchase by the issue of collateral bonds. The acquisition was of vast importance. Not only did it afford a direct connection between Ogden and the coast, but it eliminated one of the Union Pacific's four great competitors in transcontinental business, and made Mr. Harriman the dominant figure in the Southwest.

North of the Ogden-San Francisco line the conditions were less satisfactory. The Great Northern and the Northern Pacific were here supreme, and in 1901 were negotiating for the purchase of the Burlington to give them an entrance into Chicago. Mr. Harriman asked for a share in this purchase but was refused. He thereupon began to buy Northern Pacific stock in the endeavor to secure by this a half control in the more eastern road. It was the struggle which then ensued between Mr. Harriman and Mr. Hill which caused the stock exchange panic of May, 1901, and which resulted in the formation of the Northern Securities Company, in which Mr. Harriman was allotted a large though not a controlling interest. On the breakup of the Northern Securities Company the Union Pacific received back some $25,000,000 in Great Northern and $32,000,000 in Northern Pacific shares,[1] worth at market prices about $100,000,000.[2]

---

[1] Besides $824,910 in Northern Securities stubs.

[2] See B. H. Meyer, A History of the Northern Securities Case, Bulletin of the University of Wisconsin, July, 1906.

This Northern Securities episode had little effect on traffic conditions in the Northwest, but it did profoundly influence the financial policy of the Union Pacific during the following years.[1] The dissolution of the Northern Securities Company gave to the Union Pacific Great Northern and Northern Pacific shares, which were valuable as investments only. And as investments these stocks soon became undesirable. We have said that the combined value of the securities transferred approximated $100,000,000 at the time of transfer. From that time on the stocks appreciated in value till they were worth from $145,000,000 to $150,000,000, and yielded an income of less than 3 per cent on their market price. It was good policy to sell them, and $118,000,000 worth were accordingly disposed of, leaving some $30,000,000 worth still in the hands of the company.[2] What should be done with the enormous resources thus secured? Some of the cash was used to buy Chicago & Alton stock, — some of it was put out in demand loans. But beginning with June 30, 1906, the Union Pacific and Oregon Short Line began investment in stocks of other companies on a great scale. $41,442,028 were put into Illinois Central stock; $10,395,000 into Atchison preferred; $45,466,960 into Baltimore & Ohio, common and preferred; $19,634,280 into New York Central; and lesser amounts into Chicago, Milwaukee & St. Paul, Chicago & Northwestern, St. Joseph & Grand Island, and other

[1] As in the Southern Pacific purchase the acquisition of the Northern Pacific stock was financed mainly by the issue of convertible collateral bonds. Some $30,000,000 besides, it is supposed, were borrowed from the banks.

[2] Testimony of Mr. Harriman before the Interstate Commerce Commission. It is true that the Northern Securities stock held by the Union Pacific system had been pledged as security for an equal amount of Oregon Short Line 4 per cent and Participating 4s, and that when these bonds were refunded there was pledged for the new issue whatever the Union Pacific interests should receive in exchange for their Northern Securities holdings, and any other shares or bonds at not exceeding 80 per cent of their appraised value. But the purchase of the Southern Pacific and of the Northern Pacific stocks had been previously financed by an issue of convertible collateral bonds for which other collateral had been pledged. From 1904 on, the rising price of Union Pacific stock made conversion desirable and rapidly released the securities back of the original issue. These released securities, with $18,000,000 Southern Pacific preferred stock paid to the Union Pacific in 1904 (with $2,460,960 cash), proved a sufficient pledge for the Oregon Short Line refunding bonds, and the Great Northern and Northern Pacific stock shares were therefore free for other purposes.

companies. In all, $131,693,271 were invested during a little over seven months.[1] This has been the characteristic feature of recent Union Pacific finance. The large purchases of stock in other roads have assured it favorable connections in the Illinois Central and in the Baltimore & Ohio, and have modified the severity of competition with the Atchison.[2] Including the Southern Pacific, its system reaches from Chicago to Portland, San Francisco, Los Angeles, and the Gulf, and has an influential voice in two of the principal roads connecting Chicago with the Atlantic seaboard. At the same time, the extensive investment of Union Pacific funds to secure gains unconnected with increase of traffic over its lines has provoked merited criticism. A railroad is, after all, a machine for transporting passengers and goods, not an engine of speculation; and both from the point of view of the community which it serves and of the investors who hold its securities it is advisable that its income should depend on the business which its managers conduct and are responsible for, and not on circumstances over which they have no control. So far as Union Pacific purchases have been designed to open connections or to modify competition they have had a sound foundation. So far as they have been financial operations only they are not to be commended.[3]

From the point of view of operation the success of the Union Pacific has been remarkable. Like most roads it came out of its receivership in better shape than it went in, but with much lacking for the efficient and economical handling of its traffic. Since 1900 over $52,000,000 have been invested in betterments and in new equipment, of which some $15,000,000 have been withdrawn directly from income. Maintenance charges have also been liberal, particularly in the last few years. Grades and curves have been eliminated, steel bridges have been put in place of wooden, new and

---

[1] Annual Report, 1907. See also Interstate Commerce Commission, Report in the Matter of Consolidations and Combinations of Carriers, Relations between such Carriers, and Community of Interests therein, their Rates, Facilities, and Practices, 12 I. C. C. Rep. 319.

[2] The Union Pacific acquired a half interest in the San Pedro, Los Angeles & Salt Lake Railroad Company in 1904.

[3] Recent reports suggest that a holding company is to be formed, which will take over the securities now owned by the Union Pacific Railroad.

heavier rails have been laid, ballast supplied, and equipment greatly enlarged and improved. Whereas in 1896 13 per cent of all the Union Pacific system was laid with iron rails, and only 24 per cent had rails weighing more than sixty pounds to the yard, in 1907 there was no iron reported, and only 33 per cent of the track did *not* have rails weighing more than sixty pounds to the yard. The average capacity of freight cars was a shade over twenty tons in February, 1898; it was over thirty-four tons on June 30, 1907, and the new freight cars added during the last-named year averaged a capacity of sixty-seven tons apiece.

In consequence of these improvements the Union Pacific has been able to handle a very greatly increased business. Between 1899 and 1907 the tons of revenue freight carried one mile increased from 1,393,207,990 to 5,704,061,535, and the passengers carried one mile from 167,117,388 to 680,278,509. This fourfold increase has been packed away in the larger cars, which in turn have been combined into longer trains. Twenty-one tons are now put into the average freight car, and thirty-two freight cars form an average train. In 1899 the average car held twelve tons and twenty-nine of them carried a train-load. Sixty-six is the average number of passengers per train to-day; thirty-three was the average number in 1899. And so the increased business has not occasioned a proportionate growth in cost. It takes but little more than three times the outlay in conducting transportation to do over four times the work, and other railroad expenses have varied even less.

This increased business and less rapidly increasing cost has meant, finally, an increase in profits, and explains how it has been possible in seven years to take $15,000,000 from income for improvements besides liberally maintaining the property. The Union Pacific is prosperous as it never has been before. In 1907 its total fixed charges, in round numbers, were $8,600,000, and its net income was $45,000,000. Of this income $23,500,000 were paid out in dividends, $1,960,000 appropriated for betterments, additions, and new equipment, and $10,700,000 carried to surplus. There were $69,000,000 in bills payable, incurred since 1906, in part for improvements and the like, but largely in the course of the company's financial experiments; but $75,000,000 in convertible bonds have been authorized to cover them. Stock and bond issues are much larger than in 1899 and will be larger still when the new convertibles are all sold. Fixed charges, however, are less than $5,000,000 greater than they were eight years ago. In order to imperil bond interest net earnings will have to decline by 81 per cent; and even were this to happen it is probable that some margin could be retained by a decrease in the generous sums now being spent for the maintenance of equipment and of road.[1]

[1] Dividends upon Union Pacific Railroad Stock:

	1898	1899	1900	*Per Cent* 1901–4	1905	1906	1907
Common			3½	4	4½	8	10
Preferred	1½	3½	4	4	4	4	4

CHAPTER VIII

NORTHERN PACIFIC

Act of 1864 — Failure and reorganization — Extension into the Northwest — Villard and the Oregon & Transcontinental Company — Lack of prosperity — Refunding mortgage — Lease of Wisconsin Central — Financial difficulties — Receivership — Legal complications — Reorganization — Subsequent history.

THE Northern Pacific Railroad Company was chartered in 1864, and failed in 1875 and in 1893. Besides these bankruptcies it has been in frequent financial difficulty, and on the whole furnishes an instructive chapter in a study of reorganizations.

The Act of July 2, 1864,[1] empowered the Northern Pacific corporation to build a line from some point on Lake Superior, in the state of Minnesota or Wisconsin, westerly on a line north of the 45th degree of latitude, to a point near or at Portland, Oregon. It provided for organization on subscription for 20,000 shares out of an authorized capital of 1,000,000 shares with 10 per cent paid in, and granted forty alternate sections of public land per mile throughout the territories, and twenty alternate sections throughout the states across which the road should pass. This liberal donation was influenced in part by the fact that the value of lands in the Northwest was then low, and in part by the refusal of any money subsidy. The Government was to issue patents on the completion of stretches of twenty-five miles built in "good, substantial, and workmanlike manner," and was to survey lands for forty miles on each side of the line [2] as fast as the construction of the road should require. The company was to begin work within two years and was to finish the line within twelve years, and it was provided that in case of nonfulfilment of these conditions Congress could do "any and all acts and things which (might) be needful and necessary to insure a speedy completion of the road." A section which gave trouble till

[1] Entitled An Act granting Lands to aid in the Construction of a Railroad and Telegraph Line from Lake Superior to Puget's Sound, on the Pacific Coast, by the Northern Route. Statutes at Large, 38th Congress, 1st Session, chap. 217.

[2] To make possible the selection of indemnity lands.

amended forbade the issue of mortgage or construction bonds, or the making of a mortgage or lien upon the road in any way except by the consent of the Congress of the United States. The company was to obtain the consent of the legislature of any state before commencing construction through it, and finally the Act was to be void unless bona fide subscriptions of $2,000,000 to the stock, with 10 per cent paid in, should be obtained within two years.

A project so daring as the construction of a railroad through the unsettled Northwest not unnaturally found it difficult to obtain financial support. The capitalists who at first undertook the work were unable to carry it through.[1] In 1869 and 1870 two developments occurred: the prohibition of bond issues contained in the act of incorporation was removed, and Jay Cooke became interested in the building of the road. Both facts were of far-reaching importance. Mr. Cooke was one of the foremost financiers of his time. He was a man of great personal energy, large fortune, and extensive personal following, and was admirably adapted to the promotion of the work in hand. The removal of the prohibition upon bond issues made it possible, with his support, to secure some funds from a mortgage issue and to allow construction to begin.

In 1869 Jay Cooke & Company were appointed financial agents of the Northern Pacific Railroad Company. On July 1, 1870, issues of $100,000,000 in 7.3 per cent first mortgage bonds and $100,000,000 in stock were authorized. The bonds were to be sold to the agents at 88; the bulk of the stock was to go to the agents as bonus or to the syndicate interested with them. The same parties agreed to raise $5,000,000 in cash within thirty days, in order to commence the building of the line. This made a fair start possible, and by May, 1873, over five hundred miles had been completed. The situation was nevertheless a difficult one because of the reluctance of capitalists to invest in the new first mortgage bonds. In 1870 extensive plans were made to interest the European markets, but all in vain because of the outbreak of the Franco-Prussian war. In America a similar campaign was not much more successful.[2] The high price asked for

---

[1] Josiah Perham was the prime mover at first and after him certain Boston capitalists were prominent.

[2] Ellis Paxsom Oberholtzer, Life of Jay Cooke. Philadelphia, George W. Jacobs & Company, 1907. See also Smalley, History of the Northern Pacific.

the bonds,[1] the uncertain nature of the enterprise, the not altogether ill-founded rumors of extravagance and mismanagement of the construction actually under way, the presidential election of 1872, all hindered rapid sales. Failure to sell bonds meant financial stringency for the Northern Pacific. Operating expenses were high, and the interest on outstanding indebtedness was considerable. On the other hand, earnings were very small. No through business could be secured till the completion of the road at least to the Snake River, and local traffic was yet to be developed. As a result, the company borrowed more and more from Jay Cooke & Co., and that firm soon found itself heavily involved.

On September 18, 1873, Jay Cooke & Co. closed its doors. The shock to the railroad was great. The quotations of first mortgage bonds dropped from par to about 11. For a time the company struggled on. In December, 1873, a funding of interest was carried through, whereby all coupons up to and including that of January 1, 1875, were made exchangeable for five-year 7 per cent coupon bonds, convertible into the company's first mortgage bonds at par, and into the company's lands at 25 per cent off from the regular prices.[2] In April, 1874, settlement was made with Jay Cooke & Co. by the transfer of the railroad's first mortgage bonds and other securities.[3] These measures offered only temporary relief. Business was at a standstill throughout the country. Gross earnings for the year ending June 30, 1874, were reported to be $988,131, while $30,780,904 7.3 per cent bonds had been issued, and the floating debt stood at $777,335. The Northern Pacific was not only unable to meet its fixed charges, but was in default by a margin which it was hopeless to attempt to overcome. The original project had completely failed; and the only means of continuing the enterprise seemed to lie in a government guarantee of the railroad's bonds, or in a reorganization so drastic as to sweep away fixed charges and to give the company a fresh start.

In May, 1874, the first plan was tried. A bill was introduced into Congress providing that the company should be authorized to issue

---

[1] The notes were put on the market at par, though sold to the syndicate at 88.

[2] Chron. 18: 16, 1874.

[3] R. R. Gaz. 6: 135, 1874. The indebtedness of the Northern Pacific to Jay Cooke & Co. amounted to about $1,500,000.

its 5 per cent thirty-year bonds for $50,000 per mile on its entire line, complete and incomplete, and that on completed sections of the road twenty miles long it should deliver its 7.3 per cent bonds at a rate of $50,000 per mile, receiving in return $40,000 of the 5 per cent bonds with interest but not principal guaranteed by the Government, which should hold the difference of $10,000 as a reserve fund. Holders of outstanding 7.3 per cent bonds were to have the right of exchanging their bonds for new 5s on the same terms.[1] In return for the guarantee the railroad was to surrender to the United States Government its entire land grant, to be sold under the direction of the Secretary of the Interior, and to turn over semi-annually its entire net earnings. The Government was to have the right in addition to sell the Northern Pacific 5 per cent bonds whenever the combined yield of the land grant and the net earnings should not equal the interest guaranteed. Finally, Congress was to have power to fix fares, etc., provided that the government control did not impair the security of the bonds. In brief, the capitalists who had involved themselves in Northern Pacific affairs were ready to surrender their whole enterprise to the Government if the Government would carry it through. But Congress was so little willing to take the responsibility that the bill never came to a vote.

Early in 1875, while the application for government aid was still pending, the directors called a general meeting of the bondholders. When it assembled President Cass made a statement of the financial condition of the company. The outstanding debt, said he, was $30,441,300. Of the 7.3 per cent bonds issued as collateral for floating debt, mostly in 1875, there had been pledged $1,780,300 at the rate of from twenty-five to forty cents on the dollar. The interest on land warrants, bonds, and scrip given in funding of coupons amounted to $732,632. The floating debt was $634,758, of which $150,000 were arranged for settlement within a few days; and $250,-000 were due to directors for money advanced to finish the Pacific section after the failure of Jay Cooke & Co. in 1873. The total net earnings to date had been $124,056, and the capital stock was $25,-497,600. By this report it seems that some slight advance had been

---

[1] R. R. Gaz. 6: 496, 1874; Congressional Record, 43d Congress, 1st Session, May 11, 1874, pp. 3749, 3773.

made since June, 1874, but in no measure which afforded any hope for the continued solvency of the company. Most instructive were the figures for the floating debt, which in less than five years had increased to a sum more than five times the net earnings for the whole period. After some discussion the bondholders elected a committee of seven to report at a future meeting. The committee recommended a receivership, the directors did not oppose, and on April 16 General Cass was appointed receiver, resigning his position as president to accept.

By this time hope of government aid had vanished, and no time was lost in accepting the alternative of a drastic reorganization. Late in May the bondholders' committee reported a plan which was considered by the bondholders at subsequent meetings. The principle was simple, and the means sufficient. The company had earned .4 per cent on its funded debt : — *ergo*, the funded debt was to be swept away. Fixed charges had been heavy : — they were now to be completely removed. Scarcely less would have met the needs of the situation, but the merit in refusing to tinker and experiment was considerable. In more extended shape the plan was as follows : Reorganization was to be carried out through foreclosure, and a committee of six was appointed to take charge. All outstanding bonds were to be replaced by preferred stock, and all common stock was to be exchanged for new common stock. Floating debt was to be likewise exchanged for preferred stock, which was to be issued to the amount of $51,000,000 for the following purposes :

(*a*) To retire the principal of the outstanding 7.3 per cent bonds, and the interest to and including July 1, 1878, at 8 per cent, currency.

(*b*) To retire the land warrant bonds, principal and interest, to and including January 1, 1875.

(*c*) To pay the floating debt not protected under the existing orders of the court.

(*d*) Generally for the purpose of carrying the plan into effect.

Preferred stock was to have all rights and privileges of common stock, with the right to vote, and was to be entitled to 8 per cent out of net earnings before anything should be paid on the common, and to one-half the surplus after 8 per cent should have been declared on both preferred and common.[1] It was to be convertible at par into any lands belonging to the company, or thereafter to belong to it, east of the Missouri River in the state of Minnesota or the territory of Dakota, until default should occur in some of the provisions of the new first mortgage bonds, and the proceeds of all sales of such land were to be used in extinguishing the stock. Common stock was to be issued to the amount of $49,000,000, and was to be given to old stockholders share for share. To provide the means to complete and to equip the road there were to be issued first mortgage bonds not to exceed an average of $25,000 per mile of road, actually completed and accepted by the President of the United States, to be secured by a first mortgage on the whole line of road, constructed or to be constructed, and on the equipment, property, lands, and franchises, including the franchise to be a corporation, subject only to the right of the holders of the preferred stock to convert their stock into lands. The principal was to be payable in forty years, and the interest and sinking fund might be made payable in gold. No other bonds were to be issued except on a vote of at least three-quarters of the preferred stock at a meeting specially held in reference thereto on thirty days' notice. Subsequently it was resolved, and the resolution incorporated in the plan, that the holders of the common stock should have no voting power until on and after July 1, 1878, and that no assessment should be levied upon bondholders; but that the cost of purchase and the expense of foreclosure and other proceedings should be paid out of the assets and the income of the company.[2]

Applying to this plan the same tests to which all other plans have been subjected, it appears that from the point of view of the corporation it left little to be desired. The general depression throughout

---

[1] Net earnings " shall be construed to mean such surplus earnings of the said railroad as shall remain, after paying all expenses of operating the said railroad and carrying on all its business, including all taxes and assessments and payments on incumbrances, and including the interest and sinking fund on the first mortgage bonds, the expenses of repairing or replacing the said railroad, its appurtenances, equipments, or other property, so that the same shall be in high condition, and of providing such additional equipment as the said Company shall deem necessary for the business of said railroad." Annual Report, 1876, p. 45.

[2] Annual Report, 1876; Chron. 20: 522, 1875; Ibid. 21: 15, 1875.

the country and the needs of the Northern Pacific Railroad in particular were so great that for once, in the conflict of interests between the bondholders and the corporation, the latter had all the advantage on its side. As a matter of fact, had any attempt been made in this case, as so frequently in others of recent years, to unite in the exchange of new securities for old a bond and a stock as an equivalent for an outstanding bond, instead of giving stock only, the rate of interest on the new bond would necessarily have been so low as to deprive the combination of its attractiveness. That resource was not had to an income bond was perhaps due to the absence of English investment in the road. The wise course was the one pursued: — namely, to retire bonds with a fixed lien on earnings by stock which represented ownership in the enterprise, and which could claim dividends only when earned. The floating debt was not retired by an assessment but by new securities. This again, all things considered, was wise. The existing stock represented so little actual investment in the property that holders would doubtless have refused to pay an assessment, and would have surrendered their certificates instead; while it would have been both difficult to collect an assessment on the depreciated bonds, and hard to convince bondholders of the justice of a demand for such a contribution, so long as the stockholders were let off unscathed. On the other hand, whether or not an assessment would have yielded cash, the issue of stock for floating debt did not increase the fixed charges of the road, and was not, therefore, fundamentally unsound. Liberal provision was made for future capital requirements, and the only provision to which exception could have been taken was the limitation of bond issues to the moderate figure of $25,000 per mile except with the consent of three-quarters of the preferred stockholders. On the whole, the plan put the company fairly on its feet, presented it with all the work which had been accomplished, and bade it attempt again the project in which its failure had previously been so complete. The danger of future bankruptcy lay in this fact only: that a large section of the road was yet uncompleted, and through business was non-existent; that the Northwest was still unsettled, and the local business was small; in short, that so much was yet to be done that the company, with all the advantages which it now possessed, might fail again for the same reasons which had led it into bankruptcy before.

The plan was first reported on May 20,[1] and was laid before the bondholders on the 30th of June. There was some protest that it proposed giving away the property of the bondholders, and the additional sections before mentioned, concerning the expenses of the reorganization and the voting power of the common stock were added. By August nearly two-thirds of the bondholders had assented.[2] By May a decree of sale had been obtained, which was modified in August so as to give bondholders priority over claims of directors for advances made; and on August 12 all the property of the company, except the patented and certified lands,[3] with all its rights, liberties, and franchises, was sold at public auction and bought in by a purchasing committee for $100,000.[4] No upset price was set by the Court; and it was surmised that the bid was purposely made low in order to force non-assenting bondholders to accept the new stock. The new corporation was organized in October, 1875, by the election of Mr. Chas. B. Wright of Philadelphia as president, and with the denial of a petition to set aside the sale the reorganization may be said to have been concluded.

For fourteen years the company was now to be free from talk of further reorganization, and not until 1893 was there to be another receivership. During this time the mileage, owned or controlled, was to be made continuous from the Pacific coast to Chicago, and the Northern Pacific was to mount high among American railroads in its extent and in the volume of its business. In 1875 the completed mileage was, roughly, 550 miles of line; in 1893 it was 5431.92, and reached from Ashland, St. Paul, and Minneapolis on the east to Portland, Olympia, Tacoma, and Seattle on the west. In the former

[1] Annual Report, 1876.

[2] R. R. Gaz. 7: 330, 1875. Deposits of bonds kept coming in, until on June 30, 1879, when the rights of conversion into preferred stock expired, there remained outstanding but $529,000. Annual Report, 1879.

[3] These lands were reserved for the time because some of them had not been surveyed, and others which had been surveyed had not yet been deeded to the company owing to a dispute with the Interior Department over the payment of the costs of the surveys. R. R. Gaz. 7: 340, 1875.

[4] R. R. Gaz. 7: 420, 1875.

year the gross earnings were $414,722 and the net $97,478; in the latter the totals were $23,920,109 and $11,416,283. At the same time the fixed charges rose from nothing to $14,311,430, and the bonds outstanding to $133,545,500, besides $15,349,000 of bonds of subsidiary companies guaranteed. It appears, therefore, that the promoters were successful in raising funds for the completion of their enterprise, although their road suffered at first from the thin population of the Northwest and the lack of a through connection, and then from the competition of other transcontinental lines.

From the reorganization to 1879 very little was done in the way of new construction, owing to the general financial depression. Efforts to get the time allowed for completing the road extended failed, however, and it became necessary to resume in order to keep Congress contented and to avoid a forfeiture of the land grant. In 1878 a small loan was placed, and the following year one for a somewhat larger amount; and with the funds so secured construction was vigorously pushed. More liberal provision was made in 1880–1, when successful negotiations were carried through for the sale to a syndicate of $40,000,000 general mortgage 6 per cent railroad and land-grant bonds, to be issued at the rate of $25,000 per mile of finished road only, and to be secured by a mortgage on the entire property of the company except the lands east of the Missouri River, which were pledged for the redemption of the preferred stock. Provision was made for a reserve of these bonds sufficient to retire the prior issues before mentioned.[1] Under the agreement the syndicate took $10,000,000 at once and had an option of taking $10,000,000 per year in each of the next three years. The reported price was 90 for the first $10,000,000 and 92½ for the rest. As a matter of fact, the whole $40,000,000 had been turned over by the end of 1883, and though the effect on the company is seen in the increase in its bonded indebtedness from $3,881,884 in 1880 to $39,522,200 in 1883, and in its fixed charges from $334,482 to $2,478,939, it was meanwhile supplied with cash, and was enabled to advance toward the completion of the 1000 miles of line which remained unbuilt. The financial embarrassment which was felt in 1882, in spite of the syndicate contract, was due to an unforeseen cause. According to the

[1] Annual Report, 1881.

statements of the company, it was felt necessary, in order to avoid waste of time and money, to build simultaneously from both ends of the line, and to start all the heavy work on the entire route at once. "This involved the shipment of millions of dollars' worth of track material, motive power, and rolling stock to the Pacific coast many months before their actual use on the road; and on the line east of the Rocky Mountains very large expenditures of cash a long time before the works resulting from them could become parts of finished road." [1] The expenses were immediate; — the delivery of bonds to the syndicate could take place by the terms of the contract only after the completion of finished sections of road, so that great stringency easily occurred between. The trouble was only temporary, and was tided over with the help of the syndicate and of the Oregon & Transcontinental Company, a corporation of which we shall presently speak.

As the Northern Pacific pushed into the Northwest, and at the same time vigorously occupied itself in filling the gap between the ends of its main line, it came into contact with a combination of Northwestern companies known as the Oregon Railway & Navigation Company, of which Henry Villard was at the time in control. This corporation owned a line of steamboats running on the Willamette and Columbia rivers in Oregon, together with an ocean line connecting Portland and San Francisco.[2] In connection with the water routes a narrow-gauge road had been built up the left bank of the Columbia River to a connection near the mouth of the Snake River with an existing narrow-gauge road to the town of Walla Walla in Southeastern Washington; and this narrow-gauge was being widened, in 1880, to standard. This was the very territory through which the Northern Pacific expected to make its connection with the Pacific coast; and in 1880 it had passed the Rocky Mountains and had reached the confluence of the Columbia and the Snake. On October 20, 1880, a contract was signed between the Northern Pacific and the Oregon Railway & Navigation Companies whereby the former, among other things, consented to a division of territory with the Snake and the Columbia rivers as the dividing-line; in return for which the latter agreed to complete a standard-gauge road within three years

---

[1] Annual Report, 1882, p. 13.
[2] Henry Villard, Memoirs, vol. 2, pp. 272–94.

from the western end of the Northern Pacific, at the mouth of the Snake River, to Portland, and to grant the Northern Pacific the right, without the obligation, to run its own trains over it at a fixed charge per train mile. It will be remembered that the Northern Pacific was not at this time too easy in its finances, so that it was quite willing to secure connection with the coast without outlay of its own. Soon after the execution of the contract, however, the $40,000,000 loan earlier described was arranged for, and Mr. Villard feared that the road would build its own connection with Portland now that the means seemed to be at hand. To prevent it he conceived no less a plan than that of forming a new company which should purchase and hold a controlling interest in both the Northern Pacific and the Oregon Railway & Navigation Companies.[1] This was done, and the new corporation, known as the Oregon & Transcontinental Company, for a long time played a prominent part in Northern Pacific affairs;[2] aiding it in the construction of the main and branch lines, and time and again advancing money when the road was in straits.[3]

The formation of the Oregon & Transcontinental Company put Mr. Villard in control of the Northern Pacific. Mr. Villard's financial strength in later years was due mainly to the support of German interests, notably the Deutsche Bank of Berlin; but his hold on the bank and on his followers was partly due to his real ability and resourcefulness, and partly to his confident predictions of results which sometimes he was but frequently was not able to attain. One of the company's first acts after his appearance was the declaration of a scrip dividend upon the preferred stock. The question had been raised in the course of his fight for control, and he perhaps felt it incumbent upon himself to show the sincerity of his contentions; at any rate, the annual report for 1882 contained a statement that the surplus earnings since 1875 had been used for construction instead of being distributed as dividends, and that the sum of $4,667,490 was therefore properly due to the preferred stock. On the strength of this the directors resolved that a dividend

[1] Memoirs, p. 297.

[2] For the manner in which the Northern Pacific directors attempted to keep Villard from obtaining control, see notices in the Chronicle for 1881.

[3] See First Annual Report of the Oregon & Transcontinental Company; R. R. Gaz. 14: 516, 1882 (contains statement of organization and purposes).

of 11.1 per cent be declared, for which there were to be issued obligations of the company bearing 6 per cent interest, payable at the end of five years, but redeemable after one year at the pleasure of the company upon thirty days' notice, in amounts of not less than 20 per cent to each holder. The policy thus initiated was plainly non-conservative and unsound. It may be true that as a general principle new construction should be paid for out of capital rather than out of income account, yet this is subject to qualifications; and the Northern Pacific had been and was in so precarious a condition that not a dollar of its resources could safely have been alienated. The sequel came in 1883 when the annual report admitted that there had been an excess of expenditures on account of construction and equipment of $7,986,508 over the cash receipts from the proceeds of the $40,000,000 general mortgage bonds, sales of preferred stock, and other sources;[1] and when by October of the same year the deficit had been increased to $9,459,921, and a circular from President Villard stated the additional cash requirements to amount to $5,500,000.[2]

Relief had to be sought in an increase of indebtedness. On October 6, 1883, the directors authorized a second mortgage for $20,000,000 upon the property, subject to the consent of three-fourths of the preferred stock, and in a circular explained that they had accepted a proposition of Drexel, Morgan & Co., Winslow, Lanier & Co., and August Belmont & Co. to take $15,000,000 of the issue at 87½, less 5 per cent commission in bonds, with a six months' option to take $3,000,000 more on the same terms. The stockholders assented, — they could do nothing else, — a suit for an injunction was denied, and the syndicate exercised its option. The result was an increase in bonds issued from $39,522,200 to $61,635,400, of which the greater part was accounted for by the new mortgage.

By August 22, 1883, the gap in the Northern Pacific main line had been filled up, and on September 8 the formal opening occurred. The

[1] Annual Report, 1883. Arrangements had been made with the Oregon & Transcontinental Company for necessary advances in order to avoid the accumulation of a large floating debt.

[2] R. R. Gaz. 15: 716, 1883. For attempted explanation of this deficit, see Villard's statement to the stockholders in 1884, just after his retirement from the presidency.

mileage in operation was then 2365, of which 1952.5 was main line and 412.8 branches, and the rapid construction of the last 1000 miles had done credit to most of those concerned. The total capitalization per mile was $59,304, of which less than one-third represented bonds; and though the following year this percentage was increased, the proportion of mortgage to total issues remained considerably under one-half. This showing was very favorable, and accounts for the success with which the Northern Pacific withstood the panic of 1884. With the completion of its through line, moreover, earnings increased so materially as to cover the interest on the new bonds; and though the road was never to enjoy a monopoly of transcontinental traffic, in February, 1883, it had concluded an agreement with the Union Pacific concerning through rates and a division of territory, and a period of prosperity was hoped for. Meanwhile the Oregon & Transcontinental Company had been hard hit by the decline in Northern Pacific stock, due to the publication of the construction deficit. The straits of his company affected Mr. Villard; and in spite of the relief afforded by the Northern Pacific second mortgage he "became conscious that neither himself nor the Oregon & Transcontinental Company could be saved." [1] On January 4, 1884, the directors accepted his resignation, and soon after Robert Harris, then vice-president of the Erie, was elected to fill his place. [2]

The years immediately following the issue of the second mortgage and the completion of the road were not uneventful, although it is not necessary to describe them at length. The insolvency of the Oregon & Transcontinental, and continued disputes between it and the Northern Pacific over an adjustment of the two companies' financial relations, made some other means of binding the Oregon Railway & Navigation with the Northern Pacific seem advisable, and a lease of the former company to the latter was discussed. In July, 1884, an arrangement was said to have been actually arrived at on the basis of a guarantee by the Northern Pacific of 6 per cent on the Navigation stock for two years, 7 per cent for three years, and 8 per cent in perpetuity; but the interest was very high, and an injunction helped to prevent a consummation at the time. In 1885

[1] Memoirs, p. 315.
[2] Villard was back in control by 1887 with the backing of German capital.

the idea of a joint lease by the Northern Pacific and Union Pacific railroad companies came to the front. The Oregon Railway & Navigation was serving as the Northwestern outlet for both of these roads, and such a contract would have greatly simplified the competitive situation, besides taking away from the Navigation Company the power to exact an excessive pro-rate because of its double connection.[1] During the next few years negotiations were almost constantly in progress. In 1887, however, the Navigation Company was leased to the Oregon Short Line with a Union Pacific guarantee; and upon the failure of renewed negotiations Mr. Villard, who was again in power, sold the Oregon & Transcontinental Company's holdings of Oregon Railway & Navigation Company stock at a "satisfactory" price. This consummation was less unfavorable to the Northern Pacific because of its completion of a line of its own to the Pacific coast.[2] From now on the Oregon & Transcontinental Company existed only as a means of obtaining financial assistance for the Northern Pacific, and for making more easy the control of that company's stock.[3]

While these operations were going on the Northern Pacific once more found it advisable to increase its indebtedness, and added a third mortgage of $12,000,000 to the first and second mortgages which already have been described. Of the issue $8,000,000 were at once taken by a syndicate, and the $4,000,000 remaining were early disposed of to the same parties. The mortgage was said to be for the purpose of completing new work and for paying the floating debt; it also assisted in the redemption and refunding of the dividend scrip which had been issued to preferred stockholders in 1883; and the payment of $3,073,321 of this in cash, besides the extension of $1,567,500 more, now took place. The extended scrip was to be payable in 1907, to bear 6 per cent, and to be redeemable on

[1] In 1886 the Oregon Railway & Navigation was obtaining 28 cents per 100 pounds for its haul of 213 miles from Wallula Junction to Portland, leaving to the Northern Pacific 28 cents for its haul of 1699 miles from St. Paul to Wallula. R. R. Gaz. 18: 681, 1886, Report of Vice-President and General Manager Oakes.

[2] For the negotiations between the Union Pacific, the Oregon Railway & Navigation, and the Northern Pacific from 1885 to 1889, see the financial papers of that time and the reports of the railroads concerned.

[3] In 1890 it was reorganized as the North American Company.

thirty days' notice on any interest day on or after 1892; and up to January 1, 1893, holders had the option of converting it into third mortgage bonds.[1] The third mortgage itself required the consent of three-quarters of the preferred stockholders, but this there seems to have been little difficulty in securing.

The years 1886–9 saw also a considerable extension of branch and other construction. It was a time of great general activity. In another place the large additions to the Atchison system have been described; at the same time the Union Pacific grew from a system of 5825.6 miles in 1886 to one of 6996 in 1889, adding over 1100 miles; the Chicago, Rock Island & Pacific increased from 1384.2 to 1592.7; the Chicago, Burlington & Quincy from 4036 to 5140.8; and the St. Paul, Minneapolis & Manitoba from 1509.4 to 3030.1. Meanwhile the Northern Pacific added 656.8 miles, or an average of 219 miles a year.[2] In the far Northwest the great tunnel·through the Cascade Mountains was nearly completed by May, 1888; and by the end of the following year a continuous line of road was in operation from Ashland, Wisconsin, to Portland, Oregon, which was of particular service in view of the difficulties with the Oregon Railway & Navigation Company, and was the reason for the willingness of the Northern Pacific to surrender control of that connection.[3] In 1888, also, negotiations were carried on with the Canadian Government for an extension into Manitoba; and the same year the Cœur d'Alene Railroad & Navigation Company was purchased, comprising a steamship and narrow-gauge line in Northeastern Washington which extended through the mining region of the same name.[4] Generally speaking, the Northern Pacific retained its character as a single-track transcontinental route with but few branches. Where it did expand was on the east, where it reached Duluth, Ashland, Superior, St, Paul, and Minneapolis, and on the west, where it joined Wallula, Portland, and Tacoma. The principal other branches

---

[1] Annual Report, 1888, p. 8; Chron. 44: 752, 1887; Ibid. 44: 782, 1887.

[2] The preponderance of west-bound freight prior to 1888 forced the Northern Pacific to carry grain east-bound at very low rates in order to fill its empty cars. See Daniel Buchanan *vs.* the Northern Pacific Railroad Company, 5 I. C. C. Rep. 7.

[3] For immigrant traffic into the Northwest see Ry. Rev. 28: 163, 1888.

[4] The capital stock of the Cœur d'Alene Company was $1,000,000, and there were $360,000 in 6 per cent guaranteed bonds outstanding. Ry. Rev. 28: 551, 1888.

were the ones mentioned : namely, those to Winnipeg, and to the
mining districts in Montana and Washington.

In spite of its moderation the Northern Pacific was not over-
prosperous. Its passenger earnings remained small, being scarcely
greater in 1888 than they had been in 1884; and while its freight
earnings increased from $7,867,367 in 1884 to $10,426,245 in 1888,
and to $15,600,320 in 1889, this was so far offset by increased oper-
ating expenses that the increase in net earnings from both passengers
and freight was only $2,223,194. Construction meanwhile caused an
increase in funded indebtedness outstanding of $15,202,000, to say
nothing of $20,981,000 of branch-line bonds which the road by 1889
had guaranteed ; and the floating debt began to grow uncomfortably
large.[1] At the same time, if Mr. Villard is to be believed, officials in
charge of the operation of the road were eager for appropriations for
the improvement of the track, the replacement of wooden by metal
bridges, additional motive power and rolling stock, enlargement of
terminal facilities, and the purchase and construction of new lines.
The truth was that the problem of getting the road built had been
more important than that of how it was to be built; so that much
work had been done in a hasty and imperfect manner which it was
now advisable to renew.

Since, then, there was need for additional capital, while it was
unsafe to increase the fixed charges of the road, the managers felt
called upon to devise a scheme whereby these circumstances should
both, at least in appearance, be met. Their solution was the proposal
of a large refunding mortgage to retire as soon as possible existing
mortgages, and to provide a balance which could be spent upon the
line. If, they argued, bondholders could be induced to accept new
4 per cent or even 5 per cent bonds in exchange for their 6 per cent
securities, the road would be free to issue new additional bonds until
the margin of charges so obtained should have been taken up. The
plan was worthy of its ingenious promoter, Mr. Villard, and will be
criticised in the proper place.

[1] Interest due and accrued, bills payable and accounts payable for the following
years were:

| 1884 | $6,941,513 | 1886 | $4,959,406 | 1888 | $9,287,616 |
| 1885 | 4,748,235 | 1887 | 6,504,274 | 1889 | 7,858,261 |

On September 19, 1889, the managers issued a circular to the preferred stockholders. "In the opinion of the Directors," said they, "the time has come to make new financial provision on a liberal scale for the growing needs of the Company." Then followed a statement of gross earnings. "A further corresponding increase may be expected in the present fiscal year, which will bring the gross earnings up to $23,000,000 or $24,000,000. . . . But the Company could not in the past, and will not be able hereafter, to take full advantage of this auspicious situation without further large investments of capital. Secondly. — The prosperity of the road attracts competition. . . . The Company must be prepared to build additional feeders wherever and whenever the local developments warrant, and the danger of hostile occupancy appears. . . . Another strong [motive] lies in the Company's ownership of a large land grant, the benefits of which cannot be fully realized without the promotion of settlements through the construction of branch lines. The Board is also of opinion that the time has come to make such provision, that the Company may take advantage of its high credit to effect a reduction of fixed charges." [1]

It was proposed to issue a $160,000,000 one hundred-year consolidated mortgage, bearing interest not to exceed 5 per cent, to cover the entire Northern Pacific Railroad, together with its equipment, land grant, branch lines, and securities of branch lines. This was to be applied as follows:

For the retirement of $77,430,000 outstanding first, second, and third mortgage bonds	$75,000,000
For the retirement of the existing $26,000,000 branch bonds	26,000,000
For additional branches at a rate per mile not over $30,000	20,000,000
For enlargement of terminals and stations, additional rolling stock, betterments and renewals, and other expenses not properly chargeable to operating expenses	20,000,000
For premiums on bonds exchanged	10,000,000
For general purposes	9,000,000 [2]

Only a portion of these securities was, therefore, to be issued at once. The provision for enlargement of terminals, etc., was likely to call for early issues, as might a portion of that reserved for

[1] Annual Report, 1889.

[2] Annual Report, 1889; Chron. 50: 279, gives text of mortgage.

new branches and for general purposes. It was expected that a certain amount of branch-line bonds could be retired without much delay. On the whole, the bonds immediately put forth were not expected to exceed $15,000,000; though there was nothing in the plan to prevent a greater issue. The interest rate was "not to exceed 5 per cent." That this wording was deliberately adopted is shown by the terms of the mortgage, which expressly gave to the company the power to issue the new bonds, from time to time, bearing such a rate of interest as the managers might think advisable up to 5 per cent. It was understood that the issue was to be in three classes, one of $57,000,000 to bear 5 per cent, one of $23,000,000 to bear 4½ per cent, and one of $80,000,000 to bear 4 per cent; and on this basis it was thought that fixed charges would be reduced $2,000,000, to which would have to be added interest on bonds issued in excess of those previously outstanding.[1] The reserve of $10,000,000 for premiums shows that in the opinion of the directors the offer of substantially more than par in new bonds was necessary in order to induce exchanges of old bonds for new. To prevent careless use of this reserve it was provided that the $10,000,000 in bonds could be used to pay premiums only upon the affirmative vote of at least nine members (out of thirteen) of the board, and when in the opinion of the trustees, expressed in writing, a saving of interest to the company could be effected.

Not the least important part of the plan was that designed to gain the preferred stockholders' approval. It will be remembered that by the terms of the reorganization of 1875 the consent of three-quarters of these stockholders was necessary to validate any mortgage after the first mortgage then proposed. The increase in indebtedness now suggested threatened to postpone indefinitely dividends on the preferred, and could not be expected to be welcome. In consequence, the directors offered three distinct inducements: first, a promise of a distribution to the preferred stockholders of sums which had been taken from earnings and spent on the property to date; second, a promise of early and regular dividends in the future; third, a preferential right of subscription to the new bonds. By resolution of August 21, 1889, they therefore definitely declared in favor of the

[1] Ry. Rev. 29: 541, 1889. In fact the issues were all made at 5 per cent.

distribution of a sum equal to the earnings which should be found to have been applied in earlier years to the capital requirements of the property. An investigation was made, the amount was officially declared to be $2,844,430, and an equivalent amount of new bonds at 85 was set aside to cover it. For the future Mr. Villard and his associates announced a determination to begin dividends at the rate of 4 per cent, the first to be paid January 1, 1890; and declared that thereafter dividends would be paid out of the current net earnings, or, if these should be insufficient, out of a reserve fund until the net earnings should justify a larger distribution. Finally, it was provided that the common and preferred stockholders should be given the privilege of subscribing to the new bonds at 85 to the extent of 15 per cent of their holdings. That these concessions attracted attention was shown by the action of the preferred stockholders in calling for an actual distribution as soon as possible of the amounts deducted from earnings in past years. On October 17, 1889, they passed a resolution recommending to the incoming board of directors "to take into consideration the distribution of the whole amount due to the Preferred Stock, under the plan of reorganization, as soon as the Company shall be financially in a proper position to do so;" [1] and again the following year they resolved "that the incoming Board of Directors be . . . requested to set apart the additional earnings in . . . consolidated bonds . . . and to (consider) the question of either increasing the . . . dividend above 4 per cent or of declaring an extra dividend to the preferred stock." [2]

All things considered it is improbable that the refunding plan could have been put through without the promise of dividends to the preferred stock, but it remains unfortunate that such promises had to be made. The money which had been put into the road had been of necessity so invested to preserve the solvency of the company. In a sense it had increased earning power, but not all expenditures which affect earnings may be charged to capital. In the first place, if earnings are below fixed charges, or are constantly tending to fall

[1] Annual Report, 1890. For answer of directors see R. R. Gaz. 21: 759, 1889.

[2] Chron. 51: 539, 1890. The point of view of the stockholders is briefly but clearly set forth in a circular issued by Mr. Robert Harris, chairman of the board of directors. Ry. Age, 14: 658, 1889.

below, sums put into the property merely assist the company to keep its head above water, and are not a sound basis for an increase in indebtedness; and in the second place expenditures which serve to *preserve* earnings may not be charged to capital account, even when the method of preservation is the construction of branch lines, and still less when the method is the improvement of the existing plant. If, then, as was the case, the earnings claimed by the preferred stockholders had gone to preserve the solvency of the company, and to defend it against competition, the arguments of these stockholders in 1889 did not hold good.

As for the plan itself, it was simply a method for providing new capital, and should be judged as such. Its refunding provisions were mainly misleading. It proposed to secure a reduction in fixed charges by the exchange of bonds bearing 5 per cent or less for bonds bearing 6 per cent, but how the reduction was to be accomplished was not clear. The maturity of the bonds to be retired was remote, and the assured reduction was therefore also remote. The first mortgage had been issued in 1881, and ran for forty years; the second dated from 1882 and was to mature after fifty years; and the third, which had been issued only the year before, was not redeemable until 1937. The Missouri division and Pend d'Oreille mortgages matured somewhat earlier,[1] but had nevertheless a considerable time to run. The mortgage issues would therefore not soon fall in of themselves. Secondly, bondholders would evidently not consent voluntarily to surrender old unexpired bonds without such a premium in new bonds as would make their annual return approximately the same. Something they might concede in view of the more remote maturity of the new issue and the somewhat more inclusive character of its mortgage lien, but not enough to create any considerable saving.[2] The new issues for improvement of the road, moreover, involved an *increase* in the annual interest payments; which we must not, perhaps, condemn offhand, for the raising of capital was in some measure forced upon the company, but which is important in considering the railroad's financial condition and prospects. The fact was that the Northern Pacific was not self-supporting; it had been obliged

[1] In 1919.
[2] Evidence of this appears in the $10,000,000 reserved for premiums.

to issue $20,867,000 bonds of its own and to guarantee $20,981,000 besides, between 1884 and 1889, in order to secure an advance of $2,462,288 in annual net income during a period of rapidly increasing prosperity; and it was now obliged to increase this indebtedness in the attempt to maintain its solvency for the future.

Between 1889 and the end of 1892 business increased, and net earnings at first gained more rapidly than did fixed charges. Mr. Villard was again supreme in the management, and actively directed financial operations until his departure for Europe in 1890. The most important operation conducted was the lease of the Wisconsin Central, whereby the eastern terminus of the Northern Pacific system was transferred from St. Paul and Minneapolis to Chicago. The directors who were elected with Mr. Villard in 1887 controlled the Wisconsin Central and the Terminal Company, which had been formed to secure an entrance for that road into the Lake city.[1] Perhaps because of this financial interest, the conviction seems to have crept over them that the Northern Pacific would do well to make connection with the trunk lines at Chicago, instead of stopping further west; and they brought the subject up in 1889, and again in 1890. On July 1, 1889, a traffic contract went into effect, under which the Northern Pacific obtained the use of the Wisconsin Central lines in consideration of the business which it should turn over to them. Certain provisions imposed on both roads a share of the operating expenses whenever the proportion of operating expenses to gross earnings was greater than 65 per cent, and which gave both a profit whenever the proportion fell below this level. The Wisconsin Central retained entire and absolute control of its own property, except that the Northern Pacific was to share in the profits of the subsidiary Terminal Company whenever these profits should be more than $800,000.[2] This was considered unsatisfactory, because

---

[1] Memoirs, vol. 2, p. 336.
[2] Annual Report, 1889; R. R. Gaz. 21: 318, 1889. The Wisconsin Central divided its gross earnings into two parts, 65 per cent and 35 per cent; retained 35 per cent for its own use, and appropriated 65 per cent for operating expenses and for certain improvements tending to reduce operating expenses. When operating expenses were less than 65 per cent the Wisconsin Central was to pay over one-half of the difference to the Northern Pacific in consideration of the business which the latter gave it. When operating expenses exceeded 65 per cent the Wisconsin Central was to pay not ex-

the Northern Pacific had no control of the Central's operation; and on April 1 of the following year a new contract gave to the former a lease of all the lines owned and controlled by the Wisconsin Central Company and the Wisconsin Central Railroad Company between St. Paul and Chicago for 999 years; including terminal facilities at Chicago held by the Chicago & Northern Pacific Railroad Company, a subsidiary corporation.[1] "It was deemed by the Board," said the annual report, "as of the utmost importance that your road should have access to the city of Chicago by a line in its own ownership and possessed with terminal facilities which it could control and have possession of. The whole subject was most carefully considered by the Board, and the contracts and leases were adopted after deliberate and careful consideration."[2] The advantage of this lease to the Wisconsin Central lay in the large volume of traffic which the arrangement secured to it; that to the Northern Pacific was more doubtful. Connection with Chicago was desirable, but it was to prove difficult to operate the Wisconsin Central for 65 per cent, and the acquisition was to arouse the hostility of all the other roads between Chicago and St. Paul. We shall see that the lease was presently given up and that the attempt to make Chicago the eastern terminus was for the time abandoned.

The year 1891 was a good one, but during the following twelve months the situation changed for the worse. Most noteworthy was an increase in fixed charges of over $2,000,000, due in part to an increase in the funded indebtedness, but more largely to an increase in rentals paid. This increase brought charges above total net income, and shows how serious the position of the company had become. In fact, the company's repeated issues of bonds had failed so completely to put it in a stable position that in but three of the

ceeding 2½ per cent of this excess out of its 35 per cent, and to divide one-half of any excess of operating expenses above 67½ per cent equally between the Wisconsin Central and the Northern Pacific. The Northern Pacific, however, was not bound to pay its half of such excess except out of future profits received under the contract.

[1] Annual Report, 1890. For a brief statement of the complicated relations between the Wisconsin Central, the Chicago & Northern Pacific, and the Chicago & Great Western, see R. R. Gaz. 22: 350, 1890. Terms were agreed upon with the Baltimore & Ohio for the use of the Chicago terminals of the Chicago & Northern Pacific, by that corporation. Annual Report, 1891.

[2] Annual Report, 1890, p. 14; R. R. Gaz. 21: 318, 1889.

nine years from 1884 to 1892 was a surplus greater than $500,000 above fixed payments secured, while the operations of two of these same years resulted in a deficit.

The first admission by directors that the road was in difficulty consisted in the passing of the preferred stock dividend for March 31, 1892. That this action did not deprive the holders of all return was due to the previous conversion of the consols formerly reserved into a trust for ten years on which to draw whenever the road should be unable to pay the usual dividends. The directors therefore added to their declaration of suspension a resolution that the "time, manner, and method of the distribution of so many of the $3,347,000 of consolidated bonds set aside for the benefit of the preferred stockholders as may be necessary to supply the deficiency, if any, in this or any subsequent fiscal year, between the amount of net earnings and 4 per cent on the preferred stock, be submitted to preferred stockholders at the annual meeting in October next." [1] Not unnaturally stockholders were alarmed. At the annual meeting in October an investigating committee was appointed,[2] and proceeded to a careful examination of the property accompanied by certain officers of the road. The committee was not friendly to the management. Its preliminary report announced that the physical condition of the system was good, but its later criticism of the company's financial condition was severe. In the words of the London *Standard* "there has been no such scathing arraignment of Directors since the exposures of the Erie Railway." The committee stated that the bad condition of the property was due to the reckless financial methods of the directors.

[1] Chron. 54: 845, 1892. Resolutions adopted at the stockholders' meeting were in substance:

"*Resolved*, That the $3,347,000 of consolidated mortgage bonds now deposited with the Farmers' Loan & Trust Company as trustee for the preferred stockholders . . . be not sold below 90 and accrued interest.

"*Resolved*, If all the bonds be not sold as above, and smaller lots can be disposed of at 90 and interest, then the Directors may sell enough to make up the deficiency any year between the dividend actually paid to preferred stockholders and the 4 per cent which should be paid.

"*Resolved*, If 4 per cent dividends or more are declared by the Board of Directors any year, then enough bonds shall be sold to produce 1 per cent additional dividend to be paid to preferred stockholders." Chron. 55: 679, 1892.

[2] Ry. Rev. 32: 687, 1892. Members were, Henry Clews, Brayton Ives, Frank Sturges, William Solomon, and Jay Cooke, Jr.

It alleged that officers had held dual positions, and had subordinated the interests of the Northern Pacific Company to those of the Wisconsin Central, relieving themselves at the expense of the former road. It commented upon the unprofitable character of certain of the other branches. The floating debt, it maintained, had been financed by Mr. Villard personally at double the current rates of interest, and it recommended litigation in default of some assurance that the policy of the company should be changed.[1] In reply the directors issued a lengthy statement taking up the charges in detail. The policy of building branch lines, said they, was imperatively necessary in order to develop business. Although some of the branches had not earned their fixed charges, yet, if they had been credited with 60 per cent of the gross earnings on business which they had brought to the main line, they would have shown a good profit. The policy of branch-line construction had met with the unanimous approval of successive boards of directors, and had been ratified by the stockholders in 1886; and in this connection the reply defended specifically the acquisition of the Wisconsin Central and other lines. The carrying of the floating debt by officials interested in the property, instead of being subject to criticism and censure, was entitled to the highest commendation.[2]

It is difficult to pass with justice upon the conflicting contentions above outlined. However, writing in 1905, long after his retirement from Northern Pacific affairs, Mr. Villard expressed himself as follows: "In 1891 Mr. Villard . . . made . . . his last official tour of inspection of the main line and principal branches of the Northern Pacific. . . . The most alarming impression of all made upon him was the revelation of the weight of the load that had been put upon the company by the purchase and construction of the longer branch lines in Montana and Washington, which he then discovered for the first time. There was the Missoula branch to the Cœur d'Alene mines; the Cœur d'Alene Railway & Navigation, a mixed system of steamboats and rail lines; the Seattle, Lake Shore & Eastern; and the roads built into Westernmost Washington; representing a total

[1] Ry. Times, 63: 275, 1893; Chron. 56: 332, 1893.
[2] Ry. Rev. 33: 143, 1893; Chron. 56: 362, 1893; Ry. Times, 63: 302, 1893; Ibid. p. 360. See also R. R. Gaz. 25: 161, 1893.

investment in cash and bonds of not far from $30,000,000, which together hardly earned operating expenses. The acquisition and building of these disappointing lines had in a few years absorbed the large amount of consolidated bonds set aside for construction purposes, which had been assumed to be sufficient for all needs in that direction for a long time." [1] No man should have known the real profitableness of these extensions better than Mr. Villard; and the circumstances of his account give it special weight. The admitted fact that in several cases the managers of the Northern Pacific voted as directors of that corporation to buy property from themselves as whole or part owners in other enterprises also excites distrust, and this feeling is strengthened by the unsatisfactory financial condition in 1893 of the Northern Pacific system as a whole.

Even before the report of the investigating committee the directors had been busy with the floating debt. This amounted to $9,918,000 late in 1892, according to the treasurer's statement. In February, 1893, it was decided to cancel it by the sale of the stock of the St. Paul & Northern Pacific held in the treasury, but this aroused violent opposition. The St. Paul & Northern Pacific ran, it will be remembered, from Brainerd to St. Paul and Minneapolis, and had formed the eastern terminus of the Northern Pacific system until the acquisition of the Wisconsin Central. It was justly considered an extremely important section of the main line, and the possible loss of its control was regarded as disastrous. [2] Dissuaded from their first purpose, the directors considered the issue of a collateral mortgage sufficient in amount to relieve all pressing necessities, and proposed to utilize in this way treasury securities which it would have been unwise to sell. At the same time the stockholders' committee had much the same idea in mind, and wrote to President Oakes in March, and again in May. "Referring to my letter to you of March 15," said Brayton Ives, "I beg to say that the financial plan therein referred to contemplates the creation of a collateral trust in which shall be placed $10,000,000 Northern Pacific consolidated 5s, $3,000,000 Chicago & Northern Pacific firsts, and all of the St.

[1] Memoirs, pp. 359–60.
[2] Among others the investigating committee protested loudly against a sale. Ry. Rev. 33: 127, 1893.

Paul & Northern Pacific stock belonging to the Northern Pacific Company, estimated at $7,000,000. Against these securities it is suggested that notes to the extent of $12,000,000 be issued, bearing 6 per cent interest, and payable in five years, or before, at the pleasure of the company, provision being made at the same time for the increase of the amount of the notes to $15,000,000 on the deposit of additional collateral securities satisfactory to the underwriters. I am happy to be able to repeat the belief already expressed, that if the board of directors will allow the underwriters to name seven directors of the company the entire amount of notes will be subscribed for without delay." [1] This plan was backed by responsible houses, including the Mercantile Trust Company, Kuhn, Loeb & Co., the Equitable Life Assurance Company, and others, who agreed to take $7,000,000 of the new bonds at 95, less $1\frac{1}{2}$ per cent commission. The directors paid no attention to Mr. Ives's letter, and his offer was subsequently withdrawn.

The directors' own scheme was dated May 1, 1893. It provided for a collateral five-year 6 per cent mortgage to the amount of $15,000,000, of which $12,000,000 were to be issued at once. There was to be a committee of five which should take charge of the issue, and which might sell the collateral before the maturity of the notes at certain minimum prices or over. Until all the notes should have been paid the railroad company agreed not to undertake the construction of any new lines without the consent of the committee, or to purchase or lease any railroad or navigation lines, or to guarantee, endorse, or purchase the bonds or other obligations or stocks of other companies. The committee was to have the voting power on the underlying stocks, and might direct the trust company to waive any default of the railroad company in payment of interest. The railroad company might call in the notes before maturity, after May 1, 1896, and pay them off at par and accrued interest. [2] This, it will be seen, did not differ in essence from the scheme proposed by Mr. Ives: — the real contest was between parties and not between plans. In June, Mr. Villard resigned his position as director and chairman of the board, and J. D. Rockefeller was elected a

---

[1] Ry. Times, 65: 595, 1893.

[2] Chron. 56: 1017, 1893; R. R. Gaz. 25: 398, 1893.

director. Somewhat earlier, but doubtless in anticipation of this action, a syndicate agreed to underwrite the collateral issue, subject to the stockholders' right of subscription;[1] and by the end of the year $10,275,000 of the collateral notes were outstanding, of which the bulk had been taken by the syndicate.[2] The whole device was very similar to that employed by the Union Pacific in 1891. It was not designed as a permanent remedy for anything, but served to postpone a reckoning to what was hoped would be better times. As a matter of fact its effect was very small.

Receivers for the Northern Pacific Railroad Company were appointed August 15, 1893, on a petition alleging that the company was insolvent and had no funds to meet payments coming due on September 1, October 1, November 1, and December 1. The company in its answer admitted the facts, and the United States Circuit Court at Milwaukee, Wisconsin, put Messrs. Henry C. Payne, Thomas F. Oakes, and Henry C. Rouse in charge of its affairs.[3] Receivers were rapidly appointed for most of the branch lines, the intent being to put all these properties in separate hands.[4] The receivers of the main line had nothing to do with the branches, although in November they were authorized to enter into temporary traffic agreements with them. In regard to the Wisconsin Central, application was early made to compel the Northern Pacific to carry out the provisions of the lease; but Judge Jenkins of the Milwaukee court granted the receivers until September 15 to decide whether or not they desired to continue, and upon their negative reply authorized a surrender. The accounts submitted, he said, showed that since the lease had gone into effect the Chicago & Northern Pacific had been operated at a loss to the Northern Pacific of $1,304,169 and the Wisconsin Central at a loss of $1,142,316; although business during the three years in question had been generally prosperous. In accordance with the decision the property was turned over to the

---

[1] The heaviest subscribers were the Rockefellers and Villard and his friends.

[2] Annual Report, 1893; Ry. Times, 64: 290, 1893.

[3] Criticism was aroused by the alleged fact that all three receivers were adherents and virtually protégés of Henry Villard. Ry. Times, 64: 290, 1893. See also Smalley, p. 291.

[4] Except that Henry Stanton of New York was to be the Eastern receiver for all the branches.

Wisconsin Company on September 26, 1893, and the Northern Pacific for a time gave up the idea of a Chicago terminus. Of the other leases those of the St. Paul & Northern Pacific and of the Cœur d'Alene Railway & Navigation Company were at this time approved by the court, and the receivers were authorized to make the necessary payments.

The failure of the Northern Pacific was the signal for still more active and bitter personal struggles between opposing factions than had before occurred. The opposition, led by Brayton Ives and August Belmont, endeavored to get control of the company through the annual election on October 19, and to procure the removal of the appointed receivers. They displayed the greatest bitterness toward Mr. Villard, and held him responsible for the position in which the company was placed. Villard's "remarkable qualities," wrote Ives, "have been of advantage only to himself. . . . The syndicate composed of Villard, Colby, Abbott, and Hoyt, and their friends made millions [by the Wisconsin Central deal] and the Northern Pacific has suffered and is suffering a corresponding loss."[1] Circulars were sent out asking proxies, and August Belmont, J. Horace Harding, Brayton Ives, Donald Mackay, and Winthrop Smith were appointed a committee to receive proxies as they came in. On the other side the directors appealed to the stockholders, reminded them that though the company had failed while they were in office it was also during their term that it had reached its greatest prosperity, and took the cautious step of amending the by-laws so as to shorten the term of future boards from three years to one. Conditions were against the management, and the result of the election was a complete victory for the Belmont-Ives party, which was followed up by the choice of Mr. Ives for president. The real results were less than might be supposed, for the operation of the railroad and the control of its funds were to be in the hands of the receivers and not in those of the officers of the road. On January 20 President Ives filed a petition in the Milwaukee Federal Court for an order directing the receivers to surrender the seal, books and papers and stock certificates, and to pay over sufficient money to enable the president to rent rooms and pay the salaries of the auditor, secre-

[1] Ry. Times, 64: 337, 1893.

tary, and treasurer.[1] The petition was denied, and the elected officers were left in an anomalous position.

In other matters the opposition lost no time in appealing to the courts. Previous even to the election two actions had been begun against Henry Villard: the one in September by John Swope of Philadelphia to compel Henry Villard and others to restore stock and bonds obtained as a result of an illegal conspiracy:[2] the other a petition in October by the Northern Pacific Company to force the receivers to bring suit against Messrs. Villard, Hoyt, and Colby to recover nearly $2,600,000 alleged to have been made unlawfully through Northern Pacific deals.[3] The complaints were in the main the same as those which had been made by the investigating committee, and charged, *inter alia*, that Villard had secured a profit to himself by bringing about the purchase of the Chicago terminal properties by the Northern Pacific. Mr. Villard swore that his whole interest in the transaction had been as officer and stockholder and securityholder of the Northern Pacific Company,[4] and the receivers professed themselves ready and willing to bring suit, provided they were furnished with the information and evidence wherewith to prosecute the same.[5] The Court reserved the Ives motion for further consideration, and the following year directed the receivers to bring suit; but the litigation was eventually dropped.[6]

In December, 1893, the Ives faction filed a petition for the removal of the receivers. The charges were in part similar to those of the Swope suit. It was asserted that at the time the receivers were appointed the road had practically had no hearing; that its managers had in less than a year burdened it with the interest of $60,000,000 for properties which were of no value to it, but in many of which they were personally interested and out of which they made large profits, and that when insolvency was produced by this fraud they had put the road in the hands of receivers nominated by them for the purpose, with the effect of perpetuating the same control which had brought the bankruptcy. Specific charges were made against Oakes, Villard, and Roswell C. Rolston, president of the Farmers'

---

[1] These officers had resigned in consequence of the non-payment of their salaries.
[2] Ry. Rev. 33: 587, 1893.   [3] Chron. 59: 697, 1894.   [4] Ibid. 57: 765, 1893.
[5] Ry. Age, 19: 40, 1894.   [6] Ry. Age, 23: 154, 1897.

Loan & Trust Company; no charges were made against Receivers Payne and Rouse, but their removal was asked for because they happened to be in the company of and presumably in the interest of Mr. Oakes. Besides this, finally, it was alleged that separate receivers had been unnecessarily appointed for branch lines, and that the expense of administering the affairs of the company had been enormously increased.[1] The receivers filed lengthy answers on February 3; Receiver Oakes in particular answering every charge specifically, filing exhaustive documents in proof, and maintaining in general the value of the branch properties and his innocence of unlawful profits.[2] The court on the whole inclined to his view. On April 14 Judge Jenkins handed down his decision, dismissing the petition for the removal of Messrs. Payne and Rouse, and holding Mr. Oakes's conduct to have been above investigation except in three instances, to examine which a master was appointed.[3] In the course of his decision Judge Jenkins concluded that the branch lines in question, though unprofitable for a while, were necessary to the system; and that in particular the branches in Washington, Oregon, Montana, and Idaho were built as feeders, and owing to the sparsely settled district were necessarily built for the future. If Mr. Oakes were to be removed on these charges, said he, then it would make the entire board of directors of the company at that time liable to impeachment.[4] Mr. Cary, the master, reported that Mr. Oakes had had no pecuniary interest and no personal advantage or gain from any of the matters referred to him for investigation. Mr. Villard was said to have made unlawful gains in the acquisition of the Northern Pacific & Manitoba Company to the extent of $363,494, but Mr. Oakes did not know that Mr. Villard was so interested, and was not bound to take notice to prevent such gains.[5] In consequence, Judge Jenkins in October granted a motion to dismiss the petition for the removal of Oakes as receiver,[6] and the incident was closed.

[1] Ry. Rev. 33: 783, 1893; Chron. 57: 1123, 1893; Ry. Age, 19: 11, 1894.
[2] Ry. Age, 19: 89, 1894.
[3] Ibid. 19: 231, 1894.
[4] R. R. Gaz. 26: 294, 1894; Chron. 58: 683, 1894.
[5] R. R. Gaz. 26: 642, 1894; Chron. 59: 473, 1894.
[6] Chron. 59: 738, 1894; Ibid. 59: 697, 1894.

It thus appears that Mr. Ives and his friends obtained but little satisfaction in the courts up to this point. They were unable to force the receivers to turn over any share of the Northern Pacific's earnings, and they were equally unable to remove the receivers from office. So long as the road should remain in the receivers' hands their authority seemed destined to be nominal, and they were thus spurred on by their own private interests to make some attempt at reorganization. At the same time their opponents, as bondholders, were not unwilling to receive some interest on their bonds, and succeeded in this, as in other matters, in drawing substantial control into their own hands. The year 1894 was a bad one and made the importance of a reduction in fixed charges loom large. Passenger earnings decreased from $5,917,054 to $3,960,772, and freight earnings from $17,017,630 to $11,418,692; while in spite of attempted economies by the receivers, net earnings decreased by almost the same absolute amount.[1] Cuts in wages were inevitable, and a serious strike aggravated the situation. It became necessary to borrow money from the Adams Reorganization Committee, of which more will be said later, and to issue $5,000,000 in receivers' certificates to pay off $5,000,000 already authorized in 1893. On September 8 formal announcement was made that the receiverships of the twenty-four branch lines of the Northern Pacific system were to be terminated, and that the trustee was to undertake the legal management of all the lines for a stated sum per annum; while the general receivers, Messrs. Oakes, Rouse, and Payne, were to operate the separated lines under a fair traffic agreement. It was figured that $64,000 per annum would be saved; and further economies were made in the cost of the administrative staff at New York. The relief was insufficient. Net earnings for 1894 were $5,506,007, and fixed charges were $12,004,985, and the need of a reorganization was impressively shown.

The work of devising a reorganization plan was done in the various bondholders' committees. Late in 1893 a committee of consolidated 5 per cent bondholders had been formed, with E. D. Adams as chairman and General Louis Fitzgerald as vice-chairman; which

[1] This is not to be explained by more liberal expenditures by the receivers on maintenance of way and equipment, for the sums applied to both these purposes were materially less in 1894 than in 1893.

declared itself to be independent, but was regarded as affiliated with the former managers of the road. In March, 1894, this committee announced that, having received responses from the holders of a majority of the consolidated bonds, it had prepared an agreement and had secured its acceptance by the German bondholders. All consolidated bondholders were requested to deposit their securities with the Mercantile Trust Company, which would issue engraved certificates of deposit, which the committee would endeavor to have listed on the Stock Exchange. Mr. Ives was opposed to any step toward reorganization of this sort, and objected particularly to the composition of the committee; he therefore asked bondholders to withhold their acceptance of the agreement, and gave various reasons to lend weight to his request. In April, as a counter-move, he invited bondholders to send in their names and addresses to him, together with the amount of their holdings, saying that this action would not commit the bondholders, and was desired only to enable the company to furnish information respecting its affairs, and, when the proper time should arise, to confer about a reorganization plan. The rapid falling off in earnings soon imperilled the interest of the second and third mortgage bonds, superior to the consolidated mortgage. In July the Adams Committee appealed to the holders of these issues, and secured a considerable number of deposits. Henceforth it planned to act as a general reorganization committee. On the other hand a committee headed by Johnston Livingston competed for deposits of the second mortgage, and one headed by C. B. Van Nostrand for deposits of the third mortgage bonds. It was urged that holders of the earlier issues should not deposit with the consolidated committee, because its interest lay in cutting down prior liens; whereas the Van Nostrand Committee declared that the road could earn the interest on the third mortgage, and that these bonds should not accept less than par and interest in cash. Nevertheless the Deutsche Bank's London agency announced in September that it was prepared to receive second mortgage, third mortgage, and consolidated bonds on behalf of the Adams Committee, and to forward the same to New York for deposit. Various rumors were afloat at this time concerning reorganization, and suggestions were made for converting the third mortgage bonds into 5 per cent income bonds and the consolidated bonds into preferred stock;[1] but the only result was to stir up protests from the third mortgage bondholders, who still insisted in August that earnings were more than sufficient to pay the interest on all prior liens. Late in the year there was talk of selling the road under foreclosure of the second mortgage, but this too came to nothing.

Meanwhile the operation of the road went on. Receiver Rouse reported on the condition of the property in January, 1894. He estimated that $10,000,000 would be required to bring the permanent way into the most effective condition for economical operation. Exceptional causes, said he, had contributed to make the earnings for the previous three years exceptionally large, and this fact, together with the prevailing depression, the competition of the Great Northern, and reduced rates, would decrease the gross earnings in the immediate future at least 27 per cent. Although Mr. Rouse believed in the value of the Northern Pacific's branch lines, his report was not encouraging.[2] In September, on the approach of the annual election, President Ives issued a long circular. The serious decrease in the earnings of the road, he said, had affected for the worse the position of the stockholders, and these holders should understand that no one of the reorganization committees was working for their interest. He announced the appointment of a committee to receive proxies, and revealed the embarrassment of the management by a request for contributions of $12.50 per hundred shares in order to pay the expenses of the officers. So far as the officers should have any voice in the matter, President Ives assured the stockholders, contributions should be credited on any assessments which might be made thereafter. On the day of the election no opposing ticket was presented, and the Ives party were reëlected to their positions. This is where matters stood at the beginning of 1895. The hostility of the opposing committees was in no way abated; but the Adams Committee had secured deposits of nearly $21,000,000 of the consolidated mortgage bonds, $1,000,000 more than a majority of the third mortgage bonds,[3] and $3,000,000 less than a majority of the second

---

[1] Ry. Times, 65: 87, 1894.

[2] Ibid. 65: 38, 1884.

[3] R. R. Gaz. 27: 160, 1895.

mortgage bonds, and with the hearty support of the Deutsche Bank was steadily strengthening its position.[1]

In May, 1895, the Adams Committee reorganization plan came out and marked the first serious suggestion for a rehabilitation of the property. It proposed a sale, under foreclosure, of the old company and the formation of a new company under special arrangements for this purpose. The new company was to issue $100,000,000 in shares, and a maximum of $200,000,000 in gold bonds free from taxation, secured by a mortgage lien on the whole Northern Pacific system, including the St. Paul & Northern Pacific Railway, and bearing interest partly at 4 per cent and partly at 3 per cent, all under the same mortgage. A sufficient amount of these bonds was to be reserved to replace the existing first mortgage, besides a further amount to acquire independent branch lines or for new construction at a maximum charge of $20,000 per mile. The principal and interest of the new bonds were to be guaranteed unconditionally by the Great Northern Road, in return for which the Great Northern was to receive one-half of the stock of the new company. The new board was to consist of nine directors, of whom four were to be nominated by the Northern Pacific Reorganization Committee. Each $1000 Northern Pacific second mortgage bond was to receive a $1125 new Northern Pacific guaranteed bond; each $1000 third mortgage bond a new $1000 3 per cent guaranteed bond, and at least $250 in shares; each $1000 5 per cent consol at least $500 in new 3 per cent guaranteed bonds and $300 in shares. Overdue coupons of the second mortgage were to be paid in cash at the rate of 5 per cent annually, those of the third mortgage at 4 per cent, and those of the consols to be adjusted at the rate of $2\frac{1}{2}$ per cent in new 3 per cent bonds. The floating debt of the receivership was to be paid by an assessment of about $11,000,000 on the old stock. The reorganization and the raising of the necessary working capital were to be secured by a syndicate headed by J. P. Morgan & Company and the Deutsche Bank.[2]

[1] For opposing circulars by the Livingston Committee and by the directors see Ry. Rev. 35: 55, 1895. On February 20, 1896, a Stockholders' Protective Committee was appointed, consisting of August Belmont, Brayton Ives, and George R. Sheldon of New York, and Charlemagne Tower, of Philadelphia. Chron. 62: 365, 1896.

[2] Chron. 60: 930, 1895.

Briefly stated, this plan proposed to decrease somewhat the funded debt, while reducing also the interest rate from 6 and 5 to 4 and 3 per cent. The reduction in fixed charges which would have ensued it is impossible to estimate without further details. The amount which bondholders were asked to give up was, however, considerable, and for this compensation was variously given in new bonds and in new stock. The floating debt was not to be funded, but was to be paid off by the commendable method of an assessment; and provision was made for working capital, although at what cost in profits to the syndicate was not stated. But more important than the details of the plan was the guarantee of the new issues by the Great Northern Company for which it provided. The question of consolidation between the Northern Pacific and the Great Northern was said, on what purported to be good authority, to have originated on the side of the Northern Pacific among men to whom an alliance seemed necessary to the prosperity of the latter road.[1] Mr. Hill was said to have been at first reluctant, and to have consented only on condition that a majority of the Northern Pacific stock should be placed within his hands. It can scarcely be supposed, however, that he did not welcome such a union; and the petition of the Northern Pacific receivers for the cancellation of contracts with the Great Northern and the Minneapolis Union railway companies[2] made consolidation especially desirable at this time. To the end of this consolidation the Adams Committee plan was chiefly framed, and on its execution the adequacy of the plan depended. If the Great Northern could have been induced to guarantee the principal and interest of the new Northern Pacific bonds the likelihood of a default would have been reduced to a minimum, even on the indebtedness outstanding before the receivership; and a scheme for paying the floating debt and for providing a certain amount of new capital would have been all that would have been required. But it is clear that a proposal for a consolidation of two of the principal lines serving the Northwest brought the consuming and producing public to an interest in the Northern Pacific reorganization which they had not

[1] R. R. Gaz. 27: 590, 1895.
[2] For the use of trackage and terminals at and between St. Paul and Minneapolis. See Ry. Age, 20: 161, 1895; Ibid. 20: 198, 1895; Ry. Rev. 35: 209, 1895.

felt before. So long as a reorganization plan dealt merely with exchanges and manipulation of securities by and among security-holders, the influence of any settlement on outsiders was very indirect; but when it operated to reduce competition in a large section of the country the effect was plain and striking. Certain conservative financiers suggested a holding company to hold the Great Northern and Northern Pacific stock, in order to throw some sort of a veil over the proceedings, but Mr. Hill would not consent.[1] Late in August, 1895, therefore, a bill in equity was filed to prevent the proposed coöperation, and on September 17 Attorney-General Childs, for the state of Minnesota, brought suit for an injunction on the ground that the combination was contrary to the laws of the state and would prevent competition. It was said that Mr. Childs was supported by the practically unanimous sentiment of the people of Washington and Montana. The matter came before the Supreme Court on suit by one Pearsall, a stockholder of the Great Northern, and this tribunal held that the combination was contrary to the laws of Minnesota and should, therefore, be enjoined, affirming the principle for which Mr. Childs contended.[2] This settled the fate of the Adams reorganization plan; and an entirely new scheme had to be devised.

But while once more progress toward reorganization seemed to have ceased, sensational developments occurred in the factional conflicts to which we have already referred. To Mr. Ives, barred from all participation in the management of the road, denied a salary, and unable to obtain the removal of the receivers by Judge Jenkins, came the idea of appealing to another court. It will be remembered that the original receivership suit had been instituted in the circuit court of Milwaukee, Wisconsin, and that that court ever since had been regarded as possessing primary jurisdiction. Since no compulsion existed on other courts to recognize this jurisdiction of the Milwaukee court, the orders of which were supreme in its own district only, and the smooth working of the receivership was due to a respect for "comity," it was possible, as Ives well knew, for any circuit court along the line to throw existing arrange-

[1] Chron. 61: 325, 1895.
[2] Pearsall *vs.* Great Northern Railway Company, 161 U. S. 647.

ments into the direst confusion. Relying on this fact, President Ives sent the General Counsel of the company to present applications for the removal of the receivers to one court after the other along the road.[1] In September, 1895, judges willing to take jurisdiction were found in Seattle, in the far northwestern corner of the United States.[2] Petition was made in two parts: first, that the Seattle court take jurisdiction; second, that it remove Messrs. Oakes, Rouse, and Payne. Judge Hanford of the Federal Court of the Washington District called Judge Gilbert of the United States Circuit Court to sit with him, and deciding on the question of jurisdiction first, according to the request of the receivers, the two judges held that the principle of comity did not of necessity apply in the Northern Pacific case because no part of the railroad was within the jurisdiction of Judge Jenkins's court, and any court along the road could more properly and efficiently administer the trust. The court, therefore, directed the receivers to answer the charges of malfeasance, and to file their answers in Seattle by October 2; also to file their accounts with the clerk of the court at Seattle,[3] and to file each a $100,000 bond.[4]

The result was the prompt resignation of the receivers, who in a letter to Judge Jenkins made their feelings clear. "Your receivers manifestly cannot administer the trust," said they, "with justice to the parties interested, or themselves, if subject to the orders and instructions as to the general administration from two or more independent tribunals. We cannot abide, nor can we ask our sureties to abide, the danger of the differences of opinion between courts, each assuming to be controlling as to the expenditures of the receivership in the general administration, in view of the immensity of the interests involved. . . . Unless your receivers recognize, as they understand it, that that honorable court [the Seattle court] is the court of primary jurisdiction they will of necessity be in contumacy. . . . Your receivers are not willing under any circumstances to file an additional bond in such jurisdiction, nor are they willing to put

[1] Ry. Rev. 35: 461, 1895.
[2] Proceedings were begun in the Seattle court in August. See Chron. 61: 241, 1895; Ry. Age, 20: 394, 1895; Ibid. 20: 418, 1895; Ibid. 20: 430, 1895.
[3] Up to this time such accounts had been filed in the Milwaukee court.
[4] Ry. Age, 20: 442, 1895; Ry. Rev. 35: 503, 1895.

themselves in a position to endanger their right to challenge the jurisdiction of that honorable court." [1] Judge Jenkins accepted the resignations and appointed Messrs. McHenry, chief engineer of the Northern Pacific, and Bigelow, a Milwaukee banker, receivers.[2] The hitherto respected principle of comity had, however, lost all force. On September 30 Judge Sanborn at St. Paul confirmed Judge Jenkins's appointments for the states of Minnesota and North Dakota; on October 1 Judge Hanford at Tacoma refused to accept the resignation of the old receivers, but removed them and appointed Andrew F. Burleigh for the district of Washington; on October 2 Judge Billinger concurred in Burleigh's appointment for Oregon; on October 7 Judge Knowles at Helena, Montana, confirmed the above for the districts of Washington and Oregon, and appointed Captain J. H. Mills and E. L. Bonner for the district of Montana; and in the week ending October 26 Judge Beatty appointed Burleigh receiver for Idaho. The only conservative action was that of Judge Lacombe in New York, who deferred his appointments as often as the matter came before him, in the hope that the Western judges would come to an agreement.

The situation at the end of October, 1895, was as follows: in Wisconsin, Minnesota, and North Dakota there were two receivers, Messrs. McHenry and Bigelow; in Montana there were three receivers, Messrs. Mills, Bonner, and Burleigh; and in Idaho, Washington, and Oregon there was one receiver, Andrew F. Burleigh. It was a condition of affairs which could not be endured. In each of the Western States orders were made compelling all agents or persons connected with the road to deposit all money collected in that state, and it was at any time in the power of the receivers in any state to appoint operating officers distinct from those managing traffic over the other parts of the line. On January 9, 1896, Judge Gilbert simplified the situation by retiring Messrs. Mills and Bonner, and by appointing Andrew F. Burleigh sole receiver for the district of Montana. This reduced the number of receivers to three, and left Burleigh in control of the road west of North Dakota, and McHenry and Bigelow in control of the rest. Application was now

[1] Ry. Age, 20: 478, 1895; R. R. Gaz. 27: 648, 1895.

[2] Chron. 61: 611, 1895; Ry. Times, 68: 442, 1895.

made to the Supreme Court of the United States, and on January
28, 1896, four justices of this tribunal, acting as justices assigned to
the several districts in which the Northern Pacific Railroad Company had property,[1] decided that Judge Jenkins's court for the Eastern District of Wisconsin should be considered the court of primary
jurisdiction, and issued each an order to this effect to take effect in
his particular circuit.[2] The various circuit judges hastened to conform. On February 21 Judge Lacombe confirmed the appointment of F. G. Bigelow and E. H. McHenry as receivers for the
Second Judicial District, and similar action had by then been taken
by the judges of the other districts except that of the state of Washington. There Judges Gilbert and Hanford refused to discharge
Burleigh, although recognizing that the general orders for the management and control of the railroad property were henceforth to
issue from Judge Jenkins's court.[3] The judicial strife was thus at an
end. President Ives obtained the removal of the receivers to whom
he particularly objected, but did not overthrow the authority of
the Milwaukee court, nor secure any material gain to compensate
for the great trouble which he caused.

With the receivership tangle straightened out it became possible

[1] Justices Brown, Harlan, Brewer, and Field.

[2] "We are of the opinion," said Justices Field, Harlan, and Brewer, "that proceedings to foreclose a mortgage upon lines extending through more than one district
should be commenced in the Circuit Court in which the principal operating offices
are situated, and in which there is some material part of the railroad embraced by
the mortgage. Such court should be the court of primary jurisdiction. But in view
of the fact that a portion of the line of road owned by the Northern Pacific Company
is within the State of Wisconsin, and that at the time of the filing of the creditors'
bill the Northern Pacific Railroad Company was operating a road through the
Eastern District of Wisconsin, although such road was under lease to it for 99 years;
and in view of the further fact that the railroad company assented to the action
of the Circuit Court for the Eastern District of Wisconsin in taking jurisdiction,
and as such jurisdiction has been recognized by the Circuit Court in every district
. . . for the space of about two years, we are of the opinion that the Circuit Court
for the Eastern District of Wisconsin has jurisdiction to proceed to a decree of foreclosure which will bind the mortgagor company and the mortgaged property, and
ought to be recognized by the Circuit Court of every district along the line as the
court of primary jurisdiction." Chron. 62: 234, 1896.

[3] Justice Field of the Supreme Court declined to exercise his authority to remove
Burleigh, intimating that the existing arrangement was satisfactory. Ry. Age, 21:
174, 1896.

to proceed again with the work of reorganization, and on March 16, 1896, the final plan was published, endorsed not only by the Adams Committee, but by President Ives and his Stockholders' Protective Committee, and by other important interests as well. The feeling had become general that some action should speedily be taken, and that it was in the interest of all parties that the factional conflicts which had raged so long and with so little result should cease. Reorganization was proposed on the following basis:

(*a*) The abandonment of Chicago as the eastern terminus, and the limitation of the railway on the east by the Mississippi River and the Great Lakes; — the bonds and stocks of the Chicago & Northern Pacific and of the Chicago & Calumet Companies to be sold.

(*b*) The ultimate union of the main line, branches, and terminal properties through direct ownership by a single company.

(*c*) The reduction of the fixed annual charges to less than the minimum earnings under probable conditions.

(*d*) Ample provision for additional capital as required in a series of years for the development of the property and for the greater facilities necessitated by an increased business.

There were to be issued:

$130,000,000 in prior lien 100-year 4 per cent gold bonds, to be secured by a mortgage upon the main line, branches, terminals, land grant, equipment, and other property embraced in the reorganization . . . and . . . thereafter acquired.[1]

$190,000,000 in general lien 150-year 3 per cent gold bonds, with a lien junior to the previous issue, but covering the same property, of which $130,000,000 were to be reserved to retire the $130,000,000 prior lien bonds when they should fall due.

$70,000,000 in 4 per cent non-cumulative preferred stock.

$80,000,000 in common stock.

Generally speaking, the new prior liens were to go for old first and second mortgage bonds, receivers' certificates, equipment trusts, collateral trust notes, St. Paul & Northern Pacific bonds, and for new construction; the new general liens for mortgages junior to the second mortgage; the new preferred stock as additional inducement to the

---

[1] The existing general mortgage covered only the main line, land grant, and equipment so far as owned by the company.

exchanges mentioned above, and in part for the retirement of old preferred stock; and the common stock for old preferred stock (in part) and common stock. Existing first mortgage bondholders were not, however, to be forced to give up their old securities. "It is not sought in any way to enforce a conversion of the present general first mortgage bonds," said the plan, "and this offer is made solely on the belief that on the terms proposed such conversion, while advantageous to the company, is also manifestly to the advantage of the bondholders so converting." There were reserved $4,000,000 of the general liens for new construction, and $2,500,000 new preferred and an equal amount of common were set aside under the general head "to provide for reorganization purposes or available as a treasury asset." None of the new bonds were to be subject to drawing or to compulsory redemption prior to their regular maturity. The proceeds from land sales to an amount not exceeding $500,000 in any year were to be devoted to the redemption by purchase and cancellation of the new bonds, purchases to be made of prior liens so long as these could be secured at not over 110, after which to continue of the securities next in rank. The preferred stock was to have a claim for 4 per cent before anything should be paid on the common stock, and was to participate equally with the common after 4 per cent had been paid on each. There was to be a voting trust until November 1, 1901, unless closed out earlier by the voting trustees, after the expiration of which the preferred stock was to have the right to elect a majority of the board of directors whenever for two successive years 4 per cent dividends on their holdings should not have been paid. No additional mortgage was to be put upon the property, and the amount of preferred stock was not to be increased, except, in each instance, after obtaining the consent of a majority of the whole amount of the preferred stock, given at a meeting of the stockholders called for that purpose, and the consent of a majority of such common stock as should be represented at such meeting, the holders of each class of stock voting separately. During the existence of the voting trust the consent of holders of like amounts of the respective classes of beneficial certificates was to be necessary. There was to be an assessment of $10 on preferred stock and of $15 on common. Branch lines were to be consolidated with the main line, but each case was to be dealt with separately, and a fair basis of adjustment arrived at, for which general lien 3 per cents and new preferred stock were reserved. There was to be an underwriting syndicate, formed by J. P. Morgan & Company, and the Deutsche Bank of Berlin, to the subscribed amount of $45,000,000, to provide amounts of cash estimated to be necessary to carry out the terms of the plan, and to furnish the new company with some $5,000,000 working capital for early use in betterments and enlargements of its property. The syndicate's compensation was not stated in the plan, but was to be "reasonable," and in addition to it the sum of ¼ per cent of the par value of all securities deposited was to be paid to J. P. Morgan & Company and the Deutsche Bank for their respective services as managers and depositaries. Finally, at the discretion of the managers, the various properties were to be sold under one of the several mortgages in default, and a successor company was to be organized.[1]

An examination of this plan shows that the total capitalization proposed, exclusive of bonds and stock reserved for new construction, etc., amounted to $311,000,000; of which $161,000,000 were 4 per cent and 3 per cent bonds and $150,000,000 stock. The reported capitalization of the Northern Pacific Railroad in 1893 had been $218,685,631, including the bonds of branch roads guaranteed; but comparison of this figure with that given by the plan is not fair, because in 1893 the Northern Pacific property had been owned by fifty-four distinct corporations, which the reorganization proposed to consolidate into one. A comparison of the total bonds and stock issued by the fifty-four corporations with the issue under the reorganization plan reveals an increase from $271,949,044 to $311,000,000, or 14.3 per cent. At the same time fixed charges were to be decreased, according to estimates, from $10,509,690 to $6,052,660; to cover which the managers reported net earnings of $6,015,846 for the year ending June 30, 1895, and of $7,801,645 for the average of the five years ending with that date. It will be observed, therefore, that the plan left no margin between net earnings in 1895 and fixed charges, but relied upon an increase in earnings for the future to preserve the solvency of the road. It is, however, only just to say that the net

---

[1] See Circular of the Reorganization Committee, or Chron. 62: 550, 1896; Ry. Times, 69: 287–8, 1896.

earnings in 1895 were less than they had been in any year since 1887, with the exception of 1894, and that a considerable increase was probable. The large reduction in fixed charges which was to take place was to be chiefly at the expense of holders of the consolidated mortgage bonds of 1889. These unfortunate investors received but 129 per cent in new securities, of which nearly one-half was stock, in return for a reduction in their fixed annual income from 5 to 2 per cent, the reason being the inferior character of their mortgage lien. That securityholders who had consented to exchange their prior securities in 1889 for the consols then issued in the hope of benefiting the road should have fared considerably worse than bondholders who had refused to make concessions is an example of the injustice sometimes occasioned by successive reorganizations and refundings. Of the other securities the second mortgage received prior liens and stock sufficient to bring its return over 6 per cent, providing the road should earn it, and the third mortgage and dividend certificates received general liens and stock sufficient to yield something over 5 per cent except in very prosperous times, when their income would be larger. The underlying principle in these cases was the union of a security with a fixed claim on earnings with a security with a conditional claim only. The first mortgage received no stock, and so was denied participation in future profits, but in recompense gave up only some .6 per cent in the annual income received. The collateral trust notes fared nearly as badly as the consolidated mortgage, but the northwest equipment stock was paid off in cash. In brief, all securities but the equipment stock yielded something, and the greatest sacrifices were demanded from the junior securities. On the other hand, the stock was far from escaping unscathed. On January 2, 1896, the quoted prices were $3\frac{1}{2}$ for common and $12\frac{5}{8}$ for preferred. As against this the plan made assessments of $15 on common and $10 on preferred; — sums which could obviously be demanded only because of the probable future appreciation of the shares. A point in favor of the stock was the fact that the reduction in fixed charges brought it nearer a dividend; although it must be remembered that the common stock had to divide any return above 4 per cent with the preferred.

The other salient points of the plan were the provision for paying the floating debt, for supplying fresh capital for future additions and improvements, for consolidation of branch lines with the main stem, and for a voting trust. The total floating debt in 1895 amounted to over $20,000,000, of which $4,900,000 consisted of outstanding receivers' certificates and $8,329,205 of interest matured and unpaid.[1] The unpaid interest was provided for in the exchanges which have already been described; the receivers' certificates were cancelled by prior lien bonds, and the balance was provided for by assessment. This method was a sound one. The provision for new construction, betterments, etc., was liberal, consisting of $25,000,000 prior lien bonds, of which no more than $1,500,000 were to be issued in any year, and $4,000,000 general lien bonds, presumably to be used as needed. One of the great difficulties in the history of the company had been the lack of necessary capital for needed work upon the line, and it was well that future requirements were provided for. The consolidation of the branch lines into the parent company was also wise. "As it [the Northern Pacific system] now stands," the committee said, "the system, in its form of incorporation and capitalization, is a development without method or adequate preparation for growth. Scarcely any single security is complete in itself. The main line mortgages cover neither feeders nor terminals. The terminal mortgages may be bereft of their main line support. The branch lines are dependent on the main line for interchange of business and the main line owes a large part of its business to the branch lines."[2] The plan contemplated separate bargains with each branch. Negotiations were carried on during 1896, and some of the arrangements arrived at were as follows: The bondholders of the Northern Pacific & Manitoba Terminal and of the James River Valley Railroad agreed to take 50 per cent in new Northern Pacific 3 per cent bonds and 50 per cent in preferred stock, and to allow the Northern Pacific to retain their property.[3] Bondholders of the Duluth & Manitoba were given 90 per cent in cash.[4] Bondholders of the Spokane & Palouse received 52½ per cent cash, 52½ per cent in general 3s, and 25 per cent in Northern Pacific preferred stock,[5] and Helena & Red Mountain

---

[1] In addition there were $73,875 of unpaid interest on receivers' certificates.
[2] See R. R. Gaz. 28: 219, 1896, for editorial on plan.
[3] Ibid. 28: 349, 1896.
[4] Chron. 62: 1139, 1896; Ibid. 63: 155, 1896.
[5] Chron. 62: 990, 1896; Ibid. 62: 1041, 1896.

bondholders agreed to accept 100 per cent in new preferred.[1] A number of the branches were foreclosed and bought in by the Northern Pacific reorganization committee, and the net result was an exceedingly beneficial unification of the system. Finally, the voting trust was designed to secure permanence in policy during the first years of the new company's existence. The idea has been a common, and on the whole a wise one. In this case the membership represented fairly the interests which had been prominent throughout the receivership, and consisted of J. P. Morgan, George Siemans, representing the Deutsche Bank, August Belmont, Johnston Livingston, and Charles Lanier. The trustees were to fill their own vacancies, except that the successors of George Siemans were always to be nominated by the Deutsche Bank.

In the main the plan was a good one, following a sound principle, and reducing fixed charges to a point which, if not far below the danger-line, proved low enough in view of the subsequent development in business. Current opinion was generally favorable, and criticised only the amount of profits which the syndicate was to secure on the basis of its large subscribed capital. Mr. Hill of the Great Northern said: "I think the Northern Pacific reorganization plan will be successful. The promoters have adopted a conservative policy, and have marked the interest charges down. We are entirely satisfied to have the Northern Pacific securityholders run the road, pay its debts, and be charged with the responsibility of meeting all its proper obligations, rather than to have it operated by the officers of two or three courts which are continually contending as to jurisdiction." [2] By April 23, when the time for deposits expired, the reorganization committee was able to announce that it held over 92½ per cent in amount of general, second, and third mortgage bonds, dividend certificates, consolidated mortgage bonds, collateral trust notes, preferred stock, common stock, northwest equipment stock, and Northern Pacific and Montana first mortgage bonds, and that the plan and agreement was therefore declared operative.[3] By June a majority of the first mortgage bonds had been secured, and it was announced that after June 30 the basis of con-

---

[1] Chron. 62: 1088, 1896.   [2] Ry. Times, 69: 511, 1896.
[3] Chron. 62: 779, 1896.

version of this issue would be reduced from 135 to 132 per cent in new 4 per cent prior lien bonds. On July 24 the Northern Pacific *Railway* filed its articles of incorporation at St. Paul, Minnesota, and the next day the sale of the property took place, in spite of suits by the general creditors and the preferred stockholders. The sale was in three parcels, and the property was bid in for $12,500,000 by Mr. Winter, the newly elected president. After the first sale the company's lands in Wisconsin were offered and bid in for $575,000, and two days later the lands west of the Missouri were bought in for sums aggregating $600,000. Finally, on August 4, the lands in Washington and Oregon were bought in for $1,705,200 and $558,000 respectively. The property of the company was turned over by the receivers to the reorganization committee at midnight, August 31, and on November 7 the final step in the reorganization plan was taken by the formal authorization by the stockholders of the issue of $190,000,000 of bonds.[1]

From 1896 to the present time the Northern Pacific has enjoyed a development scarcely less noteworthy than that of the Union Pacific. Gross earnings have increased from $23,679,718 in 1898, the first full year after the receivership, to $68,534,832 in 1907; net revenue from $13,471,544 to $33,208,840; and mileage from 4350 to 5444. Gross earnings per mile were $5443 in 1898; they were $12,590 in 1907. The retirement of the eastern terminus of the system from Chicago to St. Paul and Minneapolis was accomplished in the course of 1897 by arrangement for connection with the Chicago & Northwestern instead of with the Wisconsin Central, and the sale of the certificates of proprietary interest in the Chicago Terminal Transfer Railroad received by the Northern Pacific under the Chicago & Northern Pacific plan of reorganization; while the improvement of the position of the new mortgages has been vigorously prosecuted by the rapid drawing for redemption of old first mortgage bonds at 110, and by the calling of the entire issue of the Missouri division bonds at par and accrued interest.

---

[1] Curiously enough the sale did not extinguish the old Northern Pacific Railroad Company. Some 25,000 or more shares did not assent to the reorganization plan and are still outstanding. They assert that it is because of them that the old organization is kept up.

In the years following 1897 large sums have been spent for betterments and enlargements. Some $68,500,000 have been invested from the proceeds of the sale of prior lien bonds and of miscellaneous assets, and over $18,000,000 have been temporarily withdrawn from income for the same purpose.[1] Grades have been reduced, lines straightened, new branches built, real estate acquired, track relaid and ballasted, bridges strengthened and renewed, equipment rebuilt and increased in amount, and other similar betterments undertaken. It is a work which all the great American systems have carried on, but the Northern Pacific has surpassed even the Union Pacific in the extent of its operations. Ordinary maintenance requirements have not meanwhile been neglected, and in 1906 and 1907 the Northern Pacific set aside $2,000,000 for depreciation of equipment, which is over and above the other sums which have been mentioned. The company owned 1255 locomotives on June 30, 1907, of an average weight of 174,000 pounds; in 1898 it had owned 542 of an average weight of 104,000 pounds. It had 42,000 freight cars in 1907 with an average capacity of over 33 tons; it had possessed 18,500 in 1898 of an average capacity of 22 tons. Seventy-five per cent of the main line was laid with track of 72 pounds or over in 1906, but only thirteen per cent in 1898. In consequence heavier trains are run,[2] at a less expense per ton, and the net revenue is correspondingly increased. Even the liberal expenditures which have hitherto been made are insufficient, however, for present conditions, and the stockholders have approved a proposal to issue $93,000,000 of new common stock at par for the purpose of extending the Northern Pacific's mileage and facilities.[3]

The endeavor to stimulate traffic to fill the trains has led to important developments. In order to increase the exchange of commodities between their territory and the Middle West, to establish stable conditions on transcontinental business and thereby to secure back loading for their cars, the Great Northern and Northern

---

[1] From 1898 to 1907 inclusive. This does not include advances to subsidiary companies, which have aggregated nearly $20,000,000.

[2] The average train load in 1907 was 406.77 tons; that in 1898 was 264.59 tons.

[3] Chron. 83: 1524, 1906; Ibid. 84: 103, 1907. The new issue is to go in part for improvements previously made out of income. The directors have adopted the questionable policy of charging all such expenditures to capital account.

Pacific in 1901 arranged for the purchase of the Burlington system which connected both their lines with Chicago. The refusal to share their purchase with Mr. Harriman led to the competitive purchase of Northern Pacific stock by rival interests, and to the retirement of the Northern Pacific preferred, but did not prevent the consummation of the deal.[1] This purchase has been a profitable one. The Burlington has paid in dividends upon its stock almost enough to cover the interest on the bonds issued to acquire it, and the indirect effects of its control have satisfied expectations. Indeed, the eastbound lumber traffic has so developed that the Great Northern has recently raised its lumber rates in order once more to equalize east- and west-bound shipments.

The Northern Pacific has been openly dominated by the Hill-Morgan interests for the last six years, and probably has been under their control since its reorganization. From the financial as well as from the traffic point of view its position is secure. The voting trust was dissolved in 1901 "by reason," in the words of the trustees, "of the evidence of financial strength, conservative management, skilful and profitable operation, superior physical condition of the property, and the reasonable prospect of continued prosperity." [2] In 1907, out of a net income of $33,208,840 only $9,575,183 were paid out for interest, rentals, and taxes, and $23,473,929 were left for dividends, improvements, and reserve. This whole sum, which amounts to 33 per cent of gross income, is available as a protection for the mortgage bonds; and a considerable portion could be dispensed with without forcing a decrease in the present rate of dividends.[3] It is likely that the coming years will see a check in the advance of national prosperity, but the Northern Pacific is in excellent condition to stand the strain.

---

[1] For this and for an account of the Northern Securities episode see B. H. Meyer, A History of the Northern Securities Case, Bulletin of the University of Wisconsin, July, 1906.

[2] Annual Report, 1901.

[3] The dividends declared by the Northern Pacific Railway have been:

	1898	1899	1900	1901	1902	1903	1904	1905	1906	1907
Common stock		2	4	4	$5\frac{1}{2}$	7	$6\frac{3}{4}$	7	7	$5\frac{1}{4}$*
Preferred stock	5	4	4	4	1					

* Including August.

CHAPTER IX

ROCK ISLAND

Charter — Early prosperity — Reorganization of 1880 — Conservative policy — Extension — Pays dividends throughout the nineties — Moores obtain control — Reorganization of 1902 — Further extensions — Impaired credit of the company.

THE original Rock Island Railroad, chartered in 1847,[1] was completed between Chicago and Rock Island in 1854. Construction was continued from Rock Island to Council Bluffs across the state of Iowa, under the charter of the Mississippi & Missouri, until 1866, when this company was merged with the original Rock Island Railroad Company, and after 1866 under the Rock Island charter until the extension was completed in 1869. Unlike the Atchison, the Rock Island passed through a fairly well-settled territory, which was at the same time one of the most fertile in the United States. In 1870, according to the census returns, Iowa produced 28,708,312 bushels of spring wheat out of a total for the United States of 112,-549,733 bushels, more than any other state in the Union; while Illinois in its yield of winter wheat was surpassed by Indiana and Ohio alone. Of Indian corn Iowa and Illinois together produced 198,-856,460 bushels against 562,088,089 for all other states combined. Manufactures were well begun, and even mining had attained a considerable development, particularly in the extraction of bituminous coal in Illinois. Naturally the road was prosperous; gross earnings increased from $3,154,236 in 1866 to $5,995,226 in 1870, and to $9,409,833 in 1879; while net earnings attained the very considerable sum of $4,548,117 in 1879, being 48 per cent of the gross receipts. At the same time the capitalization was very moderate, due to the relatively level character of the country through which the road ran, and, not less important, to the absence of speculative financial operations in the course of its construction. To build 1231 miles had cost in 1879 but $35,664,200, of which $4,702,202 had been supplied from earnings; leaving a total of bonds and stocks of

[1] Poor's Manual, 1878. The name was first the Rock Island & La Salle Railroad Company, and was changed to the Chicago & Rock Island Railroad Company in February, 1851.

$30,962,000, or $25,151 per mile. Fixed charges were, therefore, low. In 1875, when net earnings were $3,853,676, interest on bonds, taxes, and all other necessary disbursements took but $1,065,395; and in 1879 the payments were markedly less. Is it strange that the troubles of the road came from too great earnings rather than from too small, and that instead of striving to maintain solvency the directors had to seek ways and means for concealing or getting rid of earnings without arousing the hostility of legislators to whom 10 per cent dividends seemed high, and anything over 10 per cent proof of extortion? Between 1866 and 1876 four cash distributions of 10 per cent were made to stockholders, five of 8 per cent, one of 8½ per cent, and one of 7½ per cent. The dividend for 1879 was again 10 per cent, that of 1878 8 per cent, and that for 1879 9½ per cent. Meanwhile large sums were carried to surplus. The balance, after all disbursements, never after 1873 fell below $665,000, and in 1879 was nearly equal to the dividend declared; that is, while distributing $1,993,086, or 9.5 per cent, the road earned, over and above charges, $3,947,065, or 18.8 per cent.

It was inevitable that some attempt should be made to increase the distribution to stockholders; and the most obvious method was the one adopted, viz., a watering of the stock. The plan devised in 1880 was as follows: It was proposed to consolidate various branches of the railroad company, hitherto operated as separate corporations, with the main line; and to do this through the formation of a new company, which should exchange its stock for the stock of the previously existing corporations in the ratio of two to one. Practically all the stock retired was owned by the Chicago, Rock Island & Pacific Railroad Company, so that the only increase in stock outstanding came through the distribution to the stockholders of the parent company. In March the executive committee of the Rock Island passed the following resolution: "Resolved, that the proposition to consolidate the capital stock, property, rights, franchises, and privileges of the Chicago, Rock Island & Pacific Railroad Company with the capital stock, property, rights, franchises, and privileges of the Iowa Southern & Missouri Northern Railroad Company, the Newton & Monroe Railroad Company, the Avoca, Macedonia & Southwestern Railroad Company, and the Atlantic & Audubon

Railroad Company into a consolidated Railroad Company, with an authorized capital of $50,000,000, and such powers as shall be assumed in the articles of consolidation, be submitted to a vote of the stockholders of this company at their annual meeting."[1] Of the roads named only the Iowa Southern & Missouri Northern was of importance, extending 270 miles from Washington, Iowa, to Leavenworth, with branches which raised its total to 347 miles. This company had been organized as the Chicago & Southwestern Railroad Company, and the main line had been completed in 1871. The Chicago, Rock Island & Pacific Railroad Company had guaranteed its $5,000,000 main-line bonds, with a provision that it could demand foreclosure if called upon to pay either interest or principal, and in return had secured a lease in perpetuity. The road had been sold under foreclosure and reorganized in 1875 as the Iowa Southern & Missouri Northern, and had issued its stock to the Rock Island in return for money advanced by that company, the stock to be held in trust to 1926, and then to become the property of the lessee. The other roads did not together possess more than 80 miles of line, so that the operation was a genuine case of stock-watering. The opinion of the stockholders may be inferred from the quotations of their shares. Between January 2 and June 1, 1880, the quotations of Rock Island common rose from 149 to 189, with few sales, in anticipation of the distribution. On June 2 the stockholders formally gave their approval, and on June 4 the Chicago, Rock Island & Pacific Railway started on its career.[2] The price of the new stock was of course less than that of the old. It started at 106½, but by December it had reached 122¼, and by June the following year had risen to over 141.

This may be called Rock Island's first reorganization. It doubled the stock of the road, and increased its indebtedness by the assumption of the $5,000,000 bonds of the Iowa Southern & Missouri Northern; but the new stock involved no increase in fixed charges, and the new bonds a nominal increase only. Instead of being occasioned by too little prosperity it was caused by too much; and instead of being carried through after active opposition from many of the interests concerned, and reluctant acquiescence from the others,

---

[1] Chron. 30: 356, 1880.
[2] Chron. 30: 616, 1880.

it occasioned a rise in price of the common stock of 27 per cent in six months.

Between this date and 1902 no reorganization occurred. A rapid review of the period brings out, however, certain interesting features : First, that the stockholders and the directors were extremely conservative; second, that this conservatism did not keep the road from sharing in the expansion of mileage from 1887–9, which was so general in the Middle West; third, that this expansion decreased the average receipts per mile, and consequently the rate of dividends, and occasioned a fall in stock quotations from $140\frac{7}{8}$ to $63\frac{3}{8}$; fourth, that though weakened the road went through the panic of 1893 and the subsequent depression without suspending dividends; and fifth, that the year 1901 saw the beginning of a new expansion of the system, accompanied by a change in control and the carrying out of more ambitious plans than had ever occurred to the men of the previous generation.

The conservatism of the stockholders is shown in the election, year after year, of the same men to positions of authority. Rock Island was not a speculative road; the high price of its stock forbade. Stockholders regarded their shares as permanent investments, and, satisfied with the returns secured, loyally supported the management in good times and in bad. Between 1875 and 1897 there were but two presidents, Mr. Riddle holding the position until 1883, and then giving way to Mr. R. R. Cable, who, after directing the policy of the company for fourteen years, served as chairman of the board of directors from 1898 to 1901. Among the five members of the executive committee, if the reckoning is begun with the year 1881, three had been in office five years by 1886, one 2 years, and one 1 year, or an average of $3\frac{2}{5}$ years. In 1891 two members had been in 10 years, one 7 years, one 6 years, and one 1 year, or an average of $6\frac{4}{5}$ years; and in 1901 one member had been in 20 years, one 17 years, one 8 years, one 3 years, and one 2 years, or an average of 10 years. The board of directors showed the same general tendency. In 1890 seven of the thirteen directors had served for 9 years, and the average service was $6\frac{8}{13}$ years; in 1897 four of the directors had served for 16 years, and the average was $9\frac{10}{13}$.[1] It was but natural that men

---

[1] For the attempt of Vanderbilt to get representation on the board see the pamphlet

working under these conditions should have been apt to err on the side of caution rather than on the side of recklessness; and we find them, therefore, slow to extend their system, and slow to stretch into new territory where traffic returns were uncertain, and where the road had to create its business as it went. At the date of the consolidation the company had become the owner of 1038 miles and operated under lease 273 miles more, or a total of 1311 miles. By 1883 this had been increased to 1381; but in 1887 the total was only 1384.2, showing a total construction of little over three miles in four years.

This policy had to be abandoned, for other roads were extending their lines in Iowa and Illinois, and the Rock Island's share of Western business tended to fall off with the construction of rival lines west of the Missouri. As the report of 1889 expressed it, "while the lines of this company terminated at the Missouri its competitors for business had extended beyond, reaching in many cases the extreme western boundaries of population and even further. Thus the volume of traffic received by the company for carriage to and from the West was materially affected, while in order to restore the equilibrium overbalanced by the reduction in rates, the reverse was necessary, a larger rather than a smaller share of the tonnage to and from points west of the Missouri was demanded by the situation." The directors were forced against their will to take active measures in self-protection. As early as 1884 a bond issue was approved for construction from Minneapolis westward to an eventual junction with the Northern Pacific.[2] Building was to be carried on in the name of the Wisconsin, Minnesota & Pacific Railroad Company, and the securities of this company were to be received by the Rock Island as collateral for the issue which it made.[3] Two years later more extensive plans were put on foot, and the Chicago, Kansas & Nebraska Railroad Company was organized to carry out construction west of the Missouri. The new company had a capital stock of $15,000,000, and then (1887) of $30,000,000, and an indebtedness in 1889 of $25,141,-

issued by the Rock Island Company at this time; also R. R. Gaz. 16: 420, 1884; Annual Report, 1884; Ry. Age, 9: 428, 1884.

[2] R. R. Gaz. 16: 891, 1884.

[3] R. R. Gaz. 16: 709, 1884.

ooo 6 per cent first mortgage bonds; and turned over all of its bonds, and practically all of its stock to the Chicago, Rock Island & Pacific Railway in consideration of advances made to it. The Rock Island Company in its turn reserved the branch-line bonds as collateral, and issued against them its own 5 per cent collateral and extension bonds; agreeing to supply all money needed for construction and equipment,[1] and leasing the new railway at a rental of 30 per cent of its gross earnings.[2] Under this arrangement 1388 miles were built by 1889 and 276 leased, making a total of 1664.4. In 1889 it was thought more convenient to consolidate the two systems, so interest was defaulted on the Chicago, Kansas & Nebraska bonds, and foreclosure proceedings commenced; resulting in 1891, in spite of protests by municipalities along the route, in a foreclosure sale and union of the two properties in name as well as in fact. The collateral bonds of the Chicago, Rock Island & Pacific now became a direct instead of an indirect lien upon the Kansas & Nebraska mileage.[3]

Owing to these operations the mileage of the system increased from 1384 in 1887 to 3257 in 1889, and to 3408 in 1891. The greater part now lay in Kansas, Nebraska, and Colorado instead of in Illinois and Iowa, while at the same time the addition of the new mileage through sparsely settled districts decreased the density of traffic and the gross and net receipts per mile of line. In 1887 the Rock Island was earning the very high return of $8899 gross per mile operated; in 1891 this had fallen to $5126; in 1887 the net return was $3478 per mile; in 1891 it had fallen to $1484; in other words, the new mileage brought an increase in traffic, but not nearly so great a traffic per mile as the Iowa and Illinois lines had enjoyed, while the financing of the new construction swelled the annual charges from $1,795,351 to $4,775,601, and even with the larger mileage increased the charges per mile from $1295 in 1887 to $1400 in 1891. We need not, therefore, be surprised that the rate of dividends dropped from 7 per cent to $5\frac{3}{4}$ per cent and then to 4 per cent; nor that the price of common stock fell from its high level of $140\frac{7}{8}$ in May, 1887, to $63\frac{3}{8}$ in March, 1891.

It was in this weakened condition that the Rock Island encountered the panic of 1893 and the years of depression which followed;

[1] Annual Report, 1891. [2] Ibid. 1889. [3] Ibid. 1892.

and yet, in spite of the marked decrease in business in the years 1895-6-7, it continued to pay dividends, and showed no signs of financial distress except the lowering of its rate to 2 per cent. As a matter of fact the road was still in these years one of the strongest in the United States. Its lines were well located, its management was conservative, and consequently trusted, and its credit was good; so that at a time when some of the largest systems in the United States were being forced to the wall, it was enabled to preserve its solvency and even to keep up fairly liberal expenditures for maintenance of way and rolling stock. Little new construction was of course indulged in. In 1892 an extension was begun from Minco, the terminus of the Rock Island in the northwest corner of the Indian Territory, southwards; [1] in 1893 the southern boundary of the Territory was reached, and the Chicago, Rock Island & Texas Railway Company was organized to build through Texas; [2] and in 1894 a combined line was opened to Fort Worth; but exclusive of the Chicago, Rock Island & Texas, the total mileage increased by but 360 miles between 1890 and 1900, being an average of 33 miles a year.

In 1901 Messrs. William H. Moore and D. G. Reid were elected directors in place of Messrs. H. M. Flagler and H. A. Parker, and a new era in the road's affairs began. Mr. Moore had not long been interested in railroad matters. Known as a daring and successful promoter of industrial companies, he had made large profits out of the organization of the National Biscuit and Diamond Match companies; had lost almost equally large amounts in speculation which had followed, and had then regained a fortune through the organization and promotion of companies which were absorbed into the United Steel Corporation. In these last operations he had come into contact with Mr. W. B. Leeds, who, though originally

[1] Annual Report, 1892.

[2] "With the Chicago, Rock Island & Texas Railway Company this company has financial and traffic agreements under which the Chicago, Rock Island & Pacific Railway Company supplies all funds necessary to build and equip the road in consideration of receiving all the stock and all of the bonds of the Texas company, the latter issued at the rate of $15,000 per mile of completed road and additional for equipment to an amount equal to cost of the same, not exceeding $5000 per mile." Annual Report, 1893.

a railroad man, had acquired wealth through a tin-plate plant which was afterwards turned over to this same Steel Corporation. Mr. Moore was apparently in 1901 seeking for an investment. He was too well acquainted with industrial properties to care to sink his money in them, while he realized that for obvious reasons good railroad property was as safe, and might be made as profitable as anything else to which he could turn. The Chicago, Rock Island & Pacific was at the time the system most available for his purpose. It was not under the control of any large New York interests; it had an excellent financial record; its mileage was so placed as to admit of ready expansion; and, moreover, it is probable that to a man of Mr. Moore's speculative disposition the very low capitalization of the road opened up vistas of almost indefinite increase.[1] Just when Mr. Moore and his friends began their purchases, and what price they paid is of course largely a matter of conjecture: large blocks of stock were, however, undoubtedly secured in the early months of 1901, during which time quotations ranged from 116⅛ to 136; and it is probable that the larger part of the purchases were made nearer the upper than the lower level. During the following year the Moore party increased their holdings. It has been said that in April, 1901, Messrs. Moore and Reid were elected to the directorate. In November, 1901, at a special meeting of the stockholders, the directors were authorized to elect two new members to the executive committee, and Messrs. Moore and Wm. B. Leeds were chosen. In February, 1902, H. R. Bishop, Tracey Dows, and F. E. Griggs resigned, and Geo. McMurtry, F. L. Hine, and F. S. Wheeler were elected directors in their place. Mr. McMurtry had formerly been president of the American Sheet Steel Company, merged in the Moore Steel Combine, and Mr. Hines, vice-president of the First National Bank of New York, presumably brought the backing of that powerful institution.[2] Meanwhile Mr. James H. Moore had been chosen a director, and the Moore interest had gained control of the executive committee, so that a majority both of that committee and of

[1] Bonded indebtedness, 1900, amounted to $18,395 per mile.
    Capital stock, 1900, amounted to   13,711
                                           $32,106 per mile.

[2] Ry. Age, 33: 186, 1902.

the board of directors was in their hands. The new group of capitalists were not railroad men; their training had been on the financial side of corporation dealings, and the bulk of what experience they had had in actual management had been derived from industrial and not from railroad operations. It was natural, therefore, that the most striking results from their accession to power should appear on the financial rather than on the operating end, and that their ability to manipulate stocks and bonds should prove more unquestionable than their ability to handle railroad affairs. Results in the development of the Rock Island system were, however, attained, and for two reasons: in the first place, the Moores were able, and above all enterprising men, and untrammelled by traditions of conservatism, they were quick to see and bold to execute plans made possible by the admirable location of their 4000 miles of road; in the second place, they soon had large blocks of securities which they wished to sell, and were impelled to undertake large operations in the hope of raising quotations upon the Exchange.

In June, 1901, the stockholders authorized an increase in the capital stock from $50,000,000 to $60,000,000; stockholders of record June 28, 1901, to have the right to subscribe at par.[1] The proceeds were to go in part for extension from Liberal, Kansas, to El Paso, Texas, and in part for a new depot and elevation of tracks in Chicago, and for the improvement of the physical condition of the road. This El Paso extension plan was not new, since in December, 1900, the Chicago, Rock Island & Mexico, and the Chicago, Rock Island & El Paso had been incorporated to build a line from Liberal, Kansas, to Santa Rosa, New Mexico; there to connect with the El Paso & Northeastern, and to afford a through route to the Pacific coast and into Mexico. The other plans were, however, new. In April, 1903, the Chicago, Rock Island & Texas filed an amendment to its charter providing for an extension from Fort Worth to Galveston, 295 miles. The same month the sale of the Choctaw, Oklahoma & Gulf to the Rock Island was officially confirmed. This road has been, with one exception, the most im-

---

[1] Stock quotations: June 1, 1901   156$\frac{3}{4}$
                       July 1, 1901   155$\frac{3}{4}$
                       July 12, 1901   132$\frac{1}{2}$

portant acquisition of the Moores. It stretches from Memphis, Tennessee, through the Indian Territory, Arkansas, and Oklahoma, to the border line of Texas, and furnishes a nearly direct line from those states to the Mississippi River; while a projected extension to New Mexico will connect with the Rock Island main lines to the southward, and make it a valuable link in the through route from El Paso to Memphis and Birmingham. The Rock Island paid $80 a share for the common stock and $60 for the preferred,[1] and under the terms of the sale agreed to take at the same price all stock offered. The premium was very large. Choctaw preferred had been paying 5 per cent for some years, and the common had received 2 per cent in 1889, 4 per cent in 1900, and 4½ per cent in 1901, plus 10 per cent in stock; but reckoned on a basis of 120 and 160 respectively, these returns sank to a very modest rate. The property is a valuable one, but will have to show great development to justify its purchase price. Payment was made by the issue of collateral trust 4 per cent bonds to the amount of $23,520,000, in return for which practically all of both issues of stock were deposited. Certain smaller roads were also bought in. In June, 1902, the stockholders voted to increase the capital stock from $60,000,000 to $75,000,000; and in July the directors decided to allow the stockholders to subscribe at par for $8,235,000 of the new issue in amounts equal to 12½ per cent of their holdings; — the new stock to take up shares of the Burlington, Cedar Rapids & Northern, the Rock Island & Peoria, and the St. Louis, Kansas City & Colorado.[2] The first of these roads connected the Rock Island system with Minneapolis and St. Paul.[3] The Rock Island & Peoria was a short line in the state of Illinois. The St. Louis, Kansas City & Colorado was to afford, when finished, a more direct route between the important cities of St. Louis and Kansas City.

This is where matters stood when the reorganization plan of August, 1902, was brought forward. There had been a refunding put through in 1897 whereby some simplification of bond issues had

---

[1] The par was $50 for both common and preferred.

[2] R. R. Gaz. 34: 562, 1902.

[3] This line had been leased before, and the majority of its stock and that of the Rock Island & Peoria had been owned by the Chicago, Rock Island & Pacific.

been secured;[1] but this scheme of 1902 was for a different purpose and differed radically in the methods employed. Its explanation is to be found in the character of the men in control. We have seen that Mr. Moore had made his reputation in the speculative promotion of industrial combinations, that he had entered Rock Island in search of an investment, and that he had thrown himself into the extension of the system in part because he saw the opportunity for development, in part because he hoped to pave the way for profitable manipulation of the stock. The time he had awaited seemed now to have arrived. His projects had caught public attention, comment on the whole had been favorable, and the price of his shares was at a high level; all indications pointed to the probable success of a scheme of stock-watering on an enormous scale. At the same time Mr. Moore was too well pleased with the position he had attained to wish to sacrifice it by the sale of his holdings; and his desire was, therefore, to devise an arrangement whereby the stock of the Rock Island should be inflated and large blocks sold to the confiding public, while the control should remain where it had been before, — in the hands of Mr. Moore and his followers. It is to be noticed that there was no call for a reorganization by the creditors of the road, and no question of a default in interest, or even of a cessation of dividends upon the common stock; nor, on the other hand, were earnings so great that the managers felt it unwise to distribute them. The reason for the reorganization was entirely the financial ambition of the Moore group and the chance which its members saw of making larger profits than the earnings of the property would ever bring.

With these objects the following plan was put through. Instead of one Chicago, Rock Island & Pacific Company the Moores now proposed to have three companies, of which one was to operate the railroad, one was to hold the stock of the operating company, and one was to hold the stock of the company which held the stock of the operating company. That is to say, the Chicago, Rock Island & Pacific Railway Company was left undisturbed, while in Iowa a Chicago, Rock Island & Pacific Railroad Company was formed to hold the stock of the Railway Company, and in New Jersey

[1] See financial papers for 1897.

a Rock Island Company was organized to hold the stock of the Railroad Company, and of such acquisitions as might afterwards be made. The retention of the Railway Company made unnecessary the consent of creditors, for the lien and interest rate of outstanding bonds remained the same as before; the formation of the Railroad Company served apparently to meet legal requirements; and the organization of the Rock Island Company seemed likely to make more easy the purchase of parallel and competing lines. But the great advantage of the new companies lay in the opportunities for stock inflation which they presented, together with the lessening of the amount of capital required for control. This appears plainly in the following: The old Railway Company had a capital stock of $75,000,000; the new Railroad Company issued stock to the amount of $125,000,000 and 4 per cent bonds to the amount of $75,000,000. The Rock Island Company issued common stock to a total of $96,000,000 and preferred stock to a total of $54,000,000; and the aggregate, excluding the undisturbed bonds of the Railway Company, footed up to $425,000,000 instead of to $75,000,000 as before. From this total must be deducted $200,000,000, which represented issues of stock by one company to another, and $21,000,000 Rock Island Company stock and $1,500,000 Railroad Company bonds reserved for future extension, leaving a net increase from $75,000,-000 to $202,500,000. This involved some increase in fixed charges, since 4 per cent on $75,000,000 became obligatory; but the true significance lay in the inflation of principal rather than in the increase of interest charges, opening as it did an opportunity for great profit to the managers in the sale of the new securities. An incidental result was the transformation of the Rock Island shares from investment securities to media for speculation. At the same time the investment required for control was diminished. $75,000,000 of Railway stock was exchanged for $75,000,000 Railroad bonds, $96,000,000 Rock Island Company common stock, and $54,000,000 Rock Island Company preferred stock. Of these the bonds obviously had no voting rights. To both the common and preferred stock the right to vote was given, but in unequal degrees. "Until the number thereof shall be increased," read the certificate of incorporation of the Rock Island Company, "the number of directors shall be nine. There shall be five classes of directors. The first class shall contain a majority of the whole number of the directors as fixed at any time by the by-laws. . . . The holders of the preferred stock shall have the right, to the exclusion of the holders of the common stock, to choose directors of the first class. . . ." In other words, to the preferred stock, which constituted a minority of the whole, was given the right to elect a majority of the board of directors; so that whereas in the old Railway Company 51 per cent of $75,000,-000 common stock, selling at from 120 to 179, had been required for control, in the new combination of companies 51 per cent of $54,000,-000 Rock Island Company preferred stock, selling at 83½, was sufficient to the same end, in spite of a doubling of the stock outstanding.

To repeat: Two new corporations were formed, of which the Chicago, Rock Island & Pacific Railroad Company of Iowa issued $125,000,000 stock to the Rock Island Company of New Jersey, and in return received $127,500,000 Rock Island preferred and common stock. With this stock, and with $75,000,000 of its own bonds, the Railroad Company purchased the $75,000,000 stock of the Chicago, Rock Island & Pacific Railway Company, paying for every $100 in shares

> $100 in Rock Island Company common stock;
> 70 in Rock Island Company preferred stock; and
> 100 in its own 4 per cent bonds.

The Railway shares acquired were pledged for the Railroad bonds, and from them came the total income of the Railroad Company; and dividends upon the Railroad shares, together with dividends upon shares of other companies which it might chance to own, constituted the total income of the Rock Island Company. After thus receiving indirectly the earnings of the Railway Company through two sets of dividends, the Rock Island Company paid dividends on its own shares, which were held by the public; the preferred stock being entitled to 4 per cent from 1903 to 1909 inclusive, to 5 per cent from 1910 to 1916 inclusive, and to 6 per cent thereafter.

Other provisions were as follows: The Rock Island common stock might be increased from time to time according to law, but the amount of the preferred stock could not be increased except with the assent of the holders of two-thirds of the entire preferred stock and two-thirds of the entire common stock at the time outstanding, given at a meeting called for that purpose. Preferred stock was to be preferred as to principal as well as to interest; it had the right, as has been said, to elect a majority of the board of directors, but this right could be surrendered by the affirmative vote of the holders of two-thirds in amount of the preferred stock at the time outstanding at a special meeting of the holders of the preferred stock called for that purpose. A Finance Committee might be appointed from and by the directors which should have such powers as the directors and stockholders should choose to give it, and which should have all the powers of the directors when the board was not in session. The directors might accumulate working capital, but no reservation for working capital should be made in any year out of the surplus or net profits of such year until after the payments for such year of the dividends on the preferred stock of the company. The directors might also use the working capital in purchasing or acquiring the shares of the capital stock of the company as they might deem expedient, but shares so purchased might be resold unless retired for the purpose of decreasing the capital stock of the company.[1] This last provision aroused so much criticism that the directors gave up the right of dealing in the shares of their own company by resolution of November 5, 1902.

The important features of this reorganization were, as has been indicated, those in connection with the inflation of the capitalization and with the control of the property. In this connection it may be asked, first, whether the Moores made a profit by the deal; second, how large an investment they have had to keep in the property in order to retain control; and third, what cost to them this investment represents.

On January 2, 1902, Chicago, Rock Island & Pacific Railway Company common was quoted at 154. On February 1 it was $162\frac{1}{4}$, on April 1, 179, on July 1, $172\frac{1}{2}$, on August 1, 190, on October 1, 200, and on November 1, $199\frac{1}{2}$. It is safe to assume that the rise from $172\frac{1}{2}$ to 200 was due to the publication of the plan, and it may be that some of the earlier increase in value was owing to purchases by insiders, or by people who had obtained some inkling of what was

[1] Annual Report, 1903.

being considered; but a comparison of the aggregate value of the securities given for the railway common stock on January 3, 1903, with the price of the stock on July 1, 1902, shows that the former exceeded the latter by 22.3 points, with the error tending toward an understatement of the excess. That is, for every $172½ invested in July, 1902, the Moores, and other stockholders with them, held securities worth $194.8 in January of the following year. During 1903 the Rock Island securities fell with others upon the market, till on January 2, 1904, the aggregate value of the stocks and bonds in question was only $132.2; but the decline was temporary, and by January 3, 1905, recovery to $176.6 had taken place. The operations therefore did result in a chance for large profits, and gave renewed evidence that the public demand for stocks and bonds does not fall off proportionately to an increase in their volume.[1]

It is obvious that neither before nor after the reorganization could the Moores have sold all their holdings and yet have kept control. Starting again with the price of 172½ for Chicago, Rock Island & Pacific Railway common on July 1, 1902, it may be calculated that the cost of a majority of the issue then footed up to $64,687,672. If this had been carried on margin, and the brokers had demanded on every share a deposit of $40, with $40 more instantly available if needed, the total investment required for control would have been $15,000,040, with as much more held in readiness for any emergency. On January 2, 1903, Rock Island preferred stock was selling at 83½, and the cost of a majority of the whole issue would have been $22,-545,083; which, if carried on margin with a deposit of $20 a share, would have represented an investment of $5,400,020, with as much more in reserve. In other words, while all went well, less than $11,000,000 sufficed to control properties with a total mileage of 7718 miles of line, a bonded indebtedness of $201,660,475, and an outstanding capital stock of $118,249,007. It is of course improbable that the Moores in 1903 carried all, or even a large part of their holdings on margin; supposing, therefore, that all of their stock was

---

[1] Quotations of securities:

	Jan. 2, 1903	Jan. 2, 1904	Jan. 2, 1905
Rk. I. Co. common stock	49	22¾	36¼
Rk. I. Co. preferred stock	83½	61	84
C., R. I. & P. R. R. Co. 4 per cent bonds	87⅞	66¼	81⅞

bought and paid for, the fact still remains that with $22,545,083 they were able to control a system capitalized at $319,909,482.

In examining the cost to the Moores it is at once to be said that these gentlemen did not pay 172½ for their old Railway stock. What they did pay is of course uncertain. It is known that much of their holdings was acquired in the early months of 1901, when prices ranged from 116⅞ to 136. An average of 140 would represent a conservative estimate of what they paid, at which price a majority of the $75,000,000 would have cost $52,500,140. In return for this stock, at the prices of January 2, 1903, they obtained

$18,375,049 in Rock Island Company common stock,
 21,918,808 in Rock Island Company preferred stock, and
 32,765,712 in Chicago, Rock Island & Pacific Railroad Company 4 per cent
    bonds.

Since the preferred stock sufficed for control, there were left $18,375,049 of Rock Island Company common, and $32,765,712 of Railroad Company bonds, or a total of securities with a nominal market value of $51,140,761. Deducting this from the original investment, which has been estimated at $52,500,140, there is left $1,359,379 to represent the actual cost to the Moore crowd of control of the great Rock Island property. Beneath all of these figures lies, of course, the erroneous assumption that it would have been possible to unload large blocks of securities upon the market without causing a break in price; and yet, though large deductions must be made on this account, the figures are eloquent of the skill with which the Moores have manipulated Rock Island issues, and of the slender basis on which their control rests. It has been truly said that the question is raised anew as to what is legitimate in corporate finance.

All this is very different from anything described before; and so far as motives go, the two Rock Island reorganizations stand by themselves. In the matter of methods some similarities appear. The great increase in capitalization resting on the Rock Island system was accomplished mainly by an inflation of stock, not of mortgage bonds, and involved a comparatively slight increase in fixed charges; the Rock Island Company closely resembled other holding companies in its method of operation, and seemed likely to offer some facilities for the consolidation of competing lines; and though the extraordinary privileges given the Rock Island preferred stock have perhaps never been paralleled in degree, the practice of granting such stock preferential treatment in other things than dividends is not unknown. On the whole, however, this kind of reorganization stands apart, and is rather instructive as showing what may be done in the handling of corporation securities than in indicating any sound principles on which bankrupt roads may proceed.

The reorganization plan aroused sharp criticism both from Wall Street [1] and from the wider public, but met no opposition sufficient to prevent its being carried through. In September Attorney-General C. W. Mullen, of Iowa, in an opinion filed with the Governor of that state, held that the acts of the new Iowa corporation of the Rock Island, *i. e.* the Chicago, Rock Island & Pacific Railroad Company, were not outside the powers conferred by statute.[2] The Governor, in concurring with the opinion from a legal point of view, added, "the thing done is neither a merger nor a consolidation. Not a mile of track nor a dollar in value is added to the Rock Island property. It is simply a new device for watering securities; it is for the next General Assembly to say whether it is wise to permit our laws to so remain that such things are possible."[3] The various corporations were, therefore, organized, and the various issues of stocks and bonds put forth.

During the past four years the events which require mention are four: First, the acquisition of the St. Louis & San Francisco; second, the connection of the Rock Island with the Gulf; third, the temporary control of the Chicago & Alton; and fourth, the issue of a new refunding mortgage.

In October, 1903, the Rock Island operated 7123 miles of line. Its tracks stretched southwest from Chicago to Santa Rosa, New Mexico, west from Memphis to Tucumcari, and northwest from Rock Island, Illinois, to Minneapolis and St. Paul, and to Watertown, South Dakota. This extensive mileage surrounded, however, instead of occupying, a large territory in Missouri, Kansas, Indian Territory, and Arkansas, and could claim no share in the vast traffic passing up and down the Mississippi Valley. One of the first acts of the Moores was to remedy this defect. In May, 1903, the Rock Island

---

[1] Chron. 75: 212, 1902.   [2] Ry. Age, 34: 301, 1902.
[3] R. R. Gaz. 34: 750, 1902.

made a formal offer to purchase any and all shares of the St. Louis
& San Francisco Railroad Company, providing $22,500,000 in par
value should accept, at a rate of $60 par value in the common stock
of the Rock Island Company and $60 par value in a new issue of
5 per cent gold bonds of 1913 of the Chicago, Rock Island & Pacific
Railroad Company, for each $100 par value of Frisco common stock
deposited; the new bonds to be secured by the stock acquired. This
Frisco Company, it will be remembered, was the same that had previously been acquired and given up by the Atchison, Topeka & Santa
Fe. Since that time it had greatly extended its mileage, had gained
control of the prosperous Chicago & Eastern Illinois, with entrance
into Chicago, and was altogether more valuable than it had been
before. In relation to the Rock Island it possessed precisely the mileage which was required. It connected the latter's terminus at Chicago
with the terminus of the Choctaw, Oklahoma & Gulf at Memphis; it
traversed Southern Illinois, Southern Missouri, Southeastern Kansas,
and Indian Territory, to say nothing of lines in Oklahoma and in
Texas; and by means of a line from Memphis to Birmingham it gave
entrance into the heart of the South. In brief, it filled the gaps in the
southeastern part of the Rock Island system, and afforded a solid
foundation for further expansion. Good authorities consider the price
which the Rock Island gave for the Frisco to have been too high. It is
certain that the Frisco stockholders jumped at the chance. By June 1,
1903, the necessary $22,500,000 worth of stock had given their con-
sent and only technical details remained to be carried through.[1]

With the St. Louis & San Francisco under its control the Rock
Island could make a final advance to the Gulf. An attempt to complete a road through Texas occurred simultaneously with the Frisco
purchase in 1903. The Moores, that is, arranged with the Southern
Pacific for the purchase of a half-interest in the Houston & Texas

---

[1] Previous to this the stockholders of the Chicago, Rock Island & Pacific Railroad Company had approved the deal, had authorized the new bonds of 1913, and
had voted to increase the capital stock of their company $20,000,000, which increase
was turned into the treasury of the Rock Island Company of New Jersey, in return
for an equal amount of this latter company's stock. It is worth noting that the
purchase was to be made by Railroad Company and not by Rock Island Company
bonds, although the desire of the management was ultimately to see the indebtedness of all subsidiary roads replaced by Rock Island Company bonds.

Central, from Fort Worth to Houston and Galveston, with a branch to Austin, Texas; the Houston, East & West Texas, extending north from Houston to Shreveport, Louisiana; and the Texas & New Orleans, from Dallas to Sabine **Lake** on the Gulf of Mexico. As a part of the agreement the presidents of these lines were to be selected by the Rock Island Company.[1] This would have established a line to the coast in a very satisfactory manner. Connection between Dallas and Fort Worth was to be completed in December, 1903, and from this point the two lines of the Houston & Texas Central and the Texas & New Orleans would have furnished direct outlets to the Gulf. The scheme did not go through, because the Texas Railroad Commissioners pronounced the contracts contrary to the state constitution, in that they amounted to a consolidation of the corporations concerned, and to the establishment of a community of interest between the Rock Island and the Southern Pacific, which would preclude competition between them in respect to their Texas business.[2] The Rock Island was at first disposed to test part of the decision in the courts.[3] It later decided that discretion was the better part of valor, stopped the transaction, and cancelled the stock which it had issued as part of the purchase price.[4]

What the company could not do in Texas it could do, however, in Missouri, Louisiana, and Arkansas. As early as November, 1902, the St. Louis & San Francisco had purchased the entire capital stock of the St. Louis, Memphis & Southeastern Railroad, a line which was opened from St. Louis in 1904 to a junction with a branch of the Frisco above Memphis. From Memphis the Kansas City, Memphis & Birmingham stretched southeast through Mississippi into Alabama. These roads formed a basis for extension which was practicable though less convenient than the western route. Accordingly, in 1904, trackage agreements were concluded which gave to the Rock Island system:

(1) Trackage rights over the Mobile & Ohio and the New Orleans & Northeastern between Tupelo, Mississippi (on the Kansas City, Memphis & Birmingham), and New Orleans, Louisiana.

(2) Trackage rights over the St. Louis, Iron Mountain & Southern

[1] Ry. Rev. 43: 408, 1903.   [2] Chron. 76: 1192, 1903.
[3] Ry. Age, 36: 1, 1903.   [4] Ry. Age, 37: 1153, 1904.

and the Texas & Pacific from a point opposite Memphis, Tennessee, to a point opposite Baton Rouge, Louisiana.

(3) Trackage rights over the Yazoo & Mississippi Valley between Baton Rouge, Louisiana, and New Orleans, Louisiana, and over certain tracks in the latter city.

This afforded alternative routes of considerable directness from Memphis to the Gulf, while from the junctions of the Frisco with the Southern roads freight could be sent north to St. Louis and Chicago over the Rock Island system's own rails. Arrangements were made for the construction of terminals in New Orleans by a subsidiary company whose stock was to be owned and whose bonds were to be guaranteed by the Southern and the St. Louis & San Francisco companies.[1]

At the present time the Rock Island is reaching south at two points other than those so far mentioned. Under the name of the Rock Island, Arkansas & Louisiana Railroad Company,[2] it has built almost due south from Little Rock, Arkansas, while from New Orleans to Houston it has completed a line which connects at Eunice, Louisiana, with the Rock Island, Arkansas & Louisiana, and at Houston with the Trinity & Brazos Valley Railway.[3] This last line runs from Houston to Fort Worth and Dallas, Texas, and is controlled by a half-interest in its capital stock. The Rock Island is thus in fair shape to share in the south-bound grain movement from Kansas, Nebraska, and the Dakotas, and to take a part in the north and south business of the Mississippi Valley. There is no question but what the company is making a bold bid for an enormous traffic, and that failure will not be due to any narrowness of view.

About the time that it was struggling to reach the Gulf the Rock Island took hold of the Chicago & Alton in the north in order to have another and a more direct line between Kansas City and Chicago.

---

[1] See the Annual Report of the St. Louis & San Francisco Railroad for 1904.

[2] A consolidation in 1905 of the Arkansas Southern Railroad Company, the Arkansas & Louisiana Railroad Company, and the Little Rock & Southern Railroad Company. See the Annual Report of the Chicago, Rock Island & Pacific Railroad Company for 1906.

[3] See letter from Mr. C. W. Hilliard, vice-president of the Colorado Southern, New Orleans & Pacific Railroad, and comptroller of the St. Louis & San Francisco Railroad Company, in Chron. 84: 507, 1907.

A strong minority interest had previously been bought in the Alton by Mr. Harriman, and a board of directors had been elected. In 1904 the Rock Island bought within a few hundred shares of absolute control, and since the classification of the board prevented the displacement of its opponents for two years, arranged a compromise. Between them the Harriman and the Rock Island interests deposited a controlling number of Alton shares with the Central Trust Company of New York, to be held in a voting trust. Each of the rival interests was to have five directors, and the odd director was to be in alternate years first a Harriman and then a Rock Island man.[1] The Rock Island was, further, to have an option on the Harriman holdings for two years. It was an unfortunate time to buy. Mr. Harriman had previously displayed his splendid dividend producing ability in Alton finance, and the road was short of money. Market conditions were unfavorable, bonds were hard to sell, and, after all, the Alton was not of vital importance to the Rock Island, although it opened up new territory of some considerable importance. By 1907 it seems that the Moores had become tired of their bargain. In June of that year they served notice on the Union Pacific that the compromise agreement of 1904 was illegal and should be abrogated;[2] and shortly after they sold their holdings to the Toledo, St. Louis & Western.[3]

All in all the growth of the Rock Island has been astounding. Instead of the limited number of 7123 miles which the system possessed in 1903, or the 3819 of 1901, it comprises 14,270 miles of line operated in 1907. Gross earnings are $112,464,000 in 1907 as against $25,365,000 in 1901; net income $40,828,000 instead of $8,901,000; capitalization about $525,000,000 instead of $118,081,000. In fact, the very size of the system and the diverse nature of its interests make the economical management of the whole almost beyond the capacity of any one man. The Rock Island handles traffic from the West and South to Chicago, St. Louis, and Birmingham, and connects with the trunk lines to the Atlantic coast; it is also striving to receive and care for the constantly increasing business from the Northwest to the Gulf. It reaches into Mexico; it extends into Colorado, and sends branches into the Northwest; while at the other end

[1] After October, 1906.   [2] Ry. World, 51: 531, 1907.   [3] Chron. 85: 468, 1907.

it connects Kansas City, Memphis, and St. Louis by a triangle of lines. It was remarked a year ago that a contrast between the operations of the Rock Island and of the Atchison lines in the Southwest disclosed what might be called demoralization on the part of the former, and it is in the multiplicity of its operations that the cause must be sought.

It is to be expected, therefore, that the financial position of the company should not be secure. Operating expenses, fixed charges, and taxes absorbed 87 per cent of gross income in 1907 and 89 per cent the year before. We must not be blinded by the magnitude of the reported figures. Although $9,476,397 were carried to surplus in the year ending June 30, 1907, and $5,568,092 were paid out in dividends, these two items together comprise only about 13 per cent of gross income, and a bad year might readily see a decrease sufficient to sweep this margin away. Unlike the Union Pacific and the Northern Pacific, moreover, the Rock Island has not made consistently heavy improvement expenditures from income. Less than $40,000 was deducted by either the Frisco or the Rock Island & Pacific Railway in 1905 or in 1907; less than half a million in 1904; a little over two millions in 1903 and in 1906. And this in spite of the fact that the mileage of the Rock Island system is greater than that of any other road which this study has taken up. The fate of the company's refunding mortgage of 1904 probably testified as much to the distrust of the Moore group of financiers and of the soundness of the property which they control as it did to the general financial uneasiness of the time. This proposition for a refunding mortgage was first framed in July, 1903. It then comprised an issue of $250,000,000 4 per cent bonds, to be used for the refunding of outstanding obligations, future enlargements and construction, purchase of bonds and stocks of other companies, and for the reimbursing of the company for advances already made. Subscriptions were sought in New York in vain. Whereas the project was to have come up at a meeting of the stockholders on October 8, the managers obtained an adjournment of this meeting until January without action, and before that month arrived announced an indefinite postponement of operations. On March 21 the stockholders voted on and approved a modified version of the original scheme, whereby $163,000,000 instead of $250,000,000 were authorized, of which $15,000,000 were to be issued at once, and $82,025,000 were to be reserved for retiring certain outstanding obligations. It proved no easier to secure subscriptions to this than to the previous plan, and in April $5,000,000 4½ per cent notes were issued instead and taken by the First National Bank of New York, which was already closely identified with the company. Not until November, 1904, after fourteen and one-half months of persistent effort, was a firm of bankers found to take the refunding issue. $25,108,000 were then sold to Speyer & Co. Mr. Speyer became a director of the Rock Island and entered the finance committee, while the proceeds of the sale went to reimburse the treasury for capital expended, and to provide for the payment of obligations maturing in 1905. Since this time other blocks of the bonds have been sold.

It is thus evident that the Rock Island has not regained the position which it held prior to the operations of Mr. Moore and of his friends. The recent developments have done two things: they have piled upon the company a mass of excessive capitalization; and they have transformed it from a moderate sized railroad with a clearly defined flow of traffic into a great system sprawled over the Central West and handling at least three different currents of business. Neither one of these changes alone can account for the present condition of the road. Together they have made it what it is. It is only fair to say that large sums from capital account are being spent upon the property and that the managers announce an intention of bringing it up to the highest standard of physical condition. Over $4,000,000 were appropriated for additions and improvements in 1907, and nearly $3,500,000 in 1906, besides still greater sums for construction and equipment. Heavier rails have been laid down, bridges have been strengthened, equipment increased and improved. Meanwhile maintenance charges have not been unduly low, though not so high as on some other Western roads. It is true, nevertheless, that the Rock Island has lost its former stability and must await a period of lessened earnings with serious apprehension.

CHAPTER X

CONCLUSION

Definition of railroad reorganization — Causes of the financial difficulties of railroads — Unrestricted capitalization and unrestricted competition — Problem of cash requirements — Problem of fixed charges — Distribution of losses — Capitalization before and after — Value of securities before and after — Provision for future capital requirements — Voting trusts — Summary.

A GENERAL survey of railroad reorganizations may now be attempted. Eighteen different ones and no less than forty-two reorganization plans have been examined in detail. In their seemingly infinite variety may not some guiding principles be found which will assist both in interpreting the past and in directing the future? [1]

It is apparent that a readjustment of a railroad's affairs is more

[1] Date	Number of reorganizations	Name of reorganization	Number of plans	Foreclosures
1900–4	1	Rock Island	1	No
1895–9	6	Atchison	2	Yes
		Baltimore & Ohio	1	No
		Erie	3	Yes
		Northern Pacific	2	Yes
		Reading	4	Yes
		Union Pacific	3	Yes
1890–4	2	Atchison	1	No
		Richmond Terminal	3	Yes
1885–9	3	Atchison	1	No
		Reading	6	No
		East Tennessee	2	Yes
1880–4	3	Reading	5	No
		Rock Island	1	No
		Union Pacific	1	No
1875–9	2	Erie	4	Yes
		Northern Pacific	1	Yes
1859	1	Erie	1	Yes
	18		42	

Carl Snyder, American Railroads as Investments (N. Y., The Moody Corporation, 1907), offers, *inter alia*, an analysis of the results of operation of the railroads considered in the text.

difficult than the readjustment of those of an individual. A railroad is a complex financial, as well as a complex operating machine. Especially when it has been built up by the union of numerous small properties, each of which has been allowed to retain a certain individuality of its own, are the relations between the different parts intricate and involved. The obligations which have been incurred in the course of its career, and the kinds of paper which represent these obligations, disclose a variety which the debts of an individual seldom or never present. This complexity in railroad capitalization inevitably leads to clashes in interest between different classes of securityholders. Divergencies in interest seem to appear even while a road is solvent. If classes of securities exist upon which payment of interest is optional, it is to the advantage of the junior issues to prevent payment of interest or dividends upon others until earnings are such that payment may be made upon all. If common stockholders can reinvest in the property sums which normally would be paid in dividends on the preferred stock, they advance the day upon which they can secure dividends for themselves at the expense of their seniors. The same situation may also arise as between the preferred stock and the income bonds. Or, again, it may be to the advantage of speculative stockholders to pay dividends to themselves by means of the accumulation of a floating debt, and to sell out at top quotations, leaving the floating debt to take precedence even of mortgage bonds.[1] Both this and the preceding operation are facilitated by the control which the least valuable portion of the capital, the common stock, usually has over the policy of the entire company. But it is when a reorganization becomes necessary that these conflicts in interest become most apparent, and it is as a compromise between contending forces that a reorganization plan must take its shape.

The term "reorganization" is used in this study to denote the exchange of new securities for the principal of outstanding, unmatured, general mortgage bonds, or for at least 50 per cent of the unmatured junior mortgages of any company, or for the whole of the capital stock. These exchanges have been the essential features of

---

[1] The lien of a floating debt is inferior to that of a bond when unsecured, except as it represents arrears of wages and payment for supplies. But it is usually very well secured.

the operations which have been described. This exchange of securities must take place upon a considerable scale. Small readjustments may involve valuations of specific bits of property, but they do not require that comprehensive survey of the relations of all parts of the system to each other which distinguishes the general reorganization. In fact, the small adjustments are at once more simple and more difficult than the larger kind. More simple because they involve less change; more difficult because the same pressure cannot often be brought to bear. It is useful to mark a dividing-line between the small and the large. No such line can be defended as exact; but the one chosen seems to include a tolerably homogeneous group, and will lend a convenient definiteness to the discussion.

As thus defined, a reorganization may be, and generally is, accompanied by other operations essential to its success. If a large floating debt has been accumulated, provision for the cancellation of this debt must be made; [1] if unprofitable leases have been entered into, these must be abolished; [2] or if the system has been unduly hampered by inability to issue new capital, appropriate relief must be afforded. But none of these are determining features. They are means to an end, as is the exchange of new securities for old, and they may have their effect just as the economical management of the Union Pacific under Charles Francis Adams had its effect in the years prior to 1890; but they are not essential parts of that group of operations which have been characterized as reorganizations.

The exchange of new securities for old on a large scale usually takes place when a railroad is unable to meet maturing obligations.

---

[1] In the case of the Rock Island in 1902 there was no floating debt to be considered, while in 1885 the Erie funded overdue coupons and issued a 6 per cent mortgage on its Jersey City terminals to cover accumulated liabilities, but did not disturb its outstanding mortgage bonds, and cannot, therefore, be said to have reorganized.

[2] This was, in fact, a prominent feature of the reorganizations between 1893 and 1898. The Atchison surrendered the St. Louis & San Francisco; the Erie absorbed the New York, Pennsylvania & Ohio into its system instead of continuing the lease thereof; the Northern Pacific surrendered the lease of the Wisconsin Central and cancelled various unprofitable traffic contracts and traffic agreements; the Reading gave up the Lehigh Valley and its New England extensions; the Southern reduced its mileage by over one-half; and the Union Pacific shrunk from 7674 miles in 1892 to 5399 in 1899.

Of 18 reorganizations and 42 plans, 15 reorganizations and 39 plans have had to do with the extrication of companies from financial embarrassment. But though impending insolvency is the usual occasion it is not the only one. Reorganization sometimes occurs when prosperity is too great as well as when it is too little. Or a management may desire to get rid of hampering restrictions, or it may desire to manipulate the conditions of control. This last named cause — the desire to manipulate conditions of control — has been fortunately an infrequent cause of reorganization. An example is, however, afforded by the Rock Island reorganization of 1902. It will be remembered that the Chicago, Rock Island & Pacific Railway had long been a prosperous road in the Middle West, and that its control had required the ownership of between 40 and 50 per cent of $75,000,000 of common stock, quoted at over 160 in the early part of 1902. By the issue of new bonds, new preferred and new common stock to a total of $270 for every $100 of old common stock, and by giving to the preferred stockholders the right to elect a majority of the directors, the owners of the property were able to part with a large portion of their holdings and yet retain absolute control. A somewhat similar case was that of the Chicago & Alton. This road had been a conservatively capitalized enterprise, doing a large business between Chicago, St. Louis, and Kansas City. It had paid 7 per cent or better on its two classes of stock for eighteen years without a break, and had accumulated in that time an uncapitalized construction expenditure of $12,444,178. In 1899 a syndicate of Eastern capitalists bought control, and the following year reorganized the property by forming a holding company, which issued $22,000,000 in 3½ per cent bonds, $19,489,000 in preferred and $19,542,800 in common stock to exchange for the $22,230,600 old common and preferred shares outstanding. At current prices on January 3, 1899, a majority of both the old issues would have cost $19,030,048; on January 4, 1901, however, a majority of both of the new issues represented an investment of $10,729,437; and this investment it would have been possible to reduce to $2,241,377 by the sale of the new bonds received, without in any way endangering control.[1]

[1] See Interstate Commerce Commission: In the Matter of Consolidations and Combinations of Carriers, etc., 12 I. C. C. Rep. 319.

It is evident that both the Rock Island and the Chicago & Alton reorganizations were influenced by the very great prosperity of the companies concerned. It was desired to reap a profit by the sale of new securities as well as to lessen the investment required for control; although it may be remarked that the advantage of retaining control depended on the future prosperity of the roads. Reorganizations concerned with manipulation of control are therefore closely allied with reorganizations due to too great prosperity. These latter may, however, take place independently, and are likely to occur whenever profits are extraordinarily large, and a simple stock dividend is deemed inadvisable. An example was the reorganization of the Chicago, Rock Island & Pacific in 1880, when the formation of a new company and the exchange of new stock for old was deemed wise, in view of the large earnings which were to be distributed.

The desire to eliminate hampering restrictions is seldom the sole cause for a reorganization, but frequently it is a contributing one. When, for instance, the managers of the Union Pacific wished to extend their system in the years following 1880, they were forced to establish a separate organization for each branch line. By the terms of the charter nothing could be consolidated with the main stem except the Kansas Pacific and the Denver Pacific, the consolidation with which was provided for in the original acts.[1] This obviously prevented considerable economies, and could be remedied only by a new incorporation. The Northern Pacific was hampered in yet another way because the consent of three-fourths of the preferred stock was required by the terms of the reorganization of 1875 to the imposition of new mortgages;[2] and similarly the Atchison, after 1889, found it extremely difficult to issue new bonds because of the position of the outstanding income bonds. In this last case the restriction was the sole cause of the reorganization which followed. It should be remarked that the cancellation of such provisions sometimes works

[1] Testimony of C. F. Adams, United States Pacific Railway Commission Report, 1887, vol. i, p. 45.

[2] "It is only by the fullest knowledge of the affairs of the company that a correct judgment of the best manner of meeting its wants can be formed, and there is no other practicable way to manage the business of the company to its best advantage than for the stockholders to elect directors worthy of confidence, and to leave the management to them." Annual Report, 1887, Robert Harris, President.

considerable injustice. Restrictions on future increases in capital, for instance, may have facilitated the issue of bonds in the past, and in this case have formed part of the consideration given for subscriptions. The readjustment is defended on the ground of the need of the corporation, or is so accomplished as not to lessen the value of the creditors' holdings.[1]

The typical railroad reorganization, as has been said, occurs when a road ceases to be able to pay interest on its outstanding obligations. Whether because of excessive capitalization, or because of unexpectedly low earnings, or owing to an accumulation of floating debt which ties up all current resources, the reorganizing railroad finds itself incapable of meeting payments falling due. For this, experience shows that two deep-seated causes have generally been responsible. First, there is the almost entire freedom in matters of capitalization which railroads have enjoyed. Far from the recommendation of Secretary Taft that no railroad company engaged in interstate commerce be permitted to issue stock or bonds and put them on sale in the market except after a certificate by the Interstate Commerce Commission that the securities are issued with the approval of the Commission for a legitimate railroad purpose,[2] American railroads have in the past been practically unrestricted. It was open to the Erie to increase its capitalization per mile from $81,068 in 1864 to $117,760 in 1872, with no corresponding addition to its property; it was open to the Union Pacific to create a capitalization of $104,561 per mile by 1870, of which about one-quarter was in the form of government bonds; and it was possible for the Atchison to issue $129,162,350 in new bonds and stocks between 1884 and 1889 while its net earnings seriously decreased. Had there been a supervision of new issues, or had even a certain percentage of stocks to bonds in those instances been required, failures would have been less frequent and reorganizations less common. New construction would probably have been less rapid, but not so much so as is often asserted. A smaller number of new enterprises might have yielded

---

[1] In the case of the Atchison, old income bonds were retired by new second mortgage bonds, with the result that the aggregate value of creditors' holdings was largely increased.

[2] Speech at Columbus, Ohio, August 19, 1907.

larger profits; the chances for land speculation might have tempted many, and liberal regulations might have allowed a generous profit while at the same time eliminating all inflation due to fraud. Unfortunately railroad-hungry communities seldom stopped to count the cost. West, South, North, and East, privileges were offered to railroads, donations of land and money were made, and exemptions from taxation were conferred.

The second fundamental cause of railroad distress has been competition. If unrestricted capitalization has increased the load which the railroads have had to bear, unrestricted competition has impaired their ability to support any load at all. The forms which this competition has taken have been mainly two: first, the cutting of rates, either openly or by secret concessions; second, reckless extensions of line, generally followed by rate-cutting. The cutting of railroad rates is now a subject familiar to all. Illustrations may be found in the history of any great railroad system. President Hadley has made classical the theory that roads will take business until rates fall below the specific cost of hauling a given shipment; that is, below the additional cost which the articles in question impose. Even this limitation is often non-existent. Railroads which serve different cities will take freight when a war is in progress whether or not the rate repays the specific cost of hauling. If their rival imitates them they hope to wear it out by their superior ability to stand the loss. If it does not, the city which they serve will temporarily eject all others from common market, and may obtain so firm a footing that a permanent increase in business will result. All of the railroads which have been studied, in fact, have suffered more or less from rate-cutting. Repeated attempts at pooling and agreements to maintain rates have improved conditions only during the short periods in which the agreements have been of effect. In the South there have been scarcely more successful attempts to secure harmony by community of stock control. Competition by means of extensions has been also vigorously practised. The reader will recall the growth of the Atchison from 1884 to 1889. It was after the dissolution of the Southern Railway Security Company that the East Tennessee entered upon its policy of purchase and of new construction. The entrance of the Reading into New England was the direct cause of its failure in 1893; and that of the Baltimore & Ohio into New York largely contributed to its difficulties in 1887. Sometimes such extension is into territory where there is no business to justify it. Sometimes the business is there, but has to be divided among too many rivals. Sometimes the new lines are so poorly built as to be unduly expensive to work, and not infrequently they are so good that the resources of the expanding road are strained in acquiring them. In any one of these four cases new extension causes a drain upon the parent road which may readily bring about its failure.

Other conditions may lead to railroad failure. Simon Sterne alleges the following causes to be often responsible: [1]

1. The control of railroads by stock which represents little or no original cash investment.

2. The development of the territory served by individual railroads at a slower rate than is anticipated, and the influence of competition in reducing profits when the territory has developed.

3. The undertaking of railway construction when there is considerable activity in the money market, and when capital commands a high rate of interest.

4. The circumstance that railways, lacking reserve capital, can never avail themselves of a cheap market for labor or supplies, but must always buy when everything is inflated, because then only can they float their loans and borrow capital.

5. The necessity of complete reconstruction within a brief period of most railroads built through new territory, and the increase in funded and in floating debt involved.

7. The growth of railroads beyond the ability to handle them.

8. The steadily increasing expenditures required by law to accommodate the public.

9. The abuse of their position by directors and trustees.

10. The irresponsibility of railway accounts.

And it may be added that the control of American railways by foreign investors who apportion charges between operating and capital accounts in a way unsuited to American conditions has been upon occasion a cause of disaster. Unlimited freedom in matters

[1] Forum, September, 1890, and March, 1894.

of capitalization and unrestricted competition have nevertheless been the fundamental causes of bankruptcy.

It is interesting to observe that the majority of the principal railroads which failed in the nineties had taxed their resources nearly to the point of exhaustion before the panic of 1893 finally drove them to the wall. For every $100 received in 1892 the Richmond & Danville and East Tennessee systems were paying out $68.79 for operating expenses and $31.15 for interest on bonds, rentals, etc., leaving only 6 cents for dividends, necessary improvements, and the like. For every $100 received the Erie paid out the same year $66.46 for operating expenses and $31.85 for interest and other fixed charges, leaving only $1.68 as a surplus to ensure solvency in case of a decline in earnings. In 1893 the Atchison, the Northern Pacific, the Reading, and the Union Pacific had no surplus at all, but rather a deficit. The following table shows similar figures for all of our reorganized roads:

Percentage to Gross Income

	1893			1892		
	Operating Expenses	Fixed Charges	Surplus	Operating Expenses	Fixed Charges	Surplus
B. & O.	66.89	24.27	8.83	67.68	24.55	7.76
Erie	64.91	32.12	2.96	66.46	31.85	1.68
N. Pac.	59.25	43.55		53.71	36.34	9.94
Reading	57.04	45.41		52.64	33.91	13.44
Rich. & Danv. and E. Tenn.	73.49	25.63	.12	68.79	31.15	
U. Pac.	59.66	43.18		51.91	36.42	11.66
Atchison	77.47	24.96		77.16	21.59	1.24[1]

With these figures may be compared statistics for seven roads which went through the depression of 1893–7 without failure. These roads had a more extensive margin which could be cut off before interest on their bonds should be endangered. Furthermore, this margin was secured, not by low operating expenses, but by low fixed charges, including interest on bonds. Operating expenses averaged higher than for the preceding group, fixed charges averaged

[1] The percentages for the Atchison are corrected according to the report of Mr. Little. Owing to the lack of available detail it has been necessary to increase operating expenses by the total amount of the errors which he discovered, and this figure is, therefore, unduly inflated.

much lower. In the first group but one road had charges in 1893 which were less than 25 per cent of gross income; in the second group but two roads had charges which were greater. The condition of the roads of the second group referred to was as follows:

Percentage to Gross Income

	1893			1892		
	Operating Expenses	*Fixed Charges*	*Surplus*	*Operating Expenses*	*Fixed Charges*	*Surplus*
C., B. & Q.	64.46	23.12	12.41	65.17	20.86	13.96
C., M. & St. P.	65.95	20.78	13.26	64.00	22.36	13.63
C., R. I. & P.	71.72	13.31	14.96	69.88	19.83	10.28
Great No.	50.44	34.54	15.01	52.66	32.98	14.34
Ill. Cen.	61.92	25.84	12.23	64.58	23.99	11.12
N. Y., N. H. & H.	72.31	16.07	16.36	73.36	8.77	17.86
N. Y. C.	68.79	20.84	10.36	68.46	21.53	9.96

The causes which lead to railroad failure have now been mentioned. When bankruptcy has at last occurred, three groups of interests take part in the reorganization which must ensue. These are the creditors, who find interest and perhaps principal of their bonds in default; the stockholders; and the bankers and financiers who advance ready money and subscribe to necessary guarantees. Of these the creditors and the stockholders are widely scattered, and are quite unable to protect themselves by individual action. Their first impulse is, therefore, either to elect committees to represent them, or to authorize self-appointed committees of well-known men to look after their interests. Stockholders in a reorganization have little voice. They are the owners, and all that the corporation has is subject first to the bondholders from whom it has borrowed money. Occasionally they seem to make their influence felt. In 1880 the Reading actually attempted to pay off its floating debt by bonds with a lien inferior to the common stock; and in 1892 the Olcott plan for the reorganization of the Richmond Terminal Company strongly favored the junior securities. But as a rule stockholders must accept, and rightly, about what the creditors desire.

The creditors, then, are the most important factors, and they, like the stockholders, act through committees. There may be a committee for every class of bonds, or one or more classes may join together. The Union Pacific, in 1893, had committees for the consolidated first mortgage, the collateral trust 5s, the Oregon Railway & Navigation consols, the Dutch bondholders, and certain branch lines; and in 1894 for the collateral trust 4½s and the Kansas Pacific consols. As the financial situation grew worse the interest on senior mortgages became imperilled, and even the Union Pacific first mortgage bondholders deemed it wise to elect a committee; while a second committee arose for the Kansas Pacific consols, and a new committee for the Denver Extension mortgage. By April, 1895, at least fifteen committees were in active operation, of which fourteen represented not more than two classes of bonds each. The Reading reorganization of 1884 to 1886 was largely shaped by two committees representing the general mortgage bondholders; seven reorganization trustees representing the foreign creditors, the general, income, junior securities, and stockholders; and an opposition committee known as the Lockwood Committee. Within four months after the failure of the Erie in 1875 the English bondholders and stockholders each had elected a committee, and had urged all securityholders to join; a meeting of bondholders had elected Mr. John Hooper chairman of a committee in New York; and another meeting had elected Mr. N. B. Lord chairman of another committee in that city.[1] The more general a committee the greater the influence which it seems able to exert on reorganization, and the greater the likelihood that the plan which it approves may be accepted. The fact that a scheme has to meet the criticism of opposing interests during its formation renders it less likely to contain any injustice which conditions make it possible to avoid; and the endorsement of their representatives makes all classes of bondholders more ready to accord it temperate consideration. Among the numerous Union Pacific committees it was the joint committee, representing the foreign holders, the Denver & Rio Grande, the Oregon Railway & Navi-

---

[1] In 1893, after the Northern Pacific failure, the consolidated 5 per cent bond-holders formed a committee; Mr. Brayton Ives invited bondholders to send in their names and addresses to him (1894); and later in 1894 the falling off in the railroad's earnings induced the formation of the Livingston and Van Nostrand committees, and the announcement of the consolidated committee that it would accept the deposit of second and third mortgage bonds. Finally, within four months after the Atchison failure of 1893, four important reorganization committees were asking for deposits in the United States and one was soliciting deposits in London.

gation, and other interests that took the leading part. In the case of the Reading from 1884 to 1886 the seven reorganization trustees outweighed any other representatives of the creditors; in that of the Northern Pacific the Adams Committee succeeded in becoming a general reorganization committee, and took the leading part; and the Atchison reorganization was accomplished only by the union into a joint executive reorganization committee of three of the previously existing bodies.[1]

The situation which bankers and financiers occupy in relation to a bankrupt road is almost equally important. Their aid is essential to a reorganization while that of the officers and receivers of the company is not. And they are not subject to the pressure of imminent financial loss which forces creditors and stockholders to accept plans of which they do not altogether approve. It is true that these bankers may have money invested in the securities of the road. It may even happen that they have been formerly in control. In this case a certain pressure does exist. But as bankers their function is to do one or both of two things; namely, to advance cash to keep the railroad system together pending reorganization, and to underwrite assessments or the sale of securities. Either one of these involves them in new risks, and in undertaking either they will be only indirectly affected by investments which they may previously have

[1] The officers of bankrupt roads have no need of committees to make their wishes known, but only so far as they are bondholders, or in so far as they can influence bondholders by argument do their opinions carry weight. President Ives of the Northern Pacific in 1893 was able to use his position to fight his opponents through the courts, and secured besides appointment on a stockholders' protective committee, but exercised no great influence on the reorganization; President Jewett, of the Erie, gained the confidence of the visiting committee of English bondholders in 1875, and had some voice accorded him; but generally speaking officers have to rest content if they can successfully defend themselves against charges of inefficiency and mismanagement. They are, in fact, both the choice and the representatives of the stockholders, and the stockholders having no authority in the event of bankruptcy can delegate none. Officers of the courts which are in control of bankrupt railroads enjoy sometimes a different position from officers of the corporations themselves, in that they do not represent or depend on stockholders, and may not be connected with the circumstances which have caused the ruin of the road. Thus the receivers of the Union Pacific in the nineties were called to testify before Congressional committees, and those of the Erie chose a committee which prepared the first reorganization plan suggested, but in both cases the functions of the court officers were purely advisory, and so they must always be.

made. Their influence on reorganization is strong because they are necessary, and because they are free to participate or not to participate according to their opinion of the precise reorganization plan proposed. For much the same reason their influence is a wholesome one. We shall see that the primary conflict which takes place in any reorganization is between the interests of the corporation which needs a lessening of its burdens, and the interests of the security-holders which is opposed to any reduction in their claims.[1] The degree to which the former interest prevails determines the strength of the reorganized company. In this conflict the bankers naturally take the side of the company. As bankers, who advance cash, and who usually receive their pay in securities, they wish to make the corporation prosperous, and to raise the quotations of its securities to a high figure. An important factor also is that as reputable banking firms they wish the future career of corporations which they have handled to reflect credit upon themselves.

An example of the influence of bankers and financiers appears in

---

[1] In 1895 the final Atchison reorganization plan announced the following arrangement: "A contract has been made with a syndicate to furnish an amount of money equal to the assessments of non-assenting or defaulting stockholders, and such syndicate, by such payment, shall take the place of the non-assenting or defaulting stockholders, and shall be entitled to receive the new common and preferred stock, which non-assenting or defaulting stockholders would have been entitled to receive if they had deposited their stock and paid their assessment in full. Syndicates may also be formed to furnish the money needed, in case of foreclosure, to pay the non-assenting bondholders their *pro rata* share of the proceeds of sale, and to advance any cash which may be required during the reorganization and for other purposes." Chron. 60: 658–62, 1895. The reorganization plan of the Baltimore & Ohio in 1898 contained the following: "A syndicate has been formed . . . which agrees: 1st, To purchase $6,975,000 of the new preferred stock, and $30,250,000 of the new common stock, and to offer the same for sale to depositing holders of old 1st and 2d preferred and common stock of the Baltimore & Ohio Railroad Company. . . . 2d, To purchase $9,000,000 3½ per cent prior lien bonds; $12,450,000 1st mortgage 4 per cent bonds; $16,450,000 preferred stock. 3d, To protect the new company in the ownership and possession of the properties covered by $49,074,098 . . . of the existing mortgage bonds of the old company of different issues by agreeing to purchase from the new company the new securities not taken, but to which the holders of such bonds would have been entitled if depositing under the plan, at a price equal to the principal of the respective old securities, and also to make advances and perform other obligations essential for the purposes of the plan." Poor's Manual, 1898, p. 1381. Similar provisions appear in the plans of the Erie, the Northern Pacific, the Reading, the Southern, and the Union Pacific.

the case of the Union Pacific. A committee comprising General Louis Fitzgerald, Jacob Schiff, T. J. Coolidge, Oliver Ames, and two railway presidents took the road out of receivers' hands, cut charges per mile by over one-half, and paid the Government's claim in full. The Reading reorganization of 1886 to 1887 was the work of a syndicate which took hold after interests closely connected with the properties had failed to produce a satisfactory plan. The result was the best plan ever applied to the Reading Railroad. The Richmond Terminal Company was reorganized by a single banking firm. In this case the operation cut charges less than could have been desired, though the other parts of the plan were well-advised. The intervention of a syndicate has fortunately been usual of late years. And it is doubtful if the compensation accorded has been exorbitant, even for the direct services rendered. In 1886 the Reading agreed to pay a syndicate 5 per cent upon $15,000,000 of subscribed capital, plus 6 per cent on all money advanced. The Richmond Terminal paid Drexel, Morgan & Co. $100,000 in cash to cover their office expenses and $750,000 in common stock at $15 per share [1] for their work of coöperation and supervision. The Union Pacific paid the syndicate which financed its reorganization $5,000,000 in preferred stock quoted at 59, or 19 per cent at current prices on a subscribed capital of $15,000,000. All three syndicates, however, ran the risk of depreciation in the value of the stock given them, and all three rendered great service in providing large sums of cash at a time when capital was not readily to be obtained.

Payments to bankers or trust companies receiving deposits of bonds and stocks and undertaking the clerical work of a reorganization, should be sharply distinguished from those made to underwriting syndicates above described. Depositaries assume no risk, and are paid a definite sum for definite services performed. In 1895 the Erie set the compensation of Messrs. J. P. Morgan & Co. and J. S. Morgan & Co., for their services as depositaries and in carrying out the plan of reorganization, at $500,000 in addition to all expenses incurred; and the same year the Union Pacific allowed $1,000,000 in preferred stock to the bankers who managed its underwriting syndicate, as against $5,000,000 to the syndicate itself.

[1] In 1894.

It should be said that the compensation to depositaries is in part payment for the use of the name of the firms employed as well as in part payment for clerical work performed. Bondholders are more ready to deposit their securities with a well-known house than with an obscure one; and are to some extent influenced by the implied approval of the reorganization plan which acceptance of deposits by such houses involves.

At the beginning of the ordinary reorganization, then, creditors, stockholders, syndicate, and corporation find themselves face to face. The interests of the syndicate and of the corporation most nearly coincide except in so far as the syndicate is an owner of stocks or bonds. The syndicate desires a radical reorganization, — the corporation requires it. But as between stock- and bondholders and the corporation; between the stockholders and the bondholders; or between the junior and the senior bondholders; there is well-nigh complete antagonism. The corporation, to repeat, needs a reduction in the fixed charges which it has to pay. The securityholders wish to lose as little as possible. The stockholders hope to force sacrifices from the bondholders, and the bondholders to levy a heavy assessment upon the stock. The junior bondholders call upon their seniors to bear their part; and the seniors reply that they are well secured and that the juniors and the stock must take care of themselves.

The first question which arises is that of the cash requirements. How much cash must be raised to pay off the floating debt, and how much working cash capital will the new corporation require? It is almost always true that a large floating debt has accumulated prior to reorganization. The Northern Pacific in 1893 had a gross debt of no less than $15,000,000; the Reading in 1895 one of $13,800,000; the Baltimore & Ohio in 1896 one of $13,000,000; the Atchison in 1893 one of $16,000,000. In part this means simply the accumulation of unpaid bills. In part, however, it represents promissory notes or other short time paper which the corporation has issued, generally to pay current indebtedness, but occasionally for financing somewhat extensive operations. Thus Mr. McLeod carried his purchases of New England railroad stock by means of advances from brokers, and the Government Directors of the Union Pacific reported that $15,000,000 out of $21,400,000 of floating debt of that road in 1891 were the result of expenditure and advances in the construction of branch or tributary lines. The cost of carrying such indebtedness is naturally high. Mr. McLeod is reported to have paid an average of 9 per cent for his loans. The reorganization committee of the Atchison stated in 1895 that during the five years preceding, the road had paid over $1,100,000 in discounts and commissions to secure the renewal of $9,000,000 of guarantee fund notes. And floating indebtedness is by far the most dangerous as well as the easiest sort of obligation to incur. It represents a possible demand for large sums of cash on short notice which even a solvent company may find it impossible to meet; — a demand, moreover, which is likely to be made at a moment of stringency in the money market. For this reason, and on account of the high interest demanded, corporations endeavor to fund their floating debts when these reach unwieldy proportions. In 1891 the Union Pacific authorized three-year 6 per cent notes to the amount of $24,000,000 to be used in taking up its floating debt. In 1893 the Northern Pacific authorized $15,000,000 collateral five-year 6 per cent notes for the same purpose. In each case it was hoped to refund these short time issues with bonds of longer term when the date of their maturity should arrive. After a company has been in receivers' hands, issues of receivers' certificates are pretty sure to swell the current liabilities. These, again, may be issued to pay current bills, or to maintain or to improve the railroad when other resources prove insufficient. For whatever reason incurred, it is plain that the problem of the floating debt is a serious one for the creditors and owners of a bankrupt road to meet. If the provision which they make is insufficient their company will not regain a safe financial footing. And if, in addition to cancelling the debt outstanding, they do not provide a margin for working capital, the company will be forced to incur new floating debt and their work will have to be done over again.

In general there are two ways by which cash for floating debt and working capital can be raised:

(1) By assessment on securityholders.

(2) By the sale of securities.

Sales of securities may comprise the sale of securities of the bankrupt, or of other corporations held in that company's treasury, or they may be sales of part of new bond or stock issues reserved for that purpose. In 1898 the Baltimore & Ohio sold among other things $3,800,000 of Western Union Telegraph stock held in its treasury since 1887; while in 1889 the Atchison issued and sold $12,500,000 general mortgage 4s and $1,250,000 income 5s. When outside securities are sold the value of which is in no way dependent upon the prosperity of the road which sells them; and which are such, moreover, as the selling road can readily spare, this method of raising capital is open to few objections. Its chief disadvantage is that the sale is apt to be made at a time when the level of general prosperity is not high, and the price obtained is therefore apt to be low. But the question is quite different when the securities are those of the embarrassed or bankrupt road itself. In this case the credit of the company and the price of its securities are sure to be at a low ebb. The initial sacrifice entailed is necessarily great; while if the securities sold are bonds, as they are almost sure to be, the company increases its annual interest charge without receiving an equivalent value in return. If, on the other hand, the railroad endeavors to prevent a rise in charges by the use of income bonds or stock, the gain is usually neutralized by the extremely low price obtained.[1] In general we may say that sale of a railroad's securities in time of general depression is impossible except at a ruinous sacrifice; that sales should not be resorted to at all except when the road's difficulties are acute rather than chronic, as in the case of the Reading in 1896; and that when securities are to be sold the best of the available bond issues should be used and not the worst.

The case of an assessment is very different. Securities may be sold to outsiders or to present securityholders. In the one event no pressure at all can be brought to bear; in the other only that of the indirect loss which the difficulties of the reorganizing company would involve.[2] An assessment, on the other hand, is levied solely

---

[1] H. V. Poor (Manual, 1900) compiles the following statement for 57 selected companies reorganized between 1886 and 1898:

Securities provided for other corporate purposes of new companies

Capital stock: Preferred, $89,971,268	Bonded Indebt. Int.-bearing, $538,277,638
Common, 96,555,753	Income, 48,902,701

[2] Where stock- or bondholders are compelled to subscribe to an issue of new securities the operation becomes an assessment and not a sale.

on securityholders and is compulsory. Stockholders or bondholders who refuse to pay are ordinarily debarred from all participation in the reorganization, and lose all chance to recoup their losses from their share in subsequent prosperity. In return for the assessment some security is usually given, so that from one point of view an assessment and a sale resemble each other. But the element of compulsion appears in this: namely, that in the case of a sale the new securities are taken at the buyers' valuation; but in the case of an assessment the company determines what it shall give for the cash paid in. Hence the usual compensation for an assessment is an equal nominal amount of preferred stock; — while that for the purchase money in a sale is a greater nominal amount in bonds. Either an assessment or a sale of securities may be fortified by a syndicate guarantee. In the one case the syndicate agrees to substitute itself for all non-assenting or defaulting stock- or junior bondholders; in the other it engages to take and dispose of the new securities offered, or such part of them as the company is unable to sell. The advantages of syndicate assistance we have already discussed.

It will be recalled that both assessments and sales of securities have been freely employed in the reorganizations which have been considered, and that syndicate guarantees have been of ordinary occurrence. Out of eighteen reorganizations, fourteen were forced to pay attention to the raising of cash; the four which did not consisting of the consolidation of the Union Pacific with the Kansas Pacific and of the Chicago, Rock Island & Pacific with its branch lines in 1880, the income conversion reorganization of the Atchison in 1892, and the Rock Island reorganization of 1902, — each a reorganization of a more or less peculiar nature. Of the fourteen remaining, four provided cash by assessment, three by the issue of securities, and five by a combination of both methods. Adding to this the Northern Pacific reorganization of 1896 and that of the Erie in 1859, which combined an assessment with funding provisions, we have eleven reorganizations which relied on assessments in whole or in part. This preponderance is, however, due to the extensive use of assessments from 1893 to 1898; since the earlier reorganizations show assessments in only about one-half of the cases. This does not mean that the value of an assessment was not understood before

1893. For the reorganization of the Northern Pacific in 1895 was otherwise so radical that an assessment was less necessary; and that of the Atchison in 1889 took place at a time when business conditions were not in general depressed. The effect of widespread depression on the means employed for raising cash is, however, perfectly clear.[1]

Of the reorganizations of 1893 to 1898, to repeat, there was none which we have considered which did not make use of assessments. The following table shows the amount and distribution thereof:

Assessments, 1893–8

	Common Stock	1st Preferred	2d Preferred	Junior Securities
Atchison	$10		$20	4 per cent on 2d mortgage and income
B. & O.	20	$2		
Erie	12	8		
N. Pac.	15	10		
Richm. Term.	10			
E. Tenn.	7.20	3	6	
Reading	20			20 per cent on 1, 2, and 3 incomes
				4 per cent on deferred incomes
U. Pac.	15			

It thus appears that the assessments varied from $7.20 on the East Tennessee to $20 on Reading common, with less sums on the preferred stock and the junior securities.[2] The real sacrifice demanded of the stockholders is ascertained by deducting from the above the value of securities given for assessments whenever such were allowed. Taking for the purpose the market quotations of these securities six months after actual reorganization, that is, after the sale of the road, or the putting into effect of the plan proposed, it appears that the common stock of the Atchison received $1.90; that of the Baltimore & Ohio $15.20; that of the Richmond Terminal $5.02; that of the East Tennessee $3.55; and that of the Union Pacific $8.10. The Erie, the Northern Pacific, and the Reading gave nothing

---

[1] Among the reorganizations of the eighties, for instance, the Denver & Rio Grande levied $8 per share in 1885 upon its $38,000,000 common stock; the Pittsburgh & Western assessed its common stock 4 per cent in 1887; the New York, Chicago & St. Louis assessed its common $10, and its preferred an equal sum; and the Central Iowa levied 2½ per cent on its debt certificates, 5 per cent on its 1st preferred stock, 10 per cent on its 2d preferred, and 15 per cent on its common. See Chron. 40: 480; Ibid. 44: 212, 370, 653.

[2] A syndicate guaranteed the assessment in each case between 1893 and 1898. The Reading assessment is calculated on a par of $100.

for assessments in the nineties.[1] Preferred stock, whenever assessed, received the same relative amount and kind of securities for assessment as did the common stock, and the same is true of the junior securities. Since, however, these new securities had but a prospective value at the time of the issue of the various reorganization plans, it is advisable to make no attempt to determine precisely the net assessment, and to call attention to their allowance merely as a fact on which the stockholders could rely as they could count on a future rise in the value of their shares. With this qualification the relative height of assessments and stock quotations one month after the publication of each reorganization plan, and six months after the completion of each reorganization may be given.

Six Reorganizations, 1893–8

	Common Stock			*Preferred Stock*		
	Assessments	*Price 1 month after plan*	*Price 6 months after reorganization*	*Assessments*	*Price 1 month after plan*	*Price 6 months after reorganization*
Atchison	$10	$ 5¾	$13⅛			
B. & O.	20	12⅜	56¾	$20		$114
Erie	12	8½	14⅛	8	$22	36⅛
N. Pac.	15	1½	13¼	10	10	26¼
Reading	20	2½	22¼			
Richm. Term.	10	2⅞	11⅜			
E. Tenn.	7.20	½	6⅕	3	10	13¼
U. Pac.	15	10⅛	20			

Four Reorganizations before 1893

E. Tenn., '86	6	2½	5⅘			
Erie, '59	2½			2½		
Erie, '77	4		18½	2		29
Reading, '86	10	38⅜	58	10		53¼[2]

[1] The assessments before 1893 were as follows: The Erie levied 2½ per cent on its common and preferred in 1859, and a minimum of $4 on its common and $2 on its preferred in 1877, with no allowance of new securities in either case. The East Tennessee assessed its common stock 6 per cent and its income mortgage 5 per cent in 1886, and gave to the one a corresponding amount of 2d preferred, and to the other of 1st preferred stock. The Reading assessments in 1886 ranged from 2½ per cent on the deferred incomes to 15 per cent on certain junior securities, with an assessment of $10 on both classes of stock. Preferred stock was given for all assessments up to the full amount of the sums taken.

[2] The quotations six months after reorganization are for the combined securities

In every case during the nineties the amount of assessment exceeded the sum for which common shareholders could have sold their stock one month after the publication of the reorganization plan. The difference ranged from $3.50 for the Erie to $17⅔ for the Reading; in other words the assessments wiped out the whole value remaining to common stockholders, and exacted an additional contribution as the price of participation in any future prosperity. In the case of the preferred stock, where values were greater and assessments less heavy, the results were not the same; but even here the proportional demand was large, and amounted to 100 per cent of current quotations in the case of the Northern Pacific. Before 1893 assessments were fewer in number and not so great in amount. It is to the subsequent rise in stock quotations to which we must turn for an explanation of the willingness of stockholders to contribute such heavy sums. The assessments, we find, did not come out of the stockholders' pockets in the end; for their payment, in connection with other features of reorganization, so enhanced the value of shares that only six months after reorganization the price of stocks in all cases was nearly equal to the assessment plus the previous market quotation. In some instances, such as the Baltimore & Ohio, the sum amounted to much more than this total.[1] Refusal to pay would have wiped out the stockholder's interest and have kept him from benefiting from the rise. It is needless to add that quotations to-day are many times the amount of the assessments. The increase in value has occurred alike for common and preferred stock, even in times of severe depression. On the whole, it has abundantly justified the payments which stockholders were asked to make.

The use of assessments alone represents the most radical and the soundest method of raising cash. It disposes of the accumulated quick liabilities once and for all; and involves no subsequent increase given in exchange for the old preferred stock. In the case of the Baltimore & Ohio *e. g.*, this was 150 per cent in new common; for the Northern Pacific it was 50 per cent new common and 50 per cent new preferred. Only $5,000,000 of Baltimore & Ohio preferred stock were outstanding before the reorganization of 1898, and no record of quotations can be found. Quotations are similarly unobtainable for the Reading in 1886.

[1] The very large increase in the Baltimore & Ohio quotations was doubtless due to the lateness of the reorganization.

in interest charges. It was the method of the Atchison and the Union Pacific after 1893, of the Reading from 1883–6, and of the Erie from 1875–7. It was furthermore the method of the Western, New York & Pennsylvania in 1893,[1] of the Norfolk & Western in 1896,[2] and of other railroads which might be named. Probably its most drastic application was in the case of the Houston & Texas Central in 1887, where an assessment of 73 per cent was found necessary to discharge the floating debt and to provide cash payments for interest and bonus to first mortgage bondholders, and to pay the charges, expenses, and other liabilities made or incurred by the Trust Company.[3]

The sale of securities also has been relied upon for the production of cash. The most striking example of the use of securities alone is afforded by the Reading reorganization of 1883, which at the same time illustrates the possible unsoundness of the method. The floating debt of the Reading companies amounted in June, 1880, to $12,155,248, the bulk having been incurred in attempts to maintain solvency. To cover this Mr. Gowen proposed an issue of $34,300,000 deferred income bonds,[4] to be sold at 30 per cent of their par value, and to be entitled to dividends after 6 per cent had been paid on the common stock. These securities were practically worthless, and had to be set aside in favor, first, of new general mortgage bonds, and then of old unissued general mortgage 7 per cent bonds which the company happened to have in its treasury. So ineffective was even this expedient that in October, 1884, the floating debt amounted to a sum nearly one-third greater than that reported in 1880. Another example was the Erie scheme of 1886, which was not, however, a reorganization, according to our definition. The floating debt of the Erie in September, 1884, amounted to $5,455,338, of which $1,007,922 consisted of unpaid coupons. On the suggestion of English securityholders these coupons were funded; and the balance was raised by a new terminal mortgage issued and disposed of by a subsidiary terminal corporation known as the Long Dock Company. The result was an increase in fixed charges, which contributed to the

[1] Chron. Investors' Supplement, January, 1894.
[2] Ibid. 62: 641, 1896.
[3] Chron. 45: 792, 1887 (reorganization plan). See also Chron. 49: 269, 1889.
[4] Pages 84–5, *supra*.

final failure in 1893. The history of the Southern Railway affords a third example. At the end of 1888 the Richmond & West Point Terminal Railway & Warehouse Company found itself with a floating debt of $5,000,000, and proceeded to authorize an isssue of $24,300,000 5 per cent 25-year collateral trust bonds, of which $5,000,000 were to be sold to cancel this indebtedness. In subsequent years the current liabilities again increased, and for this and other reasons a general reorganization became necessary, in which both an assessment and a sale of securities were required. On the whole the result of experience bears out the statement as to the unsoundness of reliance on the issue of securities for cash even when the sale of the securities is guaranteed.

Yet another method of raising cash has been the combination of assessments with the sale of bonds or stock or both. In 1898 the Baltimore & Ohio disposed of $3,800,000 Western Union Telegraph stock. It also provided a total of $37,900,000 prior lien and first mortgage bonds and preferred stock, which was in part given for assessments, and in part turned over to a syndicate in return for cash. The Erie, in 1895, besides its assessment sold $15,000,000 in prior lien bonds; while the Reading sold $4,000,000 in new general mortgage bonds and $8,000,000 in new first preferred stock. In each case the success of the sale was ensured by a syndicate agreement. In 1886, to go outside of the reorganizations which have been particularly described, the Texas & Pacific provided funds with which to cancel a part of its floating debt by an assessment of $10 and an issue of $6,500,000 common stock. Three years later, the St. Louis, Arkansas & Texas assessed its second mortgage bondholders 5 per cent and its stock 10 per cent and sold securities to the par value of $4,490,880 to cover $3,400,000 of cash requirements.[1] In 1894 the New York & New England issued $4,355,000 in securities and levied $20 and $25 respectively upon its common and preferred shares.[2] In 1896 the St. Louis & San Francisco planned to raise $821,410 by assessment and $5,500,000 by sale of securities. Such examples might be multiplied indefinitely.[3]

[1] Chron. 50: 141, 1890.　　　　　[2] Ibid. 58: 762, 1894.

[3] Chron. 62: 829, 1896. Poor states in his Manual for 1900 that of $96,094,960 of assessments levied on securities of fifty-seven selected companies, $86,972,703 were on stock and $9,122,257 on bonds.

The problem of cash requirements must be met and solved before the parties interested can consider the fixed charges. It is the reduction in charges, nevertheless, which is usually of the more fundamental importance. A floating debt accumulated through inability to pay current expenses is the direct result of excessive charges, and a settlement which did not lower these, as well as pay off the debt, could give but temporary relief. Only when failure has been due to special causes can a decrease in the annual burden be even a matter for debate. The following tables show the absolute changes brought about by those of the reorganizations earlier considered for which precise figures are available:

FIXED CHARGES

Seven Reorganizations, 1893-8

Road	Before	After	Per cent decrease	Per cent increase
Atchison	$9,423,160	$6,486,842	31.16	
B. & O.	7,202,855	6,359,896	11.70	
Erie	8,637,700	8,126,283	5.92	
N. Pac.	13,813,945	6,761,960	51.04	
Reading	11,422,054	9,043,944 [1]	20.81	
Richm. Term. system	7,498,584	4,195,925	44.04	
U. Pac.	7,985,921	4,502,134	43.62	
	$65,984,219	$45,576,984	30.92	

Seven Reorganizations before 1893

Road	Before	After	Per cent decrease	Per cent increase
Atchison, '89	$11,157,770	$7,256,054	34.9	
Atchison, '92,	7,189,199	9,423,160		31.0
E. Tenn. '86	1,742,495	1,167,000	33.0	
Erie, '75	4,697,802	5,215,146		11.0
Reading, '80	7,734,031	11,535,078		49.1
Reading, '83	8,235,047	7,581,032	7.9	
Rk. I. '80	1,508,989	1,271,836	16.3	
	$43,276,372	$43,449,306		.53

One Reorganization, 1902

Road	Before	After	Per cent increase
Rk. I. '02	$4,780,649	$10,485,882	119.3 [2]

[1] The figure of $9,043,944 is the true figure for the Reading fixed charges after reorganization, eliminating duplications. In computing the percentage of charges to earnings in 1898, however, the unrefined figure of $12,210,291 is used in connection with a similarly unrefined figure of earnings.

[2] The reorganizations omitted are those of the Union Pacific in 1880, which did not alter fixed charges, and of the Erie in 1859 and the Northern Pacific in 1875, for which precise figures are not available. In this last charges were almost entirely removed; its exclusion, therefore, tends to lessen the percentage of reduction shown for the reorganizations before 1893.

From these tables, it appears that each of the reorganizations from 1893–8 occasioned an absolute reduction in fixed charges which varied from 5.92 per cent in the case of the Erie to 51.04 per cent in that of the Northern Pacific. On the other hand the reductions in the earlier reorganizations were more irregular and were exceeded by the increases.[1] Absolute figures, however, reveal little. Charges may be reduced and the road be worse off than before because of more than proportional reductions in mileage or in earnings. The preceding table must therefore be supplemented by one showing the changes in charges per mile of road and changes in the relations of charges to earnings.

FIXED CHARGES

Seven Reorganizations, 1893–8

	Charges per mile		Per cent of charges to net income	
	Before	After	Before	After
Atchison	$1415	$1001	110.5	80.9
B. & O.	3438	3107	98.2	86.3
Erie	4116	3824	114.7	95.8
N. Pac.	2630	1494	106.8	50.2
Reading	9856	6611	111.3	82.1
Southern	1553	955	105.1	81.5
U. Pac.	4381	1859	105.7	40.6

Seven Reorganizations before 1893

Atchison, '89	$1603	$1064		
Atchison, '92	1079	1415	85.8	110.5
E. Tenn. '86	1578	1083	134.3	79.5
Erie, '75	4984	5619	93.9	91.1
Reading, '80	9138	7287	98.1	83.0
Reading, '83	8760	7185	78.3	77.0
Rk. I., '80	1200	952	13.2	10.2

One Reorganization, 1902

Rk. I. '02	1231	1448	39.8	59.0[2]

---

[1] The six reorganizations before 1893 include that of the Atchison in 1892, which was not caused by inability to earn charges, and consequently made no attempt to lower their figure. Excluding this reorganization, the reductions in charges before 1893 overbalanced the increases. H. V. Poor calculates the absolute reduction in fixed charges for sixty-eight railroads reorganized between 1885 and 1897 at $24,-007,490. (Manual, 1900, p. cvi.)

[2] The decrease in charges per mile for the Reading in 1880 was due, not to any reduction in charges, but to an increase in mileage through the lease of the Central Railroad of New Jersey. In this case the increase in absolute charges better represents the real effect of the reorganization.

A summary of the preceding tables is as follows:

FIXED CHARGES BEFORE AND AFTER REORGANIZATION

Seven Reorganizations, 1893–8

	Per cent Decrease			Per cent Increase		
	Absolute Charges	Charges to income	Charges per mile	Absolute Charges	Charges to Income	Charges per mile
Atchison	31.1	26.7	29.2			
B. & O.	11.7	12.1	9.6			
Erie	5.9	16.4	7.0			
N. Pac.	51.0	53.0	43.0			
Reading	20.8	26.2	32.9			
Southern	44.0	22.4	37.7			
U. Pac.	43.6	61.5	57.5			
	30.9	31.2	31.2			

Seven Reorganizations before 1893

	Per cent Decrease			Per cent Increase		
	Absolute Charges	Charges to income	Charges per mile	Absolute Charges	Charges to Income	Charges per mile
Atchison, '89	34.9		33.6			
Atchison, '92				31.0	28.5	31.1
E. Tenn. '86	33.0	40.8	31.3			
Erie, '75		2.9		11.0		12.7
Reading, '80		15.3	20.2	49.1		
Reading, '83	7.9	2.2	17.9			
Rk. I. '80	16.3	22.7	20.6			
	10.3	13.1		.53		

One Reorganization, 1902

	Per cent Decrease			Per cent Increase		
	Absolute Charges	Charges to income	Charges per mile	Absolute Charges	Charges to Income	Charges per mile
Rk. I. '02				119.3	48.2	17.6[1]

[1] It is perhaps unnecessary to warn the reader that these tables can be taken as generally indicative only. The percentage of charges to earnings varies not only with charges but with earnings; and an increase or decrease in the latter may conceal a decidedly contrary movement in the former. Since the reorganizations were accomplished at different dates the error is not in all cases in the same direction, and in particular the percentage of charges to earnings for one road cannot be compared with the percentage for another. The figures of charges per mile of line are somewhat more reliable, but are nevertheless to be used with care. Different railroads report their mileage differently, and it has not been possible in all cases to use the homogeneous figure of mileage operated. Further, the significance of high charges per mile varies with the character of the mileage. A reorganization which lops off many unprofitable branch lines may conceivably cause thereby an increase in the charges per mile of road remaining, and yet place the system in a much stronger position than before. This difficulty disappears if the figure of charges per mile be used in connection with the percentage of charges to earnings, and in general the three columns given correct each other.

These tables show plainly that substantial reduction in fixed charges was the rule in the reorganizations of 1893-8, though less universal and less important in the reorganizations before that date. Even before 1893, however, the fact that reductions must be made was apparent. Three reorganizations increased absolute charges instead of decreasing them. Of these the Atchison reorganization of 1892 was not due to lack of prosperity, and the Erie reorganization was a failure. The Reading reorganization of 1880 increased absolute charges, increased mileage more than correspondingly, but was also a failure. And it is significant that only those roads which generously reduced charges regained even a temporary prosperity.

The distribution of losses which a reduction in fixed charges requires can best be made by a comprehensive redistribution of securities. All the bonds and stocks which are to suffer must be called in; and varying amounts of new securities must be given in their place. Among the important considerations to those who fix the rates for exchanges are these:

(1) Maximum charges under the new régime should approximate minimum net earnings under the old.

(2) As large a proportion of the charges as possible should consist of the one item of interest on bonds.

(3) Losses should fall most heavily on the junior securityholders.

(4) The nominal value of outstanding securities should be reduced as little as possible.

(5) Bondholders whose claims have been cut down should be afforded some chance to participate in future increased earnings of the property.

These rules may be considered in turn. The point to which the best practice should reduce fixed charges is readily understood. Nothing less than solvency under the least favorable conditions is the goal toward which a reorganization plan should strive. It appears, accordingly, that the minimum earnings of the Atchison property from 1891-4 had been $5,204,880; while the fixed charges proposed for it were $4,528,547. The lowest net earnings which the Union Pacific had ever recorded had been $4,315,077. The interest on its new bonded indebtedness was placed at $4,000,000. The net earnings for the Northern Pacific in 1895 were $6,052,660, which was the least that the road had earned for eight years. The new fixed charges were estimated at $6,015,846. The minimum net earnings of the Baltimore & Ohio from 1887 to 1898 had been $6,610,774. The fixed charges of the plan of 1898 were set at $6,252,351.

In order to simplify the charges, as well as for other reasons, it is desirable to have the item of interest bear a large proportion to the whole. The fixed charges of six of our seven reorganizations from 1893–8 amounted together to $54,562,165. Of this sum, interest on bonds comprised $35,239,146 or some 64 per cent. The charges of the same railroads after reorganization amounted to $36,533,040, of which sum interest on bonds comprised $30,926,638 or 84 per cent.

The distribution of losses should bear most heavily on the junior securities. The simplest readjustment would seem at first sight to demand a proportionate concession from all creditors. But this would be both unjust and impossible. In no sense do all bond- and stockholders stand upon an equal footing. In the first place, the cost at which senior bondholders have acquired their claims has much exceeded the cost at which junior bondholders and stockholders have acquired securities of equal nominal amount. Apparently equal claims represent very unequal investment. In the second place this increased cost has been due to certain legal provisions touching security which become prominent during reorganization. All mortgage bonds possess by law a lien upon the property pledged to secure them. Upon default in repayment of principal, and usually also upon default in payment of regular interest, their owners have the right to sell the pledged property at auction and to recoup themselves from the proceeds. After the underlying bonds have been satisfied the selling price is applied as far as it will go to the settlement in full of mortgages in the order of their issue; while the stock, representing the owners of the property, takes what is left. As a rule a railroad will not sell for anything like the sum required to pay off all its mortgages, and the junior issues are threatened with extinction. Usually, however, it is possible for the junior to guarantee interest on the senior bonds, or to buy the railroad at foreclosure sale under some senior mortgage, thus preserving to themselves the benefit of the earning power of the corporation. When this is done earnings are distributed according to the relative priority of the various junior issues on penalty of still further foreclosure and readjustment. The principle of reorganization which is followed prescribes because of this the payment in full of all claims which can be satisfied by the purchase price of the bankrupt railroad at foreclosure sale, and the distribution of losses among the remainder according to the relative priority of their liens.

The consent of securityholders to a reduction in their claim to an annual return is more easily obtained if the nominal value of their holdings be little or not at all reduced. There is a magic in the par value stamped upon a certificate which affords a certain consolation to those from whom sacrifices in interest are demanded. An unimpaired principal, moreover, constitutes a real advantage when the date of maturity arrives. But if the low earning power of the corporation compels it to ask sacrifices from the holders of its securities, it is only fair that these sacrifices should cease when the earning power improves. In other words, it is but just that old bondholders be given securities upon which payment of interest is optional, so that they may share in future prosperity, and obtain the same return which they once enjoyed whenever the road earns enough to pay it.

The foregoing rules dictate the amount of reduction to be made in charges, and also the kind and amount of new securities which are usually offered in the exchanges. Interest and rentals must be cut down without decreasing the nominal value of the securities outstanding. To reduce interest without reducing nominal value, either the interest rate on outstanding securities must be lowered, or mortgage bonds must be replaced by income bonds or by stock. To reduce rentals annual payments may be arbitrarily cut down, or rental contracts may be funded into mortgage bonds. These different methods may be taken up in some detail.

The accompanying tables (see opposite page) show for fourteen reorganizations the number and amounts of outstanding issues before and after reorganization at the various rates of interest designated.

Few collections of figures in railway finance deserve more careful attention than those given in these tables. Whereas the greatest number of the issues before the seven reorganizations prior to 1893 bore 6 per cent, and the greatest amount outstanding was similarly at that rate; the overwhelming preponderance in amount after the reorganizations of 1893–8 bore 4 per cent, and a total of 14.7 per cent of all the bonds outstanding bore a lower rate of interest than had appeared at all at the earlier date.

BOND ISSUES

Seven Reorganizations, 1893–8

| | Before | | | | After | |
Per Cent	Number	Amount	Per Cent	Number	Amount	Per Cent
7	33	$56,741,222	6.1	13	$43,942,500	4.9
6	85	300,925,695	32.7	30	82,586,000	9.3
5	51	267,623,426	29.0	23	90,853,035	10.3
4½	11	34,490,800	3.7	5	13,400,000	1.5
4	9	260,055,689	28.2	16	520,709,117	59.0
3½				2	76,733,350	8.7
3				1	53,350,000	6.0
	189	$919,836,832	99.7	90	$881,574,002	99.7
Not specified		5,141,238			1,000,529	
		$924,978,070			$882,574,531	

Seven Reorganizations before 1893

| | Before | | | | After | |
Per Cent	Number	Amount	Per Cent	Number	Amount	Per Cent
7	40	$153,251,000	23.7	21	$81,327,544	10.3
6	59	173,641,790	26.8	55	150,999,589	19.1
5	22	174,060,032	26.9	16	180,341,768	22.8
4½	2	4,611,000	.7	1	79,000	.01
4	5	140,041,700	21.6	5	375,881,614	47.6
	128	$645,605,522	99.7	98	$788,629,515	99.81
Not specified		5,712,749			8,940,939	
		$651,318,271			$797,570,454	

Graphically indicated the change was as follows:

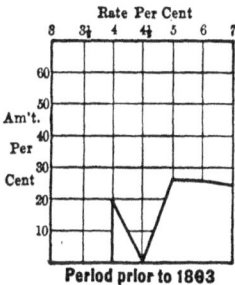

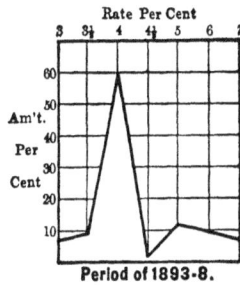

Period prior to 1893   Period of 1893-8.

Comparing the total interest with the total bond issue, we find the average rate to have decreased from 5.5 per cent to 4.9 per cent by the reorganizations prior to 1893, and from 5.1 per cent to 4.3 per cent by the reorganizations of 1893–8. Of some significance is a comparison of the rates prior to the reorganizations before 1893 with those subsequent to the reorganizations of 1893–8. The total interest payable on the issues at the later date was $38,291,319. If the same proportions of bonds had been issued at the same rates of interest as before the reorganizations prior to 1893, this interest would have amounted to $48,552,688. The total interest payable on the issues before the reorganizations prior to 1893 was $35,658,192. If the same proportions of bonds had been then outstanding at the same rates as after the reorganizations of 1893–8 the interest charge would have been $27,941,807. Thus in the first case there would have been a saving of $10,261,369 annually, and in the second case one of $8,279,775. This computation is inexact because it fails to take account of the normal reduction of interest rates due to improved credit and to increased prosperity from causes other than reorganization; but it is included here because, in the first place, a large part of the reduction was due to actual reorganization; and in the second place, because much of the improved credit is attributable indirectly to reductions of charges and other reorganization features.

It should be noticed that the new bond issues not only bore lower rates of interest, but were of greater volume and of longer term than the issues which they replaced. The greater volume is reflected in the considerable reduction in the number of issues at the same time that the total amount of bonds outstanding decreased slightly or increased. Thus the reorganizations before 1893 increased the amount of bond issues from $645,605,522 to $788,629,515, and decreased their number from 128 to 98; while the reorganizations of 1893–8 decreased the amount of bonds from $919,836,832 to $881,574,002, and decreased the number of issues from 189 to 90, or in far greater proportion.[1] The matter may be viewed in another way. Just before the beginning of the later reorganizations the predominant rate of interest for the roads concerned was 6 per cent. The number of issues at 6 per cent outstanding was 85 and the average amount per issue was $3,540,302. The predominant rate just after those reorganizations was 4 per cent. The number of issues at 4 per cent outstand-

---

[1] These figures do not include the comparatively small amount of bonds for which no interest rate was specified.

ing was 16, and the average amount per issue was $32,544,319. In other words, the process was to replace numerous small issues which bore high rates of interest, by a few comprehensive issues at lower rates; thus simplifying the financial situation, as well as lightening the burdens which the roads had to bear.

The lengthening of the terms for which the various mortgages were to run is equally apparent. Before its reorganization in 1897 the Union Pacific had no mortgage issued for more than 40 years. The first mortgage of 1897 ran for 50 years. The Reading in 1895 had four mortgages, all issued during the reorganization of 1888, with terms of 70 years. All its other mortgages were for shorter periods. In 1897 it put forth a grand divisional mortgage with a term of 100 years. The Erie in 1894 had two mortgages of 91 years each and one of 84 years, issued during the financial scandals of 1869, but no other of over $1,000,000 which ran for more than 43 years. Both its prior lien and its general mortgage bonds now outstanding are to mature 101 years from date of issue. The Atchison in 1889 could boast of only one mortgage with a term of 51 years. Its reorganization at that time gave it two of 100 years. The Northern Pacific issued one 100-year mortgage in the course of its troubles in 1889, and two mortgages for 101 and 150 years respectively in its reorganization of 1896. The reason for long terms has been the wish to make new mortgages attractive. Reorganization mortgages, as has just been said, tend to be large mortgages, at a lessened rate of interest. They are also blanket mortgages with an inferior lien. Some inducement besides the compulsion of necessity is useful in securing the assent of old bondholders to the proposed exchanges of these bonds for outstanding securities. The long-term bond protects the holder against the probable steady fall in the rate of interest on capital. It promises him advantage in the future in return for surrender in the present.

The reduction in charges by the substitution, for mortgage bonds with fixed interest, of securities upon which payment of interest is optional, has been as important as the reduction in the rates of interest just described. Such securities may be either income bonds or stock. The income bond has a lien upon railroad property similar in kind to the lien of an ordinary mortgage. Upon default in the payment of its principal it can exercise foreclosure rights. But it has no claim on earnings except in a right to receive dividends out of net earnings before any dividend shall be paid upon the stock. Stock certificates control the company by their right to vote,[1] but are entitled to its profits only after expenses of every kind have been met. When divided into preferred and common shares the former receive preference in dividends and sometimes in voting power. Among the reorganizations described in the text three made use of income bonds before 1893 and one after 1893. The amounts of the issues and the percentages of incomes to total capitalization before and after the reorganizations were as follows:

Income Bonds

	Before	After	Per cent Before	Per cent After
Atchison, '95		$51,728,000		31.8
Atchison, '89		80,000,000		35.4
Reading, '83	$22,347,227	56,389,466	21.7	39.3
Reading, '80	11,678,500	18,737,709	15.0	19.3

The East Tennessee reorganization of 1886 did away with income bonds, as did that of the Atchison in 1892. It will be noted that these bonds were more used before 1893, owing probably to the fact that the name of bond was considered to increase the salability of a security on the market. Securityholders hesitated to accept stock, but received bonds without too great a protest. The extent to which railroads catered to this preference is seen in the case of the Reading deferred income bonds, on which payment of interest was deferred to a 6 per cent dividend upon the common stock. From certain points of view, however, the income bond is inferior to preferred stock. For instance, preferred stock almost always has voting power, while income bonds usually have none. And although the income bondholder is sometimes protected from the insertion of new claims upon earnings between his bond and the underlying property, provisions in preferred stock certificates may afford an equal guarantee. In consequence, the use of income bonds has declined as a more accurate knowledge of their limitations has become widespread, and the Atchison adjustment 4s represent the sole use of this security in our reorganizations from 1893–8.

[1] Income bonds sometimes, though rarely, possess the right to vote.

The exchange of preferred stock, with or without new bonds, for old bonds which have borne a fixed interest rate represents the best current practice. Six of the seven principal railways reorganized from 1893–8 retired old bonds with fixed interest by new bonds and preferred stock or by preferred stock alone. Take for illustration the case of the Erie, which exchanged new general lien bonds and preferred stock for old second consolidated bonds; of the Northern Pacific, which exchanged new prior or general lien bonds and preferred stock for its second and third mortgages; of the Union Pacific, which gave 4 per cent bonds and preferred stock for its old first mortgage 6s; exchanges which are but typical of a widely extended use. Even the Reading, which alone refused so to lighten the claims upon its earnings, employed preferred stock in retirement of old first, second, and third income bonds.

These issues were all protected from future introduction of new bonds between them and their property. The preferred stock certificates of the Atchison in 1897 contain the following words: "No mortgage, other than its general and its adjustment mortgage, executed in December, 1895, shall be executed by the company, nor shall the amount of the preferred stock be increased unless the execution of such mortgage and such increase of preferred stock shall have received the consent of the holders of a majority of the whole amount of the preferred stock which shall at the time be outstanding, given at a meeting of the stockholders called for that purpose, and the consent of the holders of a majority of such part of the common stock as shall be represented at that meeting." Similar restrictions were imposed by the Southern in 1893, by the Erie in 1895, by the Northern Pacific in 1896, by the Reading in 1896, and by the Baltimore & Ohio in 1898; or in other words by all the large corporations except the Union Pacific, whose failures in the nineties we have described.

As for the years before 1893, in them the use of preferred stock was known, if not so widely resorted to. The East Tennessee in 1886 offered new consols and preferred stock for old consols, divisional and debenture bonds. In 1881 securityholders of the Reading proposed, and in 1886 nearly secured, the adoption of plans which comprised extensive issues of preferred stock in exchange or in partial exchange for old mortgages. The influence of English capital, however, and the liking for the name of bond to which we have referred seems to have prevented large employment of the device. Where either preferred stock or income bonds were used protection was afforded. When, in 1875, all the outstanding bonds of the Northern Pacific were replaced by stock, provision was made for an issue of first mortgage bonds to an average of $25,000 per mile of road completed; but no other bonds were to be issued except on a vote of at least three-fourths of the preferred stock at a meeting specially held in reference thereto on thirty days' notice. In the Reading reorganization of 1886 a clause provided that in calculating the net earnings from which dividends on income bonds should be paid there should be deducted from gross profits operating expenses, taxes and existing rentals, guarantees and interest charges, but not fixed charges of the same sort subsequently created. And in the case of the Atchison in 1889 the provision that no bonds could be inserted between the incomes and the general mortgage 4s was so absolute as to prove an almost complete bar to new issues.

It is this use of preferred stock and income bonds which makes it possible to realize the last and highly important rule which the engineers of exchanges have in mind. Only by the combined use of securities upon which payment of interest is optional with securities upon which payment is obligatory can the claims which their corporations are forced to meet be reduced, while at the same time former bondholders are given the chance to share in future prosperity. Such a result is deliberately sought. "The general theory of adjustment of disturbed bonds," said the Richmond Terminal reorganization plan of May, 1893, "has been to substitute for them the new 5 per cent bonds to such an extent as is warranted by the earnings and situation of the properties covered by the present mortgages, and the new preferred stock for the remainder of the principal." This purpose receives, moreover, a natural development. Justice does not demand that old bondholders be given the unlimited chance at future surpluses which old stockholders should enjoy. Their former holdings could expect but a fixed amount, and the maximum to be paid on their new bonds and preferred stock is therefore rightly restricted. But fair play dictates that they be given opportunity to receive the *same* income as before. If they must surrender 6 per cent bonds in exchange for 4 per cent bonds it is equitable to allow to them as well 50 per cent of their original holdings in new 4 per cent preferred stock. The corporation thus announces its intention of saving them unharmed if it can possibly do so, while it insists that its solvency be not dependent on the success of its attempt. This idea has been realized in a number of cases with approximate exactness. The old third mortgage 6 per cent bonds of the Northern Pacific in 1896 received 118½ per cent in new 3 per cents, 50 per cent in 4 per cent preferred stock, and 3 per cent in cash, — which together could yield nearly the same as the old mortgage. The holders of Chicago Division 5s of the Baltimore & Ohio in 1898 surrendered an annual income of $50 for a chance to receive $50.30; the Union Pacific first mortgage 6s in 1898 obtained precisely 100 per cent in new 4 per cent bonds and 50 per cent in new 4 per cent stock. It would be too much to expect that such exactness should generally obtain. The variations in security between issues, the well-founded desire to distinguish and not at the same time to swell unduly the amount of new stock put forth lead to fluctuations both above and below the point of equivalence of return. The important fact to remember is in short this: that the use of bonds with a fixed rate of interest, together with bonds or stock upon which payment of interest is optional, provides that compromise between the interests of the old bondholders and the interests of the corporation which alone can afford justice to both sides and can allow the reorganization to proceed.

The matter of rentals may now be considered. "The extent of the reduction in rentals from reorganization," says one authority,[1] "is seen where the reduction of this item of fixed charges for the entire country is considered. The net reduction in lease rentals from 1892 to 1898 was $24,527,000, and of this sum $17,768,000 appears in the South and West where the failures were most numerous and extensive. The reductions of rentals are most conspicuous in the Northwest and Pacific coast railroads. It is true that a part of this decrease in rentals is to be ascribed to the steady movement in the direction of consolidation which is constantly converting lease into

[1] E. S. Meade, Annals Amer. Acad. Pol. and Soc. Sci. March, 1901.

purchase; but coming so close together, the difference between the figures of 1892 and those of 1898 is sufficiently marked to warrant the conclusion that most of the reduction is due to the numerous reorganizations which intervened."

This conclusion is at first sight borne out by the following tables, which show the decreases or increases in absolute rentals and interest for thirteen reorganizations, of which six fall within the period covered by the quotation:

FIXED CHARGES

Six Reorganizations, 1893-8

	Interest		Rentals, etc.		Total Charges	
	Decrease	Increase	Decrease	Increase	Decrease	Increase
Atchison	40.6			13.7	31.1	
B. & O.		19.7	77.2		11.7	
Erie		33.3	62.7		5.9	
N. Pac.	14.2		88.9		51.0	
Reading					20.8	
U. Pac.	21.8		78.2		43.7	
Average decrease	4.7		58.8		25.7	

Six Reorganizations before 1893

	Interest		Rentals, etc.		Total Charges	
	Decrease	Increase	Decrease	Increase	Decrease	Increase
Atchison, '89	39.0		17.3		34.9	
Atchison, '92		38.7		3.9		31.0
Erie, '75		13.4	.5			11.0
Reading, '80		15.9		98.1		49.1
Reading, '83	13.3		.6		7.9	
Rk. I., '80	11.9		25.2		16.3	
Average decrease	1.0			9.9		5.3

One Reorganization, 1902

	Interest		Rentals, etc.		Total Charges	
	Decrease	Increase	Decrease	Increase	Decrease	Increase
Rk. I. '02	139.0		29.0			119.3[1]

It appears that while the decrease in rentals was of little import-

[1] The figure for the Reading in 1880 is affected by the lease of the Central of New Jersey, which took place simultaneously with the reorganization. Excluding the increase in rentals, the remaining increase in fixed charges amounted to only 9.5 per cent. The East Tennessee reported no rentals in either 1885 or in 1887. The data for the Southern Railway are not in such shape that rentals and interest can be compared. Its reorganization reduced rentals, however, very greatly.

CONCLUSION 371

ance in the six reorganizations before 1893, it was of great importance in the reorganizations from 1893 to 1898. Whereas absolute interest charges were reduced by none of the later reorganizations by over 40 per cent, four of the railroads cut rentals by over 60 per cent, and two others might have shown a similar result if a satisfactory division between interest and rentals could have been made. Unfortunately, both these statistics and Meade's statement are open to criticism for the reason which Meade recognized but to which he did not give sufficient weight. The relative amounts of interest and of rental paid by a railroad at any time represent the method by which its system is held together. If a parent company raises money by the sale of bonds, and purchases its branches outright, or buys a majority of their shares, its interest charges will be large and its rentals small; if it leases these same lines its interest payments will be small and its rentals large. A steady movement in the direction of consolidation doubtless existed before 1893, but this movement was certainly accelerated by, and made a prominent feature of many of the reorganizations of the following five years. Thus the Northern Pacific in 1893 reported a total length of line of 5431.92 miles; of which leased lines and lines operated under contract constituted 1912.92. In 1898, after reorganization and surrender of the Wisconsin Central, it reported 4524.45 miles owned and operated, of which 2430.42 consisted of main line, and 2030.82 of branch lines owned. The Erie in 1893 reported 551.12 miles leased and 598.51 operated for 32 per cent out of a total of 1970.32.[1] Four years later it either owned outright or held a majority of the stock of 1806.92 miles out of a total of 2162.81. The Baltimore & Ohio operated 26.5 per cent of its mileage in 1897 under lease or contract, but had reduced this by 1899 to .5 per cent. The Southern Railway proportion was 38.1 per cent in 1892 and 28.4 per cent in 1895. A reduction in rentals through reorganization has occurred, but a reduction due nevertheless largely to consolidation of systems, rather than to revision of rental contracts.

It was partly because of the difficulty of exact statement on the subject that a discussion of rentals was postponed till the matter of

[1] The 32 per cent paid has been included under rentals.

interest should have been considered. It now appears that the reduction in interest payments which was so prominent took place in spite of a reduction in rentals. If, for instance, the annual interest charges fell $10,261,369 in the course of all reorganizations, and if in later years the interest figures represented charges which at earlier date appeared as rentals, then the real reduction in interest was greater than the figures show. It is true that consolidation is not responsible for all of that decline in rentals which has occurred. It is as open to a reorganizing railroad to continue old leases at easier terms as it is to absorb the leased roads into its system; and much of this has been done. The East Tennessee, Virginia & Georgia, for instance, leased the Memphis & Charleston in 1877 for a yearly payment of $297,750; while the Southern Railway Security Company a few years before had agreed to pay $318,763.50 annually for the same property. And it is a fact that both consolidation and direct agreement have been the occasion of considerable reductions in the payments for the control of subsidiary lines. There is no reason why leased lines which have not earned their rentals should not suffer as much as portions of the main system which have not earned interest on their bonds. On the whole, then, rentals have decreased, both by means of direct negotiation and through an absorption of leased roads into the main system accomplished by exchange of new securities for old. The significance of precise figures must not be exaggerated. The losses which have occurred have been distributed according to the same principles which have already been detailed.

It is now clear that creditors, stockholders, and syndicate in practically all successful reorganizations agree that cash must be raised, fixed charges reduced, and the losses distributed according to the seniority of existing claims; and that of all methods the comprehensive exchange of new securities for old is best suited to accomplish at least the last two of these necessities. To give a comprehensive view of the operations the capitalization after reorganization of the roads which have been studied may be compared with the capitalization before. It will then be possible to see at a glance the consequences of the great variety of exchanges. The following table gives the percentages which the stock and bonds of these companies bear before and after reorganization to the total capitalization before.

CAPITALIZATION

Seven Reorganizations, 1893–8

	Before				After			
	Bonds	Preferred Stock	Common Stock	Total	Bonds	Preferred Stock	Common Stock	Total
Atchison	69.2		30.7	100	48.9	39.6	30.7	119.2
B. & O.	72.9	4.5	22.5	100	121.3	35.4	31.6	188.3
Erie	58.4	4.1	37.4	100	59.0	22.1	48.1	129.2
N. Pac.	61.0	16.5	22.4	100	71.3	34.2	36.5	142.0
Reading	80.3		19.6	100	61.2	33.2	33.2	127.6
Southern	52.5	8.8	38.6	100	43.8	23.5	59.8	127.1
U. Pac.	40.9	27.3[1]	31.7	100	50.4	45.7	39.1	135.2
Average	65.8	4.6	29.5	100	59.1	33.6	39.2	132.0

Seven Reorganizations before 1893

	Bonds	Preferred Stock	Common Stock	Total	Bonds	Preferred Stock	Common Stock	Total
Atchison, '89	67.7		31.8	100	95.6		31.8	127.4
Atchison, '92	68.8		31.1	100	70.2		31.1	101.3
E. Tenn. '86	48.2	19.2	31.9	100	22.1	34.2	31.9	88.2
Erie, '75	38.5		61.4	100	47.4		60.5	107.9
Reading, '80	69.1	1.3	29.5	100	86.3	1.3	29.6	117.2
Reading, '83	71.9	.4	27.6	100	100.4		27.6	137.7
Rk. I. '80	32.2		67.7	100	40.3		135.4	175.7
	62.5	1.7	35.7	100	73.9	2.8	37.6	114.4

One Reorganization, 1902

	Bonds	Preferred Stock	Common Stock	Total	Bonds	Preferred Stock	Common Stock	Total
Rk. I. '02	54.2		45.7	100	55.7	40.0	57.2	152.9

The most striking fact is that every reorganization but one has occasioned an increase in total capitalization.[2] The increase varies from 1.3 per cent for the Atchison in 1892 to 88.3 per cent for the Baltimore & Ohio in 1898; and the average increase is 32 per cent for the later period and 14.4 per cent for the earlier. This reflects the exchange of new securities on which a lower rate of interest is payable with securities on which all payments are optional, for old

[1] Government Debt.

[2] In considering the capitalization of the Erie before and after the reorganization of 1895 the securities of the New York, Pennsylvania & Ohio have been excluded.

securities which claim a high annual return. It is the result of the attempt to reduce the demands upon reorganized corporations without materially reducing the sums which old securityholders may in times of prosperity receive. It reflects also, however, the sale of securities for ready cash, or the exchange of these for assessments, as well as the investment of minor sums in the improvement of the roads. A closer examination of the table shows that the increase comes chiefly in bonds before 1893 and in stock after that date. The average increase in bonds of the seven reorganizations before 1893 was 11.4 per cent and of common stock .9 per cent; whereas bonds decreased between the reorganizations of 1893–8 from 65.8 cent to 59.1 per cent of the previous capitalization, although common stock increased 9.2 per cent and there was introduced a great volume of preferred stock which is scarcely found at all before. The less radical nature of the early reorganizations and the use of income bonds instead of preferred stock as a security with optional interest are here apparent. In brief, the statement of capitalization before and after reorganization summarizes and confirms the conclusions which we have reached. A few fundamental principles have underlain the complicated details of the exchanges of new securities for old. These principles appear when the reorganizations are examined one by one, and they show not less clearly when all the reorganizations are taken in two general groups.

Another question now naturally arises. If an increased capitalization has been obtained without an increase in charges, owing to the lowering of the rates of bond interest and to the liberal use of stocks or income bonds, what has been the effect on the market value of the securities concerned? Is the aggregate value of the new securities less or greater than the aggregate value of the securities which they have replaced? It has been seen that taken as a whole less annual payments can be claimed from the railroads as of right. Has this fact decreased aggregate quotations, or has the larger volume of securities and the chance for dividends over and above the minimum interest, raised such quotations higher than they were before? The following tables compare the quotations of securities disturbed by the various reorganizations one year before the failure of their railroads, with the quotations one year after reorganization of the new securities issued to exchange for them. A third column is inserted to show the effects of years of prosperity upon quotations subsequent to reorganization.

Seven Reorganizations, 1893-8

	Lowest quotation of month one year before failure	Lowest quotation of month one year after reorganization	Lowest quotation December, 1906
Atchison	$184,857,934	$129,364,451	$342,941,683
B. & O.	26,955,000	34,092,518	45,634,437
Erie	67,190,748	38,895,077	82,230,457
N. Pac.	157,555,214	135,507,699	289,557,415
Reading	88,940,250	71,607,223	179,190,107
Southern	45,653,414	35,231,356	71,411,937
U. Pac.	83,241,672	103,329,339	187,596,748
	$654,394,232	$548,027,663	$1,198,562,784

D. 16.2 per cent   I. 83.1

Four Reorganizations before 1893

Atchison, '89	$129,142,003	$113,993,417
Atchison, '92	35,100,000	42,600,000
E. Tenn. '86	17,657,377	21,746,188
Reading, '83	39,061,531	48,664,864
	$220,860,911	$227,004,469

I. 2.7 per cent

It thus appears that the increased volume of securities of the reorganizations of 1893-8 sold for a less aggregate price than did the smaller volume which it replaced. Whereas the disturbed securities of the seven roads in question, multiplied by their quotations one year before reorganization, give a product of $654,394,232, the new bonds and stock given for the disturbed securities, multiplied by their quotations one year after reorganization, give a product of $548,027,663.[1] This is not true for three of the four reorganizations

[1] The difficulties which prevent wider extension of these tables consist partly in the absence of quotations for certain classes of bonds, and partly in the lack of sufficiently detailed and precise information in some of the early reorganization plans. Thus there are no quotations recorded in 1874-5 for the 2d consols and convertible bonds of the Erie Railroad which were disturbed by the subsequent reorganization; and no detailed figures of the exchange of new bonds for old appear in the reports of the reorganization plans of the Reading in 1881-3, and of the Northern Pacific in 1875. The reorganization of the Union Pacific and of the Chicago, Rock Island & Pacific in 1880 did not disturb the bonds outstanding.

before 1893, and it is not true for the reorganizations of the Baltimore & Ohio and of the Union Pacific in the later period. Individual causes account for most of the difference. The Reading reorganization of 1886–8 took place so soon after the previous failure that our method makes it necessary to take the quotations of securities "before reorganization" only five days after the railroad has left receivers' hands. These figures are therefore unduly depressed. The Atchison reorganization of 1892 was voluntary, and was not caused by financial difficulties. The reorganizations of the Union Pacific and of the Reading in 1897 and 1898 respectively occurred later than most of the other reorganizations and benefited from the sharp increase in stock and bond quotations which began in 1897. For the seven reorganizations of 1893–8, to repeat, the aggregate market value of old securities before reorganization was greater than the market value after reorganization of the new securities given in exchange for them. The smallest changes took place in the senior securities. In the case of the Northern Pacific the aggregate value of the three prior mortgages disturbed increased from $85,498,685 one year before failure to $86,158,702 one year after foreclosure; while the consolidated or blanket mortgage of the company decreased from $36,032,360 to $29,235,111. In the case of the Reading the value of the general mortgage 4s increased from $37,160,977 to $37,383,503, while the first, second, and third income bonds decreased from $32,353,497 to $22,784,700. The reason was not generally a smaller increase in volume, but the fact that new bonds of fairly stable value were given for the better sorts of old securities, while old junior mortgages were apt to receive new income bonds or preferred stock, of which the value varied within wide limits.

The wide difference in the nature of the securities of the different roads forbids any attempt at precise classification. The following divisions may, however, be made: Three of the reorganizations from 1893–8 retired branch-line bonds for which quotations are obtainable, with a resultant increase in value for the issues of $3,256,127, or 14.2 per cent. Five of the reorganizations dealt with what may be classed as general mortgage bonds, and the value of the new securities given was to the value of the old as $182,160,406 to $196,186,382, or a decrease of 7.1 per cent. Three of the reorganizations retired junior bonds other than income. The value of the old securities was $47,874,648 and that of the new $22,272,174, or a decrease of 53.6 per cent. Four of the reorganizations retired income bonds. The value of the old securities was $40,913,662, the value of the new was $28,177,721, and the decrease was 31.1 per cent. Three of the reorganizations retired old preferred stock, and reduced the aggregate market value from $36,509,662 to $13,825,138, or 62.1 per cent. Finally, the common stock decreased 21.3 per cent from an aggregate value of $125,160,409 to one of $98,316,060. Stated in tabular form the result is as follows:

	Value one year before failure	Value one year after reorganization	Per Cent increase or decrease
Branch-line bonds	$22,840,928	$26,097,055	I. 14.2
General mortgages	196,186,382	182,160,406	D. 7.1
Junior mortgages	47,874,648	22,272,174	D. 53.6
Income mortgages	40,913,662	28,177,721	D. 31.1
Preferred stock	36,509,662	13,825,138	D. 62.1
Common stock	125,160,409	98,316,060	D. 21.3

This makes more definite the conclusion which has been outlined in general terms before. The burden of the reorganizations from 1893–8 fell on the junior securities and stockholders. The holders of prior lien bonds actually had more value than before one year only after reorganization had taken place; the general mortgage bondholders had nearly recouped their losses; while the former position of the other creditors and of the stockholders was far from being regained.

It may be objected that the decreases in market quotations were due to a general decline in prices of securities and not to reorganizations of the roads in question. This objection, however, cannot hold. It is true that a general decline began in the United States in February, 1893, and continued through 1894, reaching its lowest point in August, 1893, and, after that, in March, 1895; and that this decline was due to general conditions of panic and depression. In 1895, however, a revival took place, and, proceeding with uncertain steps through 1896, became obvious and important in 1897 and 1898. The average date of failure from 1893–8 of the seven roads described in the text was October 1, 1893, and the average date of reorganization was September 1, 1896. Since the market price figures quoted are taken one year before failure and one year after reorganization, conditions in October, 1892, should be compared with those in September, 1897. The following diagram traces the movements of twenty-six important railroad common stocks between those dates. Quotations for none of the seven railroads in question are included.[1]

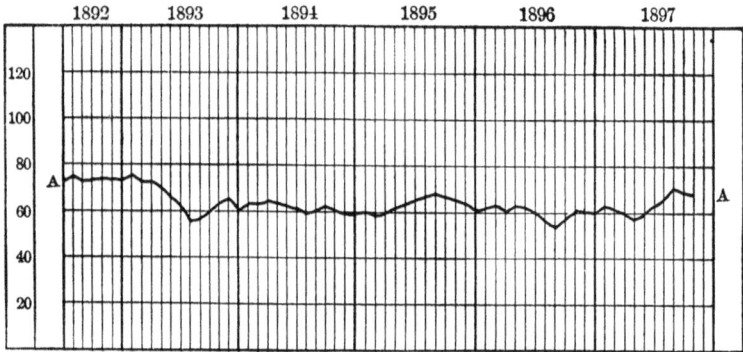

It is evident that the prices of the above stocks were not materially lower on September 1, 1897, than on October 1, 1892. The exact average was 73¾ for the earlier month, and 71⅛ for the later. The comparison may fairly, however, be carried further than this, and considerable pains have been taken to arrive at general figures which are conclusive. Such, it is believed, are the following. The market value of thirty-nine different bond issues of seventeen companies, taken at random from among those frequently bought and sold upon the New York and Philadelphia exchanges, was in October, 1892, $388,628,968. This differed little from the market value of the same securities in September, 1892, which was $388,198,432, or that in November, 1892, which was $390,170,323. The market value of these issues in 1897 was $371,125,135 in August, $373,875,293 in

---

[1] The twenty-six railroads are as follows: Canad. Pac.; Canad. So.; C. & O.; C., B. & Q.; C. & E. I.; C., M. & St. P.; C. & N. W.; C., R. I. & P.; C., C., C. & St. L.; D., L. & W.; Ill. C.; L. S. & M. S.; L. & N.; Manh. El.; Mich. C.; M., K. & T.; Mo. Pac.; Mob. & O.; N. Y. C. & H. R.; N. Y., O. & W.; So. Pac.; Wabash; Tex. & P.; C. of. N. J.; L. E. & W.; St. P., M. & M.

September, and \$372,962,239 in October. Represented in tabular form the situation appears as follows:

Market Value of Securities

	1892		1897	Decrease
September	\$388,198,432	August	\$371,125,135	4.4 per cent
October	388,628,968	September	373,875,293	3.7 per cent
November	390,170,323	October	372,962,239	4.4 per cent

In other words, the quotations for this large mass of representative securities were within 4½ per cent in 1897 of what they were in 1892. If to these are now added the same proportions of stock that existed for the disturbed securities of the seven reorganizations from 1893–8 there appears the following result:

Market Value of Securities

	1892		1897	Decrease
September	\$641,105,160	August	\$620,794,202	3.1 per cent
October	644,276,634	September	631,061,329	2.0 per cent
November	644,131,632	October	629,005,577	2.3 per cent[1]

This is, as nearly as possible, a computation comparable with figures already cited. It is made up the same way, has too broad a basis to give a non-typical result, and is not dependent upon the selection of a single month for its conclusion that security prices had nearly regained their former level by the last half of 1897. A decrease in value of 16.2 per cent for the securities of seven reorganized railroads has been determined. Less than one-fifth of this can be attributed to general causes. The significance of the decrease therefore remains.

In conclusion, two other points of interest may be mentioned. First, the provision which sound reorganization plans should make for the future development of their properties, and second, the creation of voting trusts to prevent sudden changes in control. It has been seen that restrictions on new mortgages have accompanied the issue of income bonds and of preferred stock, in order to afford to

[1] The securities in the table are taken from the following companies: St. P., M. & M.; Wabash; N. Y. C.; C., B. & Q.; C., M. & St. P.; L. & N.; D., L. & W.; Penna.; W. U. Tel.; B., R. & P.; Can. So.; Long I.; P. C. C. & St. L.; Tex. & P.; C. & N. W.; I. C.; C. & E. I.

these latter a desirable protection. If old bondholders demand these clauses, a certain amount of new issues is required by the interests of the corporation. A railroad is never finished. New extensions and improvements which shall increase earnings are generally called for to a degree which current earnings are insufficient to meet. Some provision for regular increments of new capital, without the need of stockholders' approval in each case, is highly advisable, and implies no lack of conservatism. In fact, some such provision is often forced upon a railroad. Take the case of the successive reorganizations of the Atchison properties. In 1889 no new bonds were to be allowed to be inserted between the income and the mortgage issues, but it was left optional with the management to deduct all improvements before estimating the earnings applicable to dividends on the former bonds. This proved quite inadequate, and the reorganization of 1892 provided definitely a fund of $20,000,000 second mortgage bonds, which were to be issued to a limit of $5,000,000 each year, for specific improvements on the Atchison, exclusive of the Colorado Midland and the St. Louis & San Francisco. The right was reserved to the company, when all the above should have been used up, to issue more bonds of the same sort for the same purpose, and on the same mileage up to a limit of $50,000,000. Finally, in 1895, there were reserved $30,000,000 general first mortgage bonds, to be issued each year to a limit of $3,000,000, and $20,000,000 adjustment bonds, to be issued each year to a limit of $2,000,000, after the general mortgage fund should have been exhausted. In each of the reorganizations in the nineties considered in this study, in which restrictions on new bond issues were imposed, there was concomitant provision for regular increments of mortgage bonds to be used for improvements, betterments, and new construction. Thus the Baltimore & Ohio in 1898 reserved $5,000,000 prior liens and $27,000,000 general mortgage bonds, of which the latter were to be issued at the rate of not exceeding $1,500,000 for the first four years after the organization of the new company, and not exceeding $1,000,000 a year thereafter; and the former were to be put forth at the rate of not exceeding $1,000,000 a year after January 1, 1892, for enlargements, betterments, and extensions. The Erie in 1895 provided $5,337,208 in cash to be spent at once, and $17,000,000 in general lien bonds to be issued during the years following the reorganization. The Northern Pacific in 1896 set aside $25,000,000 prior lien bonds, of which not more than $1,500,000 were to be issued in any one year, and $4,000,000 general lien bonds, presumably to be used as needed. The Reading in 1895 reserved $20,000,000 general mortgage bonds for new construction, additions, and betterments, of which not over $1,500,000 were to be used in any one year. And, finally, the Richmond Terminal reserved $20,000,000 in 5 per cent bonds to be used at the rate of $2,000,000 per year, and has recently authorized a $200,000,000 4 per cent mortgage which will raise the yearly limit of expenditure to $5,000,000.[1]

Before the nineties, as after, provision for new capital accompanied restriction on the future issue of bonds. In 1886 the Reading provided a lump sum of $9,792,000 general mortgage bonds for future use in the improvement of the railroad; and in 1875 the Northern Pacific contemplated the issue of first mortgage bonds to an average of $25,000 per mile of new road actually completed. Where, as with the Atchison in 1889, some such provision did not accompany the general restrictions placed upon new bond issues, or where, as with the Northern Pacific in 1875, the provision proved inadequate, fresh measures of relief were compelled. The Atchison reorganization of 1892 has been mentioned; in 1889 a financial operation of the Northern Pacific, which according to our definition was not properly a reorganization, provided $20,000,000 5 per cent consolidated mortgage bonds for additional branches at a rate not to exceed $30,000 per mile, and a like sum for betterments, etc.

Even where no restrictions on future bond issues are imposed, it is highly advisable that some provision for future capital requirements be made, and that the management have at its disposal a fund of bonds issuable without the approval of stockholders in each case. It is probable, therefore, that some such provision would have been a feature of some, at least, of the reorganizations even had the restrictions described not made the clauses an imperative necessity; but if we may judge from the rather restricted basis on which we are here at work, the provisions would have been far less liberal than we have found to be the case. In 1895 the Union Pacific set aside $13,000,000 4 per cent bonds and $7,000,000 preferred stock to dispose of equip-

[1] See Annual Report for 1906.

ment obligations, and for reorganization and corporate uses. Of these, corporate uses were stated to be those which would be proper to the corporation thereafter, such as the issue of securities in extension of the property. This, of course, was quite inadequate. Similarly the Rock Island in 1902 and the Erie in 1875–7 provided for a certain issue of stock or bonds to be applied to future capital requirements. It is undoubtedly true that both the Erie and the Reading railroads were hampered by the lack of adequate provision of this nature; though as the main difficulty of each corporation was the continued existence of heavier charges than it could bear, an automatic increase of indebtedness would not have proved a solution of their troubles.

The essence of a voting trust is the deposit of stock in the hands of trustees (most frequently five in number). These trustees issue certificates in return. All dividends declared on the stock are paid over to holders of certificates, but all the voting power is exercised by the trustees so long as the trust endures. Of the reorganizations which we have described, ten reorganizations with foreclosure included five voting trusts and one proxy committee; eight reorganizations without foreclosure included two voting trusts; ten reorganizations before 1893 included two voting trusts (though a third was proposed for the Atchison in 1889); seven reorganizations in 1893–8 included five voting trusts and one proxy committee. The use of voting trusts has therefore become more general, denoting a realization of the dangers of fluctuating and speculative control at critical periods in a railroad's history. This desire to secure conditions of stable control has been the dominant one in the cases under consideration. "In order to establish such control of the reorganized company for a series of years," said the reorganization plan of the Baltimore & Ohio in 1898, "both classes of stock of the new company shall be vested in . . . five voting trustees." "The importance of vesting in the present creditor class the management of the properties until their productiveness is considerably increased . . . is manifest," said the syndicate reorganization plan of the Reading in 1886. It is of supreme importance that a reorganized company be well started on its way by men who have an interest in making the reorganization plan permanently successful, and that conservative direction be assured until danger of bankruptcy be past. For this reason we should expect the use of voting trusts to increase in direct relation to the seriousness of the difficulties experienced, and to the vividness with which the need for stability is felt. If we may generalize, and say that a railroad which cannot be reorganized without a foreclosure sale is usually in more desperate straits than one which can be saved by voluntary concessions, we have an explanation of the coincidence of foreclosures and voting trusts. The teachings of experience, which have shown both the usefulness of voting trusts as tools, and the necessity of a solution such as they offer, further explain the increased prominence of the trust in later years.

It is not true that voting trusts are always used for the purposes indicated. In 1892 certain stockholders of the Baltimore & Ohio agreed to deposit their certificates in a trust for one year and five months. The stock deposited amounted to $8,975,000 out of a total outstanding of $25,000,000, and a limit of $11,000,000 was set to the amount to be so placed, the object of the arrangement apparently being to increase the influence of the stockholders concerned by concentration of their holdings.[1] Again, in 1895, to take an outside example, the stock of the Oregon Railway & Navigation Company was placed in trust with the Central Trust Company in order better to protect the preferred stock. It was provided that during the continuance of the trust the Central Trust Company should vote all the stock: first, against any increase in the preferred stock unless the holders of all the voting trust certificates of both classes should give their unanimous consent at general meetings; second, against all propositions relating to the mortgaging, selling, or leasing of the railroad and telegraph lines of the company, or to the consolidation thereof, unless a majority of each class of certificates should consent; third, on all other questions as directed by the holders of a majority of the aggregate of all voting trust certificates of both classes represented at general meetings.[2] Further provisions gave to the preferred stock control of a majority of the board of directors. These instances are of interest; but the principal purpose of the voting trusts in the reorganizations which we have considered has been nevertheless the securing of stability of control for a definite period after the rehabilitation of the bankrupt companies.

---

[1] Chron. 54: 369, 1892.　　[2] Investors' Supplement, April, 1897; Chron. 62: 41.

The duration of the voting trust varies from company to company. The most usual provision is for five years. Frequently the voting trustees may terminate the trust earlier at their discretion, as in the case of the Baltimore & Ohio trust of 1898, the Richmond Terminal trust of 1894, or the Northern Pacific trust of 1896. Frequently, also, certain conditions must be fulfilled before termination. In the case of the Erie in 1895 no stock certificates were to be due or deliverable before December 1, 1900, nor until the expiration of such further period, if any, as should elapse before the Erie Railroad Company in one year should have paid 4 per cent cash dividend on the first preferred stock.[1] In the case of the Reading in 1896 4 per cent cash dividends on the first preferred stock were required for two consecutive years, and this delayed dissolution three years beyond the time originally contemplated.[2] The Richmond Terminal trust had provisions similar to those of the Erie.

The number of trustees also varies. The scheme proposed for the Atchison in 1889 contemplated a trust of seven; the Baltimore & Ohio in 1898 and the Richmond Terminal in 1894 provided for five; and the Erie in 1896 for three; but this point is not material. When the reorganization plan requires the consent of stockholders to an increase in the issue of securities the consent of holders of trust certificates is apt to be required on similar occasions during the existence of the trust. Thus the Northern Pacific agreement of 1896 forbade the trustees to increase the preferred stock or to issue any new mortgage, except with the consent of the holders of a majority of the whole amount of preferred stock trust certificates, and of the holders of a majority of the common stock trust certificates represented at the meeting.

This ends the present treatment of the subject of railroad reorganization. The results of the discussion may be briefly summed up as follows:

First. Reorganization is most frequently an attempt to extricate an embarrassed company from its difficulties.

Second. These difficulties can generally be traced either to an unrestricted freedom of capitalization, or to destructive competition.

Third. The shape in which trouble appears is likely to be that of

---

[1] Chron. Investors' Supplement, April, 1897.   [2] Chron. 79: 2087, 1904.

a large floating debt or of excessive fixed charges; either or both of which may have brought the corporation to a critical condition some time before the actual collapse.

Fourth. The best practice favors the retirement of floating debt by assessments on securityholders, though sales of securities are sometimes resorted to, or a combination of sales and assessments is employed.

Fifth. Fixed charges are composed chiefly of interest and rentals. Interest payments are reduced by the retirement of outstanding bonds by new bonds which bear a lower rate of interest, or by income bonds or stock, or by a combination of securities with a fixed rate of interest with securities upon which payment of interest is optional. Rentals may be reduced by direct negotiation, or the leased roads may be absorbed into the main system, and their securityholders receive new stocks and bonds as above.

Sixth. The new bonds are of fewer kinds and have longer terms to run than the bonds which they displace.

Seventh. This reduction in fixed charges imposes a loss on the greater part of securityholders, both in respect to the annual interest which they can claim, and in respect to the selling price of their holdings. A similar loss is suffered by those securityholders who pay the required assessments.

Eighth. The loss falls on securityholders according to the seniority of their holdings, — those bonds escaping which can expect to satisfy their claims from the selling price of the railroad at foreclosure sale.

Ninth. The most important development in reorganization practice has been the increasing use of new securities bearing a fixed rate of interest with new securities bearing a conditional rate of interest; a use which may make the losses of junior securityholders temporary instead of permanent, and yet safeguard the interests of the corporation. In this connection preferred stock has gained in popularity over income bonds.

Tenth. This development, and the issue of new securities for floating debt and for other purposes, have caused the capitalization after reorganization in all but one of the cases which we have examined to exceed the capitalization before.

Eleventh. In order to perfect a reorganization additional provisions are often inserted, which protect junior securityholders against the reckless issue of new bonds, supply the corporation with ability to make necessary betterments from capital account, protect the corporation from sudden changes in control, and similarly supplement the main clauses.

BIBLIOGRAPHICAL NOTE

BIBLIOGRAPHICAL NOTE

INFORMATION about railroad reorganization must be gathered from a wide variety of sources. The most important are five in number. First, there are the annual reports of the railroads themselves. Second, there are the files of financial and railroad papers. Third, there are contemporaneous pamphlets. Fourth, there are memoirs and biographies containing first-hand material. And fifth, there are government documents, which comprise (1) regular reports by and testimony before bodies like the state and national railway commissions; (2) reports by and testimony taken before occasional committees; (3) legislative records; (4) state and federal court proceedings.

Of the five sources mentioned, the files of contemporary papers are the most useful. The *Commercial and Financial Chronicle*, the *Railroad Gazette*, the *Railway Age*, the *Railway and Engineering Review*, the *Railway Times* of London, the New York *Tribune*, the New York *Journal of Commerce*, the *Wall Street Journal*, and many others are generally accurate and trustworthy, though it should be noted as a limitation that they seldom have inside information, and that their comment is not always independent. These papers are supplemented by pamphlets and circulars. Many reorganization plans are published in pamphlet form. Opposition to them is not infrequently thrown into the same shape. Reports of experts are printed in pamphlets. In general, the live literature of reorganization must be put out on short notice, and so is issued in this informal way. The official statistics of railroads are to be found in the reports of the railroad companies themselves, made to stockholders or to supervisory government bodies. These statistics, like the news items in the financial and railroad papers, must be used with care. They are sometimes incomplete, and they are sometimes purposely misleading. Nevertheless, they are useful, and serious inaccuracies in any of them are usually exposed within a few years after their original publication. The material to be found in legislative records is not abundant. Railroads almost invariably, however, appear before the courts in the course of their reorganizations, and in the decisions of these tribunals some facts of interest may be found. The records of the receivership of the Union Pacific have been published in fourteen volumes. The decision of the United States Supreme Court in Pearsall *vs.* Great Northern [1] blocked the first of the reorganization plans proposed for the Northern Pacific in 1895. An earlier decision [2] enabled the Union Pacific to postpone the payment of interest upon the public debt until the principal should have fallen due. The Erie has been at times almost continuously before the courts, and the same is true of the Reading during its reorganizations, of the Northern Pacific, and of other roads. The student is most fortunate when he can uncover testimony before government committees, of men who have taken part in reorganization proceedings, or who are personally acquainted with developments which have led up to railroad failures. Mr. Blanchard, before the Hepburn Committee,[3] and Mr. Fink, before the Hepburn and the Cullom Committees,[4] helped their hearers to understand the policy which finally resulted in the failure of the Baltimore & Ohio. The report of the Poland Committee disclosed the scandal of the Crédit Mobilier.[5] The testimony of Gould, Adams, Ames, Holmes, and others before the United States Pacific Railroad Commission of 1887-8 [6] made clear the iniquity of the Union Pacific reorganization of 1880. The statements of Mr. Pierce before the Senate Committee on Pacific Railroads in 1896[7] explained the attitude of the Union Pacific towards the repayment of that company's debt to the Government. The testimony of Messrs. McLeod, Rice, Harris, and others before the Industrial Commission of 1900 threw much light upon the Reading bankruptcy of 1893. The arguments of counsel in the matter of export differentials, reprinted in the fifth volume of the Elkins Committee report,[8] gave valuable information on the subject of trunk-line competition. Many of the witnesses before these committees are frank in criticism of the railroads with which they have been connected. Others are forced to admissions

[1] 161 U. S. 647.   [2] 138 U. S. 84.
[3] New York, 1879.   [4] 49th Congress, 1st Session, Senate Report, No. 42.
[5] 42d Congress, 3d Session, House Reports, No. 77.
[6] 50th Congress, 1st Session, Senate Executive Document No. 51.
[7] 54th Congress, 1st Session, Senate Document No. 314.
[8] 58th Congress, 3d Session, hearings before the Committee on Interstate Commerce, United States Senate, in Special Session, 1905.

by the keen questioning to which they are exposed. The only similar material to be found elsewhere lies in memoirs, such as those of Henry Villard,[1] or in biographies like Oberholtzer's Life of Jay Cooke[2] and Pearson's An American Railroad Builder[3] which make use of private papers of men prominent in railroad finance. Perhaps White's Book of Daniel Drew,[4] Depew's Retrospect of Twenty-Five Years,[5] and the Life of Isaac Ingalls Stevens by his son,[6] should be included in this class.

This enumeration, while in no way exhaustive, indicates the principal sources from which material may be obtained. Secondary works do not exist which treat solely of railroad reorganization. There is an article by E. S. Meade in the *Annals* of the American Academy,[7] articles by Simon Sterne in the *Forum*,[8] and an article by A. Lansburgh in *Die Bank*,[9] but no books of which the author is aware. Mention may be made of an intelligent discussion of an industrial reorganization by A. S. Dewing in the *Quarterly Journal of Economics*.[10] *Poor's Manual* for 1900 contains the most convenient set of general statistics. On railroad receiverships, besides legal works, there is a monograph by H. H. Swain,[11] which has a brief bibliography, and articles in the *Forum*, *North American Review*, and other periodicals.

On the history of the great American railroad systems the literature is also quite inadequate. The Union Pacific has been written up frequently, because of its relations with the United States

[1] Memoirs of Henry Villard, 1835-1900. Boston, 1904.
[2] Ellis Paxon Oberholtzer, Life of Jay Cooke. Philadelphia, 1907.
[3] H. G. Pearson, An American Railroad Builder. John Murray Forbes. Boston and New York, 1911.
[4] Bouck White, The Book of Daniel Drew. New York, 1910.
[5] C. M. Depew, A Retrospect of Twenty-five Years with the New York Central Railroad and its Allied Lines. New York, 1892.
[6] Hazard Stevens, The Life of Isaac Ingalls Stevens by his Son. Boston, 1900.
[7] Annals of the American Academy for Political and Social Science, March, 1901.
[8] Forum, September, 1890, and March, 1894.
[9] Die Bank, July, 1911.
[10] Quarterly Journal of Economics, November, 1911.
[11] H. H. Swain, Economic Aspects of Railroad Receiverships, Economic Studies of the American Economic Association, April, 1898.

Government. Works by Davis,[1] von der Leyen,[2] Bromley,[3] Dillon,[4] Crawford,[5] Hazard,[6] and White[7] treat various phases of the company's development up to its final reorganization, an article by Meyer[8] describes the settlements between the Pacific railroads and the Government, and another article by Mitchell in the *Quarterly Journal of Economics*[9] deals with Union Pacific finance since that time. There may also be mentioned an account by Bailey,[10] which covers the whole of the road's history, but in a superficial way, and a vicious attack by Robinson upon all the government-aided lines.[11] The student of the Erie has at his disposal the elaborate narrative by E. H. Mott,[12] the chapters by Charles Francis Adams, Jr.,[13] and the sketch by Crouch.[14] Milton Reizenstein has dealt with the progress of the Baltimore and Ohio up to 1853,[15] and for this road there is material to be found in Smith's Book of the Great Railway Celebrations of 1857,[16] and in a com-

[1] John P. Davis, History of the Union Pacific Railroad. Chicago, 1894.

[2] Alfred von der Leyen, Die Finanz- und Verkehrspolitik der Nordamerikanischen Eisenbahnen, 2d ed., Berlin, 1895.

[3] I. H. Bromley, Pacific Railroad Legislation. Boston, 1886.

[4] J. F. Dillon, Pacific Railroad Laws. New York, 1890.

[5] J. B. Crawford, The Credit Mobilier of America. Boston, 1880.

[6] Rowland Hazard, The Credit Mobilier of America. Providence, 1881.

[7] Henry Kirke White, History of the Union Pacific Railroad. Economic Studies of the University of Chicago, 1895.

[8] Hugo R. Meyer, The Settlements with the Pacific Railways. Quarterly Journal of Economics, July, 1899.

[9] T. W. Mitchell, The Growth of the Union Pacific and its Financial Operations. Quarterly Journal of Economics, August, 1907.

[10] W. F. Bailey, The Story of the First Trans-Continental Railroad, its Projectors, Construction, and History. Pittsburg, 1906.

[11] John R. Robinson, The Octopus. A History of the Construction, Conspiracies, Extortions, Robberies, and Villainous Acts of the Central Pacific, the Union Pacific, and Other Subsidized Railroads. San Francisco, 1894.

[12] E. H. Mott, Between the Ocean and the Lakes; the Story of Erie. New York, 1899.

[13] Charles Francis and Henry Adams, Chapters of Erie and Other Essays. Boston, 1871.

[14] George Crouch, Another Chapter of Erie. New York, 1869.

[15] Milton Reizenstein, Economic History of the Baltimore & Ohio, 1827–53. Johns Hopkins University Studies, July–August, 1897.

[16] W. P. Smith, The Book of the Great Railway Celebrations of 1857. New York, 1858.

pilation of the Laws, Ordinances, and Documents Relating to the Baltimore and Ohio Railroad, published in 1840.[1] For the Northern Pacific the history by Smalley covers in popular style the period from 1864 to 1883,[2] the careful History of the Northern Securities Case, by B. H. Meyer, treats of an interesting later development,[3] chapters in von der Leyen's book contain acute and independent discussions of Northern Pacific as well as of Union Pacific finance,[4] and there is a fifteen-page pamphlet by Chapman entitled The Northern Pacific Railroad.[5] Schlagintweit in 1884 described his travels on the Santa Fe and Southern Pacific.[6] Wilson has written two volumes upon the Pennsylvania Railroad,[7] while Worthington [8] and Bishop [9] have described the internal improvements undertaken by the state of Pennsylvania. Ackerman is the author of a Historical Sketch of the Illinois Central Railroad,[10] and Hollander [11] and Ferguson [12] of works on the Cincinnati Southern. Potts [13] and Briscoe [14] have written on railroads in

[1] Laws, Ordinances, and Documents Relating to the Baltimore & Ohio Railroad Company. Baltimore, 1840.

[2] E. V. Smalley, History of the Northern Pacific Railroads. New York, 1883.

[3] B. H. Meyer, A History of the Northern Securities Case. Bulletin of the University of Wisconsin, July, 1906.

[4] Alfred von der Leyen, *v. supra*.

[5] W. W. Chapman, The Northern Pacific Railroad. Washington, 1880.

[6] Robert von Schlagintweit, Die Santa Fe und Sudpacificbahn in Nordamerika. Köln, 1884.

[7] W. B. Wilson, History of the Pennsylvania Railroad Company. Philadelphia, 1899.

[8] T. K. Worthington, Historical Sketch of the Finances of Pennsylvania. Publications of the American Economic Association, May, 1887.

[9] A. L. Bishop, The State Works of Pennsylvania. Publications of Yale University, New Haven, 1907.

[10] W. K. Ackerman, Historical Sketch of the Illinois Central Railroad. Chicago, 1890.

[11] J. H. Hollander, The Cincinnati Southern Railway: A Study in Municipal Activity. Johns Hopkins University Studies, January–February, 1894.

[12] E. A. Ferguson (Compiler), Founding of the Cincinnati Southern Railway; with an Autobiographical Sketch. Cincinnati, 1905.

[13] Charles S. Potts, Railroad Transportation in Texas. Bulletin of the University of Texas, Humanistic Series, March 1, 1909.

[14] P. Briscoe, The First Texas Railroad. Texas Historical Association Quarterly, Austin, 1904.

Texas. The Chicago & Northwestern has published a volume called Yesterday and To-day,[1] which contains some information. Hinsdale has worked up the History of the Long Island Railroad.[2] Bishop has sketched the history of the St. Paul & Sioux City Railroad.[3] Bliss is the author of a Historical Memoir of the Western Railroad.[4] Cary in 1893 described the Organization and History of the Chicago, Milwaukee & St. Paul Railroad Company.[5] Phillips discusses in excellent fashion the early history of a number of Southern carriers.[6] The autobiography of George Francis Train [7] and Smyth's biography of Henry Bradley Plant [8] are serviceable. Works like those of Van Oss,[9] Snyder,[10] Carter,[11] and Spearman,[12] and brief descriptions which have appeared in the columns of the *Railway World* and in *Moody's Magazine*, treat of a number of railroads, but make no attempt at a scholarly examination of any one. Some general works like Ringwalt's Development of Transportation Systems,[13] Adams' Railroads: Their Origin and Problems,[14] Hadley's Railroad Transportation,[15] Kupka's Die Verkehrsmittel in den Vereinigten Staaten von Nordamerika,[16] Sing-

---

[1] Chicago, 1905.

[2] E. B. Hinsdale, History of the Long Island Railroad. New York, 1898.

[3] Judson W. Bishop, History of the St. Paul and Sioux City Railroad, 1864–1881. Minnesota Historical Society, Collections, vol. x, pp. 399–415. St. Paul, 1905.

[4] George Bliss, Historical Memoir of the Western Railroad. Springfield, 1863.

[5] Cary, Organization and History of the Chicago, Milwaukee & St. Paul Railroad Company. Milwaukee, 1893.

[6] U. B. Phillips, A History of Transportation in the Eastern Cotton Belt to 1860. New York, 1908.

[7] George Francis Train, My Life in Many States and in Foreign Lands. New York, 1902.

[8] G. H. Smyth, The Life of Henry Bradley Plant, Founder and President of the Plant System of Railroads and Steamships and also of the Southern Express Company. New York and London, 1898.

[9] S. F. Van Oss, American Railroads as Investments. New York, 1893.

[10] Carl Snyder, American Railways as Investments. New York, 1907.

[11] Charles F. Carter, When Railroads were New. New York, 1909.

[12] F. H. Spearman, The Strategy of Great Railroads. New York, 1904.

[13] Philadelphia, 1888.

[14] New York, 1887.

[15] New York and London, 1900.

[16] Leipzig, 1883.

er's Die Amerikanischen Bahnen,[1] Myers' History of the Great American Fortunes,[2] Bancroft's History of the Pacific States,[3] and Chronicles of the Builders,[4] Davidson and Stuvé's Complete History of Illinois,[5] Hollander's Financial History of Baltimore,[6] Sanborn's Congressional Grants of Land in Aid of Railways,[7] Haney's Congressional History of Railways,[8] and Million's State Aid to Railways in Missouri,[9] contain incidental information about individual railroads.

These books are of service. Their number is, however, small and their scope limited. It is surprising that a field so rich as that of the history of American railroad systems should have attracted so little attention from competent students. It is not too much to say that the history of the Erie by Mott is the only comprehensive work of the kind which our literature possesses, and that is already thirteen years old.

[1] Berlin, 1909. [2] Chicago, 1910. [3] San Francisco, 1890.
[4] San Francisco, 1891. [5] Springfield, 1874. [6] Baltimore, 1899.
[7] Madison, 1899. [8] Madison, 1908 and 1910. [9] Chicago, 1896.

INDEX

INDEX

Abbott, E. H., 290, 291.

Accounts, juggling with, Baltimore & Ohio, 11, 15, 21-23; Erie, 37; Reading, 127; Southern, 169; Atchison, 208-10.

Adams, Charles Francis, Jr., 7, 232-7.

Adams Committee, 293-5, 296-7, 302.

Alabama Central, 149, 151.

Alabama Great Southern, 188.

Aldrich Committee, 221-2.

Alexander, E. P., 154, 164, 169, note.

Ames, Oliver, 250.

Anderson, E. E., 40, 244, 248.

Anthracite coal, see Coal.

Armour, P. D., 31.

Assessments, Baltimore & Ohio, 6; Erie, 35, 44, 47, 68, 70; Reading, 107, 111, 114, 139; Southern, 155-6, 181-2, 185-6 ; Atchison, 212-14; Union Pacific, 252; Northern Pacific, 269, 303, 305-6; General, 350-4.

Atchison, Topeka & Santa Fe, 192-219, 235, 259, 260, 277, 342.

Atlantic & Great Western, see New York, Pennsylvania & Ohio.

Atlantic & Pacific, 194, 195, 208, 216. See also St. Louis & San Francisco.

Atlantic Coast Line, 148, 158, 161.

Bacon, E. R., 18.

Baer, George F., 111, 142.

Baltimore & Ohio, 1-33, 38, 145, 169, 259, 260, 342.

Baltimore Committee, 24.

Baring Brothers & Co., 11, 215.

Bartol Committee, 103, 104-5.

Belen, 218.

Belmont, August, & Co., oppose Erie reorganization plan, 63-6; lead opposition to Adams Committee, 290; members of Northern Pacific reorganization committee, 296, note; of Northern Pacific voting trust, 307; underwrite Northern Pacific mortgage, 274.

Bigelow, F. G., 300, 301, 308.

Blanchard, George R., 2, 3.

Boissevain, A. H., 242-4, 245-7.

Bond, Frank S., 89, 90, 91; plan of reorganization by, 92-5; 95-6.

Boston & Maine, 122, 124, 126, 127-8.

Boston, Hartford & Erie, 36.

Branches, Baltimore & Ohio, 9-10; Erie, 51-3, 57, 59-60, 74; Southern, 168; Atchison, 196-8, 217-18; Union Pacific, 230-31, 232-3, 236, 248-9, 250-51, 253-4; Northern Pacific, 275, 276, 277-8, 286-7, 291, 292, 304,

306-7; Rock Island, 315-16, 319-20, 328-31; General, 369-71.

Brice, Calvin S., 150, 160, 244.

Brown, Shipley & Co., 9, 11.

Buffalo, New York & Erie, 38.

Burleigh, Andrew F., 300, 301.

Cable, R. R., 314.

Caldwell, Stephen A., 81, 82, 97.

Capitalization, Baltimore & Ohio, 1, 9, 11; Erie, 34, 35, 36, 39, 44, 48, 71-2; Reading, 75-6, 82, 101, 115, 138, 141; Southern, 151, 183-4, 186; Atchison, 198, 200, 211, 219; Union Pacific, 221-4, 225, 227, 229, 232, 236, 251; Northern Pacific, 264, 266, 268, 271, 275, 276, 278, 279, 302, 304; Rock Island, 311-12, 315, 318, note, 322, 331, 332-3; General, 339, 363-9, 372-4, 374-9.

Cash requirements and floating debt, Baltimore & Ohio, 11-15, 26-7; Erie, 34-5, 40, 54, 55-6, 61, 68; Reading, 79, 81-2, 101, 124-6, 127, 133, 139; Southern, 152, 156, 160, note, 168, 173, 182, 186; Atchison, 197, 199-200, 213; Northern Pacific, 266-7, 267-9, 272, 274, 276, 287-9, 295, 304-6; General, 348-56.

Cass, George W., 266, 267.

Central of New Jersey, 9, 10; leased by Reading, 97-9, 117, 120, 122; shares purchased on margin, 99-100.

Central, New England & Western, 123.

Central Railroad & Banking Company of Georgia, 162-6, 169, 175-8, 188.

Charlotte, Columbia & Augusta, 147, 159.

Chicago & Alton, Harriman buys stock in, 331; Rock Island buys stock in, 330, 331; reorganization of, 337.

Chicago & Atlantic, 52, 54, 57, 62.

Chicago & Northern Pacific, 283-4, 286, 287; loss on operation of, 289, 291-2; Northern Pacific abandons lease of, 290, 302, 308.

Chicago, Burlington & Quincy, 277, 310, 343.

Chicago, Indianapolis & Louisville, 189.

Chicago, Milwaukee & St. Paul, 259, 343.

Chicago Terminal Transfer Company, 33, 283; Northern Pacific sells stock in, 308.

Childs, Attorney-General, 298.

Choctaw, Oklahoma & Gulf, 319-20, 328.

Cincinnati, Hamilton & Dayton, 52-3, 57, 74.

Cincinnati, New Orleans & Texas Pacific, 189.

Clark, S. H., 240, 253.

Clyde, W. P., 174-8.

Coal, development of Erie's traffic in, 38, 50-1,

73; interest of Reading in, 76–81, 97, 99, 118–23, 125–6, 141, 143, 145; 311.

Coal & Iron Company, Reading, 77, 80–83, 88, 92, 97, 101, 118–20, 123, 127, 139, 141–4.

Colby, Charles L., 290.

Colorado Midland, 203, 205, 212.

Columbia & Greenville, 159, 160, note, 168.

Committee of Investigation, Baltimore & Ohio, 15–16, 21; Erie, 37, 40, 55–6; Reading, 84, 119; Southern, 152, 170, 177; Atchison, 199–200; Northern Pacific, 285–6.

Committee of Reorganization, *see* Reorganization Committee.

Competition, a cause of railroad failure, 340–1.

Consolidation, through reorganization, 370–1.

Contracts, trackage and traffic, Baltimore & Ohio, 9; Erie, 52; Reading, 121; Southern, 149; Atchison, 193–5, 217; Northern Pacific, 275, 283–4, 308.

Cooke, Jay, interested in Northern Pacific, 264; failure of, 79, 265.

Cooley, Thomas M., 7.

Coppell, George, 128, 175.

Corbin, Austin, 117, 118, 120.

Coudert, F. R., 241.

Cowen, J. K., 20, 29–30.

Crédit Mobilier, 223–4.

Cullom Committee, Albert Fink testifies before, 7.

Davis, J. C. Bancroft, 35.

Davis, John P., 222–3, 224.

Deferred income bonds, 81, 84–6, 87–8, 90, 96, 115.

Delaware, Lackawanna & Western, 120–1.

Denver Pacific, 227, 228–30.

Depew, Chauncey M., 250.

Deutsche Bank, supports Henry Villard, 273; 294; underwrites Northern Pacific reorganization plan, 296, 304; 307.

Differentials, between eastern seaboard cities, 5, 7; between stronger and weaker roads, 17.

Dillon, Sidney, 233, 234, 237.

Dressed beef, rates cut on, 17.

Doane, John W., 241.

Drew, Daniel, 34, 36.

Drexel, Anthony J., 125, 126, 134.

Drexel, Morgan & Co., take part in Erie reorganization, 62, 65, 66–9; in Southern reorganization, 167–8, 175, 178–86; underwrite Northern Pacific mortgage, 274.

Dunan, S. H., 37.

Durant, T. C., 223.

Earle, George H., Jr., 135.

East Tennessee, Virginia & Georgia, *see* Southern Railway.

Employees, reorganization of the service, 15;

234; wages reduced or delayed, 37, 39, 41, 79, 81, 100, 199, 234; wages high, 222.

Equipment, Baltimore & Ohio, 23, 28, 31; Erie, 73; Reading, 144; Southern, 168, 189, 190; Atchison, 218; Union Pacific, 261; Northern Pacific, 309.

Equitable Life Assurance Company, 288.

Erie, 2, 7, 17–18, 34–74, 342.

Erlanger Roads, 166, 167, 185.

Excelsior Enterprise Company, *see* National Company.

Express companies, 12, 14.

Fairchild, C. S., 170.

Fink, Albert, 6, 7, 10.

Fink, Henry, 154.

Fisk, Jim, 36.

Fitzgerald, General Louis, takes part in Baltimore & Ohio reorganization, 24; in Reading reorganization, 136, 138; in Union Pacific reorganization, 244–5, 250, 251–4; in Northern Pacific reorganization, 293; examines Richmond Terminal properties, 170.

Fixed charges, Baltimore & Ohio, 8, 10, 16, 20, 22, 28, 342, 357–9; Erie, 35, 36, 38, 39, 48, 58, 66, 69, 72, 73–4, 342, 357–9; Reading, 75, 82, 94, 96, 101, 115, 116, 118, 139–40, 144–5, 342, 357–9; Southern, 152, 155, 173, 180, 186–7, 342, 357–9; Atchison, 197–9, 203, 213, 216, 218, 342, 357–9; Union Pacific, 224–5, 227, 229, 235–6, 251, 253–4, 261, 342, 357–9; Northern Pacific, 266, 271, 275, 284, 293, 304, 310, 342, 357–9; Rock Island, 312, 322, 357–9; General, 357–61, 363–5, 369–72.

Fleming, Robert, 45–6, 155, 216.

Floating debt, *see* Cash requirements and floating debt.

Foreclosure, Baltimore & Ohio, 28–9; Erie, 34, 35, 49–50, 73; Reading, 82, 141; Southern, 157, 187, 188; Atchison, 216; Union Pacific, 254–7; Northern Pacific, 270, 308.

Foreign investors, Erie, 36, 37, 40–50, 55–6, 63; Reading, 82, 83, 84, 86–9, 91, 96, 119, 126; Southern, 155; Atchison, 206, 207–8, 210, 214, 215; Union Pacific 244; Northern Pacific, 264, 273.

Garrett, John, 4, 9.

Garrett, John B., 106, 114.

Garrett, Robert, 9, 16.

Gauge, on Erie, 34, 37, 38, 45, 51.

Georgia Central Company, 164, 165, 177–8.

Georgia Pacific, 149, 166.

Gorman, Senator A. H., 13.

Gould, Jay, prominent in Erie, 36; 194; causes combination of Union Pacific and Kansas Pacific, 226, 228–30; unloads branch roads on Union Pacific, 230–31; 233, 237.

Gowen, F. B., 76, 81, 84, 86, 87-91, 95-7, 99, 101, 112-15, 118-19, 120.

Grand Trunk, 2, 6, 7, 17, 18.

Grant & Ward, 54.

Great Northern, 258, 259, 277; proposes to guarantee Northern Pacific bonds, 296-8, 309-10.

Gregory, Dudley S., 35.

Guarantee fund, 199, 203.

Gulf, Colorado & Santa Fe, 196, 202, 205, 218.

Hallgarten & Co., on Reading underwriting syndicate, 139; on Southern reorganization committee, 171; oppose Erie reorganization plan, 63-6.

Harriman, E. H., 32-3, 63-6, 188, 218, 258-60, 309-10, 331.

Harris, Joseph S., 77-8, 83, 97, 125-8, 129, 131.

Harris, Robert, 275.

Hartshorne Committee, 136.

Hepburn Committee, Albert Fink testifies before, 7.

Higginson, H. L., 206, 245.

Hill, J. J., buys interest in Baltimore & Ohio, 31-2; struggle with Harriman, 258, 310; proposed guarantee of Northern- Pacific bonds, 296-8, 307.

Hollins, H. B., 165, 179, 188.

Hooper, John, 344.

Houston & Texas Central, 328-9, 355.

Houston East & West Texas, 329.

Hoxie, H. M., 223.

Huidekoper, F. W., 176, 177, note.

Huntington, Collis P., 194, 258.

Illinois Central, 19, 146, 259-60, 343.

Improvements, Baltimore & Ohio, 15, 23, 28, 30-31; Erie, 42, 51, 60, 73; Reading, 80-81, 118, 144; Southern, 152, 168, 170, 189, 190; Atchison, 202, note, 204, 212, 218-19; Union Pacific, 234, 260-1; Northern Pacific, 276, 278-9, 309; Rock Island, 332, 333.

Income bonds, 203-5; before and after reorganization, 365-6. *See also* Deferred income bonds.

Inman, John H., 164, 165.

Iselin, A. & Co., 139.

Ives, Brayton, 285, 287-8; president of Northern Pacific, 290; secures removal of receivers, 291-2, 298-9; 294, 295; endorses Northern Pacific reorganization plan, 302.

Jenkins, Judge, 289, 292, 300, 301.

Jewett, H. J., 39, 40, 41, 49, 50-53, 55, 57.

Joint Executive Committee, 6.

Joint Executive Reorganization Committee, 210-16.

Junior Securities Protective Committee, 137.

Kansas Pacific, poor condition of, 225; attempt at reorganization of, 226-7; consolidated with Union Pacific, 228-30; sale of, 256-7.

King, Edward, 206, 210-16.

King, John, 55, 57, 59, note, 61.

Kuhn, Loeb & Co., take part of securities issued under Baltimore & Ohio reorganization plan, 26; oppose Erie reorganization plan, 63-6; represented on Richmond Terminal investigating committee, 170; on Union Pacific reorganization committee, 250; agree to take Northern Pacific collateral trust bonds, 288.

Lacombe, Judge, 61, 300, 301.

Lake Shore & Michigan Southern, 3, 18, 32, 145.

Land grants, *see* State and federal aid.

Leases, Baltimore & Ohio, 2, 27; Erie, 51-3, 56, 58, 59-60, 71-2, 74; Reading, 97-9, 117, 120, 122, 123, 128, 130; Southern, 147, 148, 149, 159, 161-2, 166, 188; Atchison, 197; Northern Pacific, 276, 283-4.

Leeds, W. B., 317-18.

Lehigh Valley, 74, 75; leased to Reading, 120, 122, 123, 128-9, 130, 133.

Lehigh Valley Terminal Railroad, 128.

Lewis, Edwin A., 81-2, 97.

Lewis, Howard, 119.

Little, Stephen, report on Baltimore & Ohio, 21-3; on Atchison, 208-10, 213; set to work on the Reading, 128.

Live stock, 17.

Livingston, Johnston, 294, 307.

Lockwood, E. Dunbar, 106, 112, 117.

Logan, T. M., forms Georgia Central Company, 164; seeks control of Richmond Terminal, 164-6.

Long Dock Company, 58.

Lord, N. P., 345.

Loree, S. F., 33.

Louisville & Nashville, 146, 149.

Maben, J. C., 175, note, 178.

McCalmont Brothers, 86-91, 96.

McCormick, Attorney-General, 143.

McCullough, J. G., 61.

McGill, Chancellor, 122.

McHenry, E. H., 300, 301, 308.

McHenry, James, 39-40, 49.

McLeod, A. A., leases Lehigh Valley, 120; extends Reading into New England, 122-5; statement by, 125-6; resigns by request, 126-7; 132.

Macon & Brunswick, 149, 151.

Manville, Allen, 202.

Maryland, subscribes to Baltimore & Ohio stock, 1, 18.

Mayer, Charles F., 16, 18-20.